The Politics of Protest

The Politics of Protest

Extra-Parliamentary Politics in Britain since 1970

Peter Joyce
Department of Sociology
Manchester Metropolitan University

First published 2002 by
PALGRAVE MACMILLAN
Houndmills, Basingstoke, Hampshire RG21 6XS and
175 Fifth Avenue, New York, N. Y. 10010
Companies and representatives throughout the world

PALGRAVE MACMILLAN is the global academic imprint of the Palgrave
Macmillan division of St. Martin's Press, LLC and of Palgrave Macmillan Ltd.
Macmillan® is a registered trademark in the United States, United Kingdom
and other countries. Palgrave is a registered trademark in the European
Union and other countries.

ISBN 0–333–65766–7

This book is printed on paper suitable for recycling and made from fully
managed and sustained forest sources.

A catalogue record for this book is available from the British Library.

Library of Congress Cataloging-in-Publication Data

Joyce, Peter.
  The politics of protest: extra-parliamentary politics in Britain since 1970 /
Peter Joyce.
    p. cm.
  Includes bibliographical references and index.
  ISBN 0–333–65766–7 (cloth)
    1. Government, Resistance to – Great Britain. 2. Democracy – Great Britain.
  3. Great Britain – Politics and government – 1945 – I. Title.
  JN900 .J69 2002
  941.085–dc21   2002072518

10   9   8   7   6   5   4   3   2   1
11   10 09 08 07 06 05 04 03 02

Printed and bound in Great Britain by
Antony Rowe Ltd, Chippenham and Eastbourne

To my wife, Julie, and my daughters, Emmeline and Eleanor

Contents

1
Introduction: Extra-Parliamentary Politics

On 14 February 2002 a by-election took place in the Parliamentary constituency of Ogmore in South Wales. Slightly in excess of 18,000 of the constituency's 51,325 electors bothered to vote, a turnout of 31.3 per cent. News of this event was tucked away on page 13 of the *Guardian* newspaper on 16 February. This illustrated that the lack of public interest in conventional politics (which, as Chapter 2 discusses, was a feature of the 2001 general election) has not been subsequently remedied and that large numbers of citizens (including many of those who were previously regarded as civic-minded) (Hansard Society, 2001: 1) remain disengaged from this process, providing stark evidence of the existence of a profound 'crisis in democratic politics' (Whiteley et al., 2001: 786). This book is concerned with examining why this is the case, and evaluating alternative methods of political articulation which are collectively referred to as *extra-parliamentary political action*.

The book has a number of key themes. First, it asserts that for many individuals and groups *conventional political activity* is viewed as an insufficient way to articulate their concerns in an attempt to get policy-makers to pay attention to them. Chapters 2–6 examine the perceived problems of conventional political activity in relation to the specific form (or forms) of extra-parliamentary activity which constitute the focus of discussion. In general terms, however, individuals or groups may resort to extra-parliamentary means of political activity when they feel that reliance on conventional activity will not secure for them the changes they seek. This situation may arise because they are not institutionalised into the 'Whitehall interest group bargaining communities' (Hogwood, 1987: 40) or because policy-makers are unable or unwilling to concede to the policy changes which are sought. The use of extra-parliamentary politics is thus designed to alter the perceptions and priorities of policy-makers and in attempting to make them have regard to their views, participants are given a sense of empowerment (Hertz, 2001: 202). This is a crucial consideration affecting all forms of extra-parliamentary political activity which are discussed in Chapters 2–6.

Empowerment embraces actions which range from securing a permanent alteration in the power relationship between citizens and the state to temporarily 'getting one over' on one's perceived opponents and feeling morally uplifted even if the state subsequently reasserts its power through coercive means. Empowerment of this nature is a feature of riots and terrorism which are discussed in Chapters 4 and 5.

Extra-parliamentary political action involves a number of actions. The second theme of this book is to consider the main forms of this activity which have been used since 1970. To do this, the book is divided into a number of separate chapters which focus on different forms of extra-parliamentary political activity – protest (which embraces activities such as demonstrations, direct action, civil disobedience, physical obstruction and counter-cultural activities), industrial disputes (which constitute a specific form of protest that takes place within the workplace in the form of activities including strikes and work-ins), riots, terrorism and racially motivated violence. The aim of this aspect of the book is to present a broad picture of these activities rather than a detailed analysis of each and every event relevant to them, although key episodes (which include anti-capitalist protests, the 2000 petrol crisis, the 1984/5 miners' dispute, activities associated with animal welfare and animal rights and terrorism on mainland Britain) are dealt with in more detailed case studies.

An explanation of the emergence and use of extra-parliamentary political activity is the third theme of this book. This entails a consideration of the reasons underlying the use of this form of political action and of the social groups and political organisations with which it is associated. This issue is considered separately within each chapter which seeks to identify the key participants in each form of extra-parliamentary political activity discussed in the book. This makes it possible to identify whether specific forms of this activity are identified with different social groupings – for example, to investigate whether protest is primarily a middle-class activity, to examine whether industrial unrest is a preserve of the working class and to analyse whether rioting is chiefly associated with the underclass.

The fourth theme of this book concerns the regulation of extra-parliamentary political action by the state. Although the state consists of a wide range of permanent institutions which are responsible for organising communal life within Great Britain, attention is focused on legislation directed at the different forms of activity discussed in each chapter, promoted by governments and enforced by a range of agencies. These include the military (whose role is discussed in Chapter 3) and MI5 (which is considered in Chapter 7). However, the most important of these is the police service, which has been said to occupy a pivotal role at the junction of state–society relationships (Brewer et al., 1996: 233). Although the concept of the police as 'citizens in uniform' seeks to assert them as neutral arbiters of conflict (Brewer et al., 1996: 38), it has been argued that a symbiotic relationship exists between the police and state: the police service operates as the guardian of the state's monopoly of legitimate force and acts as the defender of its interests (Brewer et al., 1996: xv, xx) in particular when the status quo is challenged by public order situations which reflect cleavages in society (Brewer et al., 1996: 218). In these circumstances, the media may play an important role by mediating between the state and its citizens; it may, for example, create an ideological climate which justifies and encourages the use of repressive control tactics against dissenting groups (D. Waddington, 1992: 160) through the use of methods which include defining highly complex social situations as black-and-white 'issues' (Hyman, 1972: 146) or by focusing on specific events (especially when these make dramatic use of violence) to the detriment of providing any discussion as to why they occurred.

The fifth theme of this book is civil and political liberties. Restrictions on various forms of extra-parliamentary political activities may be justified by the concept of *political toleration*, but a particular concern is to assess whether the limitations discussed in Chapters 2–6 have eroded the liberties traditionally associated with a liberal democratic state. Accordingly Chapter 7 focuses attention on the key issues of paramilitary policing and the extent to which attempts to regulate extra-parliamentary political activities on the pretext of defending the state against subversion have eroded the right to privacy and the freedom of political expression.

The book concentrates on extra-parliamentary activity that has taken place in Great Britain since 1970. This date enables account to be taken of key developments affecting extra-parliamentary activity and the state's response, including the level of industrial unrest following the election of a Conservative government in 1970 – in particular the impact of the 1972 incident at Saltley on the way the state planned for future industrial disputes (issues which are discussed in Chapter 3) – and the impact of terrorism on mainland Britain in connection with the activities of the 'Angry Brigade' and with the politics of Northern Ireland (which is discussed in Chapter 5). However, the time scale is used flexibly. Some reference is made to events of relevance to the central themes of this book which occurred before this date (such as the emergence of race onto the political agenda which, as is argued in Chapter 6, occurred during the 1960s); and there is a deliberate focus on more contemporary illustrations of extra-parliamentary activity (such as the anti-capitalist protests, the 2000 fuel crisis and the 2001 urban disorders) as these are likely to be freshest in the minds of readers.

Before commencing on a discussion of the main forms of extra-parliamentary activities which form the basis of Chapters 2–6, some general observations concerning this form of political activity will be made.

The political environment of extra-parliamentary politics

The decision by an individual, group or movement to utilise extra-parliamentary rather than conventional political action is shaped by a number of factors. Chapters 2–6 focus on explanations for the use of specific forms of extra-parliamentary political activity. Here the discussion concentrates on a number of general factors which have influenced the political environment of a wide range of extra-parliamentary activities.

Political opportunity structure

The importance of the political opportunity structure is particularly emphasised in literature dealing with social movements (which are considered in Chapter 2). This is defined as 'the openings, weak spots, barriers and resources of the political system itself' (Eisinger, 1973: 11–12) and is primarily concerned with formal access to a state's decision-making machinery. This suggests that the development of social movements is influenced by a number of 'environmental opportunities and constraints' (della Porta, 1995: 10) which include the openness or closure of formal political access (openness entailing a large number of points of access), the degree of stability or instability of formal political alignments, the availability and strategic posture of potential allies, and political conflicts between and within elites (Tarrow, 1989). In order for protest to emerge, activists must believe that an oportunity exists, that they have the power to bring about change, and they must blame the system for the problem they seek to confront. Accordingly, the lense through which activists view potential opportunities is an important consideration affecting the emergence of protest (McAdam et al., 1996: 224).

A country's political opportunity structure is not, however, static and the political process theory emphasises how changes to it may encourage the formation of social movements. In particular, periods of political instability affecting the balance between 'insiders' and 'outsiders' may stimulate these movements by creating openings that they can exploit (Marx and McAdam, 1994: 83–5). Change in the legal or institutional structure which granted a more formal access to challenging groups is a key instigator of reform movements (della Porta et al., 1999: 101). One example of this was the emergence and development of the European Union (EU). The political institutions of the EU constituted a new political opportunity structure for a range of groups in a number of countries (della Porta et al., 1999: 110) by presenting the possibility of formal access to a supra-national decision-making process. Groups may find it more effective to ignore attempts to influence their own governments through the use of extra-parliamentary methods such as protest and direct action and to seek their objectives instead through the institutions of the EU, especially when their own government is hostile to their aims. The restrictions placed on trade unions by British Conservative governments after 1979 enhanced the importance of EU institutions such as the European Court of Justice as a defence of trade union and workers' interests, and the interests of British trade unions were reflected in developments such as the Social Chapter. The tactics used by groups seeking influence in Brussels was constrained by the logic and structure of EU institutions which encouraged groups to utilise conventional activities (such as institutionalised elite lobbying within established political channels) rather than uninstitutionalised, symbolic or mass protest (della Porta et al., 1999: 103). For this reason, social movements have been less active at EU level in comparison to pressure groups operating in Brussels.

Political culture

Political culture refers to an underlying set of values held by most people who live in a particular country concerning political behaviour, one important aspect of which is the degree of trust which citizens have in their political leaders, giving rise to 'a deferential civic culture' (Almond and Verba, 1963: 435). Political deference entails respect for institutions and rulers which is reflected in 'compliance with the laws, the lack of a revolutionary tradition, the absence of referenda, and the lack of controls on the administrators and public leaders' (Almond and Verba, 1989: 156). In Great Britain the tradition of evolutionary rather than revolutionary change and support for conventional rather than extra-parliamentary political activity as a means of bringing about change has tended to deprive groups which utilise various forms of extra-parliamentary methods – often resorted to out of desperation born of weakness – of legitimacy.

As with political opportunity structure, political culture is also capable of change. Factors such as deindustrialisation or immigration have fundamental significance for the existence of universally agreed sentiments underpinning political behaviour and may result in dominant attitudes coexisting with sub-cultural values, or produce a looser attachment to mainstream values by some sections of society. These changes may legitimise the use of extra-parliamentary means of political activity among some sections of the population, especially those who feel that they have no stake in society and who thus have nothing to lose by engaging in protest or violence to articulate the sense of grievance felt towards society and its institutions. Chapter 4 considers this issue in more detail in connection with rioting as an activity associated with the underclass.

Class dealignment

Class dealignment refers to the erosion of the historical identification between a voter and a particular social class (Denver, 1994: 60–6). By the 1960s changes in the social structure were observed resulting in increased working-class affluence (termed 'embourgeoisement') (Goldthorpe et al., 1968) and the social mobility of some members of the working class who took advantage of changes to the educational system inaugurated in the 1944 Education Act. Upward social mobility served to prevent a complete repetition of political loyalties across the generations (Abrams, 1962: 240).

These people were less concerned with the Labour Party's motivation in class conflict and with the historic policies such as nationalisation which were designed to solve it. Class dealignment had a particularly damaging effect on the electoral fortunes of the Labour Party which failed to win a general election between 1979 and 1997, and is one explanation why the progressive and working-class causes traditionally championed by the Labour Party were waged by extra-parliamentary means in this period.

The dominant party system

The term 'dominant party system' refers to a situation in which the government is constantly drawn from one political party. The strength of this party at the polls typically ensures that it is subject to no effective scrutiny or challenge to its actions in the House of Commons. The Conservative Party dominated British politics between 1951 and 1964 and then from 1979 until 1997 and the Labour Party won the 1997 and 2001 general elections by majorities of landslide proportions. The perception by opponents of the dominant party that their concerns cannot be effectively promoted through the conventional political system may result in the politics of opposition being removed from Parliament and taken to the streets in various forms of extra-parliamentary activity including protest, urban disorder and violence. This reasoning was utilised by organisations opposed to the poll tax in the 1990s. One organisation drew attention to 'a vicious right-wing government, elected by a minority of the population...which is undermining working class institutions, attacking and seeking to destroy local democracy, centralising state power and using that power to attack health, welfare and education and collective care and cooperation'. It was accused of 'operating in a very authoritarian way, riding roughshod over any opposition, weakening democracy and civil rights'. The use of collective civil disobedience allied to mass demonstrations was accordingly advocated to oppose this tax and the Thatcherite government which promoted it (ILP, 1990: 6). As Chapter 2 argues, since 1997 rural interests have adopted various forms of protest (including demonstrations and direct action) to voice their concern at what they perceive as the neglect of the needs of the countryside by Labour governments.

The electoral system

It is sometimes argued that Britain's first-past-the-post electoral system which is used for general elections encourages extra-parliamentary political activity as it is difficult for single issue groups to make much headway within the conventional political system. However, the converse of this argument is not necessarily valid: proportional representation does not always limit the extent of extra-parliamentary forms of activity. In the former state of West Germany, for example, a number of strong social movements emerged during the 1970s because the Social Democratic Party (which was politically dominant in that period) adopted a negative stance towards these organisations (Kriesi, 1995: 186).

Technology

Technology may have an adverse impact on conventional political activity by giving citizens the ability to influence specific policy decisions through on-line polls (termed 'e-democracy') which may be to the detriment of their participation in election contests. Additionally, the ability to organise extra-parliamentary activities has been greatly facilitated by technological developments including improvements in international travel, access to information and communications. These may increase public awareness of a wide range of scientific and technical matters, facilitate the access of groups to the general public, and make it easier for large groups of individuals to congregate anywhere in the world. Television has made it possible for groups such as Greenpeace to reach a wide audience and may encourage the use of spectacular forms of direct action as these are most likely to attract media attention.

Key developments include the internet, desk-top publishing and local television and radio stations which enhance the opportunity for groups engaged in extra-parliamentary activity to organise or obtain publicity, often on an international scale. The internet in particular has enabled the 'call for action' to be transmitted to hundreds of thousands at the 'click of a mouse' (Hertz, 2001: 1) and has made it possible to organise protests, demonstrations and more violent forms of political activity without the formal organisation which would once have been provided by political parties, but also without the discipline which these organisations impose on their members. The internet has also been used in connection with industrial disputes which are discussed in Chapter 3. What has been termed 'cyber-picketing' facilitated national and international support for industrial disputes including those of the Liverpool dockers in 1995 and Rentokil workers in 1998. The internet may inaugurate a form of populist politics in which widespread support for campaigns can be generated rapidly, thereby enhancing the opportunities for protest (see Chapter 2). For example, the environmentalist campaign to boycott Exxon/Esso in 2001 made use of the internet to advertise its campaign and seek support for it. The various groups comprising the anti-capitalist movement also make use of this form of communication to organise and plan events.

Extra-parliamentary politics and violence

Violence is often associated with extra-parliamentary politics. Some of the activities discussed in this book (including rioting, terrorism and racially motivated violence; see Chapters 4, 5 and 6) deliberately use violence to seek a reform or to publicise a grievance. However, other forms of extra-parliamentary activity (such as civil disobedience, demonstrations and industrial disputes, which are discussed in Chapters 2 and 3) do not necessarily entail violence, although this may arise. In this section crowd behaviour is focused upon in order to explain why violence may sometimes occur in association with extra-parliamentary politics where this is not an essential or inevitable consequence of these activities.

The causes of public disorder

Governments often adopt a critical view of extra-parliamentary activities which result in large numbers of people taking to the streets. Activities of this nature often result in public disorder and in extreme cases governments may be swept aside by this form of collective action. This situation occurred, for example, in the former state of East Germany when mass protests (including demonstrations, political rallies and industrial action) secured the overthrow of the Communist government and the institution of parliamentary democracy in 1989–90. This wave of popular protests eventually secured the reunification of the states of East and West Germany in the autumn of 1990. Actions of this nature also brought to an end the regime of President Slobodan Milosevic in Yugoslavia in October 2000. Thus governments will often use the pretext of public disorder to impose limitations on extra-parliamentary activity. The precise nature of these interventions is discussed in Chapters 2–6, and here the discussion seeks to provide an understanding as to why crowd situations sometimes result in serious disorder.

Psychological theories have sought to explain the emergence and nature of a group 'mind'. Early studies suggested that those involved in these collective forms of behaviour demonstrated characteristics such as excitability and emotionalism (Le Bon, 1896; Freud, 1945): the crowd was viewed as irrational, degenerate and pathological and it was argued that a human being in such a setting descended several rungs in the ladder of civilisation. People acted destructively when the 'mind of the crowd' took over, as they were motivated by instincts which were normally inhibited (Le Bon, 1896). Some social psychologists argued that individuals in a crowd became trapped in an ever-increasing spiral of excitement and emotionality which arose from mutually reinforcing reactions (Allport, 1924). The theory of de-individuation was latterly put forward as a psychological explanation for the way in which individuals submerged in a crowd relinquished their autonomy and self-restraint and exhibited diminished self-awareness and self-control (Zimbardo, 1969); alternatively, economic models or game theory approaches to the study of collective behaviour emphasised the rationality of a process in which participants seek to maximise benefits and minimise the costs involved in this activity (Berk, 1993).

A key theory grounded in the psychology of group behaviour is that of the 'J-Curve' (Davies, 1969). This put forward the 'frustration-aggression' hypothesis, which suggested that violence was most likely to occur when what was termed an 'intolerable gap' arose between the expectations of the general public and the ability of the government adequately to respond to the people's needs. This theory suggested that revolutions tended to occur following a period of reform since the 'gap' was most likely to become intolerable when expectations had been whetted by reforms which were abruptly halted. The people's desires continued to rise whereas the willingness or ability of the government to meet them was reduced. Violence was depicted as the inevitable consequence of popular frustration which was vented upon a symbol such as the police service which became regarded as the common enemy.

One main problem with psychological studies was their tendency to ignore factors external to the individual which could account for crowd behaviour. This deficiency formed the basis of sociological studies which sought to provide explanations concerning the setting in which these forms of collective activity emerged. This approach tended to place the blame for such events on the operations of society and its institutions rather than the minds of those engaged in them. A major exponent of this approach was Smelser whose analysis was grounded in structural functionalism. He emphasised the importance of social conditions and the operations of the social, economic and political system to collective action which occurred, for example, when society failed to meet the demands made upon it by certain groups of its members (Smelser, 1962). Thus deprivation (or relative deprivation, Gurr, 1969) was viewed as a major explanation for collective forms of behaviour ranging from protests to riots. Strain in the functioning of the social structure created the potential for collective violence which became an actuality as the result of a precipitating factor such as police intervention which was viewed as unwarranted. The role of the precipitator was that it galvanised already angry and frustrated individuals into taking action by providing legitimacy for their actions. The importance of effective leadership to crowds in such volatile situations was also emphasised (Smelser, 1962).

Smelser's account of crowd behaviour remained heavily influenced by earlier psychological theories. Accordingly there remained a tendency to view this form of collective behaviour as irrational (King and Brearley, 1996: 31), associated with the frustration and discontent of those adversely affected by structural strains emerging from modernisation (Mayer, 1995: 171). This approach tended to ignore historical studies which emphasised the frequently rational nature of crowd behaviour exhibited in events such as eighteenth-century bread riots (Hobsbawn, 1959; Rude, 1964). An evaluation of the setting within which disorder occurred, particularly the historical and cultural antecedents of such events, was required (Waddington et al., 1989: 174).

The 'flashpoint' model sought to remedy the deficiencies of earlier insular approaches to the study of public disorder by producing an evaluation which was multi-dimensional, and not reliant on one academic discipline. This model sought to understand a flashpoint by identifying six levels of analysis (the structural, political/ideological, cultural, contextual, situational and interactional) whose interrelationship helped to determine whether violence would or would not occur at a specific event (Waddington et al., 1989). This analysis suggested that violence might occur within communities whose members had experienced long-standing grievances which generated perpetual simmerings of discontent. A specific incident, although minor in itself, might provide the pretext for violence if it epitomised the sense of injustice widely felt within that community.

The flashpoint model has a number of strengths. It viewed the police as part of an interactive process whose actions could calm or aggravate a tense situation in which crowds had already assembled, suggesting that how a crowd reacted was largely dependent on how the police perceived and treated it. It did not view the police as primarily responsive to activity initiated by the public as was suggested by the 'riot curve' theory (Beckett, 1992). It also emphasised how the opportunity for negotiation and compromise between the police and protesters (which is afforded at the contextual level) and the behaviour adopted by the police and dissenting groups at a specific location (the interactional level) are crucial to determining whether a protest is transformed into a disorderly event. The mechanics of this process is discussed in greater detail in Chapter 2. It also provides an explanation as to why potentially disorderly events remain benign while other similar incidents 'kick off' and escalate into major confrontations (D. Waddington, 1996: 10). Important considerations relating to the outbreak of disorder occur at the political/ideological, contextual and the interactional levels. The first of these emphasises that similar events may be perceived differently in different time periods by institutions such as the political parties, media and the police. These differing perceptions may reflect factors such as political attitudes concerning the desirability of incorporating groups such as trade unions into the state's decision-making processes or stigmatising them as bodies which promote sectional concerns above the national interest. The contextual and interactional levels draw attention to the way in which crowd situations occurring at more or less the same time can be handled differently by the police by negotiation and liaison between both sides and the perception by both sides that the other is behaving reasonably. Illustrations of the importance of the political/ideological dimension of the model can be found in a comparison of miners' protests which occurred in 1984–85 and which were subsequently renewed in 1992 (Critcher, 2000). Episodes of extreme violence such as Orgreave in 1984 (which is discussed in Chapter 3) sometimes occurred in the former period whereas the later march of 50,000 miners in Hyde Park, London, witnessed no violence. Explanations for this focused on the altered context in which the latter event took place. John Major had replaced

Margaret Thatcher as Prime Minister in 1990 and the public was more sympathetic to the miners' opposition to further pit closures. The importance of the contextual and interactional levels can again be illustrated by the 1984/5 miners' dispute. Although there were violent occurrences in this dispute in which the police and striking miners clashed, there were many other occasions when no violence occurred on the picket lines. This suggests that the interrelationship between police and miners' representatives at each event (and especially the policing policies which were adopted by senior officers) had the potential for defusing or escalating tense situations.

Criticisms have, however, been levelled at the flashpoint model. It is particularly applicable when crowds possess a 'common mind'. This may not, however, always be the case. People may attend the same event for diverse reasons (McPhail, 1991). A riot, for example (as is argued in Chapter 4), may consist of elements who are protesting against social disadvantage, those who view the episode as exciting and wish to participate in it and those who wish to utilise the opportunity to engage in looting. In such circumstances, 'can it be said that there is a single crowd, or a collection of crowdlets?' (P. Waddington, 1996: 119). Additionally, it has been argued that the model is mainly applicable to spontaneous protests and offers a less satisfactory explanation when there is a gap between the precipitant of the event and its actual occurrence (Keith, 1993: 235).

Conclusion

This chapter has considered some general issues which relate to extra-parliamentary politics conducted since 1970 and the reaction of the state to activities of this nature. These are taken up in the subsequent chapters of this book. Chapter 2 considers a variety of actions which can be placed under the umbrella of protest. These include demonstrations, direct action, civil disobedience, physical obstruction and counter-cultural protest. Chapter 3 examines industrial disputes as a specific form of protest taking place within the workplace and often associated with trade unions. Chapter 4 analyses rioting (the most important episodes of which have taken place since 1980) in which violence is used as a method to draw attention to the participants' perceived neglect by the state. The theme of violence is continued in Chapters 5 and 6. Chapter 5 focuses on terrorism. Here the discussion is limited to mainland Britain since an account of politically motivated violence in Northern Ireland would require a far more detailed study than is possible in a synoptic account of this nature. Chapter 6 is concerned with a form of extra-parliamentary political activity that has been a main source of social disharmony and which is diametrically opposed to the progressive causes with which extra-parliamentary politics is often connected. This is racially motivated violence which is put forward as a political activity whose objective is to destroy a multi-racial society.

Glossary

Conventional political activity

Conventional political activity views a country's legislative assembly as the main arena in which political decisions are made: citizens indirectly participate in a state's decision-making process by their involvement in elections contested by political parties putting forward alternative ideologies or policies.

Extra-parliamentary political action

Extra-parliamentary methods offer alternative means of political action to that provided by conventional political activity. This entails actions undertaken by groups of citizens who directly involve themselves in attempts to influence a state's decision-making process by a wide range of methods. The ability to engage in extra-parliamentary political activity is an important feature of all liberal democratic political systems. Extra-parliamentary measures guard against political apathy resulting in a tendency to defer all political decisions to a country's leaders which, if carried to extremes, results in a totalitarian system of government, and may succeed in raising matters which the political parties would prefer to ignore either because they do not consider them to be mainstream political issues which generally dominate election campaigns (such as the economy or law and order) or because they are internally divisive. However, there are problems associated with extra-parliamentary politics. The notion of elections openly contested is a key aspect of liberal democratic political systems whose legitimacy may adversely suffer if extra-parliamentary politics becomes viewed as the way to inaugurate political change. Conventional politics conducted through the ballot box may be viewed as an irrelevant form of activity if other means are both widely practised and achieve success and may serve to undermine the capacity of the government to govern.

Political toleration

Although the freedom of political action and expression are key civil liberties in liberal democractic political systems, restrictions may have to be imposed in connection with views which are acceptable and those which cannot be tolerated and the methods which are used to put political views across to the general public. An important reason for placing restrictictions on political liberties in these circumstances is to protect vulnerable minorities who might be offended, or possibly physically attacked, as the result of the articulation of opinions which are detrimental to them.

References

M. Abrams (1962) 'Social Trends and Electoral Behaviour', *British Journal of Political Sociology*, 13, 238–56

F. Allport (1924) *Social Psychology* (Boston: Houghton Miffin)

G. Almond and S. Verba (1963) *The Civic Culture: Political Attitudes and Democracy in Five Nations* (Princeton, New Jersey: Princeton University Press)

G. Almond and S. Verba (eds) (1989) *The Civic Culture Revisited* (London: Sage)

I. Beckett (1992) 'Conflict Management and the Police: a Policing Strategy for Public Order', in T. Marshall (ed.) *Community Disorders and Policing: Conflict Management in Action* (London: Whiting and Birch)

R. Berk (1993) 'A Gaming Approach to Crowd Behaviour', in R. Curtis and B. Aguirre (eds) *Collective Behaviour and Social Movements* (Boston, MA: Allyn and Bacon)

J. Brewer, A. Guelke, I. Hume, E. Moxon-Browne and R. Wilford (1996) *The Police, Public Order and the State: Policing in Great Britain, Northern Ireland, the Irish Republic, the USA, Israel, South Africa and China* (Basingstoke: Macmillan – now Palgrave Macmillan, 2nd edition)

C. Critcher (2000) 'The Policing of Pit Closures', in R. Bessel and C. Emsley (eds) *Patterns of Provocation: Police and Public Disorder* (Oxford: Breghahn Books)

J. Davies (1969) 'The J-Curve of Rising and Declining Satisfactions as a Cause of some Great Revolutions and a Contained Rebellion', in H. David Graham and T. Gurr (eds) *Violence in America: a Report to the National Commission on the Causes and Prevention of Violence* (Washington DC: US Government Printing Office, Volume 2)

D. Denver (1994) *Elections and Voting Behaviour in Britain* (Hemel Hempstead: Harvester Wheatsheaf, 2nd edition)

P. Eisinger (1973) 'The Conditions of Protest Behaviour in American Cities', *American Political Science Review*, 67, 11–28

S. Freud (1945) *Group Psychology and the Analysis of the Ego* (London: Hogarth)

J. Goldthorpe, D. Lockwood, F. Bechhofer and J. Platt (1968) *The Affluent Worker: Political Attitudes and Behaviour* (Cambridge: Cambridge University Press)

T. Gurr (1969) 'A Comparative Study of Civil Strife', in H. David Graham and T. Gurr (eds) *Violence in America: a Report to the National Commission on the Causes and Prevention of Violence* (Washington DC: US Government Printing Office, Volume 2)

Hansard Society (2001) *None of the Above: Non-Voters and the 2001 Election* (London: Hansard Society)

N. Hertz (2001) *The Silent Takeover: Global Capitalism and the Death of Democracy* (London: Heinemann)

E. Hobsbawn (1959) *Primitive Rebels* (Manchester: Manchester University Press)

B. Hogwood (1987) *From Crisis to Complacency? Shaping Public Policy in Britain* (Oxford: Oxford University Press)

R. Hyman (1972) *Strikes* (London: Fontana)

Independent Labour Party (1990) *The Battle of Trafalgar: Where Next for the Anti-Poll Tax Movement?* (Leeds: Independent Labour Party)

M. Keith (1993) *Lore and Disorder in a Multi-Racial Society* (London: UCL Press)

M. King and N. Brearley (1996) *Public Order Policing: Contemporary Perspectives on Strategy and Tactics* (Leicester: Perpetuity Press, Crime and Security Shorter Study Series: Number 2)

H. Kriesi (1995) 'The Political Opportunity Structure of New Social Movements: its Impact on their Mobilisation', in J. Craig Jenkins and B. Klandermans (eds), *The Politics of Social Protest, Comparative Perspectives on States and Social Movements* (London: UCL Press)

G. Le Bon (1896) *The Crowd: a Study of the Popular Mind* (New York, Viking, 1960, originally published in 1896)

G. Marx and D. McAdam (1994) *Collective Behaviour and Social Movements* (Englewood Cliffs, NJ: Prentice-Hall)

M. Mayer (1995) 'Social Movement Research in the United States: a European Perspective', in S. Lyman (ed.) *Social Movements: Critiques, Concepts, Case Studies* (Basingstoke: Macmillan Press – now Palgrave Macmillan)

D. McAdam, T. McCarthy and N. Zald (eds) (1996) *Comparative Perspective on Social Movements: Political Opportunities, Mobilising Structures and Cultural Framing* (Cambridge, Cambridge University Press)

C. McPhail (1991) *The Myth of the Madding Crowd* (Hawthorne, New York: Aldine de Gruyter)

D. della Porta, (1995) *Social Movements and the State, a Comparative Analysis of Italy and Germany* (Cambridge: Cambridge University Press)

D. della Porta, H. Kriesi and D. Rucht (eds) (1999) *Social Movements in a Globalizing World* (Basingstoke: Macmillan Press – now Palgrave Macmillan)

G. Rude (1964) *The Crowd in History* (New York: John Wiley)

N. Smelser (1962) *Theory of Collective Behaviour* (New York: Free Press)

S. Tarrow (1989) *Democracy and Disorder: Protest and Politics in Italy 1965–1975* (Oxford: Oxford University Press)

D. Waddington, K. Jones and C. Critcher (1989) *Flashpoints: Studies in Public Disorder* (London: Routledge)

D. Waddington (1992) *Contemporary Issues in Public Disorder. A Comparative and Historical Approach* (London: Routledge)

D. Waddington (1996) 'Key Issues and Controversies', in C. Critcher and D. Waddington (eds) *Policing Public Order: Theoretical and Practical Issues* (Aldershot: Avebury)

P. Waddington (1996) 'Public Order Policing: Citizenship and Moral Ambiguity', in F. Leishman, B. Loveday and S. Savage (eds) *Core Issues in Policing* (Harlow: Longman)

P. Whiteley, H. Clarke, D. Sanders and M. Stewart (2001) 'Turnout', *Parliamentary Affairs*, 54(4), 775–88

P. Zimbardo (1969) 'The Human Choice: Reason and Order versus Deindividuation Impulse and Chaos', in W. Arnold and D. Levine (eds) *Nebraska Symposium on Motivation* (Lincoln: University of Nebraska Press)

2
Protest

The ability of individuals or groups to express their opposition to the policies pursued by governments and organisations in the public or private sectors is an important aspect of a liberal democratic political system, being underpinned by the freedom of expression. It has been argued that the rights of peaceful protest and assembly 'are amongst our fundamental freedoms' and are 'numbered among the touchstones which distinguish a free society from a totalitarian one' (Home Office, 1985: 2). This chapter examines the main tactics with which protest has been associated since 1970, evaluates the motives of those who were engaged in these actions, analyses reasons which explain why protest is utilised to further a cause or interest and investigates the response of governments and the police service to these activities.

Introduction

Protest movements use a wide range of extra-parliamentary activities in an attempt to influence the policy-making process of governments and public or private sector organisations. A study conducted in London in the early 1990s revealed the diverse range of causes with which protest was associated (P. Waddington, 1994: 14–22). This section briefly discusses some of the key events with which protest has been associated since 1970. In no sense does this seek to provide a comprehensive account of protest in this period, rather it aims to give a brief snapshot of some principal episodes to illustrate the diverse range of causes and tactics with which protest has been associated in this period. Industrial disputes and urban disorder (which are referred to in the four-fold typology of public order situations in Brearley and King, 1996: 37–69) are dealt with in more detail in Chapters 3 and 4.

Petitions

The use of petitions to the United Kingdom Parliament has declined, although facilities exist for them to be presented to this body. They have, however, formed an important aspect of protest in Scotland since the enactment of the 1998 Scotland Act. Between 1999 and 2001, 241 petitions have been lodged with the Scottish Parliament, most of which resulted in some form of positive action being taken (Lynch and Birrell, 2001). Additionally concern regarding issues of international importance may continue to be raised in this way. A coalition of 100 voluntary groups formed Jubilee 2000, which organised a four-year campaign seeking to have the debts of 52 of the heavily indebted nations cancelled, thereby releasing funds for programmes to eradicate poverty in these countries. Their tactics included a petition which was signed by 24 million people in 166 countries. In June 1999 the G7 countries promised to reduce the debt stock of the most severely affected states and in December of that year the Labour government agreed to cancel all debts owed to it by 41 poor countries.

Demonstrations

Demonstrations are associated with a wide range of causes. One study conducted in London between February 1990 and 1 January 1993 identified 61 political protests concerned with a diverse range of issues which included opposition to cuts in student grants and the poll tax, the support of gay rights, and disapproval of British involvement in Northern Ireland and in the Gulf War (Waddington, 1996: 220–1). Major examples of demonstrations have included those organised by the Campaign for Nuclear Disarmament (CND) in connection with defence policy in the 1950s and early 1960s, by those opposed to American involvement in Vietnam in the 1960s, and by organisations such as the Anti-Nazi League in opposition to racist political parties. Those opposed to the way in which the war in Afghanistan was being prosecuted articulated their disapproval by holding a large demonstration in November 2001. Additionally, demonstrations may be used in an attempt to influence the activities of the private sector.

Demonstrations have frequently resulted in major episodes of public disorder. Contentious items of government policy have provided the background for disorder at events which included the Trafalgar Square anti-poll tax rally in 1990 and the rally organised by the Coalition against the Criminal Justice Bill in 1994 at Hyde Park in London. Alternatively, disorder might arise when groups of protagonists clash. This was a feature of demonstrations connected with the politics of race in the 1960s and 1970s when members of the National Front were physically opposed by groups such as the Anti-Nazi League. A demonstrator, Kevin Gately, was killed at Red Lion Square in 1974 and the disorder in Southall in 1979 resulted in the death of Blair Peach. Subsequent protests against the British National Party and its opponents have also resulted in violence.

Direct action

Since 1970 some groups have gone beyond activities seeking to 'sell' their cause to the general public and have utilised various forms of physical action to implement their objectives. The tactics associated with direct action are varied and range from peaceful methods to violent actions which Chapter 5 identifies as 'terrorism'. Groups may also seek to influence public opinion through the publicity secured by these activities, especially when these are of a spectacular nature.

Direct action has been used by a wide range of groups operating at national and local levels since 1970 and has become especially viewed as a social movements tactic. Organisations which have used direct action include the squatters' movement (which initially emerged in Britain in 1945–46 and reappeared in the late 1960s), the organisations Shelter and Crisis, formed in the 1960s and concerned with homelessness, and groups such as Women's Aid and Rape Crisis which were inspired by the feminist movement and whose actions have also included campaigns designed to 'reclaim the night' and raids on shops selling pornography. Direct action has also been used by organisations such as the Animal Liberation Front to free animals in research laboratories and by groups such as Greenpeace to destroy genetically modi-fied crops, an example of which was the action undertaken by 28 activists in Norfolk in July 1999 who destroyed six acres of genetically modified maize. Direct action has also been used in connection with protest of a local nature. The 1980s witnessed what the media described as 'an explosion in grass roots organising' which entailed the setting-up of a large number of volun-tary action groups concerned with a wide range of locally-orientated causes (Butcher et al., 1980: 3).

The line separating direct action from terrorism is (as is argued in Chapter 5) hard to draw. Those using direct action will frequently invoke a higher moral law such as a United Nations Declaration or the desire to prevent a greater crime as the justification for breaking the law (Purkis, 1996: 200). This form of defence has evoked much sympathy in courts in the United Kingdom when trying cases which have involved environmen-tal protesters performing actions such as attacking genetically modified crops or by groups expressing their opposition to nuclear weapons. Those opposed to genetically modified food have defended direct action which involved pulling up crops by arguing that this action is legitimate when done in defence of a clear moral principle and to prevent a real and imme-diate threat such as genetic pollution (Melchett, 2000), and women pro-testers at Greenham Common in the 1980s sought to justify their actions by arguing that the government was breaking the Genocide Act.

Since 1970 direct action has been associated with a wide range of distinct activities including those which are discussed below.

Economic sanctions

Consumer boycotts have constituted an important aspect of protest and dis-sent since 1970 and have been advocated by Greenpeace to change the policies pursued by national governments and international corporations.

One example of the use of this tactic against a government was the call to boycott Norwegian goods in 1994 in order to put pressure on that government to end commercial whaling.

Frequently, however, consumer boycotts have been directed against business organisations. The mobilisation of consumers to 'insert a political or moral element into their purchasing decisions, rather than being driven by purely utilitarian concerns such as price and quality' (Jasper, 1997: 264) is potentially likely to be more effective than conventional forms of political activity seeking to get governments to enact legislation to control the affairs of large business corporations since their capacity and willingness to do this (especially in the case of large multinational companies) is extremely limited. The effectiveness of consumer boycotts is enhanced when they succeed in bringing together a diverse range of groups: in June 1999, for example, the Federation of Women's Institutes voted to join with a number of consumer and environmental groups – including Greenpeace and Friends of the Earth – to call for a freeze on growing genetically modified crops. Examples of consumer boycotts since 1970 have included action directed against Barclays Bank because of its stake in South Africa's apartheid regime. The bank lost around 50 per cent of its student accounts during the boycott and in 1986 sold its stake in Barclays National. This tactic was also deployed in the campaign to stop the Shell Oil company disposing of its disused Brent Spar oil rig in the North Atlantic in June 1995. The loss of revenue in Britain and Europe arising from a boycott of its products resulted in the company abandoning its plans to sink the installation at sea. In 2001 a campaign to boycott Exxon (which trades in the UK as Esso) was launched because it was seen by environmental activists as the biggest corporate opponent of the Kyoto Treaty to prevent greenhouse gas emissions which President Bush refused to sign up to in 2001. This campaign was accompanied by other tactics conducted by Greenpeace activists which included blocking access to tanker traffic at Esso's depot in Purfleet, Surrey, in July 2001 by bolting two shipping containers to the tarmac.

Civil disobedience

Civil disobedience is frequently referred to as 'non-violent direct action' and is generally understood to involve 'the deliberate and open act of breaking an unjust law' (Carter, 1983: 13). It may entail deploying economic sanctions against the government by a refusal to pay taxes. Examples of this included the suggestion by the national executive of the National Federation of Self-Employed to withhold VAT payments to Customs and Excise in 1975, and the 'can't pay, won't pay' stance of those opposed to the poll tax after 1990 who sought to achieve a political objective by a refusal to obey the law. Civil disobedience is also performed through the use of actions such as *vigils*, mass sit-ins or trespass where the intention is that the dignity of the protest will aid the cause with which it is associated.

Civil disobedience has been widely used by the Peace Movement. The Committee of One Hundred's use of the tactic of mass sit-down protests to further its opposition to Britain's independent nuclear deterrent constituted an example of civil disobedience in the early 1960s and at its annual conference held in Sheffield in 1982 CND voted overwhelmingly to use non-violent direct action in pursuance of the movement's aims.

Physical obstruction

Many of the actions associated with civil disobedience are primarily symbolic, characterised by avoiding the coercion of others and limiting the sacrifice to those actually involved in undertaking the action (Carter, 1983: 5). However, it may develop into tactics which physically oppose a course of action pursued by a government or private organisation to which the group objects, using methods which include sit-ins, occupations, trespass and blockades. *Physical obstruction* has been used in connection with attempts to prevent the closure of local facilities, such as hospitals, and with causes of national or international concern. The disruption of the South African Rugby tour of 1969–70 organised by the Stop the Seventies Tour Committee used activities which included holding sit-down protests on playing fields and disrupting coach journeys (Benewick and Smith, 1972: 193). The threat of actions of this nature caused the abandonment of a proposed South African cricket tour in 1970. Tactics which included occupation, trespass and blockade were used in the campaign mounted by women at Greenham Common in protest against the Cruise Missiles stationed there which commenced in 1982 (Benton, 1983). In 1983, 50,000 women gathered outside this base to express their opposition to nuclear weapons. A more recent example of obstruction inspired by these motives was the occupation by Greenpeace of the Menwith Hill base (which is under RAF jurisdiction but is operated by the American National Security Agency) in July 2001 to express opposition to the proposed 'star wars' system in which Menwith Hill was expected to play a crucial role. Blockades to prevent the movement of fuel from distribution points was the key feature of the 2000 fuel crisis which is discussed later in this chapter.

Physical obstruction has also been used in environmental and animal rights protests. This activity was initiated by those opposed to further motorway construction in connection with the M3 extension at Twyford Down in 1992 and was subsequently adopted elsewhere by 'anti-road protesters' who built and occupied 'tree houses' or burrowed underground in an attempt to prevent roads being built. Examples of other protests with similar objectives took place in connection with the construction of the M11 link road through East London in 1994, the M77 extension to link Glasgow and Kilmarnock in 1997, the A34 Newbury bypass in 1996 and the proposed A310 in Essex in 2000. Attempts to prevent motorway construction during the 1990s often involved protesters fighting pitched battles with police, bailiffs and security guards to prevent evictions from camps and tree houses. Allegations of violence were made by both sides of the dispute and particular criticism was directed against security guards whose behaviour, unlike that of the police, was not regulated by any disciplinary code.

Live animal exports became a lucrative trade in the 1990s. Groups, including Compassion in World Farming, opposed the conditions under which British animals were exported to Europe and the methods used by farms involved in veal production. Initially animals were transported to the Continent by ferry companies operating from the Port of Dover, but their withdrawal from this trade in 1995 forced animal exporters to go elsewhere – to ports which included Shoreham, Brightlingsea and Plymouth (Critcher, 1996: 54). Those opposed to the trade in live animals sought to prevent lorries reaching ports by obstructing highways and their actions resulted in major episodes of public disorder. Violence occurred when protesters who aimed to physically prevent lorries taking animals to ports clashed with police seeking to prevent obstructions to the highway. Claims of overly aggressive policing to clear the roads for lorries were made by residents of Brightlingsea whose objections included the police's use of long batons and the wearing of balaclavas. Attempts were also made to disrupt flights from airports such as Swansea and Coventry in 1995 which became involved in this trade when the volume of protest made the use of ports difficult. These latter actions led to the death of one protester, Jill Phipps, outside Coventry airport in 1995.

Counter-cultural forms of protest

Counter-culture constitutes a rejection of the dominant society and its culture (Nelson, 1989: 8) and typically entails an attack on the moral standards and material values on which the existing social order is based. The formal arrival of a counter-culture in England was signalled by the launch of the *International Times* in October 1966. Counter-cultural protest embraces a wide range of actions. It frequently promotes philosophies that are designed to form the basis of alternative lifestyles which include communes and various forms of cooperative endeavours. It may involve an attack on conventional behaviour designed to shock 'respectable' society which may be delivered in various ways including the use of the underground press, literature and music. One example of the latter was the version of *God Save the Queen* released by the punk rock group, the Sex Pistols, in 1977 to coincide with the Queen's Silver Jubilee celebrations. The causes with which counter-cultural protest have been associated are broad, and in the post-war period have included the demand for radical political change, protection of the environment (in opposition, for example, to road building) and the liberalisation of drug laws.

The activities performed by a number of groups since 1970 may be described as counter-cultural. 'New Age Travellers' (a description applied to a diverse range of groups which shared a common desire for freedom and a rejection of the state) have adopted life styles which contravened established patterns of social behaviour. Some environmental groups have also endorsed the cultural transformation of society into an ecological one based on the philosophy of social ecology (Purkis, 1996: 205).

Counter-cultural forms of activity have sometimes resulted in disorder in which those engaged in such activities clash with the police. New Age Travellers have frequently been at the centre of violence when the police have sought to prevent them occupying common land or evicted them from private land. In June 1985, 1000 officers drawn from five police forces intercepted a convoy of New Age Travellers on the border of Hampshire and Wiltshire. English Heritage and the National Trust obtained injunctions to bar them from their land and the police herded them into a field where they, their vans and buses were subjected to action described by an ITN journalist as 'the most brutal treatment of people I've witnessed in my entire career as a journalist' (Sabido, 1985). Four hundred and twenty travellers were arrested in the 'battle of the beanfield' which is generally regarded to have instigated grass-roots environmentalism. Conflict of this nature became an annual feature of the druid celebration of the summer solstice at Stonehenge. Other activities associated with counter-cultural forms of youth activity have included the illegal use of drugs. Hippies, for example, made use of psychedelic drugs.

Counter-cultural protest is distinguished from other forms of popular culture adopted by young people in that it contains a distinct political element. The latter may nonetheless be viewed as political in the sense that manifestations of popular culture in 'elaborated societies' constitute 'the culture of the subordinate who resent their subordination' (Fiske, 1989: 169). The term 'swinging sixties' denoted the existence of a youth culture which embraced large numbers of young people who rejected the dominant values of society. In the 1990s large numbers of youths adopted rave as their culture. This blended the 1970's festival movement with urban youth culture and was particularly associated with participation at events at which loud music was played and which were associated with the use of the drug, ecstasy. Youth sub-cultures have also involved physical conflict. Examples of this included the battles waged between 'mods' and 'rockers' in the 1960s and attempts by police forces to prevent the holding of acid house parties.

A case study in protest (1): the anti-poll tax movement

The anti-poll tax movement illustrates the wide range of tactics which are available to those seeking to change the direction of government policies. This movement emerged following the replacement of domestic rates as the local component of local government expenditure by a community charge commonly referred to as the poll tax. This was a flat rate tax on individual adults as opposed to the historic tax which was levied on the rateable value of property. This reform was proposed in the Conservative Party's manifesto at the 1987 general election and was implemented in Scotland in 1989 and in England and Wales one year later. The aim of this innovation was to ensure that all individuals made some contribution towards local government expenditure. This was intended to enhance the degree of accountability of local government to its electors, the belief being that what was viewed by the Conservative Party as profligate expenditure would not be approved of if all local residents were required to contribute towards it. However, opposition to this tax was widespread, principally as it imposed a disproportionate burden on poorer persons: all were required to contribute although those on benefits paid only a portion of the tax.

Opposition to this tax was mounted by the anti-poll tax movement which pursued a wide range of tactics which included petitions, demonstrations and marches, and civil disobedience which took the form of public burnings of poll tax demands issued by local authorities. On 31 March 1990 a march organised by the All-Britain Anti-Poll Tax Federation resulted in 1985 reported crimes, the arrest of 408 persons and damage to property estimated at £3 million (Mason, 1991: 476–77). The weight of opposition, coupled with administrative factors which included the high cost of collecting the tax resulted in its abandonment in 1992. It was replaced by the current community charge.

A case study in protest (2): the 2000 fuel crisis

The 2000 fuel crisis was an important example of the potent effect of protest. It also provided a good illustration of the way in which those who deem themselves to be ignored by government may engage in protest in an attempt to ensure that their concerns are placed on the policy-making agenda. It further illustrated the way in which the balance between insider and outsider groups (Grant, 1989: 14–15) can radically alter and encourage the formation of protest movements from those who traditionally felt no need to take their concerns onto the streets.

Rural interests were traditionally represented by the Conservative Party which dominated UK politics between 1979 and 1997. However, the landslide election of a Labour government in that year troubled those living in the countryside. Although the access enjoyed by the National Farmers' Union to the Ministry of Agriculture, Food and Fisheries was unchanged, many rural dwellers perceived that their interests would be neglected by government. Their concerns included the crisis affecting agriculture in the aftermath of the BSE crisis which aggravated anxieties about the industry's uncompetitiveness in global markets, the closure of rural facilities such as schools, post offices and shops, the inadequacies of rural public transport, and the extent of rural crime where rural Britain felt itself almost defence-less. They feared that a Labour administration led by a metropolitan elite which did not understand the problems of the countryside (McNaughton, 2001: 19–20) would ride rough-shod over their interests. This fear seemed to be starkly confirmed when in 1997 the House of Commons overwhelm-ingly backed a Bill put forward by a Labour backbench MP, Michael Foster, to ban foxhunting. To many in the countryside this practice epitomised the countryside way of life and the fact that legislation to outlaw it seemed a likely occurrence resulted in major demonstrations taking place in London in July 1997 and March 1998 which were joined by 100,000 and in excess of 250,000 people respectively.

Many of those who were concerned about the perceived neglect of the countryside joined movements representing rural England, most notably the Countryside Alliance (and its more militant wing, the Rural Action Group) which were formed in the mid-1990s. However, these people realised they were unlikely to undermine the government with a minority sectional inter-est of this nature. They needed, therefore, a broader issue which would include other sections of opinion. The opportunity to do this was provided by a cut in oil production sanctioned by OPEC which resulted in a rise in petrol prices in 2000.

The high price of fuel in the UK was aggravated by the high level of tax-ation levied upon it and the desire of the petrol companies to maximise their profits through high prices. Approximately 77 per cent of the cost of a gallon of fuel was accounted for by fuel duty and VAT. The Labour gov-ernment's desire not to raise income tax made it particularly reliant on this form of 'stealth tax' although the high fuel tax was also justified on envi-ronmental grounds, which suggested it encouraged the reduced use of private transport. Although the agricultural industry benefited from a large subsidy on diesel for industrial use, high fuel prices were a key issue among rural dwellers who were dependent on private transport in the absence of adequate public facilities. It was also an important issue for other groups such as road hauliers who had been involved in protests such as blocking motorways in May 1999 in response to high prices of diesel fuel and the road vehicle excise duty which had been raised in the spring 1999 budget. It was to be anticipated that a protest against the price of fuel would attract support from groups other than those immediately associated with the agricultural industry. The self-interest of every motorist would potentially be appealed to in a protest demanding a lower rate of fuel duty, thus trans-forming a sectional interest into a general tax-payers' protest in which the government could be depicted as out of touch with popular opinion by refusing to respond to what many members of the general public felt was a major concern that they wished to see addressed.

Action was initiated in France in late August when the Channel Ports and Channel Tunnel were blockaded by French fishermen protesting against escalating fuel prices. This (and the French government's subsequent caving in to this pressure) encouraged similar action in Britain in which a range of diverse groups, spearheaded by farmers and road hauliers, began to blockade petrol distribution points. The protest in the United Kingdom commenced when around 200 farmers and lorry drivers organised an impromptu blockade of the Stanlow oil refinery at Cheshire on 7 September 2000. It was organised by the People's Fuel Lobby since established groups (including the National Farmers' Union, the Countryside Alliance and the Road Haulage Association) were officially opposed to this form of action. Those who took part in these protests consisted of scattered groups who never formally met but who communicated by mobile telephones and the internet. The blockade of oil refineries subsequently spread throughout England, Scotland and Wales.

The effect of the protest was aided by a number of factors. The government failed to appreciate the seriousness of the situation for the initial days of the protest and thus did nothing to coordinate action against it. No formal or informal directions were given to the police in this period as to how the protest should be handled. The stance of the police also aided the protest. Police non-intervention was justified by the argument that the protesters were non-violent (although accusations were subsequently made that severe intimidation did occur) and readily obeyed any police request, for example to clear a road. Unlike the miners' dispute in 1984/5 (which is discussed in Chapter 3) local police officers, who had no desire to antagonise leading members of their own community, were used in these actions. Also, any vigorous action which the police may have liked to pursue was hampered by the fact that those who masterminded the protests were not part of any organised group such as a trade union. The protest was also aided by the attitude adopted by the petrol companies (and particularly by the fuel depot managers) who made no attempt to put pressure on tanker drivers to force their way through blockades to deliver fuel (thus leaving it up to individual drivers to cross or not to cross the unofficial picket lines which were manned by those who included colleagues in the road haulage industry) nor to test the legality of the protest in the courts. This inaction was perhaps indicative of the fact that the petrol companies were sympathetic to the objective of lowering fuel taxes, in part because this deflected attention away from the contribution which their profit margins made to the price motorists paid at the pump for their fuel. It subsequently emerged, however, that large organisations such as Shell did not employ their own tanker drivers (who were employed by P&O and who would have benefited from a reduction in fuel duty) and thus were in no position to issue instructions to them.

Accordingly, the nation began to run out of fuel and the credibility of the government was adversely affected since they were blamed for not being able to prevent the problems posed to motorists. The government's support dipped 20 points in the opinion polls in the period of one week. However, public support for the protest was influenced by government claims that the National Health Service would face chaos if it were not called off. The blockade was eventually ended when union officials persuaded tanker drivers at Grangemouth to resume supplies. The availability of large police escorts for tanker drivers both on leaving fuel depots and when delivering fuel to petrol station forecourts encouraged drivers elsewhere to take similar action. This prompted protesters to abandon their campaign but on their own terms. The action was terminated on the understanding that the government had 60 days to concede to the protesters' demands which were to make a considerable reduction in the duty paid on fuel. It had taken ten days to bring the protest under control.

Some immediate concessions were made to the fuel protesters. The November 2000 pre-budget statement was directed at motorists and road hauliers by proposing a freeze on fuel taxes and a cut in the cost of vehicle excise duty by up to £1000 for some lorries. The November Budget subsequently froze fuel duty until 2002, and offered a lower rate of road tax for cars up to 1500 cc. In February 2001 an emergency cut of two pence a litre on the duty for unleaded petrol to last until June was also introduced. Other areas of government activity were also directed at rural areas, including the Home Secretary's announcement of an extra £30 million to rural police forces to tackle crime in these areas.

Members of the Labour government subsequently vented their anger against those involved in the protests. The rhetoric of the protesters was anti-government which led the then leader of the House of Commons to suggest that it was a right-wing conspiracy by those who 'passionately believe, it's more than a belief, it's an emotion that there is something terribly, terribly wrong about having a Labour government' (Beckett, 2000). The leader of the Transport and General Workers' Union, Bill Morris, called for a public inquiry into why oil companies and the police appeared to collude with protesters.

More vigorous steps were taken by the government to ensure that the threatened resumption of protests on 13 November 2000 would find success harder to achieve. Following the end of the protest, advance preparations to combat its resumption were made by a Fuel Taskforce which was set up in the Cabinet Office and the Civil Contingencies Unit, chaired by the Home Secretary. New tactics were agreed with the police regarding motorway protests by lorry drivers which ensured that deliberate attempts to obstruct the flow of traffic would be treated as a criminal offence. This course of action had been adopted in some areas in September 2000 (most notably by the Greater Manchester Police) which had charged drivers with wilful obstruction. These preparations to keep major roads open were coupled with other measures to protect essential targets (such as food distribution centres for leading supermarket chains). The Home Secretary further warned drivers that those who participated in protests of this nature ran the risk of having their operating licence revoked (and thus their vehicle impounded). The police also agreed to escort tankers through unofficial picket lines and emergency heavy goods vehicle training was initiated to increase the number of soldiers who could be deployed in driving tankers in a future dispute. Emergency services (especially the National Health Service) stockpiled supplies and drew up contingency plans, and the number of essential users (who would be given priority use of petrol) was greatly increased. Petrol stations also stockpiled vast amounts of petrol. The government contemplated legislation to extend the 1976 Energy Act to the oil companies thereby imposing a legal duty on them to maintain supplies. Local special branches gathered information on protesters, and M15 (whose role is discussed in Chapter 7) infiltrated some groups involved in the earlier protest. The government also attempted to seize the initiative with public opinion, highlighting, for example, incidents of alleged intimidation against tanker drivers that had taken place at the earlier protest. These advance preparations played a major role in preventing a repeat of the crisis when the protesters' deadline expired on 13 November 2000.

Protest – the organisations

The previous section has indicated that the willingness of groups to utilise activities which include demonstrations, direct action, and counter-cultural forms of protest to further their opinions or to oppose the views of others has been a prominent feature of British political activity since 1970. These activities are commonly carried out by *pressure groups* and *minor parties*, although protest can also be channelled through the formal institutions of the state such as *local government acting as a pressure group* whose elected base makes it a potent political force. A particularly important role in contemporary forms of protest is performed by social movements.

'Social movements' may be defined as 'organised, collective efforts to achieve social change that use non-institutional tactics at least part of the time' (Burstein et al., 1995: 278) which have 'political or redistributive goals as their central mission' (Amenta and Zylan, 1995: 219) and constitute 'collective enterprises to establish a new order of life'. Four characteristic aspects of social movements have been identified – the existence of informal interaction networks between a plurality of individuals and groups/ organisations, the holding of shared beliefs and solidarity between them, the desire to engage in political and/or social conflicts to promote or oppose social transformation, and the willingness to use violence and confrontational tactics to secure change (della Porta and Diana, 1999: 14–15). Social movements were born in conditions of unrest and derived their power from dissatisfaction with the current form of life and desires for a new scheme or system of living (Blumer, 1995: 60). Social movements are associated with the left wing of the political spectrum but have substituted the traditional Marxist emphasis on the overthrow of capitalism achieved by a working-class revolution with a range of direct action tactics carried out by persons of diverse social backgrounds which seek to transform society by redefining social values and thus culturally undermine this economic system and alter patterns of mass consumption.

Social movements tend to be loosely organised in comparison to pressure groups and in particular lack the leadership and organisation which characterise pressure groups. They often have a 'nebulous organisational existence' (Clegg, 1996: 51). Indeed, the advent of technology, such as the internet, makes it possible to create movements almost on an ad hoc basis fashioned around a particular cause or objective. Further, the focus of their concern is often broader, seeking to instil new moral values within society. Social movements are denied easy access to decision-makers and thus typically operate outside mainstream political institutions using protest activities through which they seek to address public opinion (della Porta, 1995: 8). These often embrace various forms of direct action rather than methods such as demonstrations with which radical protest in Britain was traditionally associated. Social movement activity is frequently carried out on an international stage rather than being confined to any particular country. Some social movements might seek close association with a political party to advance their aims but they are generally sceptical of the value of close collaboration with these organisations. They may perceive that close association with one particular political party (which is typically a party in opposition seeking to enhance its electoral support through association with organised interests) would hamper the group's effectiveness either by tying it too closely to the political fortunes of that party or by making it difficult for the group to work with other political parties which might form the government. The incorporation of the peace movement into the Labour Party in the 1980s and that party's subsequent defeat at the polls in 1983 and 1987 provided a case study of the dangers in forging too close an identity between social movements and political parties (Maguire, 1995: 209–17). After 1987 the Labour Party began to view CND and the peace movement as an electoral liability which resulted in the abandonment of its independent nuclear disarmament policy in 1989. Additionally, some movements (such as the environmental movement) have jointly utilised extra-parliamentary forms of political activity in association with conventional methods to mobilise popular support for their objectives. Greenpeace, for example, has sought to combine a range of direct action tactics with the use of lobbying and scientific inquiry designed to alert both governments and the public to the problems facing the natural world (Brown and May, 1991: 5).

Protest: the participants

Various explanations have been offered to explain why individuals engage in protest. These include status inconsistency, cumulative deprivation, relative deprivation, rising expectations and social isolation (Orum, 1993). This section assesses the social background of those involved in the protests discussed previously and examines their motives for participating in these activities.

Middle-class dissent and progressive politics

The involvement of middle-class radicals is a particularly important aspect of protest designed to secure progressive reform in Great Britain. This situation emerged in the nineteenth century when to be a reformer placed considerable demands on a person's money and time (Huggett, 1971) and has remained a feature of a number of protest movements since 1970. The Campaign for Nuclear Disarmament had a middle-class base (Parkin: 1968) and middle-class women were involved in peace protests outside Greenham Common and Molesworth American Airforce bases in the 1980s. The feminist movement in the United Kingdom has also been described as 'white and middle class' (Clegg, 1996: 52), although support for the ideals of this movement extended beyond this social grouping. A significant feature of protests against motorway construction and the export of live animals in the 1990s was the diverse social background of the participants which included suburban housewives and property owners (Brewer et al., 1996: xxvii), and many students have been attracted into the anti-capitalist movement. Some anti-capitalist groups (such as Reclaim the Streets) have secured a degree of middle-class and professional support, and it has been argued that working-class identifiers and union members were generally less likely to engage in civil disobedience, which supported the idea that this was a middle-class protest tactic (Wallace and Jenkins, 1995: 127–31).

A major study conducted into the membership of Amnesty International, Friends of the Earth and National Farmers' Union Countryside concluded that women were disproportionately active in public interest groups (perhaps either as they had distinct policy preferences or because they were relatively disadvantaged in other political arenas), and that those who joined environmental groups tended to be more educated than the public as a whole. Most members of Friends of the Earth and Amnesty International were in professional, managerial and senior administrative occupations and the majority of members of all three groups (when pressed) described themselves as middle rather than working class, and were relatively affluent in terms of income. It was also concluded that environmental organisations tended to recruit heavily from the young, with 62 per cent of members of Friends of the Earth being below 35 years of age (Jordan and Maloney, 1997: 108–15).

Middle-class dissent and right-wing politics

Middle-class dissent is not, however, confined to seeking progressive political reform. The 1970s witnessed the emergence of a number of organisations which were defensive in nature, seeking to protect middle-class concerns which were perceived to be under threat from a wide range of challenges which were viewed as threatening to their economic status and detrimental to the cultural standards which they adhered to, in particular the importance they attached to the role of the family. Examples of groups which articulated middle-class protests of this nature included the National Association for Freedom, the National Festival of Light, the National Viewers' and Listeners' Association, groups representing the self-employed, and locally-oriented Amenity Societies and ratepayers' groups (many of which affiliated to the National Association of Ratepayers' Action Groups when it was established in 1974). Although these groups were diverse 'most shared a persisting dislike of higher taxation, bureaucratisation, the growth of government power and the decline in individualism' (King, 1979: 5). Their formation was underpinned by the level of inflation in the early 1970s and the public spending and taxation policies pursued by Labour governments after February 1974.

Populism

Populist politics advocates the pursuance of policies which are depicted as being supported by majority public opinion. Populist politicians claim that they speak for the people whom they seek to galvanise by playing on past myths or present fears (Street, 1997: 17–18). The concerns and the values which underpin populist politics are not derived from any coherent set of political beliefs but are widely varied, although a common strand is that the concerns which are articulated in populist rhetoric are depicted as resting on 'common sense' assumptions. Typically populist politics directs its appeal to the masses over the heads of other established social and political institutions (such as the family, social class, political parties and trade unions) by focusing on a cause which can be depicted as harmful and contrary to the best interests of mass public opinion. This appeal is especially directed at those at the lower end of the social scale although the leaders of such movements tend to be drawn from higher up the social ladder.

Some aspects of middle-class inspired protest in the 1970s were populist in nature, seeking to advance the cause of the 'ordinary man and woman' whose interests were allegedly overlooked by the power wielded in contemporary society by organisations such as speculators, big business, finance capitalism (King, 1979: 6) and trade unions. As is argued in Chapter 5, this stance is also associated with political parties on the extreme right of the political spectrum who oppose the elitism of the main parties. The 2000 fuel crisis (which has been discussed above) was also an example of a middle-class directed protest which had populist overtones, seeking to voice the concerns of a wide cross-section of British society against a government which was depicted as out of touch with popular opinion, and uncaring.

The working class

The political actions undertaken by the working class are dependent on a range of external influences which include the specific form of capital accumulation in particular localities and the resources and powers which they possess when acting collectively. These are historically and spatially variable (Johnson, 1996: 141). In general terms, however, working-class involvement in conventional political activity is limited. Working-class areas traditionally exhibit lower levels of turnout at elections than more affluent areas, suggesting that those of low social and economic status are least likely to vote in elections. The higher level of apathy towards conventional politics may underpin a greater willingness to engage in various forms of protest to achieve reform. There is (as Chapter 3 argues) a long history of working-class involvement in trade union activity to raise bread-and-butter concerns such as wages and conditions of labour and to promote reforms in the interests of the working class through means such as strike action. Working-class interests have also been articulated in activities which included the 'hunger marches' of the 1930s which were organised by the National Unemployed Workers' Union, in particular the Jarrow protest march of 1936. Working-class involvement in protest movements may also be based on an attempt to undermine the habits and lifestyles of those in a higher social bracket: for example, young working-class radicals were involved in attempts to ban the hunting of mammals with dogs in the 1960s as hunting was seen as an upper-class pursuit.

The concept of the moral economy historically underpinned some examples of progressive working-class protests such as bread riots, where the key issue was a sense of moral outrage directed especially against exploitive prices and unreasonable levels of taxation. A direct link between protest of this nature and the anti-poll tax movement of the 1990s has been constructed. It has been argued that the poll tax was seen as an issue of distributive inequality most frequently expressed in terms of the language of class, and that 'opposition to the poll tax was an expression of an underlying moral evaluation of the poll tax's principles' (Bagguley, 1996: 11, 19). Localised rent strikes in protest against unreasonable rent increases constituted a further example of more localised protests of this nature. Working-class involvement in various forms of protest may be defensive, for example to preserve local amenities such as schools or hospitals (an example of the latter being documented by Barker, 1996: 25–43).

However, not all forms of working-class involvement in protest movements are progressive. In 2000, following the murder of an eight-year-old school girl, Sarah Payne, the *News of the World* newspaper embarked upon a 'name and shame' policy directed at convicted paedophiles. This resulted in a number of examples of mob rule in working-class areas directed against paedophiles which included the murder of one person in his north London home and several assaults on persons suspected (sometimes wrongly) of being child abusers.

Women

The specific involvement of women in industrial protests is discussed in Chapter 3. Other protests, in particular (as has been observed above) the peace movement, also have a specifically female tradition. The perception that women had something specific to contribute to the peace movement which developed in Britain around the time of the First World War was attributed to four ideological reasons. The commitment to peace derived from the position of women as mothers, from their conditioning in nurturing and caring roles, from their position outside the major power hierarchies which allowed them a particular critical viewpoint, and from their understanding of the interdependence of peace and the emancipation of women (Eglin, 1987: 228). Although there was no independent female tradition in the British peace movement of the 1960s (Eglin, 1987: 239), a number of women became involved in the 1980s against the background of the development of an active women's movement and the view that women as biological mothers had a special concern for peace (Eglin, 1987: 243–4).

Young people

Persons below the age of 18 (who numbered 11 million in 2001) are not eligible to vote in elections. The exclusion of this large group from the liberal democratic process is one reason to explain why young people play a limited role in conventional politics even when they have reached 18: they have not been sufficiently socialised into voting when they acquire the right to do so. At the 1997 general election only 44 per cent of those aged 18–24 voted and 71 per cent of those aged 16–21 believed that the outcome of elections would make no difference to their lives (Hertz, 2001c). This pattern was repeated at the 2001 general election when six out of ten young people failed to vote (Hansard Society, 2001: 1). It has been argued that for the 18–34 year old generation, 'politics has become a dirty word' and such citizens are 'less likely to vote, to join a political party or be politically active. Under 25s are four times less likely to be registered than any other group' (findings quoted in Wilkinson and Mulgan, 1995: 17). The lack of participation by young people in conventional political activity may result in government being viewed as remote, arrogant and unresponsive to their needs, especially when their behaviour is stigmatised for political purposes and may result in their involvement in protest to secure political change. However, this scepticism towards conventional political activity does not necessarily imply total apathy towards politics. It has been suggested that 18–34 year olds expressed an interest in specific political issues and were prone to active involvement in voluntary organisations (Gaskin et al., 1996) and that in the 2001 general election, 24 per cent of those aged 18–24 who were defined as active citizens (for example by participating in a demonstration or march or attending a political or interest group meeting) failed to vote (Hansard Society, 2001: 8).

Educated young people

Radical British students were at the forefront of marches which took place in the 1960s to express opposition to American policy in Vietnam (D. Waddington, 1992: 35) and educated young people are a specific group of young people who have been involved in numerous protest movements since 1970. Factors which included the extension of higher education, and especially the development of the social sciences, have been cited as responsible for constructing and engendering 'a fundamental change in political socialisation of a significant minority of young people which has attracted them towards radical activism' (Benewick and Smith, 1972: 306), and a study in America concluded that more educated people were found to be more likely to tolerate or grant legitimacy to collective action on behalf of a cause which they themselves did not support (Hall et al., 1986: 564). Counter-cultural protests have frequently involved young persons from middle-class backgrounds. In the 1960s university students were involved in the establishment of communes or other 'alternative' social units. Students were heavily involved in the campaign against the financial stake held by Barclays Bank in South Africa's apartheid regime in the 1980s. It has been observed that activists in campaigning movements such as Earth First! were mainly young white persons from middle-class backgrounds who were well-educated but who were economically 'decommodified' in the sense that they could not expect security of employment or guaranteed access to welfare provision or accomodation (Purkis, 1996: 200). These persons were dubbed the 'educated underclass' in that they possessed 'cultural capital' but subsisted on very low incomes (Bordieu, 1984) and were sceptical of the ability of current political and economic structures to solve individual or global problems. A later study suggested that those likely to be involved in protests tended to be more middle class, younger and more highly educated than those not likely to be involved in such events. Nineteen per cent of the middle class compared with 15 per cent of the working class were quite likely to be protesters. Twenty-one per cent of persons educated beyond the age of 19 were likely to be protesters compared with 14 per cent of those who left school at 16 (Whiteley, 2000).

These were not necessarily descendants of the middle-class progressive tradition but constituted those who were attracted to protest movements and alternative lifestyles either because they rejected the success goals in Thatcher's Britain or because they perceived they were unlikely to attain them. One explanation why educated, middle-class persons protest is the notion of relative deprivation: people protest when there is a big gap between what they want out of life and what they are getting (Whiteley, 2000).

Case study: the anti-capitalist movement in the UK

The anti-capitalist movement is an example of a group which includes many young, educated middle-class persons among its participants. It is an umbrella that shelters a very wide array of groups who are opposed both to capitalism and globalisation. Groups associated with this ideal have demonstrated on numerous occasions such as May Day and when leaders of government have met. The capacity for these causes to attract a very broad base of support was illustrated at the G8 summit in Genoa in July 2001 where one umbrella group, the Genoa Social Forum, embraced 700 groups worldwide.

A particular focus of their dissent is directed at the world's trading system and its domination by the World Trade Organisation and International Monetary Fund which are perceived as being controlled by large – mainly American-owned – multinational corporations. The WTO was established in 1995 and its trade agreements, which are binding on all member countries, have been criticised for limiting the ability of national governments to safeguard the interests of their citizens (Hertz, 2001a). The present system of world trade is attacked for requiring developing countries to open up their national economies to large corporations and to subscribe to the rule of market forces which requires the reduction of state services, and the processes of deregulation and privatisation. It is thus argued that free trade does not bring about the enhanced eradication of poverty and that the current direction of trade is to the benefit of the northern hemisphere and the disbenefit of the southern hemisphere, thus increasing the disparity between the 'haves' and 'have nots'. It is also argued that attempts to secure trade liberalisation have an adverse impact on the environment by undermining measures designed to protect it which are sacrificed in order to boost production. Symbols of international capitalism are frequently attacked in demonstrations as anti-capitalists believe that these international chains are responsible for damage to the environment and prevent the development of local industries, forcing businesses to close and thus being responsible for creating poverty and debt in the developing world. These companies are also perceived as being responsible for the creation of a new global culture which is rejected by the emerging groups of cultural activists who wish to preserve local identities.

The anti-capitalist movement first appeared at the Seattle Trade Talks in 1999. In June of that year a 'Carnival against Capitalism' was held in the City of London which resulted in an estimated £2 million worth of damage, and a demonstration on May Day 2000 in London resulted in disorder in which the Cenotaph and a statue of Winston Churchill were defaced. A diverse range of groups have been involved in anti-capitalist protests in the United Kingdom, broadly divided into 'spikies' (who carried out acts of violence which they justified by arguing that these are insignificant in scale compared to the violence of global capitalism) and 'fluffies' who endorsed non-violent direct action. Groups which have been involved in anti-capitalist protests have included the 'Wombles' (White Overall Movement Building Liberation through Effective Struggle) who appeared in the May Day demonstration in the UK in 2001. This was an anarchist movement which believed in non-violent direct action. Other anarchist groups included Class War which advocated violence as the most appropriate means of overthrowing capitalism, and the Anarchist Federation which was especially concerned with opposition to Third World debt and globalisation.

Other groups have included Reclaim the Streets, a coalition of groups without a central organisation, or ideology, whose objective was to undermine (rather than overthrow) the state which it sought to do by decreasing people's dependence on it. Its tactics have included 'guerrilla gardening' in which areas such as city centres were taken over and turned over to alternative uses: on 1 May 2000, for example, guerrilla gardening involved the planting of flowers and building of ponds in Parliament Square. Additionally, anti-capitalist events in the United Kingdom have been joined by the Socialist Workers' Party, groups supporting animal liberation, Critical Mass (which was opposed to the car culture and wanted improved public transport), No Sweat! (which was involved in peaceful campaigns against sweatshop labour in the UK and overseas), Solidarity Federation (which aimed to replace capitalism and the state with direct democracy and which campaigned on a wide range of issues including the environment and homophobia), and the Urban Alliance (which was formed to oppose the Countryside Alliance and included hunt saboteurs and protesters opposed to student fees and the arms trade).

The May Day protest in London in May 2001 persuaded many businesses and banks to close for the day, costing them an estimated £20 million. These protesters claimed a major victory in 2001 when the threat of large-scale protest caused the World Bank to call off its annual conference on development economics scheduled to be held in Barcelona in June 2001. Violence at the G8 summit meeting in Genoa in July 2001 ended what the *Guardian* on 23 July 2001 referred to as the 'era of grand-scale summit jamborees'.

Explanations of protest

This previous section has considered the social background of those involved in protest movements since 1970s. Although this may suggest that certain social groups are disposed towards protest as opposed to conventional forms of political activity, the level of protest is determined by broader social, economic and political factors which create an environment within which it flourishes. This section considers those factors which stimulate popular involvement in protest movements.

Economic upheaval and social dislocation

The concept of anomie as originally put forward by Emile Durkheim suggested that social indiscipline occurred when societies were in a state of transition (Durkheim, 1933). One circumstance when anomie occurred was associated with the boom and slump of capitalist economies. This argument might suggest that protest is rooted in the operations of the capitalist economy. The enhanced involvement of women in the United Kingdom workforce after 1945 was one factor which resulted in the emergence of the feminist movement in the 1970s, one aspect of which sought to challenge male privilege and to campaign for social and economic equality. Recent developments such as deindustrialisation have resulted in existing ways of life being radically transformed for many at the bottom end of the social ladder (defined in Chapter 4 as the underclass). Protest may emerge from this situation, seeking either to formulate resistance to developments arising out of economic change and the resultant social dislocation or to articulate alternative values and strategies. In particular, the perception by a group that its position in society is being undermined might trigger protest. For example, issues such as inflation, pay policies, high taxation, the power of the trade unions (and especially trade union militancy) and the election of two Labour governments in 1974 (which were perceived as being willing to wield power despite their narrow majorities) were instrumental in explaining the development of middle-class protests in the 1970s, which were defensive in nature, designed to protect middle-class interests.

Disillusionment with political parties

The degree of popular support for the established political parties is affected by a number of factors. Some social groups (such as women and ethnic minorities) may feel marginalised by these organisations and perceive that only extra-parliamentary forms of activity will redress their particular and specific grievances. Other citizens may believe that the parties are underpinned by attitudes and values that are obsolescent. The view that the middle-class revolt of the 1960s was symptomatic of the alignment of political loyalties around outmoded and disruptive class conflict led Roy Jenkins and Peter Walker to suggest the creation of a centrist coalition (King, 1979: 154).

Protest may also be fuelled by the operations of the party system (in which discipline forces elected members to place their party affiliation above any other form of loyalty including to those who elected them) and the belief that parties concentrate on a narrow range of political policies (such as the economy and law and order) that are considered crucial to winning elections and exclude consideration of other issues which can thus only enter the political agenda through the medium of protest. Examples of this have included immigration and, more recently, animal welfare and a wide range of issues connected with the environment, such as global warming. The extent to which a party's decision-making machinery is suspectible to rank-and-file pressure may also influence the support given to conventional political activity. Parties whose policy-making processes are centralised and relatively impervious to grass-roots opinion are unlikely to serve as vehicles for minority opinions which may thus be expressed through other means such as protest.

The remainder of this section considers a number of key factors concerned with the operations of political parties which are likely to result in apathy towards conventional politics and create a vacuum in which people who seek political change might become receptive to alternative methods in order to achieve it. Protest may be used in addition to participation in conventional political activities (such as voting) or as an alternative to this form of political activity.

Ideological convergence

Ideological convergence refers to a situation in which the ideology of the parties becomes similar, which in turn tends to mean that they put forward policies which are essentially similar in many key areas. The term 'consensus politics' was used to describe the period after 1945 when the Labour and Conservative parties endorsed a range of similar attitudes and policies. This consensus began notably to break down in the 1970s (Butler and Kavanagh, 1975: 3) and was finally shattered with the election of a Conservative government headed by Margaret Thatcher in 1979. For a number of years after 1979 the ideology and policy of the two major parties evidenced considerable differences, the Conservatives being wedded to the free market economy while the Labour Party endorsed a number of left-wing policies which included the extension of nationalisation and unilateralism. However, Labour's defeat at the 1983 election and the subsequent election of Neil Kinnock as leader of the party in 1983 resulted in the ideology and policies of the Labour Party undergoing a number of changes which climaxed with the abandonment of clause 4 of the party's constitution in 1995 and the birth of 'new' Labour. These changes were underpinned by an ideological convergence whereby all main political parties in the United Kingdom accepted the free market, resulting in the development of a strong centre-right consensus which dominated conventional British politics after 1997, blurring the differences between the major parties and resulting in them all offering one solution, 'a system based on laissez-faire economics, the culture of consumerism, the power of finance and free trade' (Hertz, 2001d: 5). The main difficulty with this situation is that the general public see little to choose between the main contenders for political power at general elections. An *Observer*/ICM poll published in the *Observer* on 3 June 2001 indicated that 57 per cent of the electorate believed that it would make little difference to their daily lives whoever won the election and 45 per cent thought that a Conservative or Labour government would make no difference to themselves or their family being better off. Perceived similarities between the political parties is likely to have a negative effect on voter participation in conventional forms of political activity as electors are unable to discern any clear choice between the parties. This was evidenced in the 2001 general election by low turnout at the polls (Hansard Society, 2001: 2). This may stimulate the growth of protest movements in the early years of the twenty-first century as a way of bringing about political change especially by groups at the lower end of the social ladder who believe themselves to be sidelined by the Labour Party which had traditionally championed them in favour of the pursuit of the support of 'middle Britain'.

Ideological disjuncture

The period after 1970 witnessed partisan dealignment. This term means that a large number of electors either desert the party to which they were traditionally committed, or identify far more weakly with the party which they traditionally support. A number of factors may explain this phenomenon. These included the increased education and political awareness of many members of the electorate (making them prone to basing their vote on logical as opposed to emotional or traditional considerations), and perceptions that the party they historically supported did not reflect their views on key issues. This is termed an 'ideological disjuncture'. The middle-class inspired protest movements in the 1970s emerged against a background of dissatisfaction by many Conservative supporters of the policies pursued by Ted Heath's government between 1970 and 1974 as well as the subsequent actions undertaken by Labour governments which (as with the 1975 Social Security (Amendment) Act which imposed an additional National Insurance levy on the self-employed) prejudiced the interests of Conservative middle-class supporters. This resulted in a perception of neglect and a sense of political impotence felt by many Conservatives who channelled their energies into a wide range of protest movements at the expense of supporting the Conservative Party at the ballot box in the two 1974 general elections. For example, those Conservatives who were concerned about the abandonment of 'Selsdon Man' policies in 1972 and wished to combat collectivism and establish a free market economy articulated their views through protest movements such as the National Association for Freedom.

The growth of protest movements in this situation is not, however, an inevitable development. New political parties may be formed which attract the support of those who become dissatisfied with the views expressed by the party which they traditionally support. Thus Labour supporters who were concerned about their party's 'lurch to the left' in the years immediately after the 1979 general election defeat were able to support the Social Democratic Party (which was formed in 1981) in preference to participating in protest movements.

Pragmatism

A further reason for the failure of political parties to fire the popular imagination is the tendency to downplay ideology in favour of pragmatism, one aspect of which is that public policy proposals are based not on any ideology but, rather, on a perception as to what public opinion will find tolerable. This has resulted in 'a political system driven by product testing, opinion polls, focus groups and advertising slogans' (Cohen, 2001). The tendency of all the main political parties to move in this direction has created a further example of convergence, that of a move in the direction of populist politics which is characterised by the objective of seeking to follow rather than attempt to lead public opinion.

Sleaze, corrupt practices and abuse of power

Public support for political parties may be adversely affected by perceptions that those who play a leading part in their affairs are primarily motivated by self-interest. Allegations associated with 'sleaze' in Great Britain since the 1990s have resulted in citizens feeling cynical towards their elected representatives, viewing them as self-seekers rather than persons disposed towards promoting the public good. This may have an adverse effect on the level of support which citizens accord to a system of representative democracy and stimulate the growth of protest movements.

Sleaze describes the abuse of power by elected public officials who improperly exploit their office for personal gain, party advantage (which may especially benefit party leaders) or for sexual motives. The term also embraces attempts to cover up such inappropriate behaviour either by those guilty of such misconduct or by their political colleagues. Accusations of 'sleaze' have exerted a major influence on politics in a number of liberal democratic political systems since the 1990s. This may be because this conduct has increased in recent years or that the media has chosen to emphasise the personal and moral failings of politicians to a greater degree than had been the case previously. In Britain, the government's emphasis on the need for a return to Conservative traditional values of self-discipline and the importance of the family in its 'back to basics' policy of 1993 was undone by revelations that a number of members of the government were engaging in extra-marital affairs. The Prime Minister initially refused to intervene, arguing that these were personal matters. A further problem was the 'cash for questions' accusation in 1994 that a small number of Conservative Members of Parliament had accepted money to table parliamentary questions. This resulted in the appointment of a Committee on Standards in Public Life whose recommendations included establishing an independent Parliamentary Commissioner for Standards. One of the key functions of this official has been to examine accusations of MPs failing to register the interests and benefits they receive as MPs. Since 1997 the Commissioner has investigated the affairs of a number of senior Labour politicians including Peter Mandelson, Geoffrey Robinson and Keith Vaz, although not all complaints were subsequently upheld. Public confidence in the new system was not, however, enhanced by the departure of the then Commissioner, Elizabeth Filkin, in 2002, who claimed in an interview in the *Guardian* on 16 February 2002 that she had been forced out of the office and had been told by a government minister that she had made enemies who would stop at nothing to secure her removal.

Other factors have also served to undermine public confidence in political parties. The apparent ease of movement by politicians from one party to another might provoke a negative reaction by members of the general public. One example of this was the defection of Shaun Woodward (who had played a key role in the Conservative Party's 1992 general election campaign) to Labour, and for whom the safe seat of St Helens South was found by the Party's hierarchy for the 2001 general election. As one observer subsequently remarked, 'when politics is a matter of convenience, not conviction, only the self-interested prosper' (Monbiot, 2001a). Attempts by spin doctors to manipulate public opinion may also serve to undermine public confidence in conventional politics. One example of this was the cynical effort made by the Special Adviser (Jo Moore) to Transport Secretary Stephen Byers to secure the release of news stories which might potentially be harmful to the department in the aftermath of the 11 September 2001 terrorist attacks in New York and Washington (which are discussed in Chapter 5). This was designed to 'bury bad news' on the assumption that media concentration on events in America would ensure that information released by the Transport Department would receive minimal coverage to which the public would pay little attention. The adviser was forced to apologise for her actions and was reprimanded by the minister but allowed, on this occasion, to keep her job.

Additionally, the absence of public funding of political parties has made them heavily reliant on donations from wealthy individuals and big business which has led to perceptions that money is able to buy political influence. In 2002 the accusation of 'cash for access' was made in relation to a letter written by Prime Minister Tony Blair to support a bid by Lakshmi Mittal to take over a Romanian state-owned steel company. Blair claimed he had no knowledge when he wrote the letter that Mittal had previously made a donation of £125,000 to the Labour Party and crossly dismissed criticisms of his actions by opposition politicians as 'garbagegate'.

Loss of confidence in conventional political activity

Popular disillusionment with political parties may help to explain reduced levels of voter participation in elections and/or heightened interest in various forms of protest movements to achieve political ends. However, not all of the factors discussed above are novel factors: for example, there was a considerable degree of ideological convergence between the two major political parties in the 1950s (the 'Butskellite' period) but this had no adverse impact on voter participation in election campaigns in that period, national contests in 1955 and 1959 witnessing turnouts in excess of 75 per cent.

Indeed, it has been suggested that consensus was popular and that the move away from it after 1966 in areas such as countering inflation, pensions and industrial policy was responsible for popular disenchantment with the two major parties in the two 1974 general election contests (Butler and Kavanagh, 1975: 31). Accordingly, explanations of popular apathy towards conventional politics (which became most apparent towards the end of the twentieth and beginning of the twenty-first centuries) need to consider reasons which are additional to those discussed above. It is thus argued that the more recent manifestations of popular disenchantment with conventional politics arises from two sets of circumstances which have surfaced more or less at the same time – disillusionment with political parties coupled with a loss of confidence in conventional political activity to secure social, economic and political reform.

It should, however, be emphasised that scepticism towards conventional political activity does not automatically result in a refusal to vote in elections. One study suggested that members of Amnesty International and Friends of the Earth were members of political parties to a greater extent than was the general public (Jordan and Maloney, 1997: 117). It was subsequently observed that 77 per cent of likely voters were also likely protesters and that 75 per cent of people who were unlikely to vote were also unlikely to participate in protest (Whiteley, 2000). Although there is more recent evidence that this pattern may be changing (at least as far as young people are concerned) (Hansard Society, 2001: 8), this may suggest that many who have been involved in protest since 1970 viewed it as a supplement to rather than a replacement for their involvement in conventional forms of political activity and that those who were most disenchanted with conventional political activity express themselves through actions such as riot rather than protest. This issue is explored in more detail in Chapter 4. A loss of confidence in conventional political activity may arise for a number of reasons which are discussed below.

Inability to secure radical political change

Popular support for conventional political activity by those seeking social, economic or political reform may be influenced by the perception that this style of politics is unable to produce radical change. This belief may stimulate the growth of protest groups or social movements by those seeking this objective. Of particular importance is the stance adopted by parties on the left of the political spectrum. The failure of these parties to advance the progress of radical reform may motivate citizens to participate in protests. The growth of extra-parliamentary political activities after the 1964 general election was attributed to the disappointment felt by many radicals with the actions of the Labour governments (Hain, 1975: 83–90). Similar dissatisfaction with the Labour Party arose after 1979 following the election of a Conservative government. Initially an attempt was made by the Militant

Tendency to radicalise the Labour Party and transform it into the fulcrum of working-class politics (Johnson, 1996: 147). Although this strategy enjoyed success in some areas (most notably in Liverpool) it failed to become the dominant controlling sentiment in either the Labour Party nationally or in the trade union movement. During the 1980s, the Labour Party rewrote its policies and ultimately its ideology to evidence the emergence of a new consensus based on the free market. This provided political space for movements motivated by an alternative vision of society and is an important factor in the emergence of 'people politics' to seek influence over political affairs during the 1990s.

Inability to control national policies

Disillusionment with conventional political activity may arise when it is perceived that individual governments possess only a limited capacity to exercise control over key aspects of public policy. There are several explanations for this situation which are discussed below.

The policy-making processes of supranational government. Supranational government erodes the sovereignty of those nations which participate in these organisations. Additionally, the policy-making processes of some supranational bodies are not subject to effective mechanisms of accountability. Examples of deficiencies of this nature include the European Union's (EU) European Commission (which since the 2000 Nice Summit exercises international treaty making powers) and Council of Ministers and institutions such as the European Central Bank. Much EU policy is driven by a lobby group which is called the European Round Table of Industrialists whose prime concern is to improve their members' interests especially in eastern Europe. This body was a crucial force in securing the establishment of the single market in 1992 and has subsequently become the prime mover in the process of enlargement. This suggests that corporations exercise a dominant role over key aspects of EU policy. Outside of the EU other bodies, including agencies of the United Nations such as the International Monetary Fund and organisations founded on multilateral treaties such as the World Trade Organisation (both of which are key organs of the global economy), are virtually impervious to any conventional form of accountability. Thus citizens wishing to object to their policies are forced to utilise various forms of protest.

The power wielded by corporations over national governments. The industrial and economic policies of individual states are often dominated by large business corporations which are able to wield vast political influence and patronage thereby transforming the relationship between government and corporations to the benefit of the latter. It has been argued that '67% of the population ... now believe that big international companies have more influence over their daily lives than do their own governments' (Hertz, 2001c). Politicians now 'jump to the commands of corporations rather than of their own citizens' (Hertz, 2001d: 5) and their inability or unwillingness to defend the interests of the people against those of business has created a cycle of cynicism towards conventional political activity (Hertz, 2001d: 198). The ability of large corporations to lobby governments (and supranational organisations such as the EU) is an important aspect of their ability to exercise control over policy decisions. The perception that American politics was dominated by corporate interests prompted Ralph Nader to stand in the 2000 American Presidential election, where he polled 2.8 million votes which in a very closely fought contest between Al Gore and George W. Bush may have helped to determine the election outcome. It was subsequently asserted that President Bush's refusal to approve the Kyoto treaty to reduce the level of greenhouse gas emissions in order to slow down the rate of global warming was a decision driven by the American coal and oil industries, and it earned Bush the epithet of 'the toxic Texan' by environmental groups. In Britain, it has been asserted that public sector services have been tailored to meet the requirements of corporate demand rather than public need (Monbiot, 2001b: 4). In particular, privatisation has been depicted as a policy driven by large corporations (Hertz, 2001b). The power which business corporations exert over governments suggest that protest is the only effective way to oppose their activities (Hertz, 2001d: 11). It has also led some environmental activists (including the former director of Greenpeace UK, Lord Melchett) to assume that the most effective way of promoting progressive politics is through working within business corporations rather than through conventional forms of political action, although this course of action runs the risk of environmentalism 'being swallowed by the corporate leviathan' (Monbiot, 2002).

Globalisation.   Globalisation offers a further explanation for popular disenchantment with conventional politics. People's lives seem dominated by impersonal and anonymous institutions over which individual governments lack any meaningful control and which tend to concentrate power and deepen inequality. Anti-capitalist protesters view the International Monetary Fund and the World Bank as key agents of the global economy whose role is to manage the world economy in a manner which is advantageous to the USA and American-owned multinational corporations but which fails to benefit the citizens of countries which are subject to the intervention of these politically unaccountable institutions since wealth has not trickled down as had been predicted (Hertz, 2001d: 202). This situation has a particularly detrimental effect on countries in the developing world where it has been argued that:

> unregulated or under-regulated by governments, corporations set the terms of engagement themselves. In the Third World we see a race to

the bottom: multi-nationals pitting developing countries against each other to provide the most advantageous conditions for investment, with no regulation, no red tape, no unions, a blind eye turned to environmental degradation. It's good for profits, but bad for workers and local communities. (Hertz, 2001b)

This situation stimulates the growth of international protest movements to challenge the power wielded by these international organisations and multinational corporations (Hertz, 2001d: 201).

Elitism

Conventional politics is remote from the lives of ordinary people. Debates which are conducted in the House of Commons or in council chambers using rituals and language not readily understood by average citizens make conventional politics and politicians seem distant from the general public and make little impact on their everyday lives (Hansard Society, 2001: 5–6). The preoccupation of politicians with attendance at Westminster or local authorities means that their relationship with most voters is distant. The perception that conventional politics is the concern of elites rather than of all citizens is compounded by the control exerted over politicians by their leaders which is a feature of central and local government.

The charge of elitism also embraces the control which is exerted over conventional politics. Devices such as the party whip system in the House of Commons ensure that the views of party leaders (especially when in government) prevail (Young, 2001) and that ordinary MPs fulfil the role of lobby fodder, being forced (on pain of expulsion) to vote 'just as their leaders tell 'em to'. Election campaigns have increasingly become a game played out between elites with minimal scope for public involvement save to vote on polling day. This has become a key feature of contemporary general election contests. An editorial in the *Guardian* on 4 June 2001 commented that 'four years ago, Britain experienced the most tightly controlled and, "professional" election campaign in its history. This year the control has been even tighter and the "professionalism" more intense than ever. It is no coincidence that these campaigns have given less satisfaction and have granted less involvement to the voters than any in our history.' The new 'professionalism' entailed campaign managers deciding what issues can be discussed, who could and could not be interviewed and what access the general public could have to their political leaders whose pronouncements were delivered in soundbites and carefully crafted speeches written by professional speech writers and from whose texts leaders were loath to stray. Contemporary campaigns have become meticulously stage-managed by spin doctors whose control over the packaging of politics makes them very influential. The degree of control exerted by political elites over the conduct of contemporary conventional politics is a disincentive for ordinary members of the public to be interested in it.

The devaluation of representative democracy?

The elite control exerted over contemporary political parties has been connected with a further development associated with the Labour governments since 1997. It has been alleged that the 'third way' approach to policy-making associated with these governments sought to bypass political parties as the instrument which offered voters genuine choices which were put before them at general election contests and instead to seek to construct a direct relationship between the government and its citizens through the use of mechanisms such as focus groups to devise policies, and referendums to seek public approval to implement proposals (Mair, 2000: 26–7). Political parties and general elections thus become increasingly irrelevant to the process of government which has an adverse impact on voter participation at general elections. A key deficiency with this attempt to create 'a partyless and hence depoliticised democracy' (Mair, 2000: 22) is that policy-making becomes the preserve of an elite, and the role of the general public is merely to approve or reject propositions which are put before them. They are given no meaningful role in determining what should be included on the political agenda or in shaping the content of policy proposals and it has been argued that 'to offer citizens the choice of saying yes or no is not the same thing as offering the choice of real alternatives, and engaging them in a public competition of ideas' (Mair, 2000: 34–5). This may encourage citizens who seek a role in policy formulation to engage in protest as the way to achieve it.

The 2001 general election

The issues which have been discussed in the introduction regarding the factors which stimulate extra-parliamentary political action, and above concerning popular disenchantment both with the conduct of political parties and with conventional political action explained the low level of popular involvement in the 2001 general election which evidenced the lowest turnout in national contests since 1918. Below 60 per cent of those eligible to vote exercised their democratic right to do so and the Labour Party's alleged landslide victory was based on less than one eligible voter in four supporting them at the polls. Of particular significance was the perception that non-voting (which was traditionally associated with young people) was becoming more widespread throughout society – what was once viewed as a phenomenon affecting the under 25s, had become a problem affecting the under 35s and was fast moving to embrace the under 45s (Young, 2001). In 2001 one-third of women under 55 (who have been viewed as the most civic minded) failed to vote (Hansard Society, 2001: 1). The loss of 5 million votes between 1997 and 2001 was described as 'a crisis of democratic politics in Britain' (Whiteley et al., 2001: 786).

Voter apathy on this scale was attributed to a variety of factors, including the perception of 'policy discontent' (Whiteley et al., 2001: 786).

In particular, the government's pursuit of the votes of 'middle England' resulted in feelings that it had not been sufficiently radical. This failed to induce many of its core supporters, especially in inner city areas, to vote for the party, since it had not delivered on key issues of concern to them in particular with regard to making improvements in public services. Additionally, the emphasis placed by the government on performance measured by targets and figures as opposed to ideals designed to fire the popular imagination and inaugurate change had effectively made politics boring (Beckett, 2001). The lack of enthusiasm towards the government was mirrored by the absence of any widespread desire to replace them with the main opposition party, the Conservatives (Hansard Society, 2001: 2–3). The ideological convergence of the two main parties encouraged the Conservative Party to focus on right-wing issues in order to carve out a distinct political niche for itself. These included 'save the Pound' and the need to pursue a hard line towards asylum seekers. However, these policies were of marginal importance to the great bulk of the British electorate and resulted in the Conservative Party being viewed as too extreme by many of its centrist, one-nation supporters, many of whom switched their allegiance to the Liberal Democrats. The election contest was thus one-sided and could offer no result other than reaffirming Labour's political supremacy.

State intervention and protest

Governments have traditionally viewed protest with scepticism. The presence of people on the streets may threaten public order and pose a threat to its power, especially if violence should occur which cannot be contained by the police. Accordingly extra-parliamentary political activities such as demonstrations and direct action have been subject to state scrutiny, which in recent years has included the monitoring of groups such as motorway protesters by MI5 (whose role is discussed in Chapter 7). A variety of legislative restrictions have been imposed, justified by economic criteria such as the cost of policing protests or factors such as the level of violence which has sometimes occurred (Home Office, 1980: 1–2).

One protest group associated with disorder in Great Britain and abroad is the anti-capitalist movement. It has been linked with acts of extreme violence which frequently occur in an international setting where groups of international leaders are meeting. Anti-capitalist protests have involved confrontation with police forces and physical attacks on property owned by multinational corporations such as Macdonalds. Severe violence first occurred at the Seattle trade talks in 1999, in what was the biggest protest in America since Vietnam and required the deployment of the National Guard. A small event occurred simultaneously in London, involving protesters and police clashing at Euston Railway station. In June 2000 a demonstration in the City of London by Reclaim the Streets brought the area to a standstill and resulted in 42 injuries and £2 million worth of damage. Disorder continued subsequently at the Prague trade talks in September 2000 when anger was vented at the IMF and World Bank, and at the EU Summit at Nice in December 2000. On 1 May 2000 in London, disorder by anti-capitalist protesters resulted in twelve persons being hospitalised and £500,000 worth of damage. Anti-capitalist protests were continued at the EU summit meeting in Nice in December 2000 and at the meeting of Heads of State of North and South America at Quebec in April 2001. The EU–USA summit (at which President Bush announced his decision not to ratify the 1997 Kyoto agreement on global warming through reducing the level of greenhouse gas emissions) which took place in Gothenberg in June 2001 resulted in severe riots in which damage amounting to millions of pounds occurred to property and in which three persons were shot. Twenty-five thousand activists representing a variety of anti-EU, anti-USA and anti-globalisation groups under the umbrella of Gothenberg Action 2001 were involved in these protests.

This section discusses the way in which the state has responded to various manifestations of protest and dissent since 1945. It concentrates on the actions undertaken by governments (especially in the form of legislation) and by the police service. Some of the changes initiated by the police to respond to extra-parliamentary political activity were especially prompted by industrial disputes and are discussed in Chapter 3.

Protest and the Law

The legal regulation of protest may involve the application of common law or the enactment of statute law. This section discusses the key legal responses which have been directed at protest since 1970.

Common law

Prior to the enactment of the 1998 Human Rights Act, many of what are regarded as fundamental 'rights' (such as the ability to demonstrate) were rooted in common law. This is not fixed but may be developed by the judiciary, often in response to protest. Breach of the peace is a commonly-used charge against demonstrators. It is relatively easy to prove and carries a minor penalty which is unlikely to create martyrs to a political cause. But the nature of this offence has been subject to judicial interpretation. The case of *Duncan v. Jones* in 1936 suggested the legality of a police officer taking pre-emptive action to prevent a breach of the peace and, as is discussed in Chapter 3, this concept was further developed during the miners' dispute of 1984–85.

The 1970s witnessed a period of political turbulence to which the police responded with powers derived from common law. These included unlawful assembly (which was utilised, for example, in connection with the occupation of the Greek Embassy in 1967 to express opposition to the military coup), affray (which was used to combat picketing during the building workers' dispute in 1972) and riotous assembly (which was preferred against the 'Mangrove Nine' in 1972). One rationale for adopting this approach was that police intervention was of a blanket nature, directed at groups of persons involved in various forms of protest rather than against individuals committing specific acts.

Attempts were further made to 'develop' powers by the use of common law charges of conspiracy and incitement. A group of students from Sierra Leone who occupied their country's High Commission building in London in 1972 were charged and convicted of unlawful assembly and conspiracy to trespass. This judgement had the effect of transforming the civil offence of trespass into a criminal action (Cox, 1975: 74). The following year three persons engaged in picketing at Shrewsbury in connection with the building workers' strike were convicted of unlawful assembly and conspiracy to intimidate under the 1875 Protection of Property Act. There are, however, difficulties associated with the use of common law to regulate protest. Juries may refuse to convict defendants (as was the case with the 'Mangrove Nine' in 1972) especially when the penalties seem to outweigh the severity of the offence. The courts may also refuse to sanction attempts to develop common law. In 1972, for example, a charge of conspiracy to trespass in connection with actions undertaken during the building workers' dispute was thrown out.

Statute law

The response by successive governments to various forms of protest in Great Britain has primarily taken the form of introducing legislation to enable the police to restrict activities associated with it. Under the guise of maintaining public order, successive governments have utilised criminalisation as a mechanism to regulate protest. This section examines the key pieces of legislation which have been enacted to enable the state to respond to protest.

The 1936 Public Order Act. Legislation which relates to the obstruction of the highway (the 1980 Highways Act) or to obstructing or assaulting of a constable in the execution of his or her duties (1964 Police Act) has been frequently utilised against protesters since 1970. However, the main piece of legislation which related to extra-parliamentary political activity was the 1936 Public Order Act. This was enacted in response to the activities of the British Union of Fascists and their opponents and imposed prohibitions on the organisation of a paramilitary organisation and the wearing in public of a uniform signifying attachment to a political party. The police were empowered to impose conditions on the route taken by processions and to ban them (with the consent of the local authority outside of London) if they anticipated that 'serious' public disorder would arise. This took the form of a 'blanket' ban which applied to every procession of a political nature in the area for the period of time specified in the ban. Restrictions were further imposed on political expression: section 5 of the Act made it an offence to utter, publish or distribute words or material which were threatening, abusive or insulting. This section was subsequently amended by the 1968 and 1976 Race Relations Acts seeking to apply these actions to racial intolerance.

However, after 1970 protest was often conducted in ways which were not precisely catered for by the 1936 legislation. One major difficulty was that the power to ban or reroute events applied only to 'processions' (Home Office, 1980: 9) in which the key feature was that of crowd mobility. Static demonstrations were not catered for in the legislation. 'Counter demonstrations' were a feature of the activities of those opposed to the National Front in the 1960s and 1970s and also arose in some industrial disputes. The pickets at the Grunwick industrial dispute in 1976–78 (which is discussed in Chapter 3), for example, were sometimes supported by a large force of sympathetic demonstrators numbering many thousands. A further difficulty concerned the definition of 'procession'. In 1977 Greater Manchester's chief constable, James Anderton, banned a National Front march in Hyde. In response, Martin Webster (a leading National Front activist) decided to 'walk' through the town. On this occasion a large police presence ensured that he was able to conduct this activity without physical opposition from his party's opponents. However, he was threatened with arrest when he attempted to repeat this exercise in 1980 in the West Midlands.

The 1936 Act did not require the police to be given advance notice by an organisation of its intention to hold a procession, although this requirement was included in a number of local acts covering 107 local authority areas in England and Wales and three in Scotland (Home Office, 1980: 19). Nor was there any power of arrest for failing to comply with a police direction concerning the banning or rerouting of such an event, save the common law power to arrest where a breach of the peace seemed likely (Home Office, 1980: 17). This meant that the police tended to rely on groups wishing to organise a procession to give warning voluntarily of their intentions and to heed any advice which might be given. Further, section 5 of the 1936 Act was difficult to enforce. It had been copied from the 1839 Metropolitan Police Act which had totally failed to prevent anti-Semitic utterances by the British Union of Fascists during the 1930s. A particular problem concerned provocation of violence. If a melee developed arising from remarks made in a political speech, the police tended to take action against those who were clearly breaking the law as opposed to the person who provoked the problem. There were exceptions to this, however. Colin Jordan was arrested for making anti-Semitic utterances in a speech in Trafalgar Square which led to disorder. In the subsequent trial in 1963

Lord Chief Justice Parker ruled that a speaker had to 'take his audience as he found it' (*Jordan v. Burgoyne*) which meant that a speaker who knowingly incited an audience to violence was legally responsible for subsequent events. But this view did not consistently influence police interventions in public order situations after 1970.

The 1986 Public Order Act. The 1986 Public Order Act created or redefined a wide range of public order offences (riot, *violent disorder, affray, fear or provocation of violence* and *harassment, alarm or distress*). Its scope was subsequently extended by the 1994 Act. The main impact of the 1986 legislation was to criminalise a range of activities ranging from orchestrated civil disorder to boisterous behaviour in a public place. Approximately 40 criminal charges could be brought against transgresssors of the new legislation.

Some aspects of the new 1986 Act specifically related to extra-parliamentary political activity. Advance notice to the police of processions became a universal requirement and a new offence of participating in a banned event was introduced. The ability of the police to intervene in processions and demonstrations was also redefined. If the police believed a procession would result in serious public disorder they could apply to the relevant local authority to ban it. The police were also empowered to unilaterally impose conditions on assemblies held in the open air. The criteria used to justify the imposition of conditions were broader than those governing banning an event. They enabled the police to intervene if they believed an event would cause serious disorder, serious damage to property or serious disruption to the life of a community or that the purpose of organising the event was the intimidation of others with a view to compelling them not to do an act they had the right to do, or to do an act which they did not have the right to do. These new provisions provided increased powers for the police to intervene in a wide range of extra-parliamentary political activities including picketing at industrial disputes. The manner in which this Act could be used to stifle protest was illustrated in April 1995 when the assistant chief constable of Essex wrote to every householder in Brightlingsea advising them to desist from demonstrating in connection with live animal exports and threatening them with arrest and imprisonment if they continued to participate in these actions.

The 1994 Criminal Justice and Public Order Act. The 1994 Act was enacted against the background of a number of events which were associated with the actions of 'disorderly youths' in the 1990s and reflected the changing nature of protest in this period in which demonstrations and mass picketing (Brearley and King, 1996: 104) gave way to alternative tactics. Key events included the hippie convoys at Stonehenge, gatherings of new age travellers at Castlemorton in 1993, the activities of hunt saboteurs, environmental protest and the emergence of a rave culture. The 1994 Public

Order and Criminal Justice Act was thus particularly directed at youth sub-cultures and counter-cultural protest embraced by a diverse range of organisations and performed by a wide array of methods. Part 5 of the 1994 legislation gave the police a variety of new powers under the heading of 'collective trespass or nuisance on land' which they could utilise against these groups which included *aggravated trespass, trespass on land* and *trespassory assembly*. Additionally, powers were provided to the police to regulate *raves*.

The 1990 Entertainments (Increased Penalties) Act, had increased the punishment available to deal with rave promoters who breached the requirement to obtain public entertainment licences. The 1994 legislation empowered the police to terminate raves if they believed the loudness of the music caused 'serious distress' to the persons living nearby and authorised pre-emptive action to prevent persons within a five-mile radius travelling to these events. New powers related to trespass applied to common and privately-owned land and further provided for the removal of travellers from places which included scheduled monuments. A new offence of aggravated trespass was introduced in connection with the activities of a person who trespassed on land and sought to prevent a lawful activity taking place by intimidating, obstructing or disrupting that event. This was particularly directed at anti-hunt saboteurs and environmental protesters. Additionally the police could apply to the relevant local authority for an order to prohibit trespassory assemblies for a period of up to four days and could direct persons 'reasonably believed' to be on the way to such an assembly not to continue. This restriction was aimed at a wide range of direct action groups and could effectively prevent any demonstration, lobby, picket or vigil from taking place. Further powers were provided to make it easier for squatters to be removed by authorising a displaced or intended occupier or that person's agent to use violence to secure entry to premises once an order for possession had been given.

Both Acts introduced sanctions against unauthorised campers. The 1996 Act further removed the onus on local authorities to provide camps for gypsies by repealing Part Two of the 1968 Caravan Sites Act. Additionally section 70 of the 1980 Local Government Planning and Land Act was repealed which removed the liability of central government to pay grants to local authorities for capital expenditure incurred in providing gypsy caravan sites. The legislation defined 'gypsy' as 'persons of a nomadic habit of life, whatever the race or origin' but excluded persons who were members of organised groups of travelling showmen or were engaged in travelling circuses.

Young people and conventional political activity

In addition to attempts to regulate protest by legislative intervention, governments have also attempted to stimulate the participation by young people in conventional political activity. For example, the Labour government's decision to make citizenship a compulsory part of the schools' national curriculum by 2002 was designed to make younger people more interested in conventional politics, and some local authority experiments have also been conducted to secure this objective. These include Manchester's Young People's Council and Birmingham's Young People's Parliament.

The police and protest

This section discusses the manner in which the police service has responded to protest since 1970, in particular to minimise the extent of disorder with which this form of extra-parliamentary political activity has sometimes been associated. The developments which are discussed in this section are also of relevance to the policing of protest in the workplace and of urban disorder which are the concerns of Chapters 3 and 4.

The 'Ways and Means' Act

A key aspect of police work is the ability to formulate pragmatic responses to matters which arise, especially in connection with public order issues. This is what is known as employing the 'Ways and Means Act', a mythical piece of legislation which is invoked to justify a police action which may not be founded on any real legislation and which may conceivably be illegal. The use by the police of tactics based on guile as opposed to force (Waddington, 1996: 234) is especially motivated by the desire to avoid confrontation and disorder. One example of this was the action undertaken by the Metropolitan Police to respond to the anti-capitalist demonstration held in central London on 1 May 2001 which entailed penning demonstrators to prevent them spilling into thoroughfares and becoming involved in violent actions. This mass detention was justified by the need to prevent a breach of the peace and criminal damage to property. Several thousand police officers were involved in this operation against around 1000 demonstrators (including some allegedly innocent bystander tourists) who were denied access to facilities such as public lavatories for up to seven hours. They were released one by one after the police had searched and photographed them. These procedures are legal only if there are strong grounds to suspect that a person has been involved in criminality.

Specialist public order units

Since the 1960s a number of police forces have developed units which are not tied to a specific division or concerned with implementing routine police functions but which operate anywhere within a force's boundaries. An early example of this was the Metropolitan Police's Special Patrol Group. This was established in 1965 and was augmented in the 1970s by the creation of a number of District Support Units. Both were replaced in 1987 by Territorial Support Groups located within each of the Metropolitan Police districts. Other forces, however, have retained a centralised specialist unit such as the Tactical Aid Group of the Greater Manchester Police.

A key role of these units was to combat crime. The Special Patrol Group was at the forefront of reactive policing methods and was frequently criticised for what was regarded as 'hard' policing, derived from a rationale to make its presence felt in the area where it was deployed. Units of this nature were also utilised in public order situations. The use of the SPG (which initially possessed its own command structure) posed the potential of an operation being conducted independently of the mainstream policing of a particular event which would provide a source of confusion for participating members of the general public. This difficulty was encountered at Southall in 1979 (Ranson, 1980: 63). Groups such as the SPG also had no local knowledge of an area and its population and no need to cultivate links with them. This might give rise to aggressive policing: at Southall in 1979 the SPG were accused of playing a 'prominent role in the worst scenes of violence' (National Council for Civil Liberties, 1980: 171) which compelled the Metropolitan Police Commissioner, Sir David McNee, to introduce a number of reforms to the operations of this unit.

Police Support Units

Police Support Units consist of uniformed police officers whose main role is to perform routine police duties but who receive a limited degree of public order training on a regular basis. Police Support Units (termed District Support Units in the Metropolitan Police) are organised at divisional level and are composed of one inspector, three sergeants, 18 constables, three drivers and three personnel carriers. They train together as a unit and are available for deployment in public order situations when the need arises. The history of Police Support Units was connected with the Cold War and was developed by J. Devlin in his work, *Police Procedure, Administration and Organisations*, published in 1964. This idea was adopted in the *Police Manual of Home Defence* in 1974 which suggested that some police officers should be organised into Police Support Units and receive appropriate public order training to enable them to perform duties such as crowd control, guarding key points and protected areas and controlling essential services in the event of nuclear attack. However, the main operational use of Police Support Units was to provide a police response to public disorder, although in these situations these units do not always fulfil their potential. Spontaneous outbreaks of public disorder may be responded to by any officers who are immediately available, and sickness or holidays require personnel who are not members of the unit which trained together to be drafted in to make the numbers up.

Public order tactics

Initially police forces were ill-equipped to handle the public order problems which surfaced during the 1970s and 1980s. However, in many public order situations officers under attack were required to improvise their own defence from materials which included dustbin lids (Thackrah, 1985: 6). A number of significant developments occurred during the 1970s in connection with police equipment to enable the service to respond more effectively to public disorder. Violence in connection with a police operation against pickpocketing at the 1976 Notting Hill Carnival prompted the issue of special clothing; riot shields were first introduced on the British mainland at a protest against the National Front at Lewisham in 1977, and CS gas was used by Merseyside police (following approval by the then Home Secretary William Whitelaw) in an attempt to quell the disturbances at Toxteth in 1981. The 1981 riots also witnessed the government making available supplies of protective headgear.

The ability of the police to manage crowd situations has also been affected by several developments. An important innovation was the introduction of gold, silver and bronze command structures following the urban disorders in London in 1985 (Brearley and King, 1996: 10). These facilitate an improved police response to public order events through advanced planning and the clear demarcation of those responsible for strategic and tactical decisions relating to them. Technology has also been introduced to aid the policing of public order situations. Closed circuit television cameras found in many city centres provide a mechanism for the progress of events such as processions to be monitored, for 'trouble spots' to be identified and for corrective action to be speedily implemented.

International cooperation

The international dimension of some protest groups, especially the anti-capitalist movement, have prompted calls for enhanced levels of international cooperation. Violence at the EU–USA Summit at Gothenberg in June 2001 and the G8 Summit in Genoa the following month suggested the need for enhanced forms of international cooperation to curb future protests by this group, which could include the coordination of intelligence gathering agencies to help identify protesters and possibly arrangements to prevent known troublemakers from travelling (in line with powers currently used in Great Britain to combat football hooliganism). Violence at the G8 summit meeting in Genoa in 2001 prompted the Italian and German governments to call for the formation of an EU-wide police squad trained in riot technniques in order for future summit meetings to be able to take place without disruption from protesters.

Evaluation of the state's response to protest

This section evaluates the way in which the law was developed to manage protest after 1970 and the manner in which the police used their powers to respond to protest in that period.

Critique of the 1986 and 1994 public order legislation

The 1994 Act, in particular, prompted a wide degree of protest organised by groups such as the Freedom Network and the Coalition against the Criminal Justice Bill. A number of criticisms were voiced against the legislation passed in 1986 and 1994. As some of the criticisms apply to both Acts, they can be dealt with jointly.

It was argued that the 1986 and 1994 Acts extended the scope of police discretion to deal with extra-parliamentary activities. These included the powers to decide whether, and what, conditions to impose on a procession or static demonstration under the 1986 Act, and by enabling them to be the sole power to determine whether activities constituted 'raves', 'trespass' or 'distruptive trespass' and then to take action provided for in the 1994 legislation. The requirement of the 1986 Act that organisers of demonstrations needed to give the police advance notice of their intentions and the ability of the police to ban or impose conditions on these events has resulted in organisers having to negotiate with the police. It has been observed that while negotiation of this type might epitomise the principle of 'policing by consent', the extent to which genuine two-sided dialogue actually occurred was debatable: 'the balance of power lay firmly in favour of the police. Negotiation was less a process of "give and take" and more that of the organiser giving and the police taking' (Waddington, 1994a: 101). However, liaison between the police and protesters is not necessarily confrontational. Organisers of protests know they require the cooperation of the police to direct events such as demonstrations through traffic, and will often voluntarily agree to police suggestions. Opposition to police involvement in organising protests is most likely to come from groups who do not accept the authority of the state and who thus refuse to comply with the established rules of the game which are underpinned by the concept of 'give and take' by police and protesters.

It was also alleged that the main purpose of these Acts was to stifle protest. This argument especially related to the requirement to give advance notice of processions and demonstrations and the ability to use conditions such as 'disruption to the life of the community' contained in the 1986 Act in a restrictive manner either to prevent these activities completely or to permit them in a form designed to minimise their ability to influence public opinion. Additionally the 1994 Act introduced a wide range of pre-emptive powers which effectively provided the police with the ability to place major restrictions on the freedom of movement through their ability to define a peaceful, non-obstructive gathering on the highway as a trespassory assembly. The offence of aggravated trespass was widely used against those who objected to the construction of the Newbury bypass which commenced in 1996. During the police operation, 356 arrests were made for this offence (Bucke and James, 1998: 49).

Both the 1986 and 1994 Acts blurred the distinction between public and private, enabling the private interest to comandeer police resources (Waddington, 1996: 128). The civil liberties of those charged with offences under either Act were also adversely affected by both pieces of legislation. In a number of cases the 1986 Act reversed the burden of proof in a criminal trial. The 1994 measure eroded an accused's right to silence thus undermining the presumption of innocence which had formerly been at the heart of the criminal justice system.

The 1994 Act was criticised by some senior police officers for seeking to solve social problems such as homelessness through coercive means (Wilmot, 1994) and for enhancing the emphasis on the police enforcement role to the detriment of community-led priorities and ancillary tasks (Smith, 1994). It effectively outlawed collective activities practised by minority groups such as squatters but failed to offer any solution or alternative to the issue which initially encouraged, or forced, them to embark upon these activities or lifestyles. The 1994 Act also provided a good example of how a moral panic directed at particular scapegoats can have a far broader application: thus powers initially justified by the need to regulate the activities of a broadly-defined group of 'new age travellers' were also applied to gypsies. One study likened its potential effect on this population to ethnic cleansing (Hawes and Perez, 1995).

It must finally be acknowledged that no legislation can ever be watertight, and groups who wish to find ways to avoid restrictions which it imposes on their ability to protest have frequently been able to do so. This is the case with the statutory requirement of advance notice for holding a demonstration. As is discussed in Chapter 4, groups on the far right instigated disorders in a number of towns in Northern England in 2001 by holding, or threatening to hold, political meetings. This had the effect of inciting Muslim youths to violence. In an attempt to prevent reoccurrences of this tactic, police forces began to ban events planned by these groups. This led extreme right-wing groups to seek ways to circumvent prohibitions on their activities. This included transforming a demonstration into an assembly or series of assemblies which were outside the scope of the 1986 legislation. This tactic was used by extreme right-wing groups in Oldham in 2001 following a ban being placed on their intended march. Latterly, an organisation which called itself the National Front Social Club was formed. This planned to hold what it described as 'cultural tours' for its members of racially sensitive towns. This was intended to have the same effect on Muslim youths as a political meeting but required no advance warning to be given to the police of an intended event taking place (Harris, 2001).

The police use of public order powers

It has sometimes been perceived that when policing protest the police service is 'pro-right' and 'anti-left'. The traditional explanation for this stance is that the left poses a threat to capitalism whereas the right does not, and that the left is thus less likely to be viewed sympathetically by the police service which serves 'as an integral part of effective government' and is 'actively engaged in defining and defending the state, particularly in the court of first instance, the streets', and whose core mandate has been described as to 'provide the coercive power and the information resources necessary to maintain the hegemonic domination of the state' (Lofthouse, 1996: 40, 47). However, the tactics adopted by groups may have an important bearing on police actions. Attempts to 'kick the Nazis off the streets' unambiguously broke the law and is one explanation for the police response to confrontations between extreme right-wing groups and their opponents in the 1970s. Similarly, perceptions based on previous experience that anti-capitalist protesters would cause disorder resulted in the use of tactics at the 2001 May Day protests in London which were subsequently condemned on civil liberty grounds. These are referred to in the previous section of this chapter.

However, the perception that police action is biased against some political groups has been challenged, and in particular it has been argued that the police service have made only limited use of the new public order powers provided to them in the 1986 and 1994 public order legislation. In particular, marches are rarely banned and conditions on assemblies and marches are imposed infrequently. There are various explanations for this situation. The first concerns the practical effect of using powers such as banning marches. Since the enactment of the 1998 Human Rights Act there are doubts whether the requirement to inform the police in advance of a desire to hold a parade is compatible with the European Convention's guarantee of freedom of assembly and this may induce the police to use this power sparingly. But even before this Act was passed, the police were reluctant to use powers bestowed on them in the 1986 and 1994 legislation. This was so for a number of reasons. A group may decide to flout the law and ignore a ban thus necessitating a large and costly police operation to enforce it. Violence is highly likely to occur in such a charged atmosphere. Accordingly, the police reaction to protest is typically to let events proceed but to seek to ensure that trouble is avoided through adequate advance preparation, including the processes of negotiation and accomodation which takes place with an event's organisers (P. Waddington, 1994: 379). The paramount desire to avoid trouble in the form of public disorder or adverse reactions to police actions (P. Waddington, 1998: 127) may also induce the police service to permit events to proceed even when no prior authorisation has been obtained (an example of this being a march in London in January 1991 to express opposition to a war with Iraq), and to use all powers (including those of arrest) sparingly (P. Waddington, 1998: 118–19).

A second explanation for police reluctance to use their public order powers to the full is that groups which find themselves on the receiving end of restrictive legislation may feel threatened and this may radicalise their activities. Protest may act as a form of 'safety valve' at which advocates of minority causes can take to the streets and 'let off steam'. Those denied the ability to do this may embark upon actions which have a more adverse impact on public order. Thus protest (including industrial disputes which are discussed in Chapter 3) may be tolerated in the belief that actions of this nature are preferable to an all-out class war (Reiner, 1998: 43). Calculations related to the availability of police time and resources may also influence the use made of powers provided in public order legislation. This was one factor governing the use by police forces of powers available to them under the 1994 Act to direct trespassers illegally residing on a piece of land to leave the site. In particular the police were wary regarding the use of their power to seize vehicles under the provisions of the 1994 Act because of the high level of organisation and expense involved (Home Office, 1998: vii–viii). It should finally be observed that some protests have been treated sympathetically by the police. In the campaign against live animal exports in 1995, the Kent Constabulary removed unroadworthy lorries engaged in the trade from the roads and government veterinarians also intervened to ascertain the welfare of the animals. More stringent conditions (amounting to two sailings a week) were imposed on live animal exports by the Sussex Constabulary. In April 1995 the then Chief Constable, Paul Whitehouse, imposed restrictions on the movements of lorries engaged in this trade, and drivers who contravened them were threatened with arrest. Those affected by this decision, the International Traders' Ferry, succeeded in getting the High Court to rule in July 1995 that these police actions were unlawful under EU law.

However, although the police frequently facilitate protest there are occasions when this does not happen. One example of this concerned the state visit of President Jiang of China to the United Kingdom in October 1999. Members of the Free Tibet campaign wished to make the President face protests. However, the Metropolitan Police adopted a number of tactics to minimise their effect. This included confiscating 'Free Tibet' banners, and using police lorries, vans and cordons of police to block the President's view of protesters. Some protesters alleged they were manhandled by the police when seeking to protest. A Foreign Office source was quoted in the *Observer* on 24 October 1999 as saying that 'this whole sorry episode has undermined our commitment to human rights. The policing was ludicrously heavy handed.' In the High Court in May 2000 the Metropolitan Police admitted that it had been unlawful for individual officers to remove banners and flags solely on the basis that they wished to protect the Chinese regime. The most important issue regarding police actions was whether these were deployed by the police at their own behest or whether they were suggested by the British government in the knowledge that the Chinese government (with whom they wished to construct a closer working relationship) would be angered by the presence of protesters. In this instance, the desire to avoid 'trouble' emanating from official quarters was perhaps seen as preferable to the criticisms of police actions voiced by civil liberties groups.

Conclusion

This chapter has examined the diverse nature of protest in Great Britain since 1970. This has constituted an important form of political activity in this period and has been associated with a wide range of causes, some of which have been identified and discussed. It has been argued that many of those involved in protest are drawn from the middle classes who may undertake these activities as a supplement to conventional political activity in order to remedy its perceived deficiencies. It has been asserted that although the state may have reservations concerning the desirability of protest and, after 1970, passed measures designed to impose restrictions on it (most notably in 1986 and 1994) there is an acceptance that protest is an important aspect of political freedom in a liberal democratic state and this consideration has influenced the way in which the police have used the powers given to them. The following chapter continues with the theme of protest, but discusses specific activities which are carried out in the workplace. Unlike the protest considered in this chapter, these actions are primarily (although not exclusively) associated with the working class. An important issue to be explored is whether protest in the workplace is viewed less sympathetically by the state, government and the police, resulting in a more coercive response in comparison to the activities discussed in this chapter.

Glossary

Affray

This offence was defined in the 1986 Public Order Act. It entails a person who 'uses or threatens to use unlawful violence towards another and his conduct is such as would cause a person of reasonable firmness present at the scene to fear for his personal safety'.

Aggravated trespass

This offence was created in the 1994 Criminal Justice and Public Order Act. It concerns a person who 'trespasses on land in the open air and, in relation to any lawful activity which persons are engaging in or are about to engage in on that or adjoining land, does there anything which is intended by him to have the effect – (a) of intimidating those persons or any of them so as to deter them from engaging in that activity, (b) of obstructing that activity, (c) of disrupting that activity'.

Civil disobedience

Civil disobedience has been described as an act undertaken by a person in his or her capacity as a citizen under government, entailing disobedience which is 'passive', 'non-violent', 'courteous', and 'not uncivil' (Bedau, 1969: 19). It entails 'a nonrevolutionary encounter with the state', not seeking to challenge the legitimacy of its legal or political systems (Walzer, 1970: 24) and when it is motivated by moral, religious or political impulses it is 'almost always a collective act, and it is justified by the values of the collectivity and the mutual engagements of its members' (Walzer, 1970: 4). The aim of civil disobedience is to draw public attention to the objectives of the group (or to clarify the nature of the conflict) (Carter, 1983: 15) and it may further serve to establish a sense of solidarity amongst the members of the organisation. An important aspect of civil disobedience is non-cooperation with the government. The refusal to pay state taxes has been depicted as the last stage in non-cooperation since 'it is to deny to government its capacity to govern, to administer and enforce any of its laws' (Bedau, 1969: 22) since it is dependent on tax revenue in order to function.

Consumer boycotts

This is an economic sanction wielded by protest groups against governments or commercial organisations. Consumers are urged to desist from buying goods emanating from a particular country or manufactured by a specific business corporation in an attempt to alter national or commercial policy.

Counter-cultural protest

This term originated in America in the 1960s and was applied to middle-class youth protest which posed a revolutionary challenge to the establishment. The overt nature of counter-cultural protest differentiated it from other forms of popular culture embraced by young people although this too may be considered as political. Popular culture 'is organised around the various forms of the oppositional relationship between people and the power bloc' (Fiske, 1989: 163) and may empower those who are party to it so that 'they are able to act, particularly at the micropolitical level, and by such action to increase their sociocultural space, to effect a (micro) redistribution of power in their favor' (Fiske, 1989: 161).

Demonstrations

Demonstrations or rallies entail members of the public taking to the streets to air their opinions. These activities are usually designed to mobilise public opinion in support of a policy or cause and to use this pressure as a means to influence policy pursued by governments or business interests.

Direct action

Direct action entails some form of physical action to further a cause. It has been defined as 'primarily a way of expressing rebellion. It creates a potential for social change by releasing new energy and determination and encouraging social imagination' (Carter, 1973: 159).

Fear or provocation of violence

This offence was created by the 1986 Public Order Act. It concerned a person who 'uses towards another person threatening, abusive or insulting words or behaviour or distributes or displays to another person any writing, sign or other visible representation which is threatening, abusive or insulting with intent to cause that person to believe that immediate unlawful violence will be used against him or another person, or to provoke the immediate use of unlawful violence by that person or another, or whereby that person is likely to believe that such violence will be used or it is likely that such violence will be provoked'.

Harassment, alarm or distress

This offence was created by the 1986 Public Order Act. It entailed a person who 'uses threatening, abusive or insulting words or behaviour, or disorderly behaviour, or displays any writing, sign or other visible representation which is threatening, abusive or insulting within the hearing of a person likely to cause harassment, alarm or distress'.

Local government acting as a pressure group

The ability of local government to act as a powerful pressure group in which the views of local people can be forcibly articulated to central government was evidenced in Liverpool in the early 1980s. Here the nature of the economic crisis experienced within the city resulted in the radicalisation of many members of the working class and resulted in the Militant Tendency assuming a prominent role in the local Labour Party. Blame for the economic collapse was attributed to the economic policies of the Conservative government and this resulted in a policy of confrontation being pursued by the local council which refused to make cuts in jobs and services and sought enhanced government aid rather than introducing large rate rises to make up the shortfall in their budget. This tactic brought some short-term success, with the government making some concessions to the city in July 1984. However, the attempt to pursue confrontation in 1985 by setting an illegal deficit budget and symbolically issuing redundancy notices to council employees failed to induce further concessions from the government and ultimately resulted in Labour councillors being surcharged and disqualified for their delay in failing to set a legal rate. It also resulted in the expulsion of leading members of Militant by the Labour Party at its 1986 conference.

Minor parties

Political parties which do not realistically aspire to the formation of a government may utilise various forms of extra-parliamentary activity to advance their cause, perhaps as a complement to conventional political activity. This position was adopted by the Liberal Party in the late 1960s (Joyce, 1999: 169–83). In some cases (especially where extra-parliamentary activity takes the form of violence) an organisation may be divided into two parts – one espousing conventional political activity and the other extra-parliamentary means. An example of this is the relationship between Sinn Fein and the provisional IRA, a situation which is mirrored in Spain.

Petitions

Petitions enable members of the general public to voice their support for a reform or to oppose a course of action being pursued by governments or commercial organizations. They do so by adding their signature to a statement which signifies their approval of its aims and ideas.

Physical obstruction

Physical obstruction seeks to prevent a course of action to which protestors are opposed. It is associated with a wide range of tactics which include occupations (including the use of sit-ins and trespass) and blocking roads by 'sit down' protests.

Pressure groups

A pressure group is an organisation with a formal structure which is composed of a number of individuals seeking to further a common cause or interest. These groups operate at all levels of society. Some seek to influence the activities of local or central government. Others exist within the workplace in the form of trade unions. The factions or tendencies found within some political parties are further examples of such organisations. Many groups perform functions which are not political, for example by providing benefits or advisory services either to their members or to the general public. The range of methods at the disposal of pressure groups is subject to wide variation. Some operating at the level of national government enjoy an 'insider' relationship with the Civil Service or ministers: 'insider groups are regarded as legitimate by government and are consulted on a regular basis' in contrast to 'outsider groups' which 'either do not wish to be enmeshed in a consultative relationship with officials, or are unable to gain recognition' (Grant, 1989: 14–15). Various methods of direct action may be practised by outsider groups who pitch their appeal directly at the general public over the heads of governments and political parties.

Raves

The ability of the police to regulate raves was provided in the 1994 Criminal Justice and Public Order Act. A rave was defined as 'a gathering on land in the open air of 100 or more persons (whether or not trespassers) at which amplified music is played during the night (with or without intermissions) and is such as, by reason of its loudness and duration and the time at which it is played, is likely to cause serious distress to the inhabitants of the locality: and for this purpose – (a) such a gathering continues during intermissions in the music and, where the gathering extends over several days, throughout the period during which amplified music is played at night (with or without intermission); and (b) "music" includes sounds wholly or predominantly characterised by the emission of a succession of repetitive beats'.

Trespassory assembly

The 1994 Criminal Justice and Public Order Act extended the provisions of the 1986 Public Order Act to enable trespassary assemblies to be banned if such an assembly was likely to be held without the permission of the occupier of the land or to conduct itself in such a way as to exceed the limits of permission or the limits of the public's right of access, and may result (i) in the serious disruption to the life of the community or (ii) where the land, or a building or monument on it, was of historic, architectural, archaeological or scientific importance, in significant damage to the land, building or monument.

Trespassers on land

The 1994 Criminal Justice and Public Order Act provided the police with powers to deal with trespassers on land. This power applied to 'two or more persons ... trespassing on land and are present there with the common purpose of residing there for any period'. The police could ask them to leave after reasonable steps had been taken by or on behalf of the occupier to ask them to leave.

Vigils

Vigils are a static form of a demonstration in which members of the public voice their concerns regarding a particular issue by mounting a protest which typically takes the format of maintaining a constant presence in the vicinity of property in the possession of interests to which those involved in the protest object.

Violent disorder

This offence was created by the 1986 Public Order Act. It entailed a situation 'where three or more persons who are present together use or threaten to use unlawful violence and the conduct of them (taken together) is such as would cause a person of reasonable firmness present at the scene to fear for his personal safety'.

References

E. Amenta and Y. Zylan (1995) 'It Happened Here: Political Opportunity, the New Institutionalism and the Townsend Movement', in S. Lyman (ed.) *Social Movements: Critiques, Concepts, Case Studies* (Basingstoke: Macmillan Press – now Palgrave Macmillan)

P. Bagguley (1996) 'The Moral Economy of Anti-Poll Tax Protest', in C. Barker and P. Kennedy (eds) *To Make Another World: Studies in Protest and Collective Action* (Aldershot: Avebury)

C. Barker (1996) 'What is to be Done? Contrasting Activists' Visions in Community Protest', in C. Barker and P. Kennedy (eds) *To Make Another World: Studies in Protest and Collective Action* (Aldershot: Avebury)

M. Beckett (2000) quoted in *Guardian*, 16 September

M. Beckett (2001) 'Dulling Down', *Guardian*, 5 March

H. Bedau (ed.) (1969) *Civil Disobedience: Theory and Practice* (New York: Macmillan)

R. Benewick and T. Smith (1972) *Direct Action and Democratic Politics* (London: Allen and Unwin)

H. Blumer (1995) 'Social Movements' in S. Lyman (ed.) *Social Movements: Critiques, Concepts, Case Studies* (Basingstoke: Macmillan Press – now Palgrave Macmillan)

P. Bourdieu (1984) *Distinction* (London: Routledge)

J. Brewer, A. Guelke, I. Home, E. Moxon-Browne and R. Wilford (1996) *The Police, Public Order and the State: Policing in Great Britain, Northern Ireland, the Irish Republic, the USA, Israel, South Africa and China* (Basingstoke: Macmillan Press – now Palgrave Macmillan, 2nd edition)

M. Brown and J. May (1991) *The Greenpeace Story* (London: Dorling Kindersley, 2nd edition)

T. Bucke and Z. James (1998) *Trespass and Protest: Policing under the Criminal Justice and Public Order Act 1994* (London: Home Office Research, Development and Statistics Directorate, Research Study 190)

P. Burstein, R. Einwohner and J. Hollander (1995) 'The Success of Political Movement, a Bargaining Perspective', in J. Jenkins and B. Klandermans (eds) *The Politics of Social Protest: Comparative Perspectives on States and Social Movements* (London: UCL Press)

D. Butler and A. King (1975) *The British General Election of October 1974* (Basingstoke: Macmillan)

A. Carter (1973) *Direct Action and Liberal Democracy* (London: Routledge and Kegan Paul)

A. Carter (1983) *Direct Action* (London: Housmans, 3rd edition)

S. Clegg (1996) 'From the Women's Movement to Feminisms', in C. Barker and P. Kennedy (eds) *To Make Another World: Studies in Protest and Collective Action* (Aldershot: Avebury)

N. Cohen (2001) 'Focus Hocus Pocus', *Observer*, 3 June

B. Cox (1975) *Civil Liberties in Britain* (Harmondsworth: Penguin)

C. Critcher (1996) 'On the Waterfront: Applying the Flashpoints Model to Protest against Live Animal Exports', in C. Critcher and D. Waddington (eds) *Policing Public Order: Theoretical and Practical Issues* (Aldershot: Avebury)

E. Durkheim (1933) *The Division of Labour in Society* (New York: Free Press)

J. Eglin (1987) 'Women and Peace: From the Suffragists to the Greenham Women', in R. Taylor and N. Young (eds) *Campaigns for Peace – the British Peace Movement in the Twentieth Century* (Manchester: Manchester University Press)

J. Fiske (1989) *Understanding Popular Culture* (London: Routledge)

J. Freedland (2001) 'Rise of the Non-Voter', *Guardian*, 12 December

K. Gaskin, M. Vlaeminke and N. Fenton (1996) *Young People's Attitudes to the Voluntary Sector: a Report for the Commission on the Future of the Voluntary Sector* (Loughborough: Loughborough University)

W. Grant (1989) *Pressure Groups, Politics and Democracy in Britain* (Hemel Hempstead: Philip Allan)

P. Hain (1975) *Radical Regeneration: Protest, Direct Action and Community Politics* (London: Quartet Books)

R. Hall, M. Rodehier and B. Usneem (1986) 'Effects of Education on Attitudes to Protest', *American Sociological Review*, 51(4), August, 564–73

Hansard Society (2001) *None of the Above: Non-Voters and the 2001 Election* (London: Hansard Society)

P. Harris (2001) 'Exposed: Secret Plot to Start Race Riots', *Observer*, 2 September

D. Hawes and B. Perez (1995) *The Gypsy and the State: the Ethnic Cleansing of British Society* (Bristol: Bristol University School for Advanced Urban Studies)

N. Hertz (2001a) 'A Bad Day for Democracy', *Observer*, 6 May

N. Hertz (2001b) 'Why We Must Stay Silent No Longer', *Observer*, 8 April

N. Hertz (2001c) 'Why We Stayed Away', *Observer*, 10 June

N. Hertz (2001d) *The Silent Takeover: Global Capitalism and the Death of Democracy* (London: Heinemann)

Home Office (1980) *Review of the Public Order Act 1936 and Related Legislation* (London: HMSO, Cmnd. 7891)

Home Office (1985) *Review of Public Order Law* (London: HMSO, Cmnd 9510)

F. Huggett (1971) *What They've Said About Nineteenth-Century Reformers* (Oxford: Oxford University Press)

J. Jasper (1997) *The Art of Moral Protest, Culture, Biography and Creativity in Social Movements* (Chicago: University of Chicago Press)

A. Johnson (1996) 'Militant and the Failure of "Acherontic" Marxism in Liverpool', in C. Barker and P. Kennedy (eds) *To Make Another World: Studies in Protest and Collective Action* (Aldershot: Avebury)

G. Jordan and W. Maloney (1997) *The Protest Business? Mobilising Protest Groups* (Manchester: Manchester University Press)

P. Joyce (1999) *Realignment of the Left? A History of the Relationship between the Liberal Democrat and Labour Parties* (Basingstoke: Macmillan Press – now Palgrave Macmillan)

R. King (1979) 'The Middle Class in Revolt?', in R. King and N. Nugent (eds) *Respectable Rebels: Middle Class Campaigns in Britain in the 1970s* (London: Hodder and Stoughton)

M. King and N. Brearley (1996) *Public Order Policing, Contemporary Perspectives on Strategy and Tactics* (Leicester: Perpetuity Press, Crime and Security Shorter Studies Series, No. 2)

M. Lofthouse (1996) 'The Core Mandate of Policing', in C. Critcher and D. Waddington (eds) *Policing Public Order: Theoretical and Practical Issues* (Aldershot: Avebury)

P. Lynch and S. Birrell (2001) 'Grievances Galore', *Guardian*, 7 May

D. Maguire (1995) 'Opposition Movements and Opposition Parties: Equal Partners or Dependent Relations in the Struggle for Power and Reform?', in J. Jenkins and B. Klandermans (eds) *The Politics of Social Protest: Comparative Perspectives on States and Social Movements* (London: UCL Press)

P. Mair (2000) 'Partyless Democracy: Solving the Paradox of New Labour', *New Left Review*, 2nd series, March/April, 21–35

G. Mason (1991) 'Making Sense of Mayhem', *Police Review*, 8 March, 476–7

N. McNaughton (2001) 'Populist Movements – A New Development in the Politics of Pressure', *Talking Politics*, 4(1), September, 18–21

Lord Melchett (2000) 'Logic or Passion?', *Observer*, 24 September

G. Monbiot (2001) 'Break the Whip', *Guardian*, 12 June

G. Monbiot (2002) 'Business of Betrayal', *Guardian*, 15 January

National Council for Civil Liberties (1980) *The Death of Blair Peach: the Supplementary Report of the Unofficial Committee of Enquiry* (London: NCCL)

E. Nelson (1989) *The British Counter Culture 1966–1973* (Basingstoke: Macmillan)

A. Orum (1993) 'On Participation in Political Protest Movements', in R. Curtis and B. Aguirre (eds) *Collective Bahaviour and Social Movements* (Boston MA: Allyn and Bacon)

F. Parkin (1968) *Middle Class Radicalism: the Social Base of the British CND* (Manchester: Manchester University Press)

D. della Porta (1995) *Social Movements, Political Violence and the State: a Comparative Analysis of Italy and Germany* (Cambridge: Cambridge University Press)

D. della Porta and M. Diani (1999) *Social Movements: an Introduction* (Oxford: Blackwell)

J. Purkis (1996) 'Daring to Dream: Idealism in the Philosophy, Organisation and Campaigning Strategies of Earth First!', in C. Barker and P. Kennedy (eds) *To Make Another World: Studies in Protest and Collective Action* (Aldershot: Avebury)

D. Ranson (1980) *The Blair Peach Case: Licence to Kill* (London: Friends of the Blair Peach Committee)

R. Reiner (1998) 'Policing Protest and Disorder in Britain', in D. della Porta and H. Reiter (eds) *The Control of Mass Demonstrations in Western Democracies* (Minneapolis: University of Minnesota Press)

K. Sabido (1985) statement made on 1 June 1985, quoted in *Guardian Weekend*, 3 June 1995.

Sir J. Smith (1994) *Guardian*, 16 October

J. Street (1997) *Politics and Popular Culture* (Cambridge: Polity Press)

J. Thackrah (ed.) (1985) *Contemporary Policing: an Examination of Society in the 1980s* (London: Sphere)

D. Waddington (1992) *Contemporary Issues in Public Disorder. A Comparative and Historical Approach* (London: Routledge)

P. Waddington (1994a) *Liberty and Order: Public Order Policing in a Capital City* (London: UCL Press)

P. Waddington (1994b) 'Coercion and Accomodation: Policing Public Order after the Public Order Act', *British Journal of Sociology*, 40

P. Waddington (1996) 'The Other Side of the Barricades: Policing Protest', in C. Barker and P. Kennedy (eds) *To Make Another World: Studies in Protest and Collective Action* (Aldershot: Avebury)

P. Waddington (1998) 'Controlling Protest, a Contemporary, Historical and Comparative Perspective', in D. della Porta and H. Reiter (eds) *The Control of Mass Demonstrations in Western Democracies* (Minneapolis: University of Minnesota Press)

M. Wallace and J. Craig Jenkins (1995) 'The New Class, Postindustrialism, Neocorporatism: Three Images of Social Protest in the Western Democracies', in J. Jenkins and B. Klandermans (eds) *The Politics of Social Protest: Comparative Perspectives on States and Social Movements* (London: UCL Press)

M. Walzer (1970) *Obligation – Essays on Disobedience, War and Citizenship* (Cambridge, Massachusetts: Harvard University Press)

P. Whiteley (2000) 'Rich Pickings', *Guardian*, 19 September

P. Whiteley, H. Clarke, D. Sanders and M. Stewart (2001), 'Turnout', *Parliamentary Affairs*, 54(4), 775–88

H. Wilkinson and G. Mulgan (1995) *Freedom's Children: Work, Relationships and Politics for 18–34 Year Olds in Britain Today* (London: Demos)

D. Wilmot (1994) 'Freedom under the Law', *Police Review*, 18 November, 18–20

3
Protest in the Workplace

This chapter continues the discussion of protest initiated in Chapter 2 and focuses on the workplace as the arena of protest. It concentrates on the tactics of strike action and work-ins which are associated with this form of protest and discusses the importance of these activities by referring to a number of key events which have taken place since 1970. This chapter refers to the social groups and political organisations associated with protest in the workplace, and considers the environment within which this activity is conducted. The response of the state to protest in the workplace is analysed, which includes an examination of civil and criminal law utilised in connection with industrial unrest, the reaction of the police service and the role performed by the military.

Introduction

There are various forms of protest which are conducted in the workplace. Conflict with the employer may take the form of 'peaceful bargaining and grievance handling, of boycotts, of political action, of restriction of output, of sabotage, of absenteeism, or of personnel turnover' (Kerr, 1974: 171). Demonstrations and marches have also been used since 1970 to draw attention to related problems such as unemployment, an example of this activity being the 'Right to Work March' which commenced in Manchester on 27 February 1976 and culminated in a rally in London on 20 March. Employers may utilise *lock-outs* when faced with a labour dispute. This section concentrates on *strikes* and *work-ins*, and provides a selective range of examples of protest undertaken by workers acting collectively within the workplace which have taken place since 1970.

Strikes

Strikes are the most common and visible expression of industrial conflict (Kerr, 1964: 171). They have occurred in response to factors such as economic change in which industrial conflict is one mechanism used by working men and women 'to assert their changing needs and aspirations in the face of trends and problems that even their rulers or employers cannot control' (Cronin, 1979: 40, 195). Strikes have been depicted as 'a form of rational social action' insofar as 'they represent an explicit attempt to exert some control over the employment relationship' (Hyman, 1972: 107, 136), regardless of whether they arise from advance planning or occur spontaneously. There have been a number of major industrial disputes since 1970. The number of stoppages rose sharply in 1969 (Duncan et al., 1983: 134), and the number of working days lost through industrial action on a yearly average basis was 12.9 million in the 1970s and 7.2 million in the 1980s. However, during the 1990s the level of industrial militancy began to fall and fewer working days were lost due to strike action in 1991 than in any year since records were first kept in 1893. This was attributed to factors which included the persistence of high unemployment, the enactment of restrictive legislation during the 1980s, the decline in trade union membership and the adoption of a more assertive role by management (Metcalfe and Milner, 1993: 1). However, the level subsequently increased and 350,000 working days were lost in 1995. A feature of these later disputes was the high level of unofficial actions in which workers refused to heed the advice of their union leaders, for example, in action undertaken by the postal workers in 2001. However, although industrial unrest in the railway and postal industries in 2002 prompted the *Daily Express* to declare on 10 January 2002 that the dark age of strikes had returned, in 2001 fifteen minutes a year per worker was lost to strikes compared to one whole day per year in 1979. The remainder of this section briefly discusses a number of key strikes which occurred after 1970. It does not seek to provide a comprehensive list of these events but aims to illustrate the important role performed by the workplace as an arena of protest in this period.

- *The Ford Motor Company strike (1971).* This stoppage was in support of a pay claim. It commenced in January and was not settled until April. It was thus an 'exceptionally large and protracted' dispute with two million 'striker days' registered and a loss of production which amounted to £100 million (Hyman, 1972: 13). Further disruption in this company occurred in June 1971 following the dismissal of a shop steward at the Halewood factory. An all-out national strike was averted when he was reinstated, albeit in a different part of the factory.
- *The Post Office strike (1971).* This dispute arose in support of a demand for a pay increase of between 15–20 per cent. The Post Office Corporation offered 8 per cent, the target figure for annual rises desired by the government. The number of man-days lost in this dispute were 6,250,000 – the largest number lost in a single strike since the 1920s (Clutterbuck, 1980: 44). The strike was settled when the union leadership settled for an increase of 9 per cent.

- *The building workers' strike (1972).* This was a strike in support of a wage demand but was complicated by the use of *'lump' labour* and the relatively low level of unionisation among building workers which resulted in attempts to enforce the strike by the use of intimidation and violence. Events which took place at Shrewsbury and Telford in September 1972 resulted in prison sentences being handed out to two of the leaders of the dispute, Des Warren and Eric Tomlinson.

- *The miners' strikes (1972 and 1973–74).* The 1972 dispute was preceded by an overtime ban in support of a wage demand and a strike broke out after a national ballot took place. It was settled when a Court of Inquiry headed by Lord Wilberforce recommended a generous settlement which was further improved upon when the leaders of the National Union of Miners (NUM) met with the government at Downing Street. The main significance of this dispute was that it evidenced the ability of trade unions to defeat a key aspect of government policy which was designed to curb inflation. A further dispute occurred in 1973 following the rejection of a pay award which was in line with limits imposed by Stage 3 of the Conservative government's counter-inflation policy. The National Union of Miners launched an overtime ban and following a national ballot a strike was declared in February 1974. The government countered this by declaring a state of emergency which led to the imposition of a three-day working week, and ultimately a general election was called on the issue of 'who runs the country?' which resulted in the defeat of the Conservative government.

- *The dock strike (1972).* This arose in response to a long-standing grievance between dockers and port authorities over the loss of jobs as the result of mechanisation. In 1972 dockers 'blacked' (that is, refused to handle) lorries which were delivering goods from container firms. The imprisonment of five London dockers (the 'Pentonville Five') led to a national dock strike taking place in 1972. Private docks which were unregistered under the National Dock Labour Scheme were subject to picketing during the dispute, with mass *picketing* and violence especially taking place at Neap House Wharf in Lincolnshire.

- *The Grunwick dispute (1976–78).* This dispute was concerned with the right of workers to join a trade union and commenced in August 1976 when an Asian woman was dismissed from the mail order department at Grunwick Processing Laboratories for allegedly working too slowly. A small number of other workers walked out in sympathy and commenced an agitation for other workers at the plant to support a union. A further walkout occurred and those on strike sought the advice of Brent Trades Council as to which union they should join in order to be represented in their dispute with management. The advice they received (and followed) was to join the Association of Professional, Executive and Computer Staff (APEX) and when the company refused to recognise this union it approached the Advisory, Conciliation and Arbitration Service (ACAS) whose several approaches to Grunwick in 1976 yielded no positive results. Picketing also failed to advance the cause of those on strike and in order to secure an enhanced level of support for their cause the Brent Trades Council and APEX endorsed the mass picketing of the plant. This took place between June and October 1977 and on occasions witnessed violent clashes between police and protesters. A Court of Inquiry headed by Lord Scarman was appointed in 1977. The strike subsequently fizzled out and ended in July 1978. All but two of the remaining strikers voted to seek jobs elsewhere.

- *The power workers dispute (1977).* This event was caused by a pay dispute in the power industry. Some workers (mainly members of the General and Municipal and Transport and General Workers Unions) engaged in an overtime ban and work to rule which led to power cuts across the country. This (and the 1977 fire fighters' strike) were the key events in what was described by the then Prime Minister, James Callaghan, as a 'winter of inconvenience and dislocation'.

- *The fire fighters' dispute (1977–78).* This dispute was concerned with a demand for a pay increase of 30 per cent by the Fire Brigades' Union. The employers offered 10 per cent together with an agreement to continue discussing relativities. Troops were deployed to fight fires while the strike continued.

- *The 'winter of discontent' (1979).* This period witnessed a number of industrial disputes which arose against the background of the fourth phase of the government's policy on incomes which sought to impose a 5 per cent limit on pay increases. This was, however, rejected by the Labour Party conference in October 1978 and on 13 December of that year the House of Commons voted against deploying sanctions against employers who paid more than this target figure. In 1979 lorry drivers and tanker drivers submitted a pay claim for a 25 per cent pay increase which was settled at 14 per cent. In January 1.5 million public service workers including those responsible for water, sewerage and refuse submitted pay claims in excess of the 5 per cent and a day of action was followed by six weeks of strikes which ended when the claim was settled at 9 per cent plus £1 per week. These actions had effectively destroyed the government's policy on pay restraint and were attributed with securing the election of a Conservative government in the 1979 general election.

- *The steel strike (1980).* This strike arose when the British Steel Corporation (BSC) failed to meet a wage increase which had been asked for by the Iron and Steel Trades Confederation (ISTC) (which amounted to around 20 per cent) offering instead a 2 per cent award which was unacceptable to the ISTC. Attempts to prevent the production and distribution of steel were extended by ISTC pickets to private steel-making firms not part of the BSC such as Hadfields in South Yorkshire.

- *Laurence Scott (1981)*. This dispute took the form of the occupation of this firm's Manchester factory in protest against a decision by its parent company to close it and shift production elsewhere. The blockade mounted by pickets was broken by the use of helicopters to airlift goods and equipment and allow the firm to deliver to customers.
- *The National Graphical Association (NGA) dispute (1983)*. This dispute occurred when six members of the NGA were dismissed by the Messenger Group of newspapers headed by Mr Eddie Shaw and replaced by non-unionised labour. Mass picketing occurred in an attempt to prevent newspaper delivery vans leaving the factory in Warrington.
- *The miners' dispute (1984–85)*. This is discussed below.
- *The News International dispute (1986–87)*. This dispute was triggered by the actions undertaken by News International which moved from Fleet Street (the traditional home of the London newspaper industry) to a new plant at Wapping. This action entailed around 6000 redundancies among members of the print unions (SOGAT and the NTA) who responded by the use of tactics which included picketing the Wapping plant, advocating a consumer boycott and holding rallies and marches. Violence occurred in connection with the picketing at Wapping (in which, for example, lorries were overturned) and in the stance adopted by the police which included the use of mounted police charging crowds, the use of weaponry such as truncheons in an offensive manner and the apparent connivance with large lorries being driven at high speeds (which resulted in the death of Michael Delaney in 1987) (NCCL, 1986 and London Strategic Policy unit, 1987: 14, 19). The financial cost of the dispute to News International was considerable which prompted the organisation to use the 1980 Employment Act to obtain an injunction which required picketing not to entail the obstruction of highways. The inability of SOGAT's leadership to comply with these restrictions (and thus face the risk of contempt of court proceedings) forced it to abandon the dispute in January 1987, and the NGA followed suit the following month.
- *The Liverpool docks strike (1997)*. This dispute arose following the dismissal of a number of dockers who refused to cross a picket line. It continued for 28 months, one feature of the strike being the use of the internet to construct a worldwide network of solidarity which disrupted the city's shipping trade.

Case study: the miners' dispute (1984–85)

The miners' strike lasted from 5 March 1984 until 3 March 1985. It must be viewed in the context of Conservative economic policies pursued after 1979 which endorsed the free market economy and sought to reduce taxation and the role of the state. This entailed slimming down what was depicted as a heavily subsidised mining industry costing the taxpayer an annual £1.3 billion (although this figure was hotly contested) (Fine and Millar, 1985: 3–4). The miners' strike was instigated by the hostile response of the National Union of Miners (NUM) to a plan by the National Coal Board (NCB) to close 20 pits and lose 20,000 jobs in the mining industry in the coming year and was triggered by the sudden closure of Cortonwood Colliery in Yorkshire. The President of the National Union of Miners, Arthur Scargill, claimed that this was the start of a process which would end in the loss of 84,000 jobs. On March 8, the National Executive Committee of the NUM agreed that the areas of Scotland, Yorkshire, South Wales and Kent could have official area disputes, with immediate official status for any other area which wished to join the dispute. On the first day of the strike, all of Yorkshire's pits were idle. Within the next few days the strike was joined by about 75 per cent of miners (Miller and Walker, 1984: Volume 1, 4–6). However, support for strike action was less intense in Nottinghamshire with fewer than half the miners supporting the strike and where a call arose for a national ballot.

The government viewed the strike as political (Thatcher, 1993: 364). It proposed a national ballot of all NUM members and utilised a wide array of devices available to the state in an attempt to break the strike. The media coverage of the dispute sought to denigrate and undermine the miners' case against the government by the use of reporting practices which included an unbalanced emphasis on picket line violence and intimidation and a failure to explain the issues which were at the heart of the strike (Green, 1990: 157). Accusations were made that the civil law embodied in the 1980 and 1982 employment legislation to prevent 'secondary' and 'flying pickets' was enforced by the police through actions which included the roadblock policy, the cordoning of pickets to let working miners and convoys of coal lorries pass (NCCL, 1984: 9), and the activation of mutual aid arrangements which were coordinated centrally by ACPO's National Reporting Centre. It was alleged that the police made arbitrary arrests and often created a hostile atmosphere on picket lines through the use of dogs, horses and riot equipment (Critcher, 2000: 101–3). The courts endorsed attempts to break the strike by imposing bail conditions on persons arrested which prevented them from travelling to counties other than their own whilst awaiting trial, and the use of the sanction of binding over which prevented the need for a trial to be held. Many of the charges brought against striking miners (such as obstruction of a police officer or of the highway, breach of the peace and threatening behaviour) could be heard in Magistrates courts and did not require witnesses other than a police officer unsupported by any other form of corroborative evidence (Miller and Walker, 1984: Volume 1, 13–14).

Obscure legislation was revived against those who sought to promote the strike, including section 7 of the 1875 Conspiracy and Protection of Property Act which created the offence of 'watching and besetting'. The position of the striking miners was also weakened by changes to the payment of supplementary benefits introduced by the 1980 Social Security Act (whereby deductions were made to benefits paid to striking miners' families on the assumption that they were receiving strike pay from the NUM) and the exclusion of strikers from almost the entire range of urgent needs payments. Accusations were also made concerning the role played by MI5 to desta- bilise the NUM (which is discussed in Chapter 7), the use of soldiers mas- querading as police officers on picket lines (quoted in Miller and Walker, 1984: Volume 1, 64–6) and the tapping of telephones and the interception of correspondence of striking miners (NCCL, 1984: 16).

The dispute witnessed some episodes of extreme violence, particularly at the Orgreave coking plant where mass picketing was deployed to discour- age the British Steel Corporation from increasing daily supplies of coke to its Scunthorpe steel works above a quota which had been agreed by both miners' and steel workers' unions. The 'battle of Orgreave' on 18 June 1984 involved 4000 police and large numbers of miners who were charged by mounted police. Seventy-nine charges of riot were brought against protesters but each one was dismissed in court and the South Yorkshire Police paid £425,000 in damages to miners who were grabbed by snatch squads. The strike was a serious blow to the ability of unions to oppose the Thatcher government. It officially cost the NCB £1.75 billion but the real figure was likely to have been higher.

Work-ins

In addition to strikes, protests in the workplace may take the form of a work-in. The most important example of this activity after 1970 was car- ried out by the Upper Clyde Shipbuilders (UCS) in 1971–72. The background of this event was the end of the post-war boom and the initiation of reces- sion. In June 1971 the Conservative government allowed the UCS to go into liquidation thus threatening mass redundancies. It was proposed by the government's advisers that a smaller company should be formed with the workforce being reduced from around 8000 to 2500 (Collins, 1996: 71). The workforce responded with a work-in seeking to uphold the right to work which was led by a number of left-wing shop stewards who included Jimmy Reid. The demands of this action were no redundancies and the maintenance of all four existing shipyards. After a work-in which lasted around 14 months, Marathon (UK), a subsidiary of an American-owned company, announced its intention to take over the yards and build oil rigs. Those declared redundant by the liquidator would be re-employed. The Shop Stewards Coordinating Committee urged that the work-in should end following the announcement of these terms.

An editorial in *The Times* on 10 October 1972 suggested that a combina- tion of circumstances were necessary for success to be achieved in protests of this nature. These were palpable misery and sense of injustice, an impression of callousness which was convincing both to the workers and to public opinion, the availability of leadership and organisation to enable the workers to get their message across, and the need for someone to emerge with the enterprise to see the source of human talent which was available. Additionally, it has been argued that the support given throughout Scottish society was crucial to the success of the work-in: small and medium-sized businesses which supplied the yards were unhappy with a policy which seemed overwhelmingly geared to the interests of monopoly capital (Collins, 1996: 72).

The participants to protest in the workplace

The previous section examined some examples of protest which occurred in the workplace since 1970. This section considers some of the key social groups and political organisations which have been involved in activities of this nature.

Working-class trade unionism

Industrial unrest is traditionally viewed as an important aspect of working-class protest. As the examples discussed in the previous section indicated, protest in the workplace is generally organised by trade unions which arose 'as the collective response of working people to the economic deprivations of an inhospitable society' (Hyman, 1972: 75). Disputes may arise for a number of reasons. They may seek to improve the lot of those engaged in particular industries or occupations, most typically in the form of securing higher wages and better conditions: one study concluded that 51.4 per cent of stoppages which occurred between 1969 and 1973 concerned claims for wage increases, and 16 per cent were connected with other wage issues (Duncan et al., 1983: 159). Some industrial disputes are of a more defensive character, in which the aim of action is to defend jobs and industries which are threatened by scaling down or closure. The latter (characterised by events such as the UCS work-in 1971–72 and the miners' dispute 1984–85) has assumed considerable importance since 1970 'in a society which is moving from an expectation of relatively full employment to a situation where chronic unemployment is becoming the norm' (Collins, 1996: 85). Discipline in the workplace may also generate protest. It has been argued that a worker sells more than his labour when he works for an employer. He or she also submits to a system of authority and a lack of interest towards employers as persons can fuel disputes, as was argued to have been the case in the dispute at Pilkington's glass works in 1970 where one issue was identified as the breakdown of the firm's old order of autocratic paternalism (Lane and Roberts, 1971: 227–9). Trade unions are most successful in advancing their concerns if their case appeals to a wider political audience than that of their own members. The failure to achieve this results in these organisations being viewed as concerned only to protect their own sectional interests (perhaps by retaining unnecessary jobs and restrictive practices) regardless of the national interest.

Middle-class trade unionism

Although trade unionism is primarily associated with the working class, it is not confined to this social grouping. The 1970s witnessed a growth in middle-class (or white-collar) trade unionism: the overall non-manual union density increased from 29.6 per cent to 39.4 per cent in the period 1964–74 (May, 1979: 104). The growth of the public sector had an important impact on the development of middle-class unions since these organisations were especially active in central and local government. However, a significant organisation, the Association of Scientific, Technical and Managerial Staff (ASTMS) sought to organise white-collar workers in manufacturing industry and increased its membership by 700 per cent between 1964 and 1977 (May, 1979: 104). Further developments affecting the employment and unionisation of women (many of whom worked part time) meant that in the early years of the twenty-first century there were slightly more white-collar than blue-collar trade union members (Toynbee, 2002).

White-collar unions showed themselves willing to use the same tactics as those employed by manual trade unions, although the motives for their actions were not necessarily similar: the issue of pay differentials which had been eroded by inflation, increases in taxation and pay policies often motivated middle-class strike action (May, 1979: 122). In this sense, white-collar trade unionism reflected the defensive nature of some middle-class protests which were discussed in Chapter 2. Professional organisations may also be involved in various actions designed to further the interests of their members. In 2001, for example, the British Medical Association balloted General Practitioners on the issue of resignation from the National Health Service if the government failed to improve their conditions of work and in May a number of these doctors participated in the National Doctor Day organised by the *Doctor* magazine which entailed actions similar to those of a wildcat strike by refusing to work in protest against problems which included overwork and bureaucracy.

The feminist impulse

Feminists have been involved in some aspects of protest in the workplace. The 1968 strike by Ford machinists for equal pay is generally viewed as the starting point for campaigns by women (sometimes supported by men) to improve their lot in the workplace. Some of these campaigns were essentially fought within the trade union movement, seeking to end male domination of these organisations and ensure that women's needs were catered for on the trade union agenda. These included reforms such as equal pay for equal work, workplace nurseries, maternity (and paternity) pay, and action against sexual harassment in the workplace. These demands were articulated 'by activists who at the time defined themselves as feminists, as socialists, as trade union militants, as all three and none' (Clegg, 1996: 52). On other occasions, industrial disputes have primarily involved women. This was the case with the Grunwick dispute in 1976–77 which was led by Asian women although it was often depicted as a trade union dispute concerned with the right to organise. Women also played a prominent role in the miners' dispute of 1984–85, in particular through the group Women against Pit Closures. This campaign, which was concerned with the defence of mining communities, indicated women's shared interest with men and was not about issues which were exclusively female (Clegg, 1996: 62). Women have also been involved in leading organisations which participated in the anti-capitalist protests discussed in Chapter 2.

Socialism

Some on the left of the political spectrum view industrial actions undertaken by the working class as the main means through which socialism will be advanced. This view suggests a distrust of parliamentary politics as the mechanism through which working-class interests can be best secured and alternatively endorses the tactic of industrial militancy as the main way through which a sense of class solidarity could be developed and class conflict played out. Syndicalists (whose views were inspired by the writings of Georges Sorel) asserted the primacy of the workplace as the arena for the attainment of socialism. Although actions such as sabotage were discussed within syndicalist circles around the time of the First World War (Brown, 1977) emphasis was placed on strike action. It was believed that strikes sharpened the class struggle and that worker participation in them promoted feelings of solidarity and community, which would culminate in a revolutionary seizure of the means of production in a general strike which would lead to cooperative worker control of industry. This view was based on the presumption that a fixed pattern of behaviour would be 'called forth' by a specific social situation, thus ignoring the way in which different persons would perceive and define that situation (Hyman, 1972: 67, 69). These tactics legitimated the view that strikes may be viewed as anti-constitutional actions, which was the stance adopted by the Conservative government when faced with the General Strike in 1926.

The Socialist Workers' Party (SWP) is a political party which is inspired by Marxism and is the main inheritor of the UK pre-war communist tradition. Although a political party, the SWP is anti-parliamentarian, being sceptical of the capacity of the institutions of bourgeois democracy to bring about any meaningful redistribution of power and resources in favour of the working class. Accordingly, it seeks its objectives by involvement in campaigns which are designed to mobilise the working class thereby constructing socialism from the grass roots upwards. These campaigns included demonstrations, various forms of direct action and industrial disputes, examples of which were sponsoring the 'Right to Work March' in 1976 (by the International Socialists) and participation in the Grunwick dispute in 1976–78 (Clutterbuck, 1980: 224–5).

The causes of protest in the workplace

It has been previously argued in this chapter that industrial unrest has occurred frequently since 1970. All may be regarded as political in that they seek to restructure the power relationships located in the workplace to the advantage of workers. This section discusses the environment in which protests of this nature have occurred. This is designed to emphasise their political underpinning, in particular to explain why government policy has frequently become a key target for those engaged in an industrial dispute. This situation may arise for a number of reasons.

Attempts by governments during the 1970s to introduce wage controls as a key component of an anti-inflation strategy resulted in workers who sought improved pay and conditions having to confront government policy rather than their immediate employers. The 1973–74 miners' dispute, for example, was a direct consequence of the imposition of a statutory incomes policy by the Conservative Prime Minister, Ted Heath, in 1972. As has been observed above, labour disputes which took place in 1979 in the so-called 'winter of discontent' were caused by the attempt to impose a 5 per cent pay limit by the Labour government headed by James Callaghan. In the early years of the twenty-first century, the Labour government's desire to expand the role performed by the private sector in a number of public services (particularly health and education) is likely to meet with opposition from those unions most affected by these proposals and possibly the entire trade union movement. This may ultimately involve unions mounting a direct challenge to the government's power in which they utilise the strike weapon as a mechanism either to coerce the government to give in to their demands or to exert pressure on public opinion to induce the government to change the direction of its policy.

Industrial unrest may also be motivated by a desire to preserve what are perceived as rights and privileges which have been secured by the working class. In the years after 1945 most British people enjoyed relative affluence. Full employment, higher real wages, wider property ownership and a welfare state based upon economic growth made it possible for Prime Minister Macmillan to tell British people in 1957 that 'you've never had it so good'. He believed that by the time of the 1959 general election the class struggle had ended. Trade unions had become incorporated in the decision-making apparatus of an emerging corporate state and fundamental similarities in the policies of the two main political parties ensured that working-class interests were reflected in public policy regardless of which was in office. These gains for working people were, however, threatened by public expenditure cuts introduced by successive governments in the 1970s and had a particular impact on industrial militancy which sought to defend rights bestowed by the post-war welfare state which guaranteed a high level of employment and a wide range of social welfare benefits. The desire by Conservative governments after 1979 to reduce the powers of trade unions in order to further their economic objectives resulted in these bodies being denigrated as problematic to the national interest and ousted from the access they had enjoyed to the state's decision-making machinery. The decline of consensus spurred industrial action and also explained many of the violent episodes which occurred after 1979: in the changed political climate, 'force, not compromise, was the key political watchword, and disorder the inevitable result' (D. Waddington, 1992: 116).

A further explanation for government involvement in industrial disputes is that it is an employer with a direct interest in the pay and conditions of its own workers. Civil Service wage demands or decisions affecting conditions of work (such as the decision in 1984 prohibiting workers at the Government Communications Headquarters from belonging to a trade union) may result in industrial unrest being directed at the government.

Although protest in the workplace is a key way in which trade unions can influence political affairs, it is not the only tactic they may use. They may exert pressure on Labour Party policy through their financial relationship with the party. Following the 2001 general election, trade unions began openly to raise the issue of the money which they donated to the Labour Party and to discuss the virtues of disaffiliation in an attempt to force the government to rethink its announced intentions to press ahead with the privatisation of health and education provision.

The reaction of the state to industrial unrest

Industrial disputes involving a conflict between an employer and his or her workforce are often civil affairs in which the state need not necessarily have to become involved. However, state involvement in major industrial disputes usually occurs and may be justified for a number of reasons. These include the need for a government to uphold the national interest or to defend its own political concerns when these are threatened by industrial unrest. State intervention is also justified by the threat or potential threat which workplace protests pose to public disorder. There have been many examples of this since 1970. Those involved in industrial disputes may on occasions use militant tactics to further their aims. This occurred, for example, during the 1972 building workers' dispute which witnessed 'some very ugly intimidation and an underlying viciousness' (Clutterbuck, 1978: 77). This necessitated police intervention designed either to uphold the law (for example by preserving the peace or by keeping roads open) or to safeguard the rights of those wishing to work during an industrial dispute who may be prevented from doing so by intimidatory or violent picketing. The police thus become the subject of attack either because they are viewed as the personification of a state whose policies are seen as unjust or because their attempt to uphold public order results in accusations of police partiality for the views of one of the two 'sides' present at a specific event. In these cases the violence of those engaged in industrial disputes is frequently directed against the police who may respond aggressively. The 'battle of Orgreave' in 1984 during the miners' dispute was an extreme example of violence involving strikers and the police and was followed by other events at which disorder occurred, especially in connection with News International's dispute with the print unions at Wapping in 1986–87. This section examines the measures which have been taken by the state to respond to protest in the workplace since 1970.

Criminal and civil law

Both the criminal and civil law have been used in connection with protests in the workplace since 1970. The main developments are discussed below.

Criminal law

Breach of the peace is a commonly-used charge against those engaged in workplace protests. It is relatively easy to prove and carries a minor penalty which is unlikely to create martyrs to a political cause. But the nature of this offence has been subject to judicial interpretation. The case of *Duncan v. Jones* in 1936 permitted a police officer to take pre-emptive action in order to prevent a breach of the peace and this power was further developed during the miners' dispute of 1984–85. In this dispute the police sought to prevent pickets travelling to Nottinghamshire by introducing roadblocks or road checks. This was most frequently done in Nottinghamshire itself or on the boundary between Nottinghamshire and South Yorkshire, although some instances also occurred in Derbyshire and at the Kent entrance to the Dartford Tunnel. The sanctions deployed by the police in these situations included instructions to a vehicle's occupants to turn around or face arrest for obstructing the police. In the first twenty-seven weeks of the strike some 164,508 individuals were prevented from entering Nottinghamshire on the basis that they were 'presumed pickets' (NCCL, 1984: 20–1). This action was governed by section 5 of the 1936 Public Order Act, section 51 of the 1964 Police Act and the common law power of setting limits on the number of persons in any particular place to prevent a breach of the peace. This made a number of assumptions concerning a person's future behaviour although the courts ruled such police interventions to be lawful in the case of *Moss and Others v. McLachlan*, 1984.

Other charges associated with the common law were also used against those engaged in protests after 1972. The charge of conspiracy was used in 1972 against a group of Sierra Leonese students who occupied their country's High Commission in London. This had the effect of transforming a civil offence (trespass) into a criminal one. One difficulty with this innovation, however, was that the courts failed to consistently convict under it. Later in 1972 five members of the building workers' union UCATT were charged with conspiracy to trespass in connection with the occupation of offices of an agency employing lump workers. This prosecution was unsuccessful, although a second innovation, the charge of conspiracy to intimidate under the 1875 Protection of Property Act, was successfully applied against three building workers who had used violence in an attempt to persuade workers at Telford in Shropshire to stop work (Cox, 1975: 47–8, 74–5).

The regulation of trade union activities

Successive governments from the 1960s onwards adopted the view that trade unions needed controlling as some of their activities threatened the national interest. Actions which included 'wild cat' strikes (which became a 'serious economic problem' between 1964 and 1970) (Lane and Roberts, 1971: 232–3), 'secondary picketing' and the intimidation of those who refused to participate in an industrial dispute constituted what governments (and many members of the general public) viewed as the unacceptable face of trade unionism. Attempts to respond to these problems were initially embarked upon by a Labour government in the late 1960s. In 1965 the Donovan Commission was appointed to investigate the trade unions and following its report (Donovan, 1968) the government published the document, *In Place of Strife*, in 1969 which proposed the introduction of a number of legislative innovations to regulate trade union activities. The dissent which these proposals caused within the Labour movement led to the abandonment of its key provisions.

The defeat of the Wilson government at the 1970 general election resulted in Heath's Conservative government bringing forward legislation to restrict trade union activities in the form of the 1971 Industrial Relations Act. A newly-established National Industrial Relations Court (NIRC) was empowered to insist on a 'cooling off' period and a ballot before strike action could be demanded. The legal definition accorded to picketing was narrowed and a range of 'unfair industrial practices' were defined. The new court could sequester the assets of trade unions and employers could apply for compensation in connection with financial losses suffered through strike action not conducted in accordance with the provisions of the 1971 legislation.

The 1970–74 Conservative government's attempt to curb industrial militancy by coercive legislation did not succeed. Industrial disputes significantly increased during this period. Trade unions responded to what they regarded as an unjust attack on their rights by ignoring the legislation (either by refusing to register or through boycotting the newly-formed National Industrial Relations Court and failing to comply with its directions) or by sympathetic action which sometimes had the effect of transforming a local dispute into an all-out national stoppage. This led to absurdities in which either the government itself was forced to seek ways to undo the consequences of its legislation (such as through the use of the official solicitor in the 1972 dockers' dispute in order to prevent shop stewards blacking a container firm in the Port of London from going to prison in consequence of a contempt of court ruling following their refusal to appear before the NIRC) or when industrialists felt constrained to pay fines imposed by the Industrial Relations Court to avert national disputes. This latter situation occurred in the Con-Mech dispute involving the AEUW in 1973–74 (Clutterbuck, 1980: 53). The Conservative government was aware of the shortcomings of its attempts to secure industrial harmony by the methods contained in the 1971 legislation and would have introduced reforms to it. However, the reluctance of the electorate to approve a further period of Conservative rule in the 'who governs?' election of February 1974 resulted in the Labour party introducing reforms. Many of the key provisions of the 1971 legislation were repealed in the 1974 Trade Union and Industrial Relations Act and the 1975 Employment Protection Act.

The reforms of Conservative governments after 1979.   Trade unions exercised considerable political strength in the period after 1974 but were accused of abusing their power by placing sectional interests before that of the common good. Those on the right of the political spectrum attributed Britain's economic problems to trade union power which was alleged to be responsible for high taxation to subsidise jobs and inflation to pay for wage increases which were not supported by productivity. Popular scepticism concerning the power of the unions enabled the Conservative party to secure office in 1979 by emphasising the harm done to the nation during the 'winter of discontent'. The Conservative Party subsequently introduced a range of civil legislation after their 1979 election victory which was designed to restrict trade union activities. The 1980 and 1982 Employment Acts narrowed the definition of a trade dispute to an action between an employer and that organisation's direct workforce. This redefinition was aimed at secondary picketing: the 1980 Act made pickets liable to a range of civil actions if they attended any workplace other than their own and the 1982 legislation made the pickets' union responsible if it had authorised action of this nature. The 1980 Act was accompanied by a Code of Practice which suggested that six pickets were a sufficient number to state a union case. Both Acts also included provisions which were designed to weaken the closed shop.

Further legislation was enacted in the form of the 1984 Trade Union Act and the 1988 Employment Act. The former imposed the requirement of statutory ballots before the commencement of strike action while the latter specified the rights of individual members to participate in industrial disputes. Both 1984 and 1988 measures included provisions for the election of trade union executives and general secretaries. The 1992 Trade Union and Labour Relations (Consolidation) Act required a certification officer to keep a list of trade unions and defined their liability in proceedings in tort.

The Conservative Party's trade union legislation enabled the courts to intervene in industrial disputes. This intervention would usually take the form of an employer who was party to a dispute applying for an injunction to prevent activities which were the subject of legislative restriction, such as secondary picketing. A refusal to abide by an injunction could result in a union being fined or, in extreme cases, having its assets sequestrated. Other civil actions (such as the 'rule book' cases initiated during the miners' dispute of 1984–85) were also possible. It has been argued that legislation introduced during the 1980s was not solely responsible for reducing the scale of industrial militancy and that the attitude adopted by the courts was important. Their acquiesence to management witholding pay from employers who refused to work normally as a compensation for their breach of contract was argued to have 'altered the balance of bargaining power between employers and unions in areas where effective industrial action has ... been in the form of selective action short of a strike' (Elgar and Simpson, 1993: 105). Legal and judicial interventions of this kind were viewed by many trade unionists as an unwarranted attack on working-class political activity, particularly on the ability of one working-class person to display solidarity towards another. Measures of this nature were defended, however, by arguments which suggested that union democracy had been extended by giving rank-and-file members the ability to hold their leaders more effectively accountable for their actions.

It has been observed earlier in this chapter that civil legislation has frequently been reinforced by the intervention of the police and the use of the criminal law. One difficulty with civil law is that its application is often slow even if ultimately effective. The decision of News International to seek an injunction to place restrictions on picketing at their plant in Wapping in 1987 was responsible for ending the union activities waged by the NGA and SOGAT. Civil legislation is not confined to protests in the workplace and may be applied to other forms of protest and direct action. Those seeking to prevent the construction of the M65 in Lancashire in 1994 utilised tactics which included locking themselves to vehicles carrying plant to the route of the road. This placed them in contravention the 1992 Act which had been designed to prevent actions which would prevent people getting to work.

Industrial disputes and their impact on police organisation

The requirement of the police to handle public order situations has had a considerable impact on police organisation, training and weaponry. This section examines developments which primarily arose in connection with industrial disputes and should be read in conjunction with changes which relate to the policing of protest which are discussed in Chapter 2.

Mutual aid

In the nineteenth century, chief constables frequently called on neighbouring forces for support in public order situations which included industrial disputes. This was the genesis of what became known as 'mutual aid'. It was initially organised on an ad hoc basis until the 1890 Police Act formalised the practice, enabling police forces to voluntarily enter into standing arrangements to supply officers to each other in the event of major disorder. The arrangements governing mutual aid were not significantly altered until 1964. Section 14(2) of the 1964 Police Act effectively made it obligatory for forces to come to the aid of one another to provide an effective response to public disorder. The Home Office determined the financial arrangements for mutual aid. In the case of 'large scale' incidents, the sending authority continues to pay for the salaries of its officers with the receiving authority being responsible only for travelling and other additional costs of the deployment. 'Major' incidents are paid for by the Home Office.

Saltley, 1972. The events which occurred at Saltley Coke Depot in Birmingham in 1972 had a major impact on the police response to public disorder. In 1972 the National Union of Miners went on strike in connection with a wage dispute. One feature of this strike was the use of 'flying pickets' which sought to halt the production of coal and prevent its distribution to power stations. Saltley became the last major distribution point in Britain and the aim of the Yorkshire Branch of the NUM, headed by its then president, Arthur Scargill, was to blockade the depot and prevent further movements of coal from the premises through the use of mass picketing. The activities of the miners were responded to by the City of Birmingham police force, then headed by Chief Constable Sir Derek Capper. On 10 February his 800 officers were outnumbered by 15,000 pickets. He took the view that his resources were inadequate to keep the roads to the depot clear to enable lorries to enter and leave and that in this event injuries or deaths might occur. Accordingly he ordered the closure of the gates for the duration of the dispute in the interests of public safety. This was viewed as a major union victory, 'living proof that the working class had only to flex its muscles and it could bring government, employers, society to a total standstill' (Scargill, 1972). However, it was a success that the police service and successive governments were determined would never be repeated. The National Security Committee (later renamed the Civil Contingencies Committee by the 1974 Labour government) (Geary, 1985: 95) was established to plan the state's response to such future events which led to the reorganisation of mutual aid.

The reorganisation of mutual aid after 1972. The decision to apply for mutual aid and from where to seek it was initially in the hands of a chief constable faced with disorder. Since 1972, however, these decisions have been determined centrally. In that year the Association of Chief Police Officers established a mechanism which was initially known as the National Reporting Centre (now termed the Mutual Aid Coordination Centre). It operated from New Scotland Yard, was operationally under the control of ACPO's president and became activated when an event arose with major implications for public order. Its role was to coordinate the deployment of police officers from across the country to the area affected by disorder. This arrangement was utilised in the 1984–85 miners' dispute. The NRC/MACC performed an administrative and coordinating role and although it was responsible for sending officers from one part of the country to another, decisions related to their deployment theoretically remained in the hands of local commanders. However, the role undertaken by this body was challenged by those who viewed events in 1984–85 as demonstrating an unprecedented degree of national coordination of policing (McCabe and Wallington, 1988). It was alleged that the NRC issued operational directions to police units on the ground during the miners' dispute (Bunyan, 1985: 298–9), thus promoting a situation which 'came close to the setting up of a national police riot squad, independent of local police management and accountable to a central organisation' (NCCL, 1984: 33).

Improved police tactics

Industrial disputes led to the introduction of methods additional to the time-honoured practice of 'pushing and shoving' in order to control crowd behaviour, which involved the use of more specialised formations and the deployment of snatch squads. An initial development connected with the introduction of shields was a formation involving three officers with inter-locked shields and two further officers positioned behind them. The two without shields were able to leap out and effect arrests. Other develop-ments included the introduction of new methods of crowd control, such as the wedge which sought to separate elements engaged in a riotous assembly (Geary, 1986: 134). This entailed a close formation of police officers which was used to break up a crowd, followed by other officers who made snatch arrests. Events which took place during the 1980s (particularly the inner city disorders of 1980, 1981 and 1985, the National Graphical Association dispute at Wapping in 1983 and the miners' dispute of 1984–85) led to fur-ther innovations, termed 'paramilitary' policing (Jefferson, 1990), which is discussed in more detail in the concluding chapter. A key development was the publication in 1983 of ACPO's *Public Order Manual of Tactical Operations and Related Matters*. Each force was issued with a binder which contained 'a detailed analysis of the stages of a riot and the police responses appropriate to them'. A total of 238 tactics and manoeuvres were set out in its 30 sec-tions 'arranged in order of escalating force, from normal policing up to plastic bullets, CS gas and live firearms' (Northam, 1989: 42). The response by the police in public order situations thus became standardised across the entire police service in England and Wales.

The 2001 Anti-Terrorism, Crime and Security Act

This legislation extended the remit of the Ministry of Defence Police. This is a national force, consisting of around 3700 officers in 2001, under the direct control of a special Ministry of Defence Committee with no form of external accountability. The 2001 Anti-Terrorism, Crime and Security Act enabled them to assist police officers in the execution of their duties, in which circumstances they would exercise the same privileges and powers of a constable. This would theoretically enable them to be deployed against strikes and demonstrations anywhere in the country, thus potentially transforming the organisation into a centrally-controlled riot police.

The military and civil emergencies

The coercive response to workplace protest is not solely delivered by the police service but may involve other agencies. This section considers the role of the military in a range of civil affairs and in particular in connection with industrial unrest.

The historical position

Historically, soldiers have been utilised in industrial disputes and other forms of public order situations to augment the role of police forces or other civil bodies concerned with enforcing law and order. They did not intervene in these circumstances unless requested to do so by the civil authority. This was historically a magistrate whose power to summon military aid was derived from common law. Initially soldiers operated under the control of the magistrate who was empowered to give the order to 'open fire'. One problem with these arrangements was that magistrates who were party to episodes such as industrial disputes might seek to utilise soldiers in a coercive manner to further their own economic interests. Following the Featherstone colliery lock out in 1893 (in which soldiers killed two people and injured several others) new rules were introduced governing the use of the military to maintain public order. The request to summon troops had to be made through the mayor of a borough or the chief constable of a county force, and magistrates would no longer determine whether troops should use their firearms (Peak, 1984: 23). Troops were subsequently deployed on a number of occasions in the industrial unrest which preceded the First World War. This period witnessed the involvement of central government in the process of summoning such aid. Churchill, for example, responded to a request by the chief constable of Glamorgan and sent both troops and Metropolitan Police officers during the South Wales coal strike in 1910. The announcement of a national railway strike in 1911, however, prompted

Churchill to deploy troops without any prior local request having been submitted for such aid (Geary, 1985: 37).

The legislative framework

The 1914 Defence of the Realm Act gave the government powers to intervene in civil life. The role of troops was extended in some cases beyond maintaining public order to include performing the jobs of striking workers. The measure lapsed after the war and was replaced by the 1920 Emergency Powers Act. This authorised the monarch to proclaim a state of emergency to respond to actions which threatened to interfere with the 'supply and distribution of food, water, fuel or light, or with the means of locomotion' which would deprive the community, or any substantial section of it, of 'the essentials of life'. The proclamation is required to be communicated to Parliament within five days and be renewed on a monthly basis. It empowers the government to make regulations governing a wide range of matters connected with maintaining the safety and life of the community. The three-day working week imposed by the Heath government in 1973, which sought to conserve energy supplies in response to the miners' strike, was an example of the use to which this Act was put in Britain after 1970. Troops could be used under the provisions of this Act to maintain order or to carry out the work of those on strike. However, this legislation is not frequently used when industrial unrest has occurred.

The 1939 Emergency Powers (Defence Act) extended the role which members of the armed forces could play in a wide range of civil emergencies. Initially regulations were issued under this Act authorising their deployment in agricultural work, but in 1942 this was extended to cover 'urgent work of national importance'. This remained in force until the passage of the 1964 Emergency Powers Act which effectively gave permanent legislative sanction to the use of soldiers in situations which were not of a military nature. This Act did not give the government any specific power to summon troops to these situations but merely concerned the uses to which troops could be put once they had been summoned to an event.

The national security plan

The role performed by military personnel evolved in a piecemeal fashion. During the 1970s such situations were rationalised under three newly-devised headings collectively referred to as Military Assistance to the Civilian Authorities (MACA). The first of these was Military Aid to the Civilian Communities (MACC). This involved the deployment of military personnel in episodes such as flooding or other forms of natural disaster or major accidents, and stemmed from the uses to which soldiers had been put under the provisions of the 1939 and 1964 legislation. An emergency under this heading is described as 'an occasion when there is a danger to human life or a major breakdown of services vital to the welfare of the community' (Ministry of Defence, 1989: 3).

The second situation was Military Aid to the Civilian Ministries (MACM) which was latterly re-titled Military Aid to other Government Departments (MAGD). This frequently involved the use of troops to perform the work of those engaged in an industrial dispute. Examples of this included the use of soldiers to collect refuse during the 1975 Glasgow refuse collectors' strike and the deployment of troops (accompanied by 'green goddesses') during the 1977–78 national fire brigade strike (when 21,000 troops were used to replace 32,000 firemen) (Geary, 1985: 96) and subsequent local fire fighters' disputes such as that in Derbyshire in 1996 and Merseyside in 2001. In 1979 police, army and air force personnel were used to drive ambulances during strikes by ambulance drivers. Military personnel may provide other forms of aid to government departments, such as the use of troops to cull animals to prevent the spread of foot and mouth disease and to dispose of the carcasses of slaughtered animals in 2001. The final situation is defined as Military Aid to the Civil Power (MACP). This would entail the use of troops in situations in which disorder was occurring on such a scale that the police could not cope with it and the whole parliamentary system was threatened or 'if a minority, by violent means and armed force, was attempting to challenge the very authority of Government with a view to changing or overthrowing it'. In this circumstance the chief constable for the area concerned would summon military aid and assume control over the operations they undertook (Bramhall, 1980: 480–4), although this application would be made through the Home Secretary who would discuss the matter with the Secretary of State for Defence and this minister would determine whether to accede to the chief constable's request for troops (Mark, 1977: 30). Troops have been used in this capacity in Northern Ireland since 1969. The military may also be deployed for short-term emergencies, one example being controlling security arrangements at Heathrow airport during the Gulf War in the early 1990s. Additionally, specialist military units (such as the Special Air Services Regiment or bomb disposal teams) might perform more restricted roles, especially in connection with hostage or hijack situations (such as the Iranian Embassy Seige in 1980) or to perform surveillance and protection services to guard against terrorist attacks directed at facilities including the North Sea oil installations.

Contingency and emergency planning

The use of troops forms a part of the state's response to civil emergencies. In addition machinery exists to plan and administer services which may be required in the event of disruptions caused by protests. These are frequently industrial disputes but may involve other activities which are the subject of discussion in Chapters 2 and 4.

Contingency planning

Arrangements to handle civil emergencies are controlled by the Civil Contingencies Unit, consisting of a group of ministers and civil servants which meets under the chairmanship of the Home Secretary. It is housed within the Cabinet Office and in addition to planning the state's response to counter the effects of industrial disputes nominates 'lead departments' to respond to a wide range of civil emergencies ranging from floods to earthquakes. This advises the affected ministries of the circumstances in which they will be expected to take the lead and thus enables them to plan ahead and be ready to take immediate action when the need to do so arises (Home Office, 1994: 56–8). Additionally a Cabinet Office Briefing Room (Cobra) was established in the mid-1970s which keeps the Cabinet informed of events as they occur and helps to coordinate the response of the police and security services. Cobra was used in connection with the government's response to the fuel crisis in 2000 (which is discussed in Chapter 2) and the outbreak of foot and mouth disease in 2001.

The sub-national machinery for contingency planning consists of Regional Emergency Committees which were established in 1979 in response to the national lorry drivers' dispute. These are composed of civil servants and representatives from other public bodies including the emergency services. They may be activated by the Civil Contingencies Unit and their roles include monitoring and transmitting information back to the centre and acting as a mechanism whereby central government and local authorities and services can liaise. These bodies may perform executive functions in the event of a state of emergency being declared. The county level organisation of the home defence machinery may also be utilised in connection with industrial disputes. In the fire brigade dispute of 1977, for example, county control rooms were utilised to organise the provision of services at local level.

Emergency planning

Emergency planning is concerned with a situation in which the government loses control of all or part of the country. This would normally arise in the event of war in which enemy attack or invasion deprived the government of power. Emergency planning is designed to provide for government on a temporary or permanent basis. For a number of years emergency planning was termed 'civil defence', although in 1968 the new term 'home defence' was adopted. The machinery of home defence is superintended by the Emergency Services Division of the Home Office, situated within the Home Office Police Department. It is based on a system of regional government coupled with the use of existing local government administration. In 1986 the 'Planned Programme of Implementation' was introduced whereby local authorities were required to submit plans to the Home Office related to specific emergency functions such as feeding the local population.

The fear of revolution or internal upheaval was especially prevalent during the 1970s when a combination of political instability (including two inconclusive general elections in 1974), high levels of industrial unrest and inflation resulted in the establishment of a number of private strike-breaking organisations, including General Sir Walter Walker's Unison and Colonel David Stirling's GB 75 (News Line, 1980: 41–56). Those on the left of the political spectrum were critical of these advance preparations and machinery, arguing that they could be used in domestic emergencies such as strikes or various manifestations of public disorder, directed at the 'enemy within' (Spence, 1978: 2–3). This view was subsequently substantiated in the 1986 Civil Protection in Peacetime Act whereby Chief Emergency Planning Officers were required to adopt what is termed an 'all hazards approach' which does not distinguish between wartime and peacetime emergency planning. The integration of civil defence and emergency planning arrangements contained in the Civil Defence (General Local Authority Functions) Regulations, 1993, similarly emphasised the civil aspects of these advance preparations by reference to events such as the devastation caused by the 1987 storm and the 1988 Lockerbie air disaster (Home Office, 1994).

Incorporation of unions into a state's formal decision-making machinery

The above discussion has referred to a coercive response to workplace protest involving the use of civil and criminal law and the deployment of the police service and the military. There are, however, other ways available to the state to respond to activities of this nature. One further way to prevent industrial unrest from occurring is to provide trade unions with privileged access to the state's formal decision-making processes. This may be achieved in two ways.

The election of a Labour government may provide unions with access to the political arm of the executive branch of government. This may take the form of ad hoc meetings (an approach epitomised by the 'beer and sandwiches' relationship between the major unions and Harold Wilson's Labour government in 1964) or may be of a more structured nature (such as the social contract between the trade unions and Labour Party which was negotiated in advance of the 1974 general election in order to provide the basis for an anti-inflationary policy). There are, however, two problems with access constructed in this manner. First, Labour governments do not behave in a consistent manner in their relationships with trade unions. The relationship between business and 'new' Labour helped to ensure that Labour governments elected in 1997 and 2001 failed to give the trade unions any advantaged position in connection with the making of public policy. Secondly, privileged access to ministers may be denied when a Labour government is replaced by a Conservative administration. However, the potential marginalisation which unions may experience from this latter situation might be offset by access to the bureaucracy which provides a second avenue of access to the state's formal decision-making machinery. The development of neo-corporatism in Great Britain in the 1960s provided unions with a more constant form of access to the state's decision-making processes which was not dependent on the political composition of the government.

Neo-corporatism

United Kingdom trade unions and business organisations succeeded in cultivating a close working relationship with central government during the 1960s. Policy was hammered out in the forum of the National Economic Development Council (NEDDY) in which members of the government and leading trade unionists and employers effectively determined major issues of industrial and economic policy. Parliament was relegated to the role of rubber-stamping decisions taken elsewhere and the imminent introduction of a neo-corporate state meant that it made little difference which party won a general election (Pahl and Winkler, 1974: 72). This situation has been alleged to exert a major bearing on the level of protest in the workplace since neo-corporatism may reduce the level of protest by securing improved economic performance resulting in greater economic equality and consequent social harmony (Nollert, 1995: 139, 159–60). Thus some states which have developed corporatist bargaining encompassing national associations of capital and labour and top governmental officials have been relatively immune to outbreaks of protest and violence (Nollert, 1995: 160) especially in the workplace.

However, neo-corporatist structures do not always succeed in limiting the extent of workplace protest. This depends on factors such as the ability of those engaged in bargaining to carry their rank-and-file supporters with them. The period since 1970 has witnessed several unofficial, or 'wildcat' strikes. Further, groups not able to forge such a close link with the state's decision-making process may perceive themselves to be marginalised and thus be spurred into organising and being willing to use workplace-orientated forms of action. The development of organisations such as the National Federation of the Self-Employed, the National Association of the Self-Employed and the Association of Self-Employed People between 1974 and 1976 arose in consequence of the growth of self-employed persons between 1966 and 1973 by 255,000 (McHugh, 1979: 48) and the traditional difficulty faced by small entrepreneurs in getting their concerns addressed by government.

Evaluation of the state's response

Marxists assert that the state's response to protest in the workplace is biased. They believe that the key role of the state is to ensure that conditions exist for the accumulation of capital which is implemented by managing the 'inevitable' conflict which perennially arises between workers and their employers (Hain, 1986: 26). This situation was exemplified by the role played by the Ministry of Labour as a mediator between unions and management when industrial unrest was threatened. In 1974 the Conciliation and Arbitration Service (ACAS) was set up in an attempt to remove the government from pay bargaining. The Marxist view implies that all industrial disputes pose a threat to capitalism and that the nature of state intervention is consistent, giving rise to an accusation that bodies such as the police 'side' with owners or managers and oppose actions undertaken by trade unionists in order to sustain productivity. This situation was alleged to have been apparent in the 1984–85 miners' dispute when the views of the government, the actions of the police service, the decisions of the courts and the reporting of the media showed 'a clear coincidence of interests' (Scraton, 1985: 162–3). Liberals, however, assert that owners and workers share a common interest since both benefit from productive enterprise. They also believe that the maintenance of law and public order is in the interests of all and that it is legitimate for the state to intervene to defend individual liberties (such as the right to work during a strike) when these are threatened by behaviour which may be construed as intimidatory.

Police policy

The policing of industrial disputes has been subject to a number of criticisms. These are considered both in this section and in the concluding chapter.

Departure from minimum force

A key issue connected with developments concerned with the policing of industrial disputes is whether they should be utilised to enable the police to adopt an offensive or defensive posture in these situations. The main danger with offensive operations is that they depart from the traditional concept of minimum force and policing becomes seen as aggressive and overbearing by those on the receiving end of these procedures. This perception erodes the ideal of policing by consent. Orgreave, 1984, witnessed the first police baton charge since the 1940s and the use of tactics designed to disperse crowds rather than the more traditional policy of passive containment (NCCL, 1984: 13). It was alleged that police action at the News International dispute at Wapping, 1986–87, was designed to disperse and incapacitate people rather than arrest them. This resulted in demonstrators being struck on the head rather than on the arms, legs and torso, and truncheons being used to frighten people rather than for police officers' self-defence (London Strategic Policy Unit, 1987).

Politicisation

The use of the police in industrial disputes since 1970 has opened the service to the charge of politicisation. This suggests that a key role of the police is to further the political interests of the government as opposed to serving the community without fear or favour. This charge was especially made in connection with the policing of the miners' dispute in 1984–85 when the belief arose 'strongly felt by striking miners and their families, that among the purposes for which the police and the criminal justice system have been used (whether by design or not) has been the promotion of the interests of the National Coal Board and the Government' (NCCL, 1984: 3; Alderson, 1996: 12). In this period the police became viewed in working-class communities as 'Maggie's Boot Boys' (Smith, 1994: 101), whose loyalty had been bought by the implementation of the Edmund Davies pay award in return for which the service was expected to stifle protest expressed by those who were disadvantaged by the economic policies pursued by the Conservative Party which resulted in higher unemployment and restricted access to a range of social welfare benefits. This had an adverse effect on the image of the police in working-class communities and on the legitimacy they were accorded there.

Politicisation requires the government to be in a position to give directions to the police and to influence their actions. This flew in the face of the historic concept of constabulary independence and was not legally possible in the 1980s (although the 1994 Police and Magistrates' Courts Act subsequently enabled the Home Secretary to set national objectives which each police force was required to achieve). Accordingly, the pressure exerted on the police service during major industrial disputes such as that of the miners in 1984–85 consisted mainly of informal influences. This was facilitated by the National Reporting Centre which is referred to earlier in this chapter. This gave ministers a central body at the heart of the policing of the dispute which they could contact to express their preferences (Kettle, 1985: 30–1). Additionally, the Home Secretary wrote to, and held regular briefings with, chief constables to inform them of government expectations (Uglow, 1998).

The erosion of civil liberties

The accusation of politicisation in which the role of the police in workplace protest is alleged to be biased is closely connected with the issue of civil liberties. It has been argued that 'the police have a duty to protect the civil liberties of all sides in an industrial dispute' (NCCL, 1984: 11). This neutral stance, however, is more difficult to accomplish when the police are subject to informal or formal pressures to act in a particular way by the government of the day. It was argued that the civil liberties of striking miners (and those wishing to support them) during the industrial dispute of 1984–85 was eroded by a number of actions taken by the police. These included the 'extensive' (NCCL, 1984: 20) use of roadblocks or road checks which interfered with freedom of movement and, it was alleged, 'smacks of the Soviet internal passport system or South African pass laws' (NCCL, 1984: 23). Other tactics used by the police included recording the registration numbers of vehicles used by pickets even when no offence had been committed and which constituted an erosion of personal privacy (NCCL, 1984: 24).

Accusations were also made in the 1984–85 miners' dispute that a significant number of persons were arrested simply to remove them from a particular location, and that access to a solicitor (which was then provided for in Judges' Rules) or notification of arrest to a relative (which was a statutory right) for those who were arrested was sometimes denied or long delayed (NCCL, 1984: 25–6). The use of bail conditions (especially by the Mansfield Magistrates' Court) was also criticised for being 'routinely and uniformly' applied to widely differing cases, thus creating an impression of 'supermarket justice' – 'nothing would more rapidly bring the British system of criminal justice into disrepute than for the impression to be given that cases were dealt with according to predetermined rules without consideration of the individual merits of each case' (NCCL, 1984: 30).

Actions pursued against striking miners were in contrast to those undertaken to enable those wishing to work to do so: on one occasion on 9 November 1984 between one and two thousand police officers accompanied *one* miner who wished to return to work at Cortonwood Colliery.

Lack of democratic accountability

The activation of mutual aid arrangements which may involve police officers being utilised outside their own areas for considerable periods of time eroded the established mechanisms of accountability of police forces to their police authorities. During the miners' dispute, 1984–85, it was argued that 'police authorities have been given no say in whether, or how many, police officers should be sent from their area to police the picket lines' (NCCL, 1984: 34). This potentially conflicted with the role of these bodies to maintain an efficient police force in their area, and led some police authorities to believe that the existing system of political and financial responsibility had collapsed. However, some research suggested that the activation of mutual aid arrangements did not drastically erode the capacity of the police to perform their routine duties, albeit increased reliance was placed on probationers, special constables and female officers to undertake this work (Waddington, 1985: 17).

The use of the military in civil emergencies

There are a number of concerns connected with the use of the military in civilian affairs. Joint police–military exercises (such as those at Heathrow Airport in 1974) might shift the orientation of police work further towards a paramilitary direction. However, the main debate which has emerged in connection with the use of the military has centred on who has the ability to summon this aid.

The historic role of magistrates as the civil authority has been largely superseded by developments which have arisen on an ad hoc basis. Chief constables became redefined as the civil authority in Queen's Regulations for the Army when these were redrafted after Saltley in 1972 (Vogler, 1991: 56). Additionally, the government may itself authorise the use of troops by declaring a state of emergency under the provisions of the 1920 Emergency Powers Act, but there has been a recent tendency to invoke the 1964 Act where the use of troops to respond to situations referred to in this legislation is secured through the exercise of the royal prerogative exercised by the Secretary of State for Defence. This course of action possesses a number of advantages which include the government not having to declare a state of emergency nor having to meet the costs of such operations. However, the use of the royal prerogative in such circumstances has been questioned (Peak, 1984: 53–5). It has also been argued that the use of soldiers in local emergencies is not compatible with work of 'national' importance referred to in the 1964 measure (Peak, 1984: 59–61) which suggests that the use to which successive governments have put troops may on occasions have been *ultra vires*. A final difficulty with the summoning of military aid in civil affairs has been the absence of democracy in existing arrangements. Requests for military aid made by chief constables or individual government departments connected with an industry affected by unrest may (as happened in the 1977–78 fire brigade dispute) override the views of other affected parties including the employers.

Conclusion

This chapter has focused on protest in the workplace which has mainly taken the form of industrial disputes organised by trade unions. The high level of working-class involvement in actions of this nature is in contrast to other forms of protest which were discussed in Chapter 2, where there was a significant degree of middle-class participation. The following chapter discusses a further form of protest, that of riot, which can be viewed as an activity designed to influence the content of the political agenda. In contrast to the social profile of those engaged in protest or workplace-orientated actions, rioting is an activity which is especially identified with those at the bottom end of the social ladder, whom the following chapter identifies as the underclass. Chapter 4 defines this term and seeks to explain why people engage in disorder.

Glossary

Lockouts

Employers may seek to deal with industrial unrest by what is termed a 'lockout'. This involves preventing a workforce from being able to work during an industrial dispute, for example by closing a factory.

'Lump' labour

This term is applied to self-employed workers in the building trade, an important feature of which is their low level of trade union membership.

Picketing

Strike action usually entails the use of pickets whereby representatives of those pursuing a course of industrial action seek to ensure that no work is carried out until the dispute is resolved. They do this by seeking to persuade persons not to enter premises where a strike is ongoing. Blockades to prevent the movement of goods and materials may also be mounted by pickets. During the 1970s picketing was affected by a number of developments. These included the use of 'flying pickets' in which workers were bussed around the country in an attempt to ensure that no work could proceed in places where strike action was taking place. This tactic was used, for example, in the 1972 miners' strike. Mass picketing was a further tactic which was developed in this period, which involved physical obstruction rather than peaceful persuasion which had previously been the main intention of picketing. This was used in the dock strike in 1972, the Grunwick dispute in 1967–68 and the NGA dispute at Warrington in 1983. Secondary picketing was also developed in this period which entailed workers in a concern affected by industrial action seeking to advance their cause by preventing work from taking place in other areas of industry (usually with some connection with the subject of the initial strike action). The secondary picketing of Saltley Gas Works in 1972 to further the miners' dispute was an example of this form of action.

Strike

A strike entails a temporary stoppage of work by a group of employees in order to express a grievance or enforce a demand (Griffin, 1939: 20–2). The workforce withdraws its labour and refuses to return to work until its demands have been met. This view was based on the presumption that a fixed pattern of behaviour would be 'called forth' by a specific social situation, thus ignoring the way in which different persons would perceive and define that situation (Hyman, 1972: 67, 69). There are several reasons why strikes occur among which are hours of labour, demarcation disputes, employment and dismissal questions (including redundancy), other personnel questions, other working arrangements, rules and discipline, trade union status, and sympathetic action (Department of Employment, quoted in Hyman, 1972: 115–16). However, the grievances expressed by workers in strike situations centre primarily around wages (Hyman, 1972: 117) even if there are other issues at stake (Knowles, 1952: 228). Strike action typically is organised by trade unions, although unofficial actions have also occurred since 1970. An unofficial strike is 'one which is not recognised by the Executive Committee of a Union' (Knowles, 1952: 30). This form of action may be planned or occur spontaneously, in which case the term 'wildcat' is applied. One example of a wildcat strike was the seven-week dispute at Pilkington's Glass Works at St Helens in 1970 (Lane and Roberts, 1971).

Work-in

A work-in entails the workforce taking control of the means of production, typically to prevent the closure or scaling down of an industrial enterprise.

References

J. Alderson (1996) 'A Fair Cop', *Red Pepper*, May, 6–12

E. Bramall (1980) 'The Place of the British Army in Public Order', *Journal of the Royal Society of Arts*, June, 480–6.

G. Brown (1977) *Sabotage: a Study in Industrial Conflict* (Nottingham: Spokesman Books)

T. Bunyan (1985) 'From Saltley to Orgreave via Brixton', *Journal of Law and Society*, 12(3), Winter, 293–304

S. Clegg (1996) 'From the Women's Movement to Feminisms', in C. Barker and P. Kennedy (eds) *To Make Another World: Studies in Protest and Collective Action* (Aldershot, Avebury)

R. Clutterbuck (1980) *Britain in Agony: the Growth of Political Violence* (Harmondsworth: Penguin, 2nd edition)

C. Collins (1996) 'To Concede or to Contest? Language and Class Struggle', in C. Barker and P. Kennedy (eds) *To Make Another World: Studies in Protest and Collective Action* (Aldershot, Avebury)

B. Cox (1975) *Civil Liberties in Britain* (Harmondsworth: Penguin)

C. Critcher (2000) 'Policing Pit Closures 1984–1992', in R. Bessel and C. Emsley (eds) *Patterns of Provocation: Police and Public Disorder* (Oxford: Berghahn Books)

J. Cronin (1979) *Industrial Conflict in Modern Britain* (London: Croom Helm)

Lord Donovan (1968) *Report of the Royal Commission on Trade Unions and Employers' Associations, 1965–8* (London: HMSO, Cmnd 3623)

J. Duncan, W. McCarthy and G. Redman (1983) *Strikes in Post-War Britain: a Study of Stoppages of Work due to Industrial Disputes* (London: George Allen and Unwin)

J. Elgar and B. Simpson (1993) 'The Impact of the Law on Industrial Disputes in the 1980s', in D. Metcalfe and S. Milner (eds) *New Perspectives on Industrial Disputes* (London: Routledge)

B. Fine and R. Millar (1985) 'Introduction: the Law of the Market and the Rule of Law', in B. Fine and R. Millar (eds) *Policing the Miners' Strike* (London: Lawrence and Wishart)

R. Geary (1986) *Policing Industrial Disputes 1893–1985* (London: Methuen)

P. Green (1990) *The Enemy Without. Policing and Class Consciousness in the Miners' Strike* (Oxford: Oxford University Press)

J. Griffin (1939) *Strikes: a Study in Quantitative Economics* (New York: Columbia University Press)

P. Hain (1986) *Political Strikes: the State and Trade Unionism in Britain* (Harmondsworth: Penguin)

Home Office (1994) *Dealing with Disaster* (London: HMSO, 2nd edition)

R. Hyman (1972) *Strikes* (London: Fontana)

T. Jefferson (1990) *The Case Against Paramilitary Policing* (Milton Keynes: Open University Press)

C. Kerr (1964) *Labour and Management in Industrial Society* (New York: Doubleday)

M. Kettle (1985) 'The National Reporting Centre and the 1984 Miners' Strike', in B. Fine and R. Millar (eds) *Policing the Miners' Strike* (London: Lawrence and Wishart)

K. Knowles (1952) *Strikes: a Study in Industrial Conflict* (Oxford: Blackwell)

T. Lane and K. Roberts (1971) *Strike at Pilkingtons* (London: Fontana)

London Strategic Policy Unit (1987) *Policing Wapping: an Account of the Dispute 1986/7* (London: London Strategic Policy Unit, Police Monitoring and Research Group Briefing Paper Number 3)

Sir R. Mark (1977) *Policing a Perplexed Society* (London: George Allen and Unwin)

T. May (1979) 'Middle Class Unionism', in R. King and N. Nugent (eds) *Respectable Rebels: Middle Class Campaigns in Britain in the 1970s* (London: Hodder and Stoughton)

S. McCabe and P. Wallington (1988) *The Police, Public Order and Civil Liberties: Legacies of the Miners' Strike* (London: Routledge)

J. McHugh (1979) 'The Self-Employed and the Small Independent Entrepreneur', in R. King and N. Nugent (eds) *Respectable Rebels: Middle Class Campaigns in Britain in the 1970s* (London: Hodder and Stoughton)

D. Metcalfe and S. Milner (eds) (1993) *New Perspectives on Industrial Disputes* (London: Routledge)

S. Miller and M. Walker (1984) *A Stage of Seige: Policing the Coalfields in the First Six Weeks of the Miners' Strike* (Yorkshire: Yorkshire Area NUM)

Ministry of Defence (1989) *Military Aid to the Civilian Community* (London: HMSO, 3rd edition)

National Council for Civil Liberties (1984) *Civil Liberties and the Miners' Dispute* (London: NCCL)

National Council for Civil Liberties (1986) *No Way in Wapping* (London: NCCL)

News Line (1980) *Britain's State within the State* (London: New Park Publications)

M. Nollert (1995) 'Neocorporatism and Political Protest in the Western Democracies: a Cross-National Analysis', in J. Jenkins and B. Klandermans (eds) *The Politics of Social Protest: Comparative Perspectives on States and Social Movements* (London: UCL Press)

G. Northam (1989) *Shooting in the Dark: Riot Police in Britain* (London: Faber and Faber)

R. Pahl and J. Winkler (1974) 'The Coming Corporatism', *New Society*, 30(627), 10 October, 72–6

S. Peak (1984) *Troops in Strikes: Military Intervention in Industrial Disputes* (London: Cobden Trust)

A. Scargill, speech at Saltley Gas Works 9 February 1972, quoted in R. Clutterbuck (1980) *Britain in Agony: the Growth of Political Violence* (Harmondsworth: Penguin, 2nd edition), 70

P. Scraton (1985) *The State of the Police* (London: Pluto Press)

Sir J. Smith (1994) 'Police Reforms', *Police Journal*, LXVII(2), April–June, 99–104

M. Spence (1978) *Region 1: an Examination of the State's Plans for Repression in the North East* (Newcastle upon Tyne: Black Jake Collective)

M. Thatcher (1993) *The Downing Street Years* (London: HarperCollins)

P. Toynbee (2002) 'All Out For a Change', *Guardian*, 11 January

S. Uglow (1988) *Policing Liberal Society* (Oxford: Oxford University Press)

R. Vogler (1991) *Reading the Riot Act: the Magistracy, the Police and the Army in Civil Disorder* (Milton Keynes: Open University Press)

D. Waddington (1992) *Contemporary Issues in Public Disorder: a Comparative and Historical Approach* (London: Routledge)

P. Waddington (1985) *The Effects of Police Manpower Depletion during the NUM Strike, 1984–85* (London: The Police Foundation)

4
Urban and Non-Metropolitan Disorders

The previous two chapters have discussed various forms of protest which emerged after 1970. This period (especially after 1980) witnessed a considerable degree of disorder in which rioting was used by those at the bottom end of the social ladder to voice their grievances with the aim of forcing policy-makers to address them. This chapter considers the social background of those involved in actions of this type and the factors which motivated them to act as they did. It considers the response by the state which was designed to reduce the likelihood of further disorder occurring, paying particular attention to the issue of police reform whose impact is further discussed in Chapter 6.

Introduction

Riots occcurred sporadically in the 1970s. In 1976, 325 police and 131 civilians were injured in disturbances in Notting Hill, London which prompted organisations including the West Indian Standing Conference to call for a Royal Commission into relationships between the police and public in that area. Disturbances of this nature occurred more regularly after 1980 in what has been termed 'a decade of disorder' (Joyce, 1992).

In 1980 a riot occurred in the St Paul's area of Bristol. In 1981 a disturbance arising from a demonstration organised by the New Cross Massacre Action Committee was followed by a wave of disorders affecting a large number of Britain's major cities including Brixton in London, Moss Side in Manchester and Toxteth in Liverpool. In the latter riot 150 buildings were destroyed, 800 police officers were injured, 500 arrests were made and 1000 crimes were reported. Although rioting was not a new phenomenon in Britain (Kettle and Hodges, 1982: 11) the scale and intensity of events in 1981 required the attention of public policy-makers. In 1985 a further series of riots took place. A police officer was murdered in Haringey's Broadwater Farm Estate and serious violence occurred in Handsworth in Birmingham in which two people died and damage of £16 million was caused. Most of the places affected by these riots were deprived, inner city locations with multi-ethnic populations in which African-Caribbean youths played a prominent (but not exclusive) role.

However, in 1987 disorders took place in areas with different profiles. These primarily occurred in southern England in places of relative affluence. The lack of leisure facilities for young persons and their propensity for alcohol consumption were cited as explanations for these events which were termed '*non*-metropolitan disorders', and gave rise to the social problem posed by the 'lager lout', a phrase coined in the *Guardian* on 6 April 1989.

In 1991 rioting returned to Britain's inner cities and between then and 1992 thirteen serious disorders occurred. These included disturbances in Oxford, Cardiff, Tyneside, Toxteth and Handsworth in 1991 and in places which included Bristol and Salford in 1992. With the exception of Blackburn a racial dimension was largely absent from these events. This violence was mainly confined to specific housing estates such as Newcastle's Meadow Well Estate, Bristol's Hartcliffe Estate and Salford's Ordsall Estate which were occupied by white working-class persons.

Minority ethnic communities were involved when a further series of disorders occurred in Bolton, Bradford, Leeds and Brixton in 1995. Unlike the disorders of the 1980s, a leading (but not exclusive) role was played by Muslim youths. Disorder subsequently occurred in Bradford in April 2001 following a fight at a Hindu wedding reception which triggered rumours of a racist attack against Muslims. Disorder in the Glodwick district of Oldham in May 2001 was commonly described in the media as a 'race riot' in which Muslim youths clashed with groups of whites. The disorders which took place in the Harehills and Chapeltown areas of Leeds in 2001 also involved large numbers of Asian and African-Caribbean youths, and some whites and young Asians were involved in serious disorder which occurred in Bradford and Stoke in July 2001. An important feature of some of these later disorders was the way in which a perceived act of racial injustice (such as a clumsy arrest, a racial attack or provocative acts undertaken or perceived to be about to be embarked upon by right-wing extremists) triggered a violent response, especially by young Muslims. Serious disorder took place in the Stoneyholme district of Burnley in June 2001, for example, following a white attack on an Asian cab driver to which the police did not immediately respond, and the riots which occurred at Stoke in 2001 were triggered by a racist attack and the (erroneous) belief that the British National Party planned to hold a march in the area. In July 2001 a small riot occurred in Brixton after an unarmed man was shot dead by a police officer.

Case study: the Brixton riot 1981

During the weekend of 10–12 April 1981 serious disorder occurred in Brixton, South London, 'the like of which had not previously been seen in this century in Britain' (Scarman, 1981: 1). Violence occurred against the background of a police stop and search operations (termed 'Swamp '81') and was precipitated when a police officer (who was subsequently joined by a colleague) observed a black youth being chased by other black youths. When it was apparent that the first youth had been stabbed the officers sought to obtain medical attention but their actions were perceived by onlookers as an attempt to arrest the injured youth. A crowd gathered and the injured youth was taken from the police and on to hospital. Other police officers who attended the scene were attacked. This violence petered out but reoccurred the following day, the key event being the search of a black mini-cab driver and his car on suspicion of possession of drugs. This resulted in a hostile crowd gathering and the subsequent escalation of violence.

The police were attacked with petrol bombs (the first time this weapon had been used outside Northern Ireland) and law and order temporarily collapsed. The violence was at its worst on 11 April when 279 police officers and at least 45 members of the general public were injured, a large number of police and other vehicles were damaged or destroyed and 28 buildings were damaged or destroyed by fire. One observer 'described the scene as comparable with the aftermath of an air raid' (Scarman, 1981: 1). Widespread looting occurred in the shopping centre of Brixton. Similar disorders to those which occurred in Brixton subsequently took place in Southall in London, Toxteth in Liverpool and Moss Side in Manchester.

Urban disorder – the participants

This section examines the key social groups involved in urban and non-metropolitan disorder and seeks to establish why they articulated their needs through the medium of riot rather than conventional political activity. This suggests that riots are viewed by those who participate in them as a form of protest, 'a rational response to genuine grievances' (Rowe, 1998: 153). However, this view is not universally accepted. It has been asserted that rioters do not enter into any rational calculation concerning the objectives they seek through their actions (Eisinger, 1973: 13) and are thus engaged in 'an expressive rather than instrumental form of activity' (P. Waddington. 1994: 6). Rioting has been depicted as lacking a focused central objective but as being 'a frequent resort by those who have been denied a substantial identity in the world: it is a vehicle for prowess, assertiveness, and a new set of standards for gauging character' (Rock, 1981: 20). Additionally, there is often a lack of evidence which directly links factors such as deprivation and discrimination with disorder or for substantiating any common motivation governing the the actions of all participants (P. Waddington, 1994: 4–5). It may be argued, however, that rioting is political in the sense that riots evidence the sense of anger and frustration felt by those who engage in activities of this nature who feel rejected by society (whatever the nature or consequence of that rejection) and who are willing to use violence as, in the current state of affairs, they have nothing to lose by doing so.

Minority ethnic groups

Minority ethnic groups have been involved in a number of riots which have occurred since 1980, and it might be argued that this is because the conventional political system does not adequately cater for their needs. Initially those who migrated to Britain in the 1940s remained passive in the face of racial injustice, but their children and grandchildren have been far less willing to adopt this stance. Disorders in the 1980s (involving second and third generation African-Caribbeans) and in the 1990s (involving second and third generation Asian Muslims) attest to the failure of the conventional political system adequately to respond to the prejudice and discrimination experienced by ethnic minorities, and the increased unwillingness of these communities to be treated as second-class citizens. This issue is explored in more detail in Chapter 6 in the context of the discussion of racial violence.

The main explanation for this situation is the relatively small size of Britain's ethic minority communities. The 1991 census (which was the first to ask a question concerning the ethnic group to which residents belonged) indicated that this population comprised approximately 3.1 million or 5.6 per cent of the total population. The main minority ethnic groups within Great Britain (totalling approximately 2.3 million) were Indians (876,997), Pakistanis (500,295), Bangladeshis (171,516), Black Caribbean (522,242) and Black African (219,169) (Office for National Statistics, 1996: 79–82).

The relatively small size of this electorate was historically compounded by perceptions that members of ethnic minority communities were reluctant to join political parties and that registration rates for members of these communities were lower than for white electors. Research into the nature of this problem produced divergent results. It has been asserted that the situation regarding the registration of ethnic minorities improved from the low levels which were estimated in the 1960s (Deakin, 1965) and that by 1983 the differential between white and minority ethnic voters had narrowed (primarily due to reduced rates of registration for the former category of voters) (Anwar, 1984). However, later findings suggested a higher rate of non-registration (Operation Black Vote, quoted in the *Guardian* on 21 May 2001, gave a figure of 25 per cent non-registration for black and Asian voters) and subsequent studies reasserted the disinclination of ethnic minorities to participate in conventional political activity. The *Guardian* on 2 December 1996 quoted a MORI poll which stated that 86 per cent of black people aged 18–25 did not intend to vote in the 1997 general election.

However, although the involvement of ethnic minority communities was prominent in some disorders which have occurred since 1980, this is has not consistently been the case. Many disorders in the 1990s, for example, occurred in areas which were almost exclusively inhabited by white working-class persons. This might suggest that the disorders of the 1980s and 1990s were of a different character or it might imply the importance of the concept of an underclass as a factor which applied to events which occurred in both decades.

The 'underclass'

There was a tendency to refer to racial disadvantage as a key explanation of urban unrest in the early 1980s. This view may, however, obscure the economic basis of these events. Factors which included global economic restructuring and the relocation of industry away from inner city locations coupled with the economic policies pursued by Conservative governments after 1979 resulted in recession whose initial impact hit racial minorities, especially African-Caribbeans, hard and accounted for the location of urban disorders in multiracial areas. The decline of employment in the textile industries by the late 1970s (due to factors which included the increased use of technology) had a detrimental impact on the economic position of many Asians and contributed towards a situation whereby only 'about four in ten adult, non-retired Pakistani and Bangladeshi men have any form of paid employment' (Madood, 1997: 99) which resulted in the emergence of an Asian underclass consisting of Muslim men of Pakistani and Bangladeshi origin. Whites also experienced high levels of unemployment as the economic recession became deeper and in the 1990s the existence of an 'underclass' was increasingly used in accounts of unrest which occurred in both multi-ethnic urban areas as well as those inhabitated primarily or exclusively by whites.

There is no accepted definition concerning the meaning of 'underclass' and it has been observed that 'there are as many definitions of the underclass as there are sociologists' (Macnicol, 1994: 30). The concept refers to factors which include low educational attainment, a lack of adequate skills to become a member of the labour force, shared spatial location, dependency on welfare, unemployment or joblessness and an unstable relationship with the labour market, pathological family structures and the inter-generational transmission of poverty, involvement in the unreported economy, and a predisposition to criminal or disorderly behaviour (Townsend, 1990; Walker 1991 and Westergaard 1992, summarised in Crowther, 2000: 3). The term was first used by the Swedish sociologist, Gunnar Myrdal (1964) in connection with poverty in America, and in Britain it was initially applied to the position of racial minorities who were marginalised by not being part of the 'welfare state deal' (Rex and Tomlinson, 1979: 328). This accorded other members of the working class access to a range of rights and privileges such as employment, housing and social services which were denied to ethnic minorities or allocated in a discriminatory fashion. In the late 1980s and early 1990s the term 'underclass' became broadly applied in one of two ways providing it with either a cultural or a structural meaning.

First, the underclass has been depicted as a group of persons demonstrating social behaviour which is at variance with the conduct of other, 'normal', members of society. It is seen to consist of people making the wrong moral choices. This definition is consistent with the view (which is discussed later in this chapter) that those who take part in riots are morally depraved. Their behaviour is particularly characterised by illegitimacy, involvement in crime (especially violent crime) and unemployment (Murray, 1989: 4). The absence of fathers was put forward as a key explanation for disorders which occurred in places such as Tyneside in the early 1990s (Dennis, 1993: 113). The main cause of such pathological behaviour was attributed to the operations of social policy which encouraged immoral choices but which absolved individuals from any blame for the consequences of their actions. This view suggested, for example, that the decision of a single woman to have a child was encouraged by legislation such as the 1977 Homeless Persons Act and the level of social welfare benefits which 'lifted a large proportion of low-income young women above the threshold where having a baby becomes economically feasible'. Involvement in crime was blamed upon inappropriate penalties which have 'fallen in severity... swiftness and certainty' and unemployment arose from a refusal to accept jobs even when these were on offer (Murray, 1989: 21–22, 27, 30). The belief that the prime culprit for such cultural malaise was the culture of dependency led to solutions which included 'authentic self government', involving communities being given responsibility for the institutions affecting their everyday lives (Murray, 1989: 34). It was argued that increased personal responsibility within the framework of a cohesive community would result in moral improvement whereby the activities characterising the underclass (such as children 'running wild', refusal to work and involvement in crime) become unacceptable.

An alternative view of the underclass adopted a structural definition which emphasised the importance of employment opportunities. It included groups such as frail elderly pensioners, single parents with no chance of escaping welfare, and the long-term unemployed (Field, 1990: 38–9). Structural definitions of the underclass asserted the importance of the latter factor: the underclass was said to consist of the economically unproductive, the unemployed and the unemployable: family units which 'do not have a stable relationship with legitimate employment' (Smith, 1992: 4) and who were thus economically dependent on state welfare benefits. This emphasis on conditions as opposed to behaviour attributed the existence of the underclass to the operations of society and in particular the extent of inequality. This opinion is compatible with the view which is discussed later in this chapter that riots have been fuelled by social and economic deprivation. Particular blame was placed on the policies associated with the Thatcher governments after 1979 (Field, 1989). Those who were unlikely ever to find jobs in post-industrial society and thus share in its rewards or prospects were treated as 'unwanted' (in the sense of being irrelevant to the process of production). Their rejection by society resulted in their violently reacting to the situation in which they found themselves.

Much of the blame for social disharmony during the 1990s was blamed on the growth of the underclass during the 1980s. One estimate suggested that in 1979 the underclass numbered 1.96 million (4.2 per cent of the population) and had risen to 4.58 million (9.9 per cent of the population) by 1986 (Buck, 1992: 16). Although problems in defining the term have resulted in such a figure being disputed (Heath, 1992: 33–4), it suggested the inclusion of large numbers of white Britons. The tendency for the underclass to be concentrated on inner city local authority housing estates (Buck, 1992: 18) was compatible with the location of urban disorders in the early 1990s.

Young people

Rioting is an activity associated with young persons. Age as opposed to race was given as the explanation for poor police–public relationships in Moss Side and the subsequent disorders in 1981 (Tuck and Southgate, 1981: 44) and the areas affected by rioting in 1991–92 contained a disproportionate number of young people below the age of 24 years (Power and Tunstall, 1997: x). Oldham (which experienced disorder in 2001) had a young population, 25 per cent being under 16 years of age (50 per cent in minority ethnic communities) (Oldham Independent Review, 2001: 41) and those involved in all the disorders which occured in 2001 were overwhelmingly young men, those arrested mainly being aged between 17–26 (Home Office, 2001b: 8). Disaffected young people are an important component of the underclass (which has been referred to above) as school leavers were particularly adversely affected by the collapse of employment opportunities between 1979 and 1997. This resulted in a situation in which 'there have been many parts of Britain, such as Liverpool, where particularly disadvantaged groups of school leavers, the least qualified whites and member of some ethnic minority groups, have faced persistent unemployment levels well in excess of 30 per cent since the 1970s' (Roberts, 1997: 45). The relationship between the police and young people is often based on aggression, and the communication of young people with the police often takes place in a confrontational setting (Loader, 1996).

Age and race can be combined as explanations of urban disorder. Views associated with the Chicago School of Human Ecology suggested that the children of first generation immigrants were likely to experience tensions between the values of their parents and those of the host community. Those caught in this situation were unable to adapt to either culture fully and became caught in a cultural 'no man's land' which was conducive to crime or other forms of delinquent behaviour. Explanations based on this view might account for disorders in a number of northern towns in 2001 where it could be argued that young Muslim men (but not women) lacked the links to their family's previous country but were prevented through racial prejudice from enjoying full participation in British society. This resulted in the formation of territorial enclaves, and their unwillingness to adopt the subservient attitudes of their elders resulted in disorders taking place when they, or the areas in which they lived, were perceived to be under attack.

Case study: urban disorders 1991–92

The complex nature of the conditions which predispose persons to engage in rioting was revealed in a study of the thirteen disorders which took place between 1991 and 1992. This suggested that all the affected areas were low-income with long-standing social problems and poor reputations. Unemployment levels were far above the national average and local authorities regarded the neighbourhoods where riots occurred as among the most difficult in their areas, often using them as 'dumping grounds' for those perceived to be 'problem families'. They contained a very high concentration of young people and in some of the affected areas over half of all residents were below 24 years of age.

It was argued that the combination of large numbers of out-of-work young males with no status or stake in society, living in low-income, work-poor households, in areas suffering from high social stigma was a dangerous one. 'The special characteristics of these areas concerned the economic and social status of inhabitants and, in particular, the young men. Levels of unemployment were three times as high as for the local authority area as a whole and more than twice as high as other areas comprising social housing' (Power and Tunstall, 1997: ix). All the affected areas had a previous history of disorder whereby the police and community had tolerated, or were forced to put up with, unusual levels of violence and law-breaking by young men prior to the riots: 'disorder had gradually mounted and there was weak social control, serious intimidation, an unwillingness by residents to act as witnesses, and irregular policing' (Power and Tunstall, 1997: x).

It was thus concluded that the underlying causes of the 1991–92 riots stemmed from demographic, economic and social factors.

> The demographic factors were an unusually youthful population with high levels of transience and very high numbers of lone-parent families separated into large isolated areas. The economic factors are lack of work opportunities for young males, lack of marketable skills, and lack of any useable work experience. The social factors are poverty, family breakdown, weak social controls, an acceptance of law-breaking, and poor relations with the police. These factors can act together to undermine normal community controls. (Power and Tunstall, 1997: xi)

Rioting is typically performed by males with little or no involvement of females. A feminist perspective on the events in 1991 on the Meadow Well and Blackbird Leys Estates emphasised the importance of the male trait of masculinity as the explanation for them. It was observed that in these areas women sought to hold the community together and maintain the last vestiges of its structures. The preference of young males to respond to their loss of masculinity when unemployment eroded their economic power by turning to crime and disorder and the desire of the police to adopt a confrontational stance towards them were depicted as major factors accounting for the disorders which took place in these areas. The calming and creative reconstruction of these communities demanded something from both the police and the young men which seemed impossible – 'Cooperation with women' (Campbell, 1991: 23).

The causes of disorder

Riots which have mainly occurred since 1980 have been attributed to various causes. This section examines the key explanations which have been put forward to explain these events.

Social and economic causes of disorder

Social and economic explanations of rioting emphasise the linkage between crime and disorder, with the police often playing the intermediary role – their attempts to prevent crime lead to disorder involving (or being orchestrated by) those with a vested interest in continuing these activities.

Lord Scarman had linked social disadvantage and rioting in his 1981 report. He referred to many of the young people of Brixton being born and raised in insecure social and economic conditions and in an impoverished physical environment. He suggested that protest on the streets and crime were caused by the accumulation of anxieties, frustrations and the limited opportunities which existed for airing grievances at national level (Scarman, 1981: 11, 16). He concluded that 'where deprivation and frustration exist on the scale to be found among the young black people of Brixton, the probability of disorder must ... be strong' (Scarman, 1981: 16). The view that deprivation was the fundamental cause of social unrest became increasingly advocated during the 1990s by political parties on the left of the political spectrum and formed a key component of what was described as the 'liberal perspective' of the causes of riots (Benyon, 1987: 27).

Deprivation could be evidenced by various indicators. These included unemployment, housing standards, achievement in the educational system, or leisure and recreational facilities. The existence of a combination of these factors in specific geographic areas ensured that those who lived there were labelled as social outcasts and treated aggressively by agencies which included the police service. It was in the sense that these deprivations arose from 'policy and administrative decisions that are made by some and which adversely affect others' that they have been termed 'structural violence' (Burton, 1997: 32). Unemployment was viewed as a key measure of deprivation. In Toxteth unemployment had been steady for a number of years but suddenly rose from 18,000 to 22,000 in the month before the 1981 riot. On 11 September 1985 the *Guardian* referred to an estimate that only 9 per cent of all school leavers in Birmingham in the summer of 1986 were likely to get jobs. The figure for members of minority ethnic communities was estimated to be 4 per cent. On 21 November 1988 the same newspaper estimated that in Toxteth the unemployment rate among black youths was 90 per cent. Similar disadvantages were apparent in areas which experienced disorder in 2001. Youth unemployment in Oldham stood at 40 per cent, and in Burnley 40 per cent of homes were dependent on some form of state benefit and 42 per cent of children were eligible for free school meals. Poor educational and skills attainment were also evident in Burnley: four of its 16 wards were within the worst 20 per cent in England, and six out of eight secondary schools were below the English average for attaining five GCSE 'A' to 'C' grades. Inadequate housing was also an important factor underpinning the disorders in Burnley. It was estimated that 'there are only four local authority areas in the country where private sector housing is in a worse condition or where there is a lower demand for private sector housing' (Burnley Task Force, 2001b: 4). The belief that underlying social and economic conditions have an impact on crime was given official sanction in a report which stated that while most poor people do not behave in such a manner, three-fifths of all offenders came from the last fifth of the very poor who do commit crimes (Audit Commission, 1996).

Various explanations might be put forward to link crime and the emergence of the underclass. Merton's theory of anomie has relevance to urban disorder in the 1980s and 1990s. This suggested that those in a disadvantaged position to obtain society's success goals legitimately by virtue of being unemployed or paid low wages may turn to crime for economic reasons (Alderson, 1995) in order to achieve them through illegal means, thereby avoiding social exclusion and facilitating their participation in society. The crimes associated with urban areas (such as drug trading, 'ram raiding', racketeering, extortion and 'ringing' cars) offer considerable economic benefits to those engaged in them. Gang warfare may break out in an attempt to exert dominance over lucrative forms of crime. The inevitable intervention by the police to curb these criminal activities might then lead to serious disorder (as occurred in the Hyde Park area of Leeds in 1995) possibly orchestrated by those who gain most through them and who wish to keep a police presence at a distance so they can pursue these activities without official hindrance. The riot in Salford in 1992 was blamed on factors of this nature. The ability of criminals to orchestrate disorder may be enhanced by the absence of legitimate opportunity structures which make some youths susceptible to the influence of adult criminals who act as their role models. This explanation is compatible with arguments alleging that the crime-orientated gang is one response to blocked opportunity structures (Clohard and Ohlin, 1960) whose existence may provide one explanation as to why riots occur in some deprived areas but not in others. Additionally, organised crime of this nature provides a source of employment for those who operate on the margins of criminality (perhaps by acting as lookouts) while riots provide opportunities for a wider cross-section of the public to obtain luxury items through the looting which frequently accompanies them.

Sub-cultural theories also offer some explanations for the lawlessness and social unrest which has occurred since 1980. Involvement in crime and disorder may provide the participants with street credibility and status among peer groups which formerly educational success and work achievements would have secured. Additionally, unemployment is a cause of boredom which may result in young persons seeking relief by engaging in actions such as 'joyriding' which offer them excitement, especially when accompanied by a police 'chase', but which bring no obvious economic benefit to the perpetrators. This factor is a key reason why some youngsters use drugs and alcohol – it helps to pass the time and provides a temporary 'buzz'. Crime also provides an opportunity for the existence of a perverted form of 'career structure' organised around gangs in which those who perform the most audacious actions are held in esteem by their peers. The apparent rejection of private property ownership which underlies these activities may further imply that newly-devised cultural values invert (or at least aggressively challenge) those adhered to by mainstream society from which they feel excluded. The development of alternative values is likely to be accompanied by attempts to establish physical control over the areas in which these are put into practice. In these circumstances any form of police intervention will be resisted as it poses a threat to the territorial control over the area which is required to sustain their activities. Disorders also constitute a source of entertainment or excitement for those who engage in them and may attract participants or bystanders who were not a party to the action which sparked them off.

The suggestion that disadvantage may result in challenges to society's mainstream cultural values reconciles cultural and structural explanations of the underclass. The problem originates as a structural issue, characterised by high unemployment. The experience by affected groups of this structural phenomenon leads to them becoming isolated from contact with employed people and the world of work: 'they begin to adopt a new style of life; and their culture begins to change as a consequence of their life experience' (Smith, 1992: 91). These two viewpoints were both embraced in one definition of the underclass which referred to it as:

> a social group of people located at the bottom of the class structure who, over time, have become structurally separate and culturally distinct from the regularly employed working-class and society in general through processes of social and economic change (particularly de-industrialisation) and/or through patterns of cultural behaviour, who are now persistently reliant on state benefits and almost permanently confined to living in poorer conditions and neighbourhoods. (MacDonald, 1997: 3–4)

Non-metropolitan disorder

The view that deprivation is the root cause of urban disorder seems not to be substantiated by events which took place in non-metropolitan areas in the late 1980s and which did not occur in deprived areas inhabited by an underclass. One study examined 251 incidents that took place in 1987 and pointed to factors such as boredom and the lack of recreational facilities which led to excessive drinking and subsequent violent conduct. While most of those actively engaged in such activities came from middle-class homes, they were typically white males who were either unemployed (often through their own choice) or who had unskilled jobs (Tuck, 1989). Although the profile of those involved in such disorders bore some similarities to that of these who participated in various forms of protest in the 1980s and 1990s (discussed in Chapter 2), their lack of education perhaps channelled energies into destructive as opposed to constructive forms of dissent. Non-metropolitan disorders also bore witness to the concept of relative deprivation perhaps accompanied by downward social mobility whereby the prospects of some children from middle-class homes were below the achievements of their parents. This situation might provide an explanation of the 'lager lout' phenomenon and also link non-metropolitan disorders with events in inner city areas by suggesting that, although these events were not caused by poverty and absolute deprivation, they were fuelled by resentment derived from blocked avenues of opportunity which denied some people the ability to fully participate in the consumerism and ownership associated with Thatcher's Britain of the 1980s.

Biological and psychological explanations of disorder

The above section has considered explanations of public disorder underpinned by criminological theories based on social disorganisation (which asserts that crime may occur as the result of an individual's or group's response to adverse social circumstances). In addition other aspects of criminological theory have been suggested as explanations for the riots which occurred since 1980.

Psychological theories of crime and disorder link these activities to frustration which, it is argued, leads to aggression. Thus it is asserted that persons in deprived social and economic circumstances who feel they have no stake in society will react violently to this situation. A further theory focused on the impact of climate on aggressive behaviour. Urban disorders have frequently occurred in the summer. Examples of this linkage included the Notting Hill riot in 1976, the riots of 1981, the Brixton and Handsworth riots in 1985, the Toxteth riots of the following month, and the Oldham riots in May 2001. This situation may be explained by the assertion that hot weather caused people to become irritated, especially in densely populated urban areas, and this irritation resulted in acts of violence. Excessive alcohol consumption in hot weather may be a further factor which increased the likelihood of disorderly conduct. Alternatively, a biological explanation may account for the occurrence of riots in hot weather as in these climatic conditions levels of serotonin released in the brain are increased, heightening the likelihood of aggressive behaviour.

Moral depravation

Conservative governments did not accept that deprivation was an acceptable explanation for urban crime and public disorder and instead attributed them to 'mindless hooliganism and yobbery for which there can be no excuse' (J. Patten, 1991). This belief has been frequently justified by the assertion that, both historically and in the period since 1970, most deprived people neither commited crime nor rioted. Thus the Conservative Party rejected solutions seeking to substantially redistribute money and resources to the inner cities and instead directed attention at the alleged deviant values and life styles of those who committed unsocial acts. These were depicted as mindless acts of criminality which occurred because some people did not know right from wrong.

There was a tendency in the early 1980s to draw attention to the occurrence of disorders in multi-ethnic areas. Although this factor could suggest that the social problem of racial discrimination underpinned these events, some Conservatives viewed rioting as a consequence of the lack of cultural commitment by minority ethnic communities to mainstream British values, one important dimension of which was obedience to the law (Rowe, 1998: 4). The attempt to racialise the disorders which took place in the 1980s constituted a 'denial of the social, economic and political causes' of these events (Rowe, 1998: 3, 158, 162) and an attempt to instead foist the blame for them on Britain's minority ethnic communities and their 'alien' behaviour. This opinion ignored the British tradition of rioting (Kettle and Hodges, 1982: 11; Rude, 1967; Thompson, 1968), the involvement of whites in many of these disturbances (at St Pauls, Bristol, in 1980, for example, 88 black persons and 44 whites were arrested) (Joshua and Wallace, 1983: 142), and the fact that black people who were involved were mainly youths who had been born in Britain and adhered to many facets of British cultural behaviour. Nonetheless the spectre of the 'black rioter' of the 1980s was a politically convenient folk devil which was used to justify a wide range of innovations seeking to provide a law and order response to the delinquent behaviour which was especially associated with the underclass. The initial emphasis which was placed on the link between race and riotous behaviour gave way to a more general critique of the moral values of young people as an explanation for events which by the 1990s occurred in white as well as in multi-ethnic areas. Social unrest was attributed to their personal short-comings. It was argued that traits such as the loss of respect for authority, greed or drug abuse could be explained by factors which derived from the permissive values associated with the 1960s. In particular the responsibility of the family to teach children right from wrong behaviour was emphasised and adverse comment was made concerning the relative breakdown of this social unit in urban areas.

Police–community relationships

Styles and methods of policing have been at the forefront of explanations of public disorder. These events frequently arose following some form of police intervention. The ferocity of the response by the public gave credence to allegations of a loss of legitimacy by the police in areas which experienced rioting and a rejection of the role they performed there. The move to reactive policing methods in the 1960s resulted in loss of contact with the public, especially in urban areas, and the tendency for police powers to be used in a random manner. This led to poor relationships between the police and members of inner city communities which especially affected youths. The intensification of hostility towards the police and their response by methods and operations deemed unacceptable to those on the receiving end resulted in an ever-downward spiral of the collapse of consensus policing (Lea and Young, 1982: 10–13).

Poor relationships between the police service and minority ethnic communities were regarded as key explanations for the initial occurrence of urban disorders. A report written following the 1981 riots in Brixton asserted that many people in the area, especially young black people, believed that the police 'cannot be trusted, harass people for no reason, often arresting them for offences they have not committed and that following arrest will assault them and humiliate them if the opportunity arises' (North Kensington Law Centre, 1982: 1). In 1981 the riot in Manchester was alleged to have occurred as the result of an 'intimidatory style of policing, deeply stained with racial prejudice' (Moss Side Defence Committee, 1981: 3) and saturation policing methods preceded the disorders which occurred in Brixton and Toxteth. The 'catastrophically bad relationships' between police and public were cited as the main factor behind all the 1981 disorders (Kettle and Hodges, 1982: 247), and it was argued that relations between the local police and the people of Broadwater Farm were 'central' to the events which took place there in 1985 (Rowe, 1998: 136). Police misbehaviour towards members of ethnic minority communities was stated to include passport raids and checks, unwarranted interventions in political and social life, deficient treatment of those held in custody and inadequate responses to racial attacks. It was further alleged that the police complaints system worked less satisfactorily for black persons than it did for whites (Gordon, 1983: 24–59).

Particular criticism was levelled at stop and search powers. It was alleged that these were used in a discriminatory fashion, underlaid by police stereotyping of persons and communities. This resulted in a form of policing deemed oppressive and unjust by those on the receiving end of it. Official figures accepted that black men were three times more likely to be stopped than whites (Willis, 1983) and it was perceived that the aim of this over-policing was to criminalise black youths (London Borough of Lambeth, 1981: 17–23): in the operation 'Swamp '81' slightly more than one half of the 943 'stops' were of black people (Scarman, 1981: 57). The Special Patrol Group (which frequently exercised stop and search powers in inner city areas of London) was also accused of racist conduct (Rollo, 1980: 186–97). The explanation for these actions requires an examination of the factors which governed the attitude of the police towards ethnic minority communities.

Potential problems between police and ethnic minority communities had been identified in the 1960s and led to the appointment of a number of consultative committees. Local studies which were conducted in inner city areas such as Handsworth suggested violence might arise because of the breakdown in relations between police and the black community (John, 1970). Clashes of this nature did materialise in areas of London including Brockwell Park in 1973 and at Notting Hill in 1976 and 1977. A major explanation for these problems was the 'politicisation of the debate about race and crime' in the 1970s (Solomos, 1994: 123). The media propagated a negative view of black people, especially black youths. This occurred against the background of a more general concern regarding law and order out of which arose the view that the areas inhabited by black people contained society's key social problems which were epitomised by the involvement of black youths in crimes such as 'mugging'. The underlying racism within society (which is an issue discussed more fully in Chapter 6) coupled with the lack of power (especially of an economic nature) within such disadvantaged communties were major explanations for the instigation of a moral panic which sought to divert attention to one symptom of society's problems rather than its underlying causes.

For these reasons the 'black youth-crime' linkage (Gutzmore, 1983: 27) arose in police circles. This suggested that much urban crime was perpetrated by black youths who became additionally associated with disorderly activities often involving physical confrontations with the forces of law and order. This legitimised a coercive style of policing in these areas directed against those who lived there. Thus one major explanation for the disorders of the early 1980s was that those on the receiving end of such methods rioted to display their antagonism towards their treatment and to indicate they were unwilling to accept this situation any longer.

The operations of the political system

Urban disorders may be underpinned by the operations of the political system, in particular the failure of conventional politics to address the specific problems of minority groups (which may be defined on grounds of class, race or age). This section considers a number of key political considerations affecting disorder.

The end of post-war consensus

Major episodes of public disorder (including violent confrontations on picket lines which are discussed in Chapter 3) occurred following the election of a Conservative government in 1979 and recurred following the subsequent re-election of that party to office in 1983, 1987 and 1992. The end of the post-war consensus and the commencement of a new approach to the role of the state underlaid by monetarist economics was initiated after 1979. Davies's J-Curve theory (which is considered in the introductory chapter) has some relevance to urban disorders in the 1980s and 1990s. Those who became frustrated by government policy which entailed the loss of what they perceived as their 'rights' (including the 'right' to work and the 'right' to benefit from ever-improving public services) took to the streets in a display of anger. A different argument connected with the end of the post-war consensus emphasised the importance placed on individualism by these Conservative governments at the expense of collectivism. Individualism may result in the destruction of communal norms and values and behaviour which is stylised by selfishness. This point was emphasised by some Labour politicians during the late 1980s who stated that disorders, especially the events in non-metropolitan areas, indicated a belief by the participants that 'I can do anything I like provided I'm willing to pay for the damage in the morning'.

Political marginalisation

Public disorder may also explained by the concept of political marginalisation. Although members of minority ethnic groups who feel themselves to be disadvantaged possess the ability to vote in elections, their vote does not give them sufficient clout within the political system to exert any effective influence on the political agenda and ensure that political leaders represent their views, needs and concerns effectively. They may thus turn away from conventional political activity and resort to disorder as a mechanism to place their specific needs onto the political agenda. A study of black Americans noted they were 'literally powerless to get their demands into the channel of policy choices' or to 'participate actively in the formulation of policies with significant consequences for them' (Bachrach and Baratz, 1970: 74) and in this sense riots could be viewed as purposeful, meaningful acts. They have been described as 'the collective bargaining of the dispossessed' (Young, 1992) entailing deliberate actions to force governments to sit up and take notice of social problems they would otherwise prefer to ignore.

One study of the 1991–92 disorders drew attention to the lack of voice of those who participated in these events. It was argued that:

> their exclusion from work, from education, from ownership, from family status and from the wider society gave them virtually no voice, even within their very local community, let alone the wider city. Their negative sense of identity, their alienated and therefore hostile views of the wider society guaranteed a lack of voice through conventional channels. No one wanted to face their aggression and hostility. The fear these youths invoked guaranteed their exclusion but also offered an alternative expression of their pent-up feelings of inadequacy, hostility and violence. The acts of violence, law-breaking and destruction were statements about themselves and the society that surrounded them. Damage and disorder *were* a form of expression. Denial of basic status or recognition, breakdown in controls and lack of voice led young men who were marginalised and beyond control to claim power through an attack on society. (Power and Tunstall, 1997: 53)

Groups in politically marginalised situations may direct violence against structures and institutions within their own community. Youth clubs, libraries and other public amenities may be attacked because they represent an attempt to secure allegiance from some local people to the operations of what remains an unjust society and with which they are unwilling to enter into any accomodation. The attack on such neighbourhood facilities was a feature of the riots in the 1990s.

It might thus be concluded that the perceived inadequacy of conventional political action by social groups which included minority ethnic communities and young people (both of whom were key components of the underclass) gave rise both to non-voting in elections and the use of public disorder to articulate their political needs. Rioting is not, however, the only response to political marginalisation and the following section discusses the range of responses which have been practised by one politically marginalised group, minority ethnic communities.

Minority ethnic groups and political marginalisation

It has been argued above that disorder is especially associated with the underclass. It may occur for two reasons. First is the perceived need to overcome the reluctance of policy-makers to pay attention to the needs of those at the bottom end of the social ladder by undertaking actions which will force them to sit up and take notice of those they would by preference chose to ignore. Second, groups in this position have no established leaders in mainstream politics who could act as a brake and 'bring reason' to those who engage in rioting. It has been observed that there is an inherent contradiction in being the leader of a dispossessed ethnic minority group whilst being in a position of power within local or national political hierarchies (Sewell, 1985: 12–13). However, disorder is not the only means of political expression available to the politically marginalised and this section discusses the range of methods which these groups may use to voice their needs. Some, but not all, of these possess the potential for disorder.

The formation of specific ethnic minority parties. Members of ethnic minority communities who engage in conventional political activity tend to support the major parties. At the 1992 general election three British Islamic candidates contested Bradford constituencies but failed to save their deposits. However, a survey carried out by Amenta Marketing quoted in the *Guardian* on 20 September 1996 indicated that four in ten black persons believed that a separate black party or organisation would benefit them.

The formation of pressure groups. The perceived deficiencies of conventional political activity may persuade minority ethnic communities to form pressure groups in order to articulate their needs to policy-makers. These are usually promotional groups, such as the Coordinating Campaign against Racial Discrimination (CARD) which was active during the 1960s and sought to harmonise the activities of existing communal organisations. It played an influential part in securing the enactment of the 1965 Race Relations Act. This group faced a number of difficulties in securing political influence, a major problem being that minority ethnic communities did not all think, feel or act as a cohesive body. CARD was primarily an organisation which represented the African-Caribbean community and was not associated with other existing minority organisations, including the Indian Workers' Association (Benjamin Heineman, 1972).

During the 1990s other pressure groups emerged to articulate the needs and concerns of minority ethnic communities. These included the National Black Caucus (NBC) and the Anti-Racist Alliance (ARA). The NBC sought to unite Asians and Africans for progressive action designed to improve the lives of black people. Its aims included the development, promotion and implementation of local, regional and national strategies for the economic regeneration of their communities and the advocacy of black economic and political independence. Although the NBC was willing to pursue its objectives through any political party which would aid their cause, it rejected organisational, administrative or political structures which were based on seeking approval, membership or funding from white institutions. Problems have impeded the effectiveness of such organisations, including internal disputes, which especially occurred within the ARA.

Self-help as a political tactic.   Politically marginalised groups may develop self-help responses which involve them seeking control of their own destinies and rejecting the society which they feel discriminates against them. In this case disorder may arise through attempts by these groups to establish control over a geographic area (which may entail the creation of no-go areas possibly enforced by some form of ethnic cleansing to drive out those who do not share their views) and/or attempts by the state to regain control of these areas. There are various aspects to self-help which include the formation of *self-defence organisations, power-sharing, segregation, withdrawal* and the formation of a West Indian enclave community, which is termed the *'colony'*. The relationship between segregation and social disharmony is discussed more fully below. Other terms are discussed in more detail in the glossary.

Political orchestration

The view that riots are orchestrated for political purposes has been asserted within police circles and is reflective of an opinion that communities are either docile or incapable of such behaviour when solely reliant on their own resources. These allegations divert attention away from the actual causes of urban unrest and shift the focus on to short-term triggering factors. A Metropolitan Police report into the Broadwater Farm Estate riots in 1985 alluded to the existence of lakes of petrol in garage basements (Richards, 1985). Specific accusations of political orchestration have been made alleging that disorders since 1980 have been incited by political extremists who sought to utilise street violence in order to achieve revolutionary upheaval. Events in Handsworth, Birmingham in 1981 were attributed to the activities of the Socialist Workers' Party (Brown, 1982: 130–3) while on 8 October 1985 the *Daily Express* alleged that 'street fighters trained in Moscow and Libya' were responsible for organising the violence which occurred on Haringey's Broadwater Farm Estate. In 1992 accusations were made that groups such as Class War contributed to the disorders. However, while political extremists may intervene once a disorder is underway and attempt to provide leadership and channel it in the direction they wish it to proceed in, their presence does not indicate that they possess any influence over the initial outbreak of disorder.

A related argument to political orchestration concerned the role of the media in inciting rioting after 1980. It was asserted in 1981 that many of the riots which took place after the initial event in Brixton were of a 'copycat' nature and arose primarily because of the dramatic television and press coverage which but for such attention would not have occurred. Although this assertion was challenged (Tumber, 1982), the possibility that sustained media coverage could result in further acts of violence led the Home Secretary in his speech to the 1991 Conservative party conference to urge the media to refrain from pandering to the 'vanities of the violent'.

The reaction of the state

State intervention has been justified by the extent of violence occurring at urban disorders. At Burnley in June 2001 petrol bombs were discovered and 22 persons were arrested. Subsequently an Asian shop was firebombed. At Bradford in July 2001 two people were stabbed and 80 persons injured and according to the *Guardian* on 11 July 2001, damage estimated at £25 million was caused. The following section discusses some of the policies which have been pursued by successive governments since 1970 in an attempt to prevent riots from occurring.

Social reform

A number of attempts have been made since the mid-1960s to combat the racial discrimination and social and economic deprivation which have been cited in the previous section of this chapter as important underpinnings to the riots which occurred after 1980. This section discusses some of the main initiatives which were pursued to achieve these objectives.

Race relations legislation

Unlike other European governments, Britain made little specific provision for immigrants. In particular there was no attempt to coordinate immigration with other public sector services, especially housing. Those who came to Britain were thus forced to live in run-down property in the privately rented sector of urban areas where work was available. There was no official attempt to deal with racial discrimination until the passage of the 1965 Race Relations Act which (as has been argued above) was a development asssociated with the organisation CARD. This legislation made it illegal to discriminate on grounds of colour, race, ethnic or national origins in what were termed 'places of public resort' (such as restaurants and theatres). Racial discrimination in the transfer of tenancies was outlawed and incitement to racial hatred became a new criminal offence. A Race Relations Board and Conciliation Committees were established to enforce the legislation. These investigated complaints and sought to ensure that acts of discrimination would not be repeated. If this intervention failed, a prosecution could be initiated provided that the Attorney General consented to this course of action. The legislation was, however, limited in scope and the majority of cases which formed the subject of complaints to the Race Relations Board were outside its remit. The National Commission for Commonwealth Immigrants and local Voluntary Liaison Committees were additionally established to help immigrants overcome problems of social adjustment, to alert local communities to the realities of racial inequality and to offer opportunities to ethnic minorities to become more involved and integrated in the wider community.

Following the passage of the 1965 Act, the organisation Political and Economic Planning investigated the extent of racial discrimination in Britain. The findings contained in its 1967 report formed the basis of the 1968 Race Relations Act which sought a more vigorous response to racial discrimination. This legislation defined discrimination as arising where 'a person on racial grounds treats another less favourably than he treats or would treat other persons on racial grounds' and covered a range of activities relating to employment, housing, the provision of goods, facilities and services to the general public and the publication of discriminatory advertisements. It also established the Community Relations Commission to coordinate the work of local voluntary community relations organisations and to promote harmonious community relations. Between 1972 and 1975 Political and Economic Planning conducted research into the disadvantage experienced by racial minorities and the sources of this problem. It was estimated that the weak enforcement powers of the Race Relations Board (which was unable to summon witnesses, issue orders or initiate an investigation unless an individual complained) had hindered the alleviation of discrimination and that black unskilled workers had a one in two chance of being discriminated against when applying for a job (Smith, 1973). The Race Relations Act of 1976 sought to make racial discrimination unlawful in most areas of public life including employment, education and training, housing, the provision of goods, facilities and services and advertisements. Complaints concerning discrimination in employment are made to industrial tribunals and other matters are dealt with through County Courts.

The Act covered both direct and indirect discrimination. The latter was defined as conditions or requirements which had a discriminatory effect and which could not be justified without reference to race, colour, nationality or ethnic or national origin of the person affected. It also abolished the Race Relations Board and the Community Relations Commission and established the Commision for Racial Equality (CRE). This was given the duties of working towards the elimination of racial discrimination, promoting equality of opportunity and good relations between members of different ethnic groups and reviewing the workings of the Race Relations Act, with a view to making proposals for changes to the government. It is empowered to conduct formal investigations into any subject of its choice and could be required by the Secretary of State to carry out such an enquiry. In discharging this function the Commission can compel persons to give evidence or provide documents. Formal investigations may give rise to the issuance of a non-discrimination notice which required the discriminating person or organisation to cease unlawful discrimination. The impact of this notice is monitored and if discrimination continues the CRE may apply for an injunction through the courts ordering the person or organisation to desist. Breach of such an injunction constitutes contempt of court.

The stigmatisation of the underclass

One reaction of governments to urban crime and disorder has been to stigmatise those who engage in these actions in order to secure popular support for coercive actions against them. This approach was especially associated with Conservative governments between 1979 and 1997 which refused to endorse social reform in order to prevent further outbreaks of violence and who attributed disturbances to moral depravation rather than social and economic deprivation. The use of language and imagery which (as with racism) sought to deny humanity to those whose crime and disorderly acts threatened social harmony constituted an important aspect of Conservative policy to secure legitimacy for punitive action against those who transgressed key social values. Car thieves, for example, were depicted as 'hyenas' in campaigns mounted by the Home Office. These views were coupled with the intention to respond to riots with forceful action, and the latter approach was endorsed by subsequent Labour ministers. In July 2001, for example, the Home Secretary, was alleged to have considered the use of water cannon and tear gas to help police tackle the riots (which he characterised as 'mindless violence') (Blunkett, 2001) which had occurred in Bradford and other towns in northern England.

Additional policies (such as the 'Back to Basics' crusade of 1993 which emphasised 'traditional' family values of marriage and family life) were pursued by Conservative governments, the total effect being to stigmatise, ostracise and isolate the underclass, ensuring that they remained in inner city areas from which there was little chance of escape. The *Observer* on 3 November 1996 argued that opportunities for mobility by children of disadvantaged parents was receding: 'the steady march of league tables, hotchpotch selection, and opting out create an educational system in which there are sink schools at the bottom'. The perception that school league tables were a mechanism of social isolation was later emphasised by the *Independent on Sunday* on 8 December 1996 which observed that parents who wished to get their children into comprehensive schools which fared well in the league tables were willing to pay above the market price for property in order to move into the catchment area for such schools.

Teaching children right from wrong. The belief of Conservative governments that rioting could be attributed to moral depravation also resulted in suggestions for enhanced surveillance of those whose anti-social actions threatened social harmony.

A study of delinquency conducted in the 1970s asserted that many of the features apparent among older delinquents were 'demonstrably present by the age of ten' (West and Farrington, 1973: 189). This notion was resurrected in the 1990s to justify intervention in the lives of young children who were deemed likely to commit crime in their later lives. On 26 February 1992 Kenneth Baker spoke of the need to 'address crime at its very roots' in a speech delivered at the annual conference of the Association of Chief Officers of Probation (ACOP). He suggested the methods to achieve this involved directing aid to individuals whose potential for anti-social behaviour could be detected at a very early age by parents, teachers, churches and social workers and thus be nipped in the bud. He made clear his belief that the root cause of crime was moral failing and that a comprehensive strategy to counter crime required influencing the attitudes and behaviour of individuals.

Social inclusion

The Conservative attempt to marginalise and stigmatise the underclass was largely abandoned by the Labour government which was elected in 1997. Unlike its Conservative predecessors who believed that this group of citizens were surplus to the requirements of the labour market and thus excluded from social citizenship (Crowther, 2000: 81), the Labour government used the language of inclusion and sought to make the previously unemployed and unemployable stakeholders through their participation in the market economy. They believed that the smooth working of the market economy required a pool of labour which could constantly adjust to its ever-changing requirements thus being able to take advantage of new forms of work which became available when employment in existing occupations dried up. Thus training and education to enhance employment opportunities were at the forefront of Labour's policies designed to secure social inclusion. In particular the government set itself the task of reversing the trend which had taken place between 1979 and 1997 (when the number of people living in poverty increased from 5 to 14 million) and to abolish child poverty within 20 years (Piachaud, 1999). The main initiatives which were put forward to provide for social inclusion are discussed below.

'Welfare to work'. In April 1998 the New Deal programme for the young long-term unemployed aged 18–24 was initiated. This offered four options – a job, full-time education or training, voluntary work, or work with the government's environmental task force. This scheme was subsequently extended to those aged over 25 in the 2000 budget and was made permanent in the 2000 Comprehensive Spending Review. It subsequently incorporated a 'rapid response' New Deal programme to help areas affected by severe job losses and also embraced the 'New Deal for Lone Parents' which utilised personal advisers to aid lone parents to find employment. The objective of reducing the number of lone parents on benefit was also aided by the government funding of childcare facilities which aimed to provide a childcare place for

every lone parent in a disadvantaged area by 2004. In 2001 unemployment fell below 1 million for the first time in 25 years and in March 2001 the government announced proposals to extend the New Deal scheme by creating seven teams of troubleshooters to target unemployment blackspots.

Financial aid to poorer families. The main aim of directing help to poor families was to tackle child poverty. The Working Families Tax Credit was launched in 1999 to replace family credit and sought to increase state aid to those in work on low incomes which would guarantee a minimum income of £200 per week for a family with one full-time worker, which, additionally, would not pay income tax before £235 a week. Ministers envisaged that this would lift 800,000 children out of poverty, and that when parents were also included the total would be around 1.5 million persons (Elliott, 1999). Additionally, the 2000 budget announced the introduction of the Integrated Child Credit. All families would continue to receive child benefit but additional aid would be directed at poor families. A key objective of this reform was to bring the children of unemployed parents into line with those whose parents were undertaking low-paid jobs. A further reform contemplated by Labour to aid poorer families was the integration of the tax and benefit system and the extension of tax credits to cover all of the working poor. This would enable recipients of this aid (which would become the main form of state support) to keep more of their income after tax thus increasing incentives to work. It was intended to introduce these changes in 2003.

Education. The Labour government also undertook action to raise educational standards, to combat the problem of bullying and to tackle the issues of truancy and school exclusion. The initiatives which were put forward included the Sure Start Programme which was modelled on the American Head Start Programme. It targeted the parents of every child below the age of four in the most deprived areas of the United Kingdom, offering them advice on parenting and their children's health and providing access to play centres and child care. Investment in this scheme was doubled in the 2000 Comprehensive Spending Review. In 1999 intensive nursery schemes supplemented the Sure Start programme.

In 2001 the government announced its approval to provide 45,000 new childcare places in 900 nursery centres in deprived areas. These would be funded by the Department for Education and Skills and from Lottery cash via the New Opportunity Fund. The government also promised new capital funding to provide education for three- and four-year-olds in other disadvantaged areas and funding from the European Social Fund for training childcare workers. These measures were designed to help meet Labour's target of providing a childcare place in the most disadvantaged areas for every lone parent entering employment by 2004. By the same date it also sought an additional 100,000 places for three- and four-year-olds.

A further initiative to improve educational standards was the announcement in March 1999 that extra resources would be injected to improve the educational attainment of children attending inner city comprehensive schools. Some of this aid would be spent on providing 'masterclasses' at specialist schools for the ablest children, and the number of specialist and beacon schools would be greatly expanded. Other education policies included the Fresh Start Programme which was designed to rescue chronically failing schools by reopening them under a new name with new management and staffing arrangements. In March 2000 the Secretary of State for Education and Employment proposed to develop the previous Conservative initiative of City Technical Colleges and to set up a network of City Academies which would replace failing or underachieving schools. These would operate outside the control of local authorities and be supervised and sponsored by business, the churches or charities. The 2000 Comprehensive Spending Review increased the overall size of the education budget and established the cross-departmental Children's Fund. This was operated by voluntary organisations and was designed to identify and provide services for children who were manifesting signs of difficulty.

Neighbourhood regeneration.   The revival of neighbourhoods was viewed as a key measure in Labour's attempts to ensure social inclusion: 'the goal must be to reduce that gap between the poorest neighbourhoods and the rest of the country and bring them for the first time in decades up to an acceptable level' (Social Exclusion Unit, 1998: 10). The 'New Deal for Communities' which was launched in 1998 aimed to tackle poverty in urban areas by measures which included targeting a number of 'pathfinder' districts (initially 17) with resources, developing a regeneration programme in which the private, community and the voluntary sectors would work in partnership, and securing a more effective coordination of the activities pursued by various government departments. Additionally, research was initiated in 1998 by 18 Policy Action Teams (PATs) acting under the auspices of the Social Exclusion Unit (SEU). This research resulted in the publication of a wide-ranging renewal programme in 2000 which was directed at the levels of crime, unemployment, mortality rates and skills in the 44 poorest local authority districts in Britain (embracing 3000 communities) which the *Guardian* on 13 April 2000 dubbed as 'concentration camps in the midst of civilised society'. Areas of acute social need might also qualify for Single Regeneration Bids, which were designed to aid regeneration.

Legislative reform

The legal definition of riot was initially provided by the 1715 Riot Act which made it an offence for twelve or more persons to be 'unlawfully, riotously and tumultuously assembled'. This legislation was repealed by the 1967 Criminal Law Act. A riot then became 'a tumultuous disturbance of the peace by three or more persons assembled together with an intent mutually to assist one another by force, if necessary, against anyone who opposes them in the execution of a common purpose, and who execute or begin to execute that purpose in a violent manner so as to alarm at least one person of reasonable firmness and courage' (Scarman, 1981: 42). After 1967, police conduct to deal with riotous situations was governed by section 5 of the 1936 Public Order Act, the common law power of breach of the peace and the common law duty to move people on in order to prevent a disturbance from occurring. This situation persisted until the enactment of the 1986 Public Order Act. This described a riot as a situation 'where twelve or more persons who are present together use or threaten unlawful violence for a common purpose and the conduct of them (taken together) is such as would cause a person of reasonable firmness present at the scene to fear for his personal safety'. This legislation also provided a number of other offences which could be used against those engaged in various levels of public disorder. These were affray, violent disorder, causing the fear or provocation of violence, or occasioning harassment alarm and distress.

Rioting is, however, frequently dealt with by less serious charges including the common law charge of breach of the peace, one reason for this being (as was argued in Chapter 3) that the penalties associated with it are unlikely to have the effect of creating martyrs to a cause. An additional reason (which was especially apparent in 1981) was that police officers who made arrests found it difficult to identify their particular prisoner when faced with large numbers of arrested rioters at a police station. A lesser charge was thus likely to produce a guilty plea and circumvent lapses in identification procedures.

Police reform

It has been noted above that many urban disorders took place following some form of police intervention in a community. This might suggest that poor police–public relationships played a major role in these events and emphasised the importance of implementing reforms directed at the working practices of the police service.

The Scarman Report

The belief that policing methods contributed to public disorder in 1981 was given official recognition in Lord Scarman's report into these events which particularly concerned those in Brixton. His report suggested that the attitude displayed by the police towards members of the general public may intensify the feelings of alienation felt by disaffected groups thus contributing towards crime and disorder. It was thus anticipated that reforms to the working practices of the police would result in improved relationships with minority ethnic communities and the public in general, thereby reducing the likelihood of riotous behaviour in such areas. Scarman's investigation was an enquiry constituted under the 1964 Police Act and thus the bulk of his report concentrated on the policing of the affected areas which resulted in the introduction of a wide range of initiatives designed to improve police–public relationships. Particular attention was devoted to multi-ethnic communities. He noted that the police had failed to adapt themselves adequately to operate in these areas and that existing training arrangements were inadequate to prepare officers for policing a multiracial society (Scarman, 1981: 79). To address problems of this nature he suggested the modification of police training programmes to incorporate an increased emphasis on community relations. He further proposed that the composition of police forces should become more reflective of the society they served, although he rejected a quota system or the lowering of entry standards as mechanisms to achieve this ideal (Scarman, 1981: 76–7). He argued that racially prejudiced or discriminatory behaviour should become a specific disciplinary offence which, if substantiated, would normally lead to dismissal from the police service, and suggested amendments to the procedures involved in handling complaints made against the police including the introduction of a conciliation process for minor issues (Scarman, 1981: 87, 115–20). He reinforced the recommendation of the Royal Commission on Criminal Procedure in 1981 that stop and search powers should be rationalised across the country and include a number of safeguards (Scarman, 1981: 113). His proposals included the recommendation that the conduct of officers on the streets should be more effectively monitored (Scarman, 1981: 84–7). He also argued that there should be enhanced consultation with the general public, provided this did not undermine the principle of constabulary independence (Scarman, 1981: 63–4). He proposed that the emphasis placed on law enforcement as the prime role of the police service should be reconsidered since law enforcement could jeopardise the maintenance of public tranquillity which he regarded as the priority of police work (Scarman, 1981: 62–3). In this respect he placed considerable importance on the role of community policing and the activities performed by home beat officers (Scarman, 1981: 88–92).

The implementation of the Scarman Report.   The police service was receptive to the introduction of reforms in the wake of the 1980 and 1981 disorders. Some developments (such as community policing initiatives which were designed to bring the police and public closer together and thus undo some of the damage associated with unit beat policing) preceded Scarman but received increased attention within the police service in the early 1980s. It was contended that community policing could operate effectively in multi-ethnic inner city areas such as Handsworth in Birmingham (Brown, 1982). Other pressures at this time to reform police practices included the Policy Studies Institute's examination of policing in London (Smith and Gray, 1983).

Increased attention was placed on interviewing procedures to ensure that officers, and particularly recruits, were sensitive to the background of the people with whom they would come into contact in multi-ethnic urban areas. The length of the initial training period was extended to help achieve these aims. Vigorous attempts were also made to increase the number of police officers drawn from minority ethnic communities. In July 1981 the House of Commons Home Affairs Committee recommended that police forces should take 'vigorous steps' to recruit minority ethnic officers following which a Home Office circular stated that police forces in areas with substantial minority ethnic communities 'should keep in mind the need to attract recruits from those minorities'. In July 1982 a Home Office study group made suggestions for improved publicity directed at minority communities concerning police work and the prospects it offered. Moves in the direction of positive discrimination were endorsed in the suggestion that chief officers should use their discretion to accept an otherwise suitable candidate who was below the national minimum height limit and that black or Asian candidates who failed the educational tests should be given advice in order to help them re-apply. It was recommended that chief officers should scrutinise their force selection procedures and that HM Inspectors of Constabulary should monitor the progress made in this direction by individual forces (Home Office, 1982). Following the publication of this report the height requirement was formally abandoned. Further pressure from the Home Office to increase the level of ethnic minority recruitment was exerted in circular 87/1989 (which concerned equal opportunities within the police service) and circular 33/1990. The latter suggested that chief constables should consider a number of matters which included setting targets for the level of ethnic minority representation in each force, devising performance indicators for force policy on ethnic minority recruitment and the establishment of a programme of special recruitment initiatives (Home Office, 1990).

Reforms were also introduced to training programmes. Scarman had made a number of criticisms of the Metropolitan Police's probationer training course (Scarman, 1981: 81–2) which resulted in reforms, including a key role being played by tutor constables. In 1982 probationer training in race relations was examined and attention was drawn to the detrimental impact that police culture and experiences on the streets could exert on its long-term value (Southgate, 1982). In 1983 a more comprehensive examination of community and race relations training was published (Police Training Council Working Party, 1983). This made a number of criticisms concerning arrangements for providing training in these areas including a tendency to teach these subjects academically and in a manner which failed to integrate them into mainstream police activities. Accordingly it was recommended that future training in community and race relations should be provided to all officers up to the rank of chief superintendent and delivered at regular intervals throughout an officer's career, closely related to the responsibilities of each rank.

Following the publication of this report, the Home Office established the Centre for the Study of Community and Race Relations to provide police trainers with appropriate skills, knowledge and awareness and to aid police training schools to develop relevant curricula. This was closed in 1988 and replaced by a Home Office Specialist Support Unit in 1989 which also provided courses for police trainers. Additionally, four short courses in racism awareness training were sponsored by the Home Office in the Autumn of 1983. Their objective was to develop a heightened awareness of the nature of racism in society and also within the individual. It was concluded that problems had arisen concerning unclear course objectives resulting in trainers and participants having different expectations. The discussion of an individual's experiences and attitudes rather than participants being imparted with information by trainers lacked popularity and it was further observed that some of the tutors displayed hostile attitudes towards the police (Southgate, 1984).

In 1982 the Metropolitan Police introduced a course in human awareness training for recruits. This involved devoting about one-quarter of the 20-week initial training course to three broad areas of study (interpersonal skills, self-awareness and community relations) in order 'to improve the social skills and street wisdom of police officers'. The effectiveness of this course was challenged, a significant number of participants believing that human awareness training was inadequate or unsatisfactory to prepare them to perform their duties as police officers. It was observed that once initial training had ended officers underwent experiences which tended to make them police in ways which were not compatible with its philosophy. However, fewer complaints were made against police officers who had received human awareness training, which suggested that it possessed some beneficial consequences (Bull and Horncastle, 1986).

The 1984 Police and Criminal Evidence Act introduced a range of safeguards relating to the use of contentious powers such as the stop and search of persons and vehicles, and the police complaints system was reformed with the introduction of the Police Complaints Authority in that legislation. Liaison between the police and public was also enhanced by the establishment of local consultative committees provided for in the 1984 Act and by police-driven initiatives which included the setting up of community contact departments and the permanent allocation of police officers to specific neighbourhoods.

Tension indicators

A further reform to police methods which was introduced in the wake of urban disorders was the development of tension indicators. The ability of the police to effectively respond to public disorder is dependent on a variety of factors which include prior knowledge of the likelihood of a problem arising. As has been previously referred to in Chapter 2, the 1986 Public Order Act introduced a universal requirement that advance notice of an intention to organise a procession or demonstration should be given to the police, but this clearly did not cater for spontaneous forms of activity such as riots. It was thus necessary to devise means to assess community feelings. In 1982 the Metropolitan Police introduced District Information Officers (DIOs) whose role was to gather information in order to head off potential disorder (Brewer et al., 1996: 22). They monitored the rise and fall of a number of specified tension indicators which were reported to the Central Information Unit in the Metropolitan Police's Public Order Branch (D. Waddington, 1992: 183). Subsequently the Home Office proposed the use of tension indicators to monitor communities and this was adopted by the police service in the 1986 ACPO manual on public disorder. The manual listed eight of these – abuse and attacks on police officers and their vehicles, increases in complaints against the police, heightened levels of conflict between groups, racial attacks, marches or demonstrations, all-night parties by ethnic minority groups, anniversaries or significant events, and the attitude of the media or underground press (quoted in Northam, 1989: 79). The concept of tension indicators was not new. They were developed by the Metropolitan Police following the 1981 riots and involved each district transmitting reports concerning the level of tension in an area to a Central Information Unit housed in Scotland Yard's Public Order Branch. Additionally, a list of housing estates throughout London where a potential for disorder was perceived to exist was compiled by this Branch (Greater London Council, 1986: 41). One difficulty with tension indicators is that the attitudes and behaviour of police officers working in areas officially identified as disorderly may result in aggressive behaviour towards those singled out as potential rioters. This may trigger such events rather than forestall them.

Reforms directed at addressing political marginalisation

Rioting is an activity associated with young people, and one way to divert their energies into institutional channels is to ensure that they are provided with an effective voice in shaping their local communities (Home Office, 2001a: 14). One way to achieve this is by developing the Youth Parliament Scheme (Home Office, 2001b: 32). This recommendation was endorsed in Bradford where youth forums were set up for young people aged 11–25 in each of the city's Parliamentary constituencies. Each forum would nominate young people to sit on the Bradford Youth Parliament which was established in 2002. Bradford would also elect three representatives to the United Kingdom Youth Parliament in 2002 (City of Bradford, 2001: 1). A further initiative addressed to young people to interest them in conventional political activity has been the Labour government's commitment to the teaching of citizenship in schools (which became a compulsory curriculum subject in 2002) which aims to educate young people in civic involvement.

The following section addresses the issue of the political marginalisation of minority ethnic communities in more detail and discusses measures which have been designed to encourage minority ethnic groups to participate in the conventional political system.

Racial minorities and the major political parties

Although the size of the total minority ethnic vote is small, its significance is enhanced by three factors. The first of these is that it is a growing force in British electoral politics. The 1991 census figures considerably underestimate the size of the minority ethnic vote and it has been calculated that this electorate increased by 12 per cent between 1991 and 1996 and would grow by a further 20 per cent between 1996 and 2001. The comparable rise in the size of the white electorate was between 1–2 per cent in these periods (Saggar, 1997a: 695). The second of these is the clustering of this vote and its consequent ability to play a significant part of the outcome of election contests in areas where it is sizeable. It was estimated that in the 1987 general election 100 Parliamentary constituencies had a black population in excess of 10 per cent (figures referred to in Skellington, 1996: 55–6) and that in the 2001 general election minority ethnic communities were in the position to swing the result in around 100 constituencies where the ethnic minority vote was greater than the sitting MP's majority.

The final consideration is the changing nature of the support given by the minority ethnic vote to the major parties. Historically a disproportionate level of support was given by minority ethnic groups to the Labour Party, which suggested that this vote was an important component of the support which it obtained. There were exceptions to this; for example, local factors provided the Liberal Party/Liberal Democrats with support from minority ethnic communities in areas which included Rochdale where the Asian vote was crucial to Cyril Smith's by-election victory in 1972 and his five subsequent general election successes. However, the Labour Party was the main beneficiary of the ethnic minority vote and derived particular support from African-Caribbean communities (Anwar, 1984). A study of the October 1974 general election suggested that the ethnic vote played a significant part in obtaining Labour its overall victory (Anwar and Kohler, 1975) although the significance accorded to the black electorate was questioned by other studies (for example, Crewe, 1979). However, the support given by all minority ethnic voters to the Labour Party subsequently declined, from around 85 per cent in 1979 to around 72 per cent in 1987, with the Conservative Party securing its highest share of this vote in the 1987 election, around 18 per cent (CRE, 1994; Saggar, 1997b: 152). The Labour Party's share of the minority ethnic vote increased in 1992 (81 per cent to the 10 per cent obtained by the Conservative Party) but in 1997 the Conservative Party obtained 17 per cent of this vote (compared to Labour's 78 per cent), polling especially well in Asian communities (Saggar, 1997b: 152–3) at an election where the Conservative Party suffered a major defeat. The voting behaviour of minority ethnic groups may be underpinned by socio-economic factors, suggesting that increased levels of affluence could increase the support given to other political parties. This may suggest that this electorate should be carefully cultivated by the Conservative Party in future contests.

The above three factors have encouraged the main political parties to seek the support of ethnic minority voters. In 1976 the Conservative Party established a Department of Community Affairs in Central Office which launched an Ethnic Minorities Unit. This was designed to encourage minority participation in Conservative politics and resulted in the establishment of Anglo-Asian and Anglo-West Indian organisations to cultivate relationships between the party and these communities. The Anglo-Asian Society enjoyed brief success (measured in terms of membership) in achieving this objective until, riven by internal disputes, it was dissolved in 1986. It was replaced by the One Nation Forum, which acts as an advisory body of the National Union of Conservative and Unionist Associations. The black middle-class vote was courted for the 2001 general election by the party's Cultural Unit.

In 1975 the Labour Party Race Action Group was formed to act as a lobby for black issues. Perceptions that this party was sidelining black political interests and was failing to deliver policies required by ethnic minorities resulted in the Black Sections Movement, a development encouraged by reforms to the internal democracy of the Labour Party during the late 1970s. The proposal to establish black sections was debated at the 1983 and 1984 party conferences and although it was rejected, an NEC working party chaired by Jo Richardson expressed support for this development in 1985. But the National Executive Committee failed to endorse this recommendation. A black section was set up in 1990 which subsequently became known as the Black Socialist Society. In 1994 new rules enabling the party to rescind membership were drawn up to prevent ethnic minority groups gaining control of safe inner city constituencies. This followed episodes which included an attempt by in excess of 600 Asians to join the Manchester, Gorton, party (Skellington, 1996: 236).

Local government

Conventional political activity at national level has yielded few opportunities for minority ethnic groups to place their needs on to the political agenda, but local government has offered better prospects. The clustering of the minority ethnic vote in urban areas has encouraged political parties to select minority candidates and the number of black councillors has risen since 1970, particularly in London. In 1992, 287 councillors (1.5 per cent of the total) were members of minority ethnic communities (Geddes, 1993), a figure rising to 2.5 per cent in 2002. There are local variations, London in 1994 boasting 10.5 per cent of councillors who were South Asian, African-Caribbean or African (Runnymede Trust, 1994). Local government has also been at the forefront of initiatives designed to counter racial prejudice and inequality. Some of these policies have been funded by financial contributions from central government paid under the provisions of section 11 of the 1966 Local Government Act or section 137 of the 1972 Local Government Act. The role performed by local authorities in this area of activity was further enhanced by section 71 of the 1976 Race Relations Act which gave them the statutory role of eliminating racial discrimination and promoting equality of opportunity in all of their functions. Accordingly, it is now common for local government (and other public sector bodies) to operate a policy of equal opportunities in their employment policies while the usage of policies such as contract compliance can be used to further this objective in companies within the private sector with which a local authority has dealings. Some local authorities have moved towards affirmative action and set targets for their employment of members of ethnic minority communities.

Nonetheless, the role played by local government in this field has not been without criticism. It has been argued that the approach of many local authorities is affected by 'colour blindness' in which racial inequality is explained by the more general problem of class injustice arising from the operations of capitalism. This approach fails to acknowledge the specific dimensions of racism and racial inequality and thus resists any attempt to tackle racism independently of patterns of urban deprivation or class inequality (Ben-Tovim et al., 1986: 108). The changing nature of local government brought about by Conservative reforms between 1979 and 1997 tended to reduce the role of local authorities as direct employers of labour which may have an adverse effect on their ability to pursue equal opportunity initiatives.

One difficulty faced by local government when seeking to ameliorate racial injustice is the perception of unfairness felt by white residents. This situation is agravated by racial segregation whereby any form of public policy directed at these areas can be depicted as preferential treatment being accorded to minority groups. The belief that Asian areas of Oldham were unduly favoured by the distribution of local authority administered funds was believed to have resulted in a white backlash, one feature of which was a high poll for the BNP in the 2001 general election. Accordingly, a meeting between police, civic leaders and the Home Secretary in June 2001 resolved that funding targeted at Asian areas (which constituted some of the most deprived areas of Britain with higher rates of unemployment than neighbouring white districts) would be redirected into borough-wide schemes to avoid perceptions of unfairness. No representative from the town's large Asian population attended the meeting which arrived at this decision.

Consultative and project-orientated machinery

Political marginalisation may to some extent be overcome by the development of consultative machinery designed to enable the leaders or members of minority ethnic communities to place their concerns on the agendas of a range of public sector agencies. A number of public sector bodies, including the police, have established consultative machinery of this nature. Additionally organisations such as Community Relations Councils have been involved in projects and campaigns designed to promote racial equality. The CRE provides funding for a number of Racial Equality Councils. These operate at a local or regional level and numbered 88 in 1995 (CRE, 1995: 36).

The effectiveness of policies to combat riots

The previous section referred to a number of initiatives pursued after 1970 to reduce the likelihood of riots reoccurring in urban areas. This section evaluates the effectiveness of the measures which were put forward. Additional discussion regarding the the success of police reforms implemented after the publication of the Scarman report in 1981 is provided in Chapter 6.

Social reform

This section examines the effectiveness of social reform discussed in the previous section to tackle the racial discrimination and social and economic deprivation which were important underpinnings of occurrences of rioting after 1980.

Race relations legislation

It has been argued that racism requires the forces of economic and political power and cultural domination that cause it to be addressed. This involves immigrants organising themselves into a powerful force in the country's economic and political life and recreating their black identity through the recomposition of their historical heritage (Parekh, 1974: 239–42). This approach would result in minority groups being placed in a position which commanded respect from the host society rather than having to rely on its benevolence, and also having pride in their own culture and heritage rather than having to seek social acceptance by adopting the traditions and behaviour of those who had previously colonised them. This approach suggests that self-help is potentially the most effective tactic through which to challenge racism, an additional weakness of the public policy that was introduced to counter this problem being that it was mainly directed at the symptoms of racial injustice (prejudice and discrimination) rather than at its root cause which Chapter 6 identifies as the unequal power relationship existing between black and white people.

The effectiveness of race relations legislation enacted since 1965 is also debatable. The CRE can offer advice and assistance to people bringing individual complaints who may secure financial redress if the discrimination is proven. In 2000 around 11,000 people approached the CRE for advice and 1553 submitted formal applications for assistance. CRE complaints officers settled 83 cases at an early stage of the process for a total sum of £418,320, and the CRE secured compensation of £1,362,444 in 77 out-of-court settlements (CRE, 2001: 13). The amount which can be paid was increased following the removal of the upper limit for awards by the 1994 Race Relations (Remedies) Act. However, it is not easy to win a case since the onus of proving the allegation is on the complainant. Further, access to the courts is available only to individuals. This means that the 'class actions' which are a feature of American anti-discrimination legislation (and the large fines which have sometimes been awarded) are absent in Britain (Bowers and Franks, 1980: 6–7). These factors might explain why ethnic minorities have generally fared worse than the white population on grounds of unemployment, pay, housing or as victims of crime (Office for National Statistics, 1996).

The policy pursued by Conservative governments between 1979 and 1997 is an additional factor which explains the continued existence of racial prejudice and disadvantage in Great Britain. An ICM poll published in the *Guardian* on 20 March 1995 stated that an overwhelming majority of people in Britain believed that there was widespread racial prejudice in the country: 79 per cent of white respondents believed that there was prejudice towards black people. The advocacy by Conservative governments of the Citizens' Charter and the 'active citizen' was alleged to have had an adverse effect on the role of the state to protect civic and social rights and remedy social and political injustices (Solomos and Back, 1996: 172). Many Conservatives contended that over-concentration on racial discrimination removed personal responsibility and enabled the blame for a range of problems ranging from educational underachievement to delinquency to be foisted on 'the system' rather than the individual. The educational system was also accused of racial bias in this period. A report by OFSTED in 1996 asserted that the rate of expulsion of African-Caribbean pupils was six times higher than for white children which was likely to result in the emergence of an alienated, underqualified group (Gillborn and Gipps, 1996). The exclusion of black pupils from schools arose from, and served to support, a perception that these pupils posed a problem for the school and were educationally subnormal.

In an attempt to remedy racial disadvantage, the Race Relations (Amendment) Act 2000 was enacted. This required public bodies to promote good race relations in all of their activities and to have due regard to the need, when performing their duties, of eliminating racial discrimination and promoting racial equality. Further action may, however, be necessary since a government report in 2001 concluded that inequality between ethnic minorities and whites would continue to widen over the next 20 years unless fresh action was taken. The failure to reduce racial inequalities was attributed to factors which included an intolerant culture, weak anti-discrimination laws, and a labour force with relatively few non-whites (Cabinet Office, 2001) and led to proposals that everyone should be encouraged to realise their potential and to challenge prejudice where it became apparent in behaviour (Department of Trade and Industry, 2001).

Segregation

Although the 1991 census revealed that residential segregation varied between minority groups and that the African-American model of inner city segregation could not be applied to Britain (Office of National Statistics, 1996: 132–3), by the early years of the twenty-first century Bangladeshis and Pakistanis have become the most segregated groups in British society. Segregation was the key underpinning of disturbances which took place in Oldham and Bradford in 2001 when a number of incidents arose of white persons allegedly being attacked for entering Asian areas which was perceived as 'invading their territory'. Disorders subsequently occurred in, or on the margins of, areas predominantly inhabited by Pakistani or Bangladeshi communities, and in most cases occurred against the background of preceding racial tensions and racial attacks (Home Office, 2001a: 8).

Thus in the early years of the twenty-first century the objective of eliminating racial discrimination has been replaced in many urban areas by a new goal, that of tackling segregation. The existence of 'strong pressures... which prevent young people of different backgrounds from exploring life... together' (Allen and Barratt, 1996: 14) was depicted as one underlying explanation for the Bradford disorders in 1995 and was regarded as a key underpinning of the riots which occurred in a number of town in northern England in 2001, where it was argued that 'many communities operate on the basis of a series of parallel lives' (Home Office, 2001b: 9). This meant that members of the white and Asian communities had very few ways of 'learning from and understanding one another's culture and beliefs' (Burnley Task Force, 2001b: 9). It was argued that segregation may result in enhanced fear and intolerance, effectively splitting a city into two warring camps. This situation could be exploited by extremist groups (Home Office, 2001b: 9). A further problem is that segregation may result in the formation of 'no-go' areas which may become a barrier behind which unacceptable forms of criminal activity are practised (such as drug trading) to which the state will ultimately be forced to respond. This was alleged to have been one factor in explaining the disorders in 2001 at Bradford (Sutcliffe, 2001) and Burnley (Burnley Task Force, 2001b: 9), but was not accepted as a significant factor in these events by the police service or drug action teams (Home Office, 2001a: 9, 17).

The urgent need to deal with issues such as racial disadvantage and segregation was underpinned by projected increases in the size of minority ethnic populations in areas affected by disorders in 2001. In Oldham, for example, it was anticipated that by 2011 the overall white population in the town will have fallen by 8.8 per cent whereas Pakistani, Bangladeshi, black and Indian populations will have substantially increased, the Bangladeshi population from 7230 in 1996 to 15,340 in 2011 and the Pakistani population from 11,600 to 21,940 in the same period. By 2011 it was estimated that whereas the majority of the white population would be over 40 years of age, the ethnic minority populations would be mainly under 30 (Oldham Metropolitan Borough, 2001). Nationally, people within minority ethnic groups increased by approximately 500,000 between 1992–94 and 1997–99 (Office for National Statistics, 2001). A number of initiatives have been proposed to combat segregation which are discussed below.

The provision of public services.   The changing demography of towns such as Oldham has significant implications for local authority services, especially in education and housing where in addition to changes in local authority housing allocation and education provision it was proposed that equal opportunities policies should be pursued to enable the most able classroom assistants from Asian and black heritage backgrounds to qualify as teachers, and that more young women especially from Asian and black heritage backgrounds should be recruited as crèche workers and classroom assistants to provide bilingual services and culturally senstive support. It was also proposed that the quality and accessibility of housing services to Asian heritage communities in the borough should be improved, and that more staff should be employed by social services from Asian and black heritage backgrounds so that the profile of the workforce reflected the community (Oldham Metropolitan Borough, 2001).

The above policies, which rested on the promotion of equal opportunities, could be supplemented by other initiatives, including the suggestion that every submission, paper or document which came before Oldham Council for a decision should include a section on 'effects on integration within Oldham' (Oldham Independent Review, 2001: 61). It was suggested that voluntary sector initiatives which transcended racial/ethnic boundaries should be endorsed (Burnley Task Force, 2001a: 14; Home Office, 2001b: 72). The need to build trust and confidence across all communities was emphasised, an important aspect of which was the teaching of citizenship in schools to educate children to respect and understand diversity (Ouseley, 2001: 24–8; Home Office, 2001b: 74). It was also suggested that mono-cultural schools could be balanced by initiatives to foster an understanding of other communities: the twinning of these schools or holding joint sports developments under the auspices of inter-faith networks were put forward as developments to aid the attainment of this objective (Home Office, 2001b: 30). Additionally it has been proposed that equality and diversity conditions should be attached to all contracts of grant-aid public investments, and that all supplies and contracted services should be required to promote social and cultural mixing as well as good race relations (Ouseley, 2001: 32–5).

Political leadership. It was noted that 'Oldham lacks strategic direction, and a vision for the way it should develop in the future' and that there had been 'a persistent failure to face up to the deep seated issues of segregation in the town' (Oldham Independent Review, 2001, 14). In Burnley, it was observed that 'leadership, vision and civic pride are lacking at all levels of society in Burnley in both Asian and white communities' (Burnley Task Force, 2001b: 9). Comments of this kind directed attention to the weakness in local political leadership in areas affected by disorders in 2001. It was argued that this was reflected by factors which included the absence of an agreed vision of how things could be made better and an inability to broker relations between key interests and to work up agreed solutions (Home Office, 2001a: 13). Thus the need for local political leaders to promote community cohesion was emphasised. It was proposed that this should be developed on a sub-local authority basis (perhaps by Local Strategic Partnerships) and should be effectively articulated, updated and translated into action (Home Office, 2001b: 22).

Compulsion? A final issue concerns whether segregation should be compulsorily broken down. This approach was urged by one of Oldham's MPs who suggested forced integration to avoid geographical segregation (Woolas, 2001) and also by the Chairman of the Commission for Racial Equality (Singh, 2002). There are, however, numerous problems with this approach. The imposition of policies to achieve this objective without the full consent of all citizens affected by them may lead to opposition. In particular, attempts to reverse the process of segregation may antagonise minorities if they perceive that the policies concerned with this objective constitute an attack on their culture, values and beliefs. What might be perceived as a compulsory policy of assimilation is unlikely to be any more palatable than the constrained choices which forced segregation upon minority ethnic communities in the first place.

Stigmatising the underclass

The approach adopted by Conservative governments between 1979 and 1997 in responding to what they perceived as moral depravation by an approach which targeted young children in deprived areas evoked a considerable degree of criticism. It was viewed as a means of exercising surveillance over working-class children in these places, especially those from single-parent families, whilst ignoring broader social factors which might account for delinquency (West, 1982). Fears were also expressed that a child who was labelled as a potential delinquent at an early age might feel the need to live up to this designation, thus resulting in a self-fulfilling prophecy. However, this approach was not abandoned and the presumption that young people in certain categories or circumstances were at a much greater risk of becoming involved in crime latterly gave rise to the 'cycle of anti-social behaviour' which legitimised pre-emptive action undertaken by a wide range of agencies (Audit Commission, 1996: 57–9).

Social inclusion

A number of criticisms have been put forward concerning the policies pursued by Labour governments since 1997 to secure social inclusion. The rhetoric used by previous Conservative governments who attributed disorder to moral depravation was not entirely absent from pronouncements made by Labour ministers after 1997. The need to remoralise society was most prominently articulated in the Prime Minister's call for a moral crusade which was voiced following media attention to two 12-year old girls in South Yorkshire becoming pregnant, one by a 14-year old boy. He urged 'a partnership between Government and the country to lay the foundations of that moral purpose' (Blair, 1999). This entailed placing considerable store on the role of the family in teaching children right from wrong, backed up by provisions (such as curfews) provided for in the 1998 Crime and Disorder Act, the provision of effective sex education to prevent teenage pregnancies, and the targeting of boys who fathered children by the Child Support Agency who would be forced to accept responsibility for the upkeep of their children by contributing from their earnings or benefit. The government also contemplated the possibility of introducing legislation to require teachers to emphasise the benefits of marriage and the traditional family unit when discussing moral or sexual issues.

The effectiveness of Labour's policies designed to combat social exclusion has also been questioned. Problems which included the decision by the 1997 Labour government initially to stick to the spending plans of its Conservative predecessor led to accusations that insufficient money was being devoted to these tasks and created the impression that the government's prime concern was to court the support of middle England at the expense of the poor and dispossessed, even though increased public funding was provided for in subsequent budgets. In June 2001 the unemployment rate officially fell to 976,800, the lowest since November 1975 and seeming evidence of the success of Labour's desire to reinstate full employment. However, these official figures did not tell the full story: for example, the tendency during the Thatcher years to sign off workers as sick (who therefore receive incapacity benefit) in order to hide the true level of unemployment has resulted in large numbers of economically inactive households persisting into the early years of the twenty-first century. It is also unclear whether Labour policies such as the New Deal were responsible for the increased levels of employment or whether this would have occurred in any case as the consequence of economic growth. If this argument is valid, it might suggest that the economic downturn which occurred soon after Labour's victory in 2001 would result in higher levels of unemployment regardless of the 'welfare to work' policies. In 2000 there were 667,000 redundancies, one feature of which is foreign-owned firms having fewer qualms about throwing employees out of work (MacErlean et al., 2001). The overall figures for unemployment also mask the disproportionate level of unemployment existing in certain areas and among certain categories of people. Housing estates with large concentrations of persons at the lower end of the social scale continue to exhibit levels of unemployment which are far above the national average. The government's intention to eradicate child and pensioner poverty and to take 1 million children out of poverty by 2004 also seems ambitious and unlikely to be realised. One reason for this is that it is hard to reduce inequality in a period of relatively sustained economic growth.

Labour's social reform policies have also been criticised for being concerned as much with preventing crime and disorder (especially by juveniles) as with the pursuit of social justice for its own sake. It has been argued that the success of programmes to combat youth crime, disorder and vandalism is dependent on the extent to which young people are actively involved (Local Government Information Unit, 2000). Labour's policies fail to do this and might thus fail to cultivate the enthusiastic support of those on the receiving end. Labour's educational reform was especially concerned with addressing the social causes of crime. The intensive nursery scheme was allocated to high crime areas, directed at children whose upbringing led them to be perceived as potential future offenders. The aim of these programmes was to teach children of pre-school age how to think ahead and organise their lives. It was anticipated that that this would produce observable benefits by the time the child reached ten, measured by indicators which included improved school behaviour and achievement, and fewer signs of criminality. There were, however, considerable problems attached to accurately assessing those at risk, including the possibility of self-fulfilling prophecies.

Labour's emphasis on truancy and school exclusions was also underpinned by a desire to curb crime as these factors were regarded as key causes of crime. The Excellence in Cities Programme provided money to help prevent school exclusions (for example, by extending school-based learning support units whereby troublesome pupils could be dealt with in schools) and funded the appointment of mentors to address the problem of children who were excluded from schools and those who left with no qualifications. It was intended that this scheme would subsequently be extended into primary schools. Punitive measures were also directed at tackling truancy. On 1 December 1998 new powers came into force whereby the police could remove truants to designated premises and the 2000 Criminal Justice and Court Services Act proposed additional penalties for parents who failed to make their truanting children attend school.

The emphasis placed on dealing with drugs is a further example of social policy whose main objective was to reduce crime. It was calculated that offenders feeding their drug habits committed one in three burglaries and street robberies, together with a high amount of crack-related violence and prostitution. The estimated cost of drug-driven crime was between £3–4 billion a year, and the punishments imposed on drug users rarely stopped their drug use (NACRO, 1999a). The 1995 white paper, *Tackling Drugs Together*, and the subsequent 1995 legislation, resulted in a number of new initiatives which included the use of multi-agency approaches to drugs and drug-related crime in which police forces became important actors in local Drug Action Teams. Arrest referral schemes were also introduced to arrange treatment for arrested drug users, and the police also became involved in education programmes in schools designed to discourage youngsters from becoming involved with drugs. The Labour government built on these earlier approaches by the appointment of Keith Hellawell who became the UK anti-drugs coordinator in charge of the UK Anti-Drug Coordination Unit (UKADCU). In 1998 UKADCU published its 10-year plan for tackling drug misuse whose aims were to help young people resist drug abuse, to protect communities from drug related anti-social and criminal behaviour, to enable people with drug problems to overcome them and to stifle the availability of illegal drugs (UKADCU, 2000).

Heavy emphasis was devoted in the government's anti-drugs policy to treatment, education and prevention as opposed to the traditional approach which placed pre-eminent focus on the enforcement of the drug laws: its 10-year strategy included an additional £217 million over the next three years for treatment and support services for drug misusers, treatment programmes in prisons, education and prevention programes, and extra funding for the treatment-based court sentence (the treatment and testing order) which was introduced in the 1998 Crime and Disorder Act. Additional money was also provided for arrest referral schemes. The new policy attached considerable importance to multi-agency cooperation and provided for corporate performance measures. It was augmented in 2000 by the then Home Secretary's announcement of the creation of a national Drug Treatment Agency to impose national standards for treatment and rehabilitation on local drug action teams and voluntary and charitable drug treatment centres and to act as a clearing house for residential rehabilitation places for the toughest cases which involved offenders and long-term addicts. This preventive approach was balanced against more punitive proposals in the 2000 Criminal Justice and Court Services Act. This introduced a new drug abstinence order whereby the courts could require a proven drug abuser using a Class A substance to stay clean and be regularly tested. Non-compliance would attract a further penalty. This Act also empowered the courts to order the drug testing of defendants who had been charged with property crime, robbery and Class A drug offences or with any offence which was suspected of being linked to the misuse of heroin or cocaine/crack. The result of these tests would be used to inform bail decisions.

Police reform

Although reforms to policing were initiated after the publication of the Scarman Report, disorders continued throughout the 1980s. In 1985 a further wave occurred in which police action was again the subject of adverse comment. The riot in Handsworth, Birmingham followed a number of confrontational situations between the police and young black people, the police shooting of Cherry Groce resulted in a major riot in Brixton, and in Haringey's Broadwater Farm Estate a major disorder took place following the death of Cynthia Jarrett from a heart attack following a police raid on her house in connection with enquiries related to her son. The effectiveness of police reforms were further challenged by events in the 1990s. The spread of public disorder to new areas (many of which did not contain racial minorities of any numerical significance) further questioned the success of police reform which had been initiated in the 1980s. Many of the events which occurred during the 1990s were triggered by police interventions: the Meadow Well Estate riot in Tyneside in 1991, for example, followed a police chase resulting in the death of a 'joyrider' and the disorders on Oxford's Blackbird Leys Estate followed an attempt by the police to clamp down on '*hotting*'. A report into the Bradford disorders in 1995 referred to an 'inadequate relationship between the police and the people of Manningham' creating a disposition to violence (Allen and Barratt, 1996: 155).

Although the depth of feeling by minority ethnic communities towards the police service were not as intense in the 2001 riots as had been the case in previous events of this nature (Home Office, 2001b: 40), 'perceptions... that the police are partial and discriminatory, disrespectful, indulge in racist language and are sympathetic to far right extremists' affected the relationship between the police service and young Asians in Oldham (Oldham Independent Review, 2001: 41) and may be one explanantion for the disorders which took place there. The riot which occurred in Leeds in 2001 was sparked by the arrest of a Bangladeshi man. According to the *Guardian* on 6 June 2001, an onlooker stated that 'they took this man, they arrested him, kicked him and sprayed CS gas at him in front of Asian people'. At the disorder which occurred in Burnley in June 2001, a commissioner for the Commission for Racial Equality and son of the town's deputy mayor,

Shahid Malik, was allegedly assaulted by police officers when he attempted to appeal for calm on the streets by telling Asian youths to go home to prevent further street violence. He stated in the *Guardian* on 27 June 2001, 'I was hit two or three times by the same officer and three or four others and was unconscious for two or three seconds. When I came round I heard an officer saying "stop...acting and get up". I could see in their eyes all logic had gone.' Persisting problems of this nature thus suggest that the reforms proposed by Lord Scarman failed to achieve the objective of improving the relationship between the police service and ethnic minority communities. A number of reasons may explain this apparent failure of police reform which will be discussed below.

Failure to address the culture of the police

Scarman's report specifically denied that the police service was racist and instead he attributed the problem of poor police–public relationships in multi-ethnic areas to the existence of a few 'rotten apples in the barrel' who should be weeded out of the police service (Scarman, 1981: 64–5). In this key respect his package of reforms did not go far enough and helped to explain why his report failed to attain its objective of improving the relationship between the police service and ethnic minority communities. This meant that the police continued to have some blame attributed to them when urban disorders occurred. This issue is explored in more detail in Chapter 6.

Recruitment

Changes in the racial make-up of Britain's police forces proved very difficult to achieve and there was no striking success in making Britain's police forces more socially representative. In 1981 there were 132 black police officers serving in the Metropolitan Police (0.5 per cent of the total strength) (Scarman, 1981: 76). The expenditure of £1 million to attract ethnic minority recuits resulted in this figure increasing to only 467 (less than 2 per cent of the total number of officers) by 1990. At the end of 1993 there were 1814 police officers from ethnic minority origins in England and Wales, representing 1.5 per cent of all police officers. Recruitment rates stood at a slightly higher figure, constituting 3.8 per cent of all appointments to English and Welsh forces in 1993 (Oakley, 1996: 13–14).

A number of reasons may explain this situation. The attempt to improve police–ethnic community relationships was to a large extent based on the assumption that the recruitment of more black officers would achieve this goal. However, the negative image of the police within such communities (which was acknowledged by the then Home Office minister Douglas Hogg in a speech delivered to a National Conference of Police Recuiting Officers in Derby in 1986) meant that members of minorities who joined the police ran the risk of rejection by their own peers as well as the possibility of being subjected to racial prejudice from white officers who constituted the bulk of Britain's police officers. These difficulties explain both the low numbers of members of ethnic minorities joining the police and the high wastage rate of these recruits. In 1993, 66 ethnic minority officers in England and Wales left the service, constituting 32 per cent of the numbers appointed in that year (Oakley, 1996: 14).

Training

The various attempts that were made after 1981 to reform probationer training in general and community and race relations training in particular failed to achieve immediate dramatic improvements in police attitudes. In addition to the arguments presented by the reports discussed in the previous section, other explanations might be offered for these apparent failings. A particular problem concerned the philosophy which underpinned the approaches which were adopted. A considerable difference exists between multi-cultural and anti-racist training programmes. The former suggest that the problems which sometimes occur between races are based upon misunderstandings and can be remedied by providing information on the history and background of minority communities. The latter, however, insists that racial intolerance will only be rectified when members of the dominant culture become aware of their own racism so that they become receptive to suggestions designed to remedy their acknowledged defects. The approach required by these initiatives is challenging, and may lead to a classroom situation which is tense but not creative, especially when programmes of this type were delivered by non-police personnel.

The discriminatory use of police powers

Allegations of the persistence of abuses by the police towards black people continued to be made including the discriminatory use of police powers such as stop and search of persons and vehicles (Institute of Race Relations, 1987: 1–55). One explananation for this was that the key reforms such as safeguards governing the use of contentious police powers were contained in Codes of Practice rather than in the 1984 legislation itself. This meant that an officer who chose to disregard the new constraints on his or her behaviour was not guilty of a criminal offence although he/she might be the subject of a disciplinary charge. The amended stop and search provisions of the 1994 Criminal Justice and Public Order Act (which removed the condition of reasonableness that a prohibited article would be found) could serve to intensify perceptions of racism unless they were effectively monitored in accordance with the safeguards contained in the 1984 Police and Criminal Evidence Act or the 1991 Criminal Justice Act.

Police–community liaison

A number of reforms to practices concerned with police–community contact were introduced, but their effect was limited. Formal consultation with the community was a requirement incorporated into section 106 of the 1984 Police and Criminal Evidence Act but this failed to produce any substantial improvement in police–community relationships (Morgan and Maggs, 1985) one reason being that consultation is merely the right to be heard and did not alter the existing power relationship between police and public. Reforms were also introduced in the specific area of police contact with ethnic minority communities. By the late 1980s most police forces had established discrete units concerned with race and community relations, typically based at headquarters and divisional level. These, however, failed to permeate all aspects of policing, implying that race relations issues were matters of concern only to a small number of specialist officers.

Policing methods

Following the Scarman Report, most police forces sought to introduce community policing methods into multi-ethnic, inner city areas. However, these failed to secure any significant overall improvement in police–public relationships in these areas in particular because of the relatively lowly status of these officers in the police service which raised questions about 'issues such as pay and career progression to ensure that good officers were attracted to, and retained in, this role' (Home Office, 2001a: 41). The support that residents were willing to give to the police service because of the role performed by area police officers tended to be offset by the use of complementary police tactics (Gifford et al., 1989: 163–71) involving an aggressive response based on the presumption that black people were violent. Additionally the move towards what has been regarded as 'paramilitary policing' in urban areas resulted in the deterioration of police–public relationships. This style of policing involved the 'application of (quasi) military training, equipment, philosophy and organisation to questions of policing' (Jefferson, 1993: 374) and resulted in the increased tendency to utilise confrontational tactics to respond to threats (apparent or actual) posed to law and order enforcement in inner city areas. This issue is returned to in the concluding chapter.

The use of these diverse tactics reflected a division within police circles as to which style of policing was most likely to quell social unrest. The view that 'hard' policing methods caused disorders was not accepted by many rank-and-file officers. Metropolitan police officers quoted in the *Sunday Times* on 20 October 1985 expressed the view that the escalation of violence in Haringey in 1985 had been caused by an official 'hands off' policy not to arrest law-breakers which deprived officers who worked on the Broadwater Farm Estate of their authority and legitimised a more coercive approach to the enforcement of law and order in these areas.

Policing was not the major cause of rioting

It must finally be observed, however, that the continuance of public disorder following the Scarman Report and its subsequent implementation might suggest the rioting was caused by the failure to devote sufficient attention to other underlying grievances which contributed to this problem and was not solely attributable to deficiencies in policing. One study drew attention to the role of the police in triggering disorder in Brixton in 1981 but asserted that the ability of police actions to precipitate violence out of all proportion to the incident itself 'can only be explained by a complex tangle of broader causes – by unemployment and the prospect of unemployment; by a system of schooling which has failed particularly to meet the needs of black youth; by the degrading conditions of many inner-city areas; by the racism of individuals and authorities which robs black people of dignity; and by a system of policing which is widely felt to be brutal and unjust' (NCCL, 1981: 9).

The police service does not operate in a vacuum and it has been argued that police–society relationships mirror the quality of state–society relationships (Brewer et al., 1996: 4) and that policing by consent is impossible without the underlying condition of government by consent (Joyce, 1992: 238). This may suggest that while the police might be the agency which triggered events by acting in a manner viewed as 'unreasonable', it was their personification of an unjust society which resulted in them serving as the focus for the pent-up frustrations of inner city dwellers and becoming the target of their aggression. This view was articulated by Norman Bettison, Assistant Chief Constable of West Yorkshire, in the wake of the Bradford riots in 1995 who stated in the *Guardian* on 12 June 1995 that the police were the 'anvil' on which youths beat out their 'frustration and anger'. This interpretation implies that the Conservative government in 1981 used the police as a barrage balloon, seeking to highlight police inadequacies which were discussed in Lord Scarman's report in order to deflect criticism away from its economic and social policies.

Political marginalisation and conventional political activity

It has been argued above that some of Labour's policies to secure social inclusion were underpinned as much by the desire to prevent crime and disorderly activities by young people as by the concern to pursue social justice for its own sake. This criticism could also be made in connection with the emphasis placed on citizenship which may help to combat crime and disorder. This was most obviously the concern of the crime project which was launched by the Howard League for Penal Reform in 1998. This was directed at 11,000 schoolchildren aged 13 and 14 in London and was designed to foster a sense of citizenship to reduce crime and anti-social behaviour. The emphasis of this project may not encourage young people to become interested in conventional political activity. Similarly, the aim of encouraging minority ethnic groups to become involved in mainstream political activity has been adversely affected by perceptions of racism in the major parties especially regarding the selection of parliamentary candidates (Ali and O'Cinneide, 2002). The attitude of these parties is briefly assessed below.

The Conservative Party

The Conservative Party in particular has a tradition of nurturing racist senti-ments. In 1963 the Conservative backbench MP, Sir Gerald Nabarro, asked listeners to the BBC radio programme, *Any Questions*, how they would feel 'if your blonde, blue-eyed daughters ... came home with a great buck nigger and said "I am going to marry this man"' (Nabarro, 1963). At the 1964 general election a leading Labour politician, Patrick Gordon Walker, lost his seat at Smethwick to a campaign mounted by his Conservative oppponent, Peter Griffiths, which was overtly racist. During the campaign Griffiths had promised to speak out against a multiracial society and call for a complete and immediate ban on immigration (Foot, 1965: 48) and the slogan 'if you want a nigger for your neighbour, vote Labour' was circulated during the contest (Solomos and Back, 1996: 54). This led the Prime Minister, Harold Wilson, to challenge the Conservative leadership to refuse Griffiths the party whip so that he would spend his time in Parliament as a 'Parliamentary leper'. The activities of the then Conservative MP, Enoch Powell were also based on racialism. His 1968 'rivers of blood' speech intensified existing racial prejudice by suggesting that the streets of Britain would eventually run red with blood arising from factional fighting. He referred to white Britons being made to feel strangers in their own country by the influx of immi-grants which resulted in neighbourhoods being changed beyond recogni-tion. The then leader of the Conservative Party, Ted Heath, responded by throwing Powell out of the Shadow Cabinet.

Sentiments of this nature, however, continued to be articulated within Conservative circles. In April 1990 the then Conservative MP, Norman Tebbit, referred to British Asians cheering on the cricket team representing their country of origin rather than the English team. This inferred disloyalty towards Britain by ethnic minority communities. In 1990 a black barrister, John Taylor, suffered racial abuse from local party members when selected as Conservative candidate for Cheltenham. He contested this seat in the following year's general election but lost it to the Liberal Democrats. In the lead-up to the 2001 general election a number of issues suggested the Conservative Party harboured racist sentiments. Some leading Conservatives (including Michael Portillo) refused to sign up and commit themselves to the Comission for Racial Equality's anti-racist pledge by which signatories promised not to exploit race issues or to stir up prejudice at the general elec-tion and committing party leaders to disciplining anyone found to be play-ing the race card in future campaigns. One retiring Conservative MP, John Townend, attacked multi-culturalism and asserted his belief that immigra-tion was undermining Britain's homogenous, Anglo-Saxon society. He criti-cised a speech by the then foreign secretary, Robin Cook (which had hailed Britain's varied communities), for expressing a ministerial desire to transform Britons into 'a mongrel race'. His views were echoed by another retiring Conservative MP, Christopher Gill, who argued that rising numbers of asy-lum seekers were diluting Britain's 'national character'. John (now Lord)

Taylor insisted that Townend should be thrown out of the Conservative Party but the then leader of the Party, William Hague, refused this course of action and at one stage it appeared that Taylor himself might be disciplined for articulating views which were critical of the party leadership. Townend was, however, eventually required to apologise for his 'ill-chosen words', withdraw them, undertake not to repeat them and accept that racism had no place in the Conservative Party.

The Conservative Party has been associated with a range of other actions which have been seen as racist. The 1948 British Nationality Act permitted all citizens of the British Commonwealth to enter Britain to settle and seek work with their families. Limits on immigration were first introduced by a Conservative government in 1961: the 1971 Immigration Act (which required those coming to Britain having to prove a close connection with the country) particularly pandered to these feelings and tended to institutionalise racism, presenting black people as a problem for society and a threat to British culture and traditions. Since 1979 examples of black criminality (such as 'mugging' and rioting) have been used to epitomise changing patterns of social behaviour and to justify coercive interventions designed to restore 'traditional' British values (Barker, 1981). The introduction of a tiered system of citizenship in the 1981 Nationality Act, further restrictions on immigration contained in the 1988 Immigration Act and attempts to impose limitations on asylum seekers in the 1993 Asylum and Immigration Act have further reinforced the negative view of immigrants as the source of social problems whose entry should only be permitted in an ever-narrowing range of circumstances.

The Labour Party

Many working men's clubs operated a colour bar in the 1960s and 1970s, trade unions were accused of playing a role in promoting hatred of immigrants who came to Britain after the Second World War (Tompson, 1988: 71–5) and the abandonment of Labour's outright opposition to all forms of immigration control was perceived as pandering to racist sentiments (Foot, 1965: 161–94). Additionally, little attempt was made to recruit a larger number of Parliamentary candidates drawn from minority ethnic communities to contest constituencies which were winnable for the Labour Party, a situation perhaps influenced by David Pitt's failure to retain Clapham and Wandsworth for the party in the 1970 general election which gave the impression that minority candidates were an electoral liability (Saggar, 2001: 769). At the 1997 general election nine Labour MPs were derived from ethnic minority communities and at the 2001 general election this figure increased only to 12, and accusations were made that some local Labour parties (such as Bolton) had few black or Asian members in senior positions such as serving as local councillors. A later study suggested that Labour and Liberal Democrat black or Asian parliamentary candidates secured a smaller share of the vote for their parties at both the 1997 and 2001 general elections and that minority ethnic candidates depleted Labour's share of the vote by 3.5 per cent in these two contests (Mortimore, 2002).

Asylum seekers and the 2001 general election.   One issue which received prominence in the lead-up to the 2001 general election was that of asylum seekers. The attitude adopted by both of the major parties towards these people was underpinned by racism.

In the 2000 local elections a Conservative leaflet warned of bogus asylum seekers flooding Britain's shores and at the party's spring conference in 2001 its then leader, William Hague, promised to lock up all asylum seekers and to immediately deport those losing their claims. In a later speech he suggested the compulsory detention of all asylum seekers in special reception centres and a new 'removals agency' to track down people whose claims had been rejected but who remained in the country (Hague, 2001). The stance adopted by the Labour government towards asylum seekers (whereby persons of Kurd, Roma, Albanian, Tamil, Pontic Greek, Somali and Afghan origin were required to be subjected to 'a more rigorous examination than other persons in the same circumstances' on the grounds that they were more likely to be illegal immigrants or bogus asylum seekers) could also be viewed as racist (Young, 2001). These instructions were contained in orders issued by the government to immigration officers. During the election campaign the then Home Secretary, Jack Straw, announced his desire to introduce a quota of refugees who were permitted to settle in Britain (Straw, 2001) and his successor, David Blunkett, proposed the introduction of new powers to crack down on illegal immigrants.

It was subsequently asserted that politicians (from the government and opposing Conservative Party) and media alike had been encouraging racist hostility in their public attitudes towards asylum seekers. The slandering of refugees 'has not only led to direct attacks on asylum seekers but also to an underlying hostility to all those from ethnic minority communities, and heightened racial tensions. In our view the recent race riots in Oldham and Bradford are to an extent directly linked to the above' (Liberty, 2001).

The Liberal Democrats

The activities of some Liberal Democrat councillors in the London Borough of Tower Hamlets was also tainted with racism. An internal party enquiry conducted by Lord Lester in 1994 into alleged racist election leaflets recommended the expulsion of three local party members.

Conclusion

This chapter has examined a form of protest, rioting. This has a long tradition in Britain but in recent years has been identified as an activity principally carried out by the underclass in order to get policy-makers to respond to concerns which might otherwise be neglected or ignored completely.

Key issues of this nature have been identified, including the nature of policing in inner city areas. The response by the state to disorders has also been examined, including coercive measures undertaken by governments (in the form of legislation) and implemented by the police service. However, this response also embraces other reforms designed to reduce the likelihood of occurrences of this nature. These include attempts to increase the appeal of conventional political activity to marginalised groups (especially ethnic minority communities) and social reform directed at deprivation, social exclusion, racial discrimination and racial segregation. The importance of the latter issue was suggested by the riots which occurred in 2001 and is likely to assume an important aspect of public policy in the early years of the twenty-first century.

Riots involve collective actions directed against property and persons (especially those such as police officers who epitomise the unjust nature of the state) (Joyce, 1992: 235–6). The following chapter continues with the theme of the use of violence as a political tactic, and focuses on terrorism.

Glossary

The colony

The formation of a West Indian enclave community, the 'colony', in urban areas characterised by a 'range of informal dealing, semi-legal practices, rackets and small-time crime' (known as 'hustling'), was one defensive response to racism. Nurtured on heritage and tradition, it provided the basis for the growth of internal cultural cohesiveness within the black population, 'the winning away of cultural space in which an alternative black social life could flourish' (Hall et al., 1978: 351). This sought to avoid those who lived in such areas becoming relegated to society's 'underclass'. The colony aided the development of a distinct culture expressed in music, dress and in particular the 'apocalyptic religio-politics of Ras Tafarianism', the 'religion of the oppressed'. It was observed that the 'dress, beliefs, philosophy and language of this ... group ... has provided the basis for the generalisation and radicalisation of black consciousness amongst sectors of black youths in the cities' and was the 'source of an intense black cultural nationalism' (Hall et al., 1978: 357). Ras Tafarianism sought to sever ties with white dominated society and cultivate an attitude of hostility and resistance towards it. This religion, which emerged in Jamaica in the 1930s, attached a positive value to blackness, seeing black people as an elite rather than a minority in white dominated society. Africa formed the focus for a new identity and the religion preached withdrawal from, and rejection of, white society (Cashmore, 1977). Suffering forms an important aspect of Ras Tafarianism and particular hatred is bestowed on those perceived as oppressive agents of white society. The term 'Babylon man' is a term of abuse directed at the police (Bishton et al., 1980: 10–12).

'Hotting'

This involves the performance of elaborate manoeuvres at high speed in stolen, expensive cars.

Power sharing

Power sharing involves the development of community structures around which a separate identity based upon the religion and culture of ethnic minority groups can be nurtured and sustained. It may be justified by the argument that 'if...minorities are placed in a setting in which they have an identity and feel secure, such as a separate autonomy, they can reach out and establish positive functional relationships with other communities' (Burton, 1997: 25). Examples of this approach include the formation of a Muslim parliament in 1992 by Dr Kalim Saddiqi to act as a body to put forward the views of members of the Asian Muslim community, and attempts to utilise the provisions of the 1944 Education Act and establish voluntary-aided Muslim schools as occurred in October 2000 when permission was given for a Muslim secondary school in Bradford to be set up. One difficulty with power sharing is that it may result in a white backlash based on sentiments of seeking to preserve 'traditional British values'. This aggression is likely to produce a counter response from those being attacked and, if unchecked, will fuel serious racial disorder.

Riots

A riot often involves disorder which may be spontaneous or involve a degree of organisation which results in the police temporarily losing control over public spaces. It commonly involves a crowd of persons who disturb the peace and which requires police intervention to restore order. Individuals or companies who suffer damage in events of this nature may sue the police under the provisions of the 1886 Riot Damages Act.

Segregation

Segregation entails the multi-faceted separation of communities (in areas which include leisure and recreational pursuits, culture, religion, housing and education), usually based on choices which are not freely made. It is underpinned by residential segregation which arises in the absence of competition between different groups within the urban social system for a particular type of housing. This may occur through choice or constraint. A study of Asians in Bradford and Birmingham conducted in the 1970s revealed that residential segregation arose through choice. Many Asians did not wish to settle in Britain permanently and sought to live in a manner in which they could maintain their culture and values whilst living abroad in order to be accepted when they returned home (Dahya, 1973). Although the voluntary desire to remain segregated may have diminished as the intention or ability of immigrants to return home lessened, segregation was subsequently intensified by a range of additional factors most of which were forced upon minority ethnic communities. Initially discrimination in the job market resulted in many members of minority ethnic communities becoming trapped in inner city areas. The problem was intensified by racial discrimination denying minorities equal opportunities in the private and public housing sectors (S. Smith, 1989). One aspect of this was the policy pursued by some local authorities whereby housing allocation was governed by a desire to keep white and minority ethnic families apart, and another was the 'white flight' from multi-ethnic areas. Residential segregation also arose from racially motivated violence which compelled members of ethnic minority communities to band together for self-protection. What is termed 'ghetto security' (which encourages people to locate in areas where their community has concentrated) was a particular cause of the high level of segregation of Bangladeshis within the London Borough of Tower Hamlets. Residential segregation has resulted in other forms of segregation, most notably in education (Kundnani, 2001).

Self-defence organisations

Perceptions that the police were indifferent to racial violence against members of ethnic minority communities resulted in the formation of defence organisations to protect those who were the subject of attack. Examples included the East London Workers against Racism which was formed in Newham in the early 1980s. The police, however, often displayed a negative attitude towards the actions of those they perceived to be engaged in vigilante action. For example, in 1981, eight youths associated with such organisations were charged with the serious offence of 'conspiracy to assault persons unknown' in Newham. The organisation Combat 786 was formed by Asian youths as a defence against racial attacks by members of the extreme right which occurred in places such as Oldham in 2001. This organisation was alleged to have had young supporters in Asian communities in Bradford and Oldham (Harris, 2001).

Withdrawal

Withdrawal is based upon extreme sentiments of opposition to white-dominated society. These may result in a desire by minority ethnic groups to abandon their country of residence completely, a view which is held by Ras Tafarians (who seek a return to an African Zion) and was also put forward by the late black Labour MP, Bernie Grant, who suggested in 1993 that consideration should be given to allowing some ethnic minorities a 'conditional return' to their country of origin with financial assistance. Alternatively, withdrawal might result in disaffected communities endorsing violence to rid themselves of the power exerted over them by the dominant society, perhaps entailing activities associated with liberational terrorism (a term which is considered in more detail in Chapter 5) conducted within first world countries. The ideology of Black Power emerged in America during the 1960s and 1970s whose leading activists included Malcolm X and Stokely Carmichael. The Black Power movement consisted of a range of bodies which attempted to implement the goals of black economic and political power, black unity, black self-determination and racial pride for blacks and in which the locus of decision-making power, control of funds and ownership of property was in, or was shifting to, the hands of blacks (Gerlach and Hine, 1970: 31–2). These views have met with little response in Britain since 1970. A Black Panther movement briefly appeared in Brixton in the early 1970s but failed to generate much support (Vogler, 1991: 115). However, more recently the Nation of Islam (led by Louis Farrakhan) secured some support among younger Muslims. This organisation utilised racial anger as a mechanism to mobilise blacks and serve as a platform to develop the strategy of separatism. Additionally, the Islamic Liberation Party, *Hizb ut Tahrir*, has also attracted some support among young Muslims. Its beliefs include a rejection of the nation state and national boundaries in favour of a global Islamic state. It preaches against integration, perceiving Muslims as members of the Islamic world community.

References

J. Alderson (1995) quoted in C. Crowther (2000) *Policing Urban Poverty* (Basingstoke: Macmillan Press – now Palgrave Macmillan)

A. Ali and C. O'Cinneide (2002) *Our House? Race and Representation in British Politics* (London: Institute of Public Policy Research)

S. Allen and J. Barratt (1996) *The Bradford Commission Report: Report of an Inquiry into the Wider Implications of Public Disorders which Occurred on 9, 10 and 11 June 1995* (London: HMSO)

M. Anwar (1984) *Ethnic Minorities and the 1983 General Election* (London: Commission for Racial Equality)

M. Anwar and N. Kohler (1975) *Participation of Ethnic Minorities in the General Election of October 1974* (London: Community Relations Commission)

Audit Commission (1996) *Misspent Youth ... Young People and Crime* (London: HMSO)

P. Bachrach and M. Baratz (1970) *Power and Poverty: Theory and Practice* (Oxford: Oxford University Press)

M. Barker (1981) *The New Racism* (London: Junction Books)

G. Ben-Tovim, J. Gabriel, I. Law and K. Stredder (1986) *The Local Politics of Race* (Basingstoke: Macmillan Press – now Palgrave Macmillan)

J. Benyon (1987) 'Interpretations of Civil Disorder', in J. Benyon and J. Solomos (eds) *The Roots of Urban Unrest* (Oxford: Pergamon Press)

D. Bishton, B. Homer and P. Nanton (1980) *Talking Blues: the Black Community Speaks about its Relationship with the Police* (Birmingham: AFFOR)

T. Blair (1999) 'My Moral Manifesto for the Twenty-First Century', *Observer*, 5 September

D. Blunkett (2001) quoted *Guardian*, 9 July

J. Brewer, A. Guelke, I. Hume, E. Moxon-Browne and R. Wilford (1996) *The Police, Public Order and the State: Policing in Great Britain, Northern Ireland, the Irish Republic, the USA, Israel, South Africa and China* (Basingstoke: Macmillan Press – now Palgrave Macmillan, 2nd edition)

J. Brown (1982) *Policing by Multi-Racial Consent: the Handsworth Experience* (London: Bedford Square Press)

N. Buck (1992) 'Labour Market Inactivity and Polarisation: a Household Perspective on the Idea of an Underclass', in D. Smith (ed.) *Understanding the Underclass* (London: Policy Studies Institute)

R. Bull and P. Horncastle (1986) *Metropolitan Police Recruit Training: an Independent Evaluation* (London: The Police Foundation)

Burnley Task Force (2001a) *Burnley Speaks, Who Listens? Burnley Task Force Report on the Disturbances in June 2001* (Burnley: Burnley Task Force)

Burnley Task Force (2001b) *Burnley Speaks, Who Listens? A Summary of the Burnley Task Force Report on the Disturbances in June 2001* (Burnley: Burnley Task Force)

J. Burton (1997) *Violence Explained* (Manchester: Manchester University Press)

Cabinet Office (2001) *Reducing Racial Disadvantage* (London: Cabinet Office)

B. Campbell (1991) 'Kings of the Road', *Marxism Today*, December

E. Cashmore (1979) 'The Rastaman Cometh', *New Society* 41(777), 25 August

City of Bradford (2001) *Community Pride*, Issue 2, Winter 2001–2002

R. Cloward and L. Ohlin (1960) *Delinquency and Opportunity* (New York: Free Press)

Commission for Racial Equality (1994) *CRE Connections* (London: Commission for Racial Equality)

Commission for Racial Equality (2001) *Annual Report 1 January 2000 to 31 December 2000* (London: Commission for Racial Equality)

I. Crewe (1979) 'The Black, Brown and Green Votes', *New Society*, 12 April, 76–8

B. Dahya (1973) 'Pakistanis in Britain: Transients or Settlers?', *Race*, 14(3), 241–77

N. Dennis (1993) *Rising Crime and the Dismembered Family* (London: Policy Studies Institute)

Department of Trade and Industry (2001) *Towards Equality and Diversity* (London: Department of Trade and Industry)

P. Eisinger (1973) 'The Conditions of Protest Behavior in American Cities', *American Political Science Review*, 67(1), March, 11–28

L. Elliott (1999) 'Labour Widens War on Poverty', *Guardian*, 8 September

F. Field (1989) *Losing Out: the Emergence of Britain's Underclass* (London: Blackwell)

F. Field in C. Murray (1990) *The Emerging British Underclass* (London: Institute of Economic Affairs Health and Welfare Unit, Choice in Welfare Series No. 2)

P. Foot (1965) *Immigration and Race in British Politics* (Harmondsworth: Penguin)

A. Geddes (1993) 'Asian and Afro-Caribbean Representation in Elected Local Government in England and Wales', *New Community*, 20(1), 43–57

L. Gerlach and V. Hine (1970) *People, Power, Change: Movements of Social Transformation* (Indianapolis, Indiana: Bobbs-Merrill)

T. Gifford (1989) *Loosen the Shackles: First Report of the Liverpool 8 Inquiry into Race Relations in Liverpool* (London: Karia Press)

P. Gordon (1983) *White Law: Racism in the Police, Courts and Prisons* (London: Pluto Press)

Greater London Council (1986) *Policing London*, November/December

C. Gutzmore (1983) 'Capital, Black Youth and Crime', *Race and Class*, XXV(2), Autumn, 13–30

W. Hague (2001) speech at Dover 18 May, quoted *Guardian*, 19 May

S. Hall, C. Critcher, T. Jefferson, J. Clarke and B. Roberts (1978) *Policing the Crisis: Mugging, the State and Law and Order* (London: Macmillan)

P. Harris (2001) 'Far Right Plot to Provoke Race Riots', *Observer*, 3 June

A. Heath (1992) 'The Attitudes of the Underclass', in D. Smith (ed.) *Understanding the Underclass* (London: Policy Studies Institute)

J. Benjamin Heineman (1972) *The Politics of the Powerless: a Study of CARD* (London: Oxford University Press)

Home Office (1982) *Report of a Study Group: Recruitment into the Police Service of Members of the Ethnic Minorities* (London: HMSO)

Home Office (2001a) *Building Cohesive Communities: a Report of the Ministerial Group on Public Order and Community Concern* (London: Home Office)

Home Office (2001b) *Community Cohesion: a Report of the Independent Review Team Chaired by Ted Cantle* (London: Home Office)

T. Jefferson (1990) *The Case against Paramilitary Policing* (Milton Keynes: Open University Press)

G. John (1970) *Race in the Inner City: a Report from Handsworth* (London: Runnymede Trust)

H. Joshua and T. Wallace (1983) *To Ride the Storm – the 1980 Bristol Riots and the State* (London: Heinemann)

P. Joyce (1992) 'A Decade of Disorder', *Policing*, 8, Autumn, 232–48

M. Kettle and L. Hodges (1982) *Uprising! The Police, the People and the Riots in Britain's Cities* (London: Pan Books)

A. Kundnani (2001) 'From Oldham to Bradford: the Violence of the Violated', in A. Kundnani (ed.) *The Three Faces of British Racism* (London: Institute of Race Relations)

J. Lea and J. Young (1982) 'The Riots in Britain 1981: Urban Violence and Political Marginalisation', in D. Cowell, T. Jones and J. Young (eds) *Policing the Riots* (London: Junction Books)

Liberty (2001) quoted *Observer*, 1 July

I. Loader (1996) *Youth, Policing and Democracy* (Basingstoke: Macmillan Press – now Palgrave Macmillan)

Local Government Information Unit (2000) *Taking Part* (London: Local Government Information Unit)

London Borough of Lambeth (1981) *Final Report of the Working Party into Community–Police Relations in Lambeth* (London: Public Relations Division, London Borough of Lambeth)

R. MacDonald (1997) 'Dangerous Youth and the Dangerous Class', in R. MacDonald (ed.) *Youth, the 'Underclass' and Social Exclusion* (London: Routledge)

N. MacErlean, J. Insley and T. Boles (2001) 'The Sack Strikes Back', *Observer*, 29 April

J. Macnicol (1987) 'In Pursuit of the Underclass', *Journal of Social Policy*, 16(3), 293–318

T. Madood (1997) 'Employment', in T. Madood et al. (eds) *Ethnic Minorities in Britain: Diversity and Disadvantage* (London: Policy Studies Institute, The Fourth National Survey of Ethnic Minorities)

R. Morgan and C. Maggs (1985) *Setting the PACE: Police–Community Consultation Arrangements in England and Wales* (Bath: University of Bath, Bath Social Policy Paper Number 4)

R. Mortimore (2002) *Effect of Candidate Ethnicity in the British General Elections of 1997 and 2001* (London: MORI)

Moss Side Defence Committee (1981) *The Hytner Myths* (Manchester: Moss Side Defence Committee)

C. Murray (1989) *Sunday Times Magazine*, 26 November, reprinted in C. Murray (1994) *Underclass: the Crisis Deepens* (London: Institute of Economic Affairs Health and Welfare Unit, Choice in Welfare Series No. 20)

G. Myrdal (1964) *The Challenge to Affluence* (Chicago: Victor Gollancz)

Sir G. Nabarro (1963) *Any Questions?* BBC Radio, 5 April, quoted in Sir G. Nabarro (1969) *Portrait of a Politician* (Oxford: Maxwell)

NACRO (1999) *Drug Driven Crime* (London: NACRO)

National Council for Civil Liberties (1981) *Civil Disorder and Civil Liberties: Evidence to the Scarman Enquiry* (London: NCCL)

North Kensington Law Centre (1982) *Police and the Notting Hill Community* (London: North Kensington Law Centre)

G. Northam (1989) *Shooting in the Dark: Riot Police in Action* (London: Faber and Faber)

R. Oakley (1996) *Race and Equal Opportunities in the Police Service* (London: Commission for Racial Equality)

Office for National Statistics (1996) *Ethnicity in the 1991 Census* (London: HMSO, Volume 3, edited by P. Radcliffe)

Office for National Statistics (2001) *Population Trends* (London: TSO, Autumn)

Oldham Independent Review (2001) *One Oldham, One Future* (Manchester: Government Office for the North West)

Oldham Metropolitan Borough (2001) *Projected Population Change in Oldham – Implications for the Council and the Borough* (Oldham: Social Development Sub-Committee, Report of the Joint Officers, 31 July 2001, Item No. 4(7))

H. Ouseley (2001) *Community Pride not Prejudice: Making Diversity Work in Bradford* (Bradford: Bradford Vision)

B. Parekh (1974) 'Postscript', in B. Parekh (ed.) *Colour, Culture and Consciousness: Immigrant Intellectuals in Britain* (London: George Allen and Unwin)

D. Piachaud (1999) 'Wealth by Stealth', *Guardian*, 1 September

Police Training Council Working Party (1983) *Community and Race Relations Training for the Police* (London: Home Office)

A. Power and R. Tunstall (1997) *Dangerous Disorder: Riots and Violent Disturbances in Thirteen Areas of Britain, 1991–92* (York: Joseph Rowntree Foundation)

J. Rex and S. Tomlinson (1979) *Colonial Immigrants in a British City* (London: Routledge and Kegan Paul)

M. Richards (1985) *Report by Deputy Asst Commissioner Michael Richards to the Haringey Police/Community Consultative Group into events in October 1985*, quoted *Guardian* 14 January 1986

K. Roberts (1997) 'Is There an Emerging British "Underclass"?' in R. MacDonald (ed.) *Youth, the 'Underclass' and Social Exclusion* (London: Routledge)

P. Rock (1981) 'Rioting', *London Review of Books*, 17–30 September, 19–20

J. Rollo (1980) 'The Special Patrol Group', in P. Hain (ed.) *Policing the Police*, Volume 2 (London: John Calder)

M. Rowe (1998) *The Racialisation of Disorder in Twentieth Century Britain* (Aldershot: Ashgate)

G. Rude (1967) *The Crowd in History* (New York: Wiley)

Runnymede Trust (1994) *Multi-Ethnic Britain: Facts and Trends* (London: Runnymede Trust)

S. Saggar (1997a) 'Racial Politics', *Parliamentary Affairs*, 50(4), October, 693–707

S. Saggar (1997b) 'The Dog That Didn't Bite: Immigration, Race and the Election', in A. Geddes and J. Tonge (eds) *Labour's Landslide: the British General Election 1997* (Manchester: Manchester University Press)

S. Saggar (2001) 'The Race Card, Again', *Parliamentary Affairs*, 54(4), October, 759–74

Lord Scarman (1981) *The Brixton Disorders, 10–12 April 1981, Report of an Inquiry by the Rt. Hon. Lord Scarman, OBE* (London: HMSO)

T. Sewell (1983) 'Contradictions that Freeze Black Leadership', *New Statesman*, 18 October, 12–13

G. Singh (2002) statement in *Guardian*, 18 March

R. Skellington (1996) *'Race' in Britain Today* (London: Sage, 2nd edition)

D. Smith (1973) *Racial Disadvantage in Britain* (London: Political and Economic Planning)

D. Smith (1992) 'The Future of the Underclass', in D. Smith (ed.) *Understanding the Underclass* (London: Bedford Square Press)

D. Smith and J. Gray (1983) *Police and People in London* (London: Policy Studies Institute)

S. Smith (1989) *The Politics of Race and Residence* (Cambridge: Polity Press)

Social Exclusion Unit (1998) *Bringing Britain Together: a National Strategy for Neighbourhood Renewal* (London: TSO)

J. Solomos (1993) 'Constructions of Black Criminality: Racialisation and Criminalisation in Perspective', in D. Cook and B. Hudson (eds) *Racism and Criminology* (London: Sage)

J. Solomos and L. Back (1995) *Race, Politics and Change* (London: Routledge)

P. Southgate (1982) *Police Probationer Training in Race Relations* (London: Home Office, Research and Planning Unit paper 8)

P. Southgate (1984) *Racism Awareness Training for the Police* (London: Home Office, Research and Planning Unit paper 29)

J. Straw (2001) quoted *Observer*, 20 May

G. Sutcliffe (2001) quoted in *Guardian*, 10 July

E. P. Thompson (1968) *The Making of the English Working Class* (Harmondsworth: Penguin)

K. Tompson (1988) *Under Seige: Racial Violence in Britain Today* (Harmondsworth: Penguin)

P. Townsend (1990) 'Underclass and Overclass: the Widening Gulf between the Social Classes in Britain in the 1980s', in G. Payne and M. Cross (eds) *Sociology in Action* (Basingstoke: Macmillan Press – now Palgrave Macmillan)

M. Tuck (1989) *Drinking and Disorder, a Study of Non-Metropolitan Violence* (London: HMSO, Home Office Research Study 108)

M. Tuck and P. Southgate (1981) *Ethnic Minorities, Crime and Policing* (London: HMSO, Home Office Research Study Number 70)

H. Tumber (1982) *Television and the Riots* (London: British Film Institute)

United Kingdom Anti-Drug Coordination Unit (2000) *Tackling Drugs to Build a Better Britain – the Government's 10-Year Strategy for Tackling Drug Misuse* (London: TSO)

R. Vogler (1991) *Reading the Riot Act: the Magistracy, the Police and the Army in Civil Disorders* (Oxford: Oxford University Press)

D. Waddington (1992) *Contemporary Issues in Public Disorder: a Comparative and Historical Approach* (London: Routledge)

P. Waddington (1994) *Liberty and Order: Public Order Policing in a Capital City* (London: UCL Press)

A. Walker (1991) 'The Strategy of Inequality: Poverty and Income Distribution in Britain 1979–89', in I. Taylor (ed.) *The Social Effects of Free Market Policies* (Hemel Hempstead: Harvester Wheatsheaf)

D. West (1982) *Delinquency, its Roots, Careers and Prospects* (London: Heinemann)

D. West and D. Farrington (1973) *Who Becomes a Delinquent?* (London: Heinemann)

J. Westergard (1992) 'About and beyond the "Underclass": Some Notes on Influences of Social Climate on Sociology Today', *Sociology*, 26(4), 575–87

C. Willis (1983) *The Use, Effectiveness and Impact of Police Stop and Search Powers* (London: HMSO, Home Office Research and Planning Unit paper 15)
P. Woolas (2001) 'Beating the BNP', *Guardian*, 15 June
H. Young (2001) 'Labour's Law of Ethnic Punishment Shames Us All', *Observer*, 8 May
J. Young (1992) 'Riotous Rage of the Have-Nots', *Independent on Sunday*, 19 July

5
Terrorism

The previous chapter focused on the way in which violence in the form of rioting has been used to enable the 'underclass' to seek the recognition by policy-makers of their grievances or concerns. The violence demonstrated in these events may be seen as a way to force policy-makers to sit up and take notice of social groups who would otherwise be ignored. This chapter continues with the theme of violence in the form of *terrorism*. This, as with rioting, may be viewed as a means to secure political, social or economic change and provide for the empowerment of those who perceive themselves or the cause they advocate to be marginalised by those who wield power, but there are a number of significant differences between the two forms of violence. Rioting is often (although not always) (Keith, 1993: 235) spontaneous in nature, involving large numbers of persons willing to take to the streets in order to demand some kind of reform. Terrorism, however, typically involves a small number of persons whose actions are usually more meticulously planned. Unlike rioting, terrorism is generally pursued in the name of an ideology and may involve extreme violence causing the death and injury of large numbers of persons as happened on 11 September 2001 when the attack by Muslim extremists on the World Trade Centre in New York and the Pentagon Building in Washington caused the deaths of several thousand people all of whom were the victims of indiscriminate violence.

Introduction

This chapter focuses on the use of violence to achieve political purposes. This is often referred to as terrorism although groups which engage in these activities may alternatively describe themselves as practitioners of *guerrilla warfare* carried out by *rural guerrilla movements* or *urban guerrilla movements*. Alternatively, they may view their activities as a form of direct action (a term which is discussed in Chapter 2). This chapter discusses why groups resort to the use of terrorism and analyses the response of the state to these activities. The discussion is centred on mainland Britain but examples from other countries are used where this aids the evaluation of issues being considered and because the response of any one country to political violence has increasingly assumed international dimensions.

The strategies and tactics of politically motivated violence

This chapter considers terrorism through the use of selected case studies which discuss the activities of a number of groups which have been associated with this form of activity in Britain since 1970. As a prelude to this discussion, this section considers the ideologies with which terrorism has been historically associated and examines the tactics which may be used to further this cause. This will provide a context for a more detailed consideration of issues specifically related to Great Britain.

Terrorist strategies

Politically motivated violence has historically been utilised to achieve a wide range of objectives. The main ones are discussed below.

Revolutionary objectives. Revolutionary objectives are designed to overthrow the state and institute an alternative economic, political or social order. Violence is typically directed against the government – the political arm of the state – although it may involve sectarian or ethnic warfare in which groups vie with each other to determine the fundamental nature of the state. In the nineteenth century, revolutionary violence was often directed against absolutist monarchs in the belief that their deaths would result in an alternative system of government offering a greater measure of social justice. An example of this was the assassination of the Russian Tsar Alexander II in 1881 by the organisation, *Narodnaya Volya*. In the twentieth century, revolutionary groups espousing socialist ideology have utilised violent methods in an attempt to bring about the downfall of capitalism.

In more recent years, revolutionary violence has been guided by religious impulses. In 1979 the fundamentalist party *Hezb-Allah* came to power in Iran. This placed Iran at the forefront of Islamic revolutionary movements whose aim is to secure the worldwide implementation of Islamic law. The main mechanism to achieve this is the *Jihad* (or Holy War) whose implementation may involve acts of violence against secular governments and their populations. Activities associated with Islamic fundamentalists have included the assassination of President Sadat of Egypt in 1981 and the placing of bombs at an American airforce base in Saudi Arabia in 1996. It has been observed that those motivated by the religious imperative are more lethal than their secular counterparts, as they regard violence as a divine duty or sacramental act, conveyed by sacred text and imparted by clerical authority (Hoffmann, 1995).

Sub-revolutionary objectives. Other terrorist organisations possess objectives which can be secured within the existing economic, political or social system but are faced by a government which is unwilling to concede reforms of this nature. Accordingly, some form of violence may be used in an attempt either to directly coerce the government into introducing changes or to mobilise public opinion to put pressure on the government to grant them. There are numerous examples of reforms which have been brought about in Britain by such mechanisms. The campaign for female enfranchisement at the beginning of the twentieth century occasionally deployed violence, including attacks on churches. Groups with sub-revolutionary objectives have often been pitted against forces other than governments. These include business and commercial interests. The activities mounted by organisations such as the Animal Liberation Front, for example, (whose activities are discussed in more detail later in this chapter) are frequently directed against private individuals and companies.

Liberational objectives.   Some individuals and organisations are motivated by a desire to rid their country of foreign rule. The use of violence to secure self-rule has met with a number of successes across the world, most notably in opposition to colonial rule exercised by a number of European countries in Africa and Asia. Nelson Mandela (the President of South Africa), and Yasser Arafat (President of the Palestinian Authority), were both leaders of organisations (the African National Congress and the Palestine Liberation Organisation) associated with politically motivated violence. Success is achieved because nationalism is likely to find support among some sections of the population who view violence as a legitimate means to achieve this goal. The campaign by republican groups to remove the British presence from Northern Ireland has constituted a key post-war example of the use of violence to achieve what they (but not their Unionist neighbours) perceive as liberation. In Spain, the ETA has utilised violence since 1959 to advance its objective of an independent Basque socialist state.

State-sponsored violence.   Terrorism has frequently been a tactic used by one country to wage war against a technologically superior nation. However, states may also utilise coercion in their everyday activities, both legitimately or in a manner which apes terrorism. It is thus necessary to draw a distinction between force involving the legitimate use of state power to prevent, restrain or punish breaches of the law, and violence lacking the legitimation of constitutional and legal sanctions which is thus essentially arbitrary (Wilkinson, 1986: 23). Although states are frequently on the receiving end of terrorism, they may also conduct similar activities themselves against either their external or internal opponents. In the former case, state-sponsored violence may substitute for a formal declaration of war by one country against another. As an alternative, states carry out a war of attrition against each other, sometimes conducted by intermediaries rather than groups or individuals which can be directly traced back to the government of a particular state. States have practiced such 'deniable and clandestine acts to effect changes in the policies of other nations' (Wardlaw, 1989: 182) throughout history and evidence that terrorism is not a new political phenomenon associated with left-wing political causes.

States may additionally seek to respond to opposition to the conduct of their internal affairs through the use of violence. The deployment of the 'Black and Tans' and the Auxiliaries in 1920 was designed to respond to the campaign mounted by the Irish Republican Army during the war of independence. Following an ambush in December 1920 when one of their number was killed, Auxiliaries and Black and Tans retaliated by burning down a substantial part of the city of Cork. Governments who wish to eliminate internal opposition may resort to the use of 'death squads'. Units within the Brazilian police were accredited with 1000 murders between 1964 and 1970 (Arblaster, 1977: 414). This form of activity was alleged to have occurred in Northern Ireland in both the 'shoot to kill' policy of the 1980s and through the collusion of the security forces with Loyalist paramilitary groups in order to eliminate prominent republicans in the 1990s.

Terrorist tactics

The prime aim of political violence is to cause a state of 'disorientation'. In particular it 'erodes the relatively stable patterns of expectations required by social organisms' (Bowden, 1977: 284). Violence undermines the authority and credibility of the government and destroys community cohesiveness. Individual citizens become uncertain as to who they can trust and rely upon and in this situation conduct their lives in an insular fashion. It has been concluded that 'the purpose of terrorism is not military victory, it is to terrorise, to change your behaviour if you're the victim by making you afraid of today, afraid of tomorrow and in diverse societies...afraid of each other' (Clinton, 2001). A broad range of tactics are associated with terrorism although a key distinction exists between selective and indiscriminate actions. This section briefly seeks to demonstrate how these various forms of violence 'work' in the sense of helping to attain the objectives of those who perpetrate them.

Selective violence.   Violence seeking to secure revolutionary or liberational objectives is often of a selective nature, directed against those whose activities are deemed to be crucial to the functioning of the state and its institutions. Murder has been depicted as 'politics pursued by other means' (Toolis, 1995: 22). Politicians, police officers, soldiers, informers and members of the judiciary may be targeted in an attempt to reduce the capacity of the state to respond to violence and in general terms to disrupt its smooth running. Additionally, this form of violence which is targeted at 'the social and political "adversaries"' (della Porta, 1995: 12) is designed to stimulate the political will and resolve of those who perpetrate it by demonstrating the extent to which the state and its key personnel are vulnerable to a concerted campaign of violence. One example of this was the assassination of two senior RUC officers (Chief Superintendent Harry Breen and Superintendent Bob Buchanan) by the provisional IRA in South Armagh in 1989. Ultimately the level of violence may undermine a government's desire to retain power since, as Clausewitz argued, 'the required outlay becomes so great that the political object is no longer equal in value [and]...must be given up' (Von Clausewitz, quoted in Elliott-Bateman, 1974: 351–2).

Indiscriminate violence. Indiscriminate violence is directed at the general public in a random fashion. This may result in a tremendous loss of life and devastation of property as occurred in a number of separate incidents in America on 11 September 2001. A government which is unable to counter these activities will be accused of failure to perform its prime function of safeguarding the lives of its citizens. The psychological impact of violence makes it impossible for them to conduct their everyday lives in a normal manner. Those who carry out such acts of violence hope that in a state of panic, intimidated citizens will put pressure on the government to give in to the demands of the terrorists: 'therefore, by definition, a terror campaign cannot succeed unless we become its accomplices and out of fear, give in' (Clinton, 2001). Some aspects of the campaign of violence conducted by Northern Irish republican organisations on mainland Britain constituted an attempt to use violence to secure political objectives through fear. The ability to do this has been considerably enhanced by developments affecting what have been described as the 'weapons of terror' (Dobson and Payne, 1979). The contemporary combination of weapons of destruction and 'universal vulnerability' (Clinton, 2001) have made terrorism a particularly potent force in the late twentieth and early years of the twenty-first century. Semtex, for example, has made it possible to carry out acts of violence against both persons and property on a devastating scale which further serve to provide publicity for a group and the cause with which it is associated. Indeed, the quest for publicity may stimulate extreme acts of violence in the sure knowledge that the global media network will report incidents of this kind, thereby publicising the views of those responsible for them.

Violence directed at economic targets. Groups may target a country's economic life in order to further a political objective. This may involve attacks against property connected with the nation's trading, business or commercial life. In Northern Ireland the objective of the Provisional Irish Republican Army's (PIRA) commercial bombing campaign conducted during the 1970s was to discourage investment and destroy jobs which had been created in order to secure support for the political status quo from moderate nationalists. On mainland Britain campaigns waged by Northern Irish republican groups have included attempts to disrupt the tourist industry, the commercial life of the City of London and to cause damage and disruption in shopping centres. The key reasons for doing this are to stretch the government's resources and to place it under pressure from key economic interests whose profitability suffers from the destruction of business and commercial property. One difficulty with violence of this nature is that attacks directed against property may result in the death or injury of persons in the vicinity and thus cause adverse publicity for the group responsible for the attack.

Kidnapping, hijacking and robbery. Politically motivated violence has also taken the form of kidnapping, hijacking and robbery. These tactics might be advanced to secure various ends which include raising money, securing publicity, discrediting the government or obtaining concessions (such as the release of jailed comrades). In the early 1990s the IRA needed to raise between £5–£7 million each year. Declining contributions from America meant that this money was chiefly derived from the proceeds of robberies, drinking clubs, cross-border smuggling between Northern Ireland and the Irish republic and fraud. In response to activities of this nature Operation Madronna was launched in April 1995 on both sides of the border.

Political violence on mainland Britain: some key events

The previous section examined some general issues related to the aims of terrorist groups and how they perceive that violence will advance the cause they espouse. This provides an underpinning for this section's discussion of terrorism on mainland Britain since 1970. As has been argued in the introduction, events in Northern Ireland have been deliberately excluded from this discussion as it would not be possible to do justice to the subject matter in a general work of this nature.

Campaigns of politically motivated violence have periodically occurred in Britain since 1970. The 'Angry Brigade' (who were dubbed 'Britain's first urban guerrilla group') (Carr, 1975) carried out a series of bombings between August 1970 and August 1971 (25 attacks being attributed to them) (Bright, 2002: 17) on targets which included the homes of Robert Carr (then Secretary of State for Employment) and John Davies (Secretary of State for Trade and Industry). They were described as anarchists who wished to overthrow the government but advocated no alternative (Walker, 1986: 1). The absence of links between them and other radical movements or the public in general ensured that the severe terms of imprisonment served on its leading members in 1972 terminated its activities. Other examples of campaigns of politically motivated violence which occurred in this period included the campaign launched by the Welsh Language Society in 1972 against holiday homes in Wales which included the fire-bombing of properties. This section will concentrate on two campaigns of violence waged in mainland Britain since 1970. The first is associated with the politics of Northern Ireland and the second with the activities carried out by those who advocate the cause of animal rights.

Case study (1): the republican campaign on mainland Britain since 1972

The initial campaign of violence connected with the politics of Northern Ireland was waged by republican paramilitary organisations who operated in the Province and whose objective was to secure the withdrawal of the British presence there. However, the effects of this campaign were limited. In 1972, the then Home Secretary, William Whitelaw, was alleged to have informed a meeting of ministers and a delegation from the PIRA that 'we can accept the casualties...we probably lose as many soldiers in accidents in Germany'. This attitude was asserted to have been 'a major factor in the IRA's decision to have a bombing campaign in England – where casualties would not be "acceptable"' (Coogan, 1980: 492). Although the government might dismiss violence in Northern Ireland, it was considered that it would be harder to ignore it on mainland Britain.

The campaign of the Provisional Irish Republican Army (PIRA)

The campaign of violence was principally waged by the PIRA although groups such as the Irish National Liberation Army and, more recently, the Real IRA have also been involved. It commenced in February 1972 when a bomb was planted at Aldershot and continued with a car bomb exploding outside the Old Bailey the following month. The violence intensified following the abortive talks between the IRA and government in July 1972 and subsequently utilised a wide range of tactics. The willingness to frequently alter tactics (which have included indiscriminate and selective terrorism, a focus on prestige and 'soft targets' and the use of weapons such as car bombs and incendiary devices) reflects policy especially designed to hinder the work of security agencies by throwing them off balance.

Selective terrorism was directed against members of the security forces and leading politicians. These attacks included the M62 coach bombing in February 1974 (when nine soldiers, a mother and her two children were killed) and the planting of bombs in London in 1982 (which killed four soldiers, six bandsmen and seven horses) and Deal, Kent, in 1989 (which killed 11 Royal Marine bandsmen). These attacks were confined to Britain but other campaigns of violence carried out between 1978 and 1980 and 1987–90 targeted the personnel and facilities used by the British army serving in Europe. A further campaign of this nature was relaunched in 1996 with a mortar attack on a British army base at Osnabruck, Germany. Selective violence was also pursued in attacks on politicians and others who were supportive of government policy towards Northern Ireland. These actions included the assassination of Ross McWhirter in 1974 (who had sponsored a reward scheme for the apprehension of those involved in terrorism), the killing of Airey Neave (a Conservative MP and party Northern Ireland spokesman) in 1979 and an attack on the Grand Hotel, Brighton, housing a number of leading members of the government, including the Prime Minister, who were attending the 1984 Conservative party conference. In 1990 another Conservative MP, Ian Gow, was killed by an act of selective violence.

The republican campaign also included numerous acts of indiscriminate violence such as the planting of a bomb in the Tower of London in July 1974 (which injured 41 children and killed one person) and the Birmingham public house bombings the same year (which killed 21 persons and injured 182). In March 1993 an explosion in the city centre at Warrington killed two children and injured 56. Violence has also been designed to disrupt the commercial and social life of London and other major cities. Examples of this were the campaign carried out in the West End of London between 1974–75 and in the City of London in 1992–93 where violence was directed against both persons and property. The latter campaign included attacks on the Baltic Exchange (which killed three persons and caused £350 million of damage) in 1992, and the placing of a bomb outside the Hongkong and Shanghai Bank in Bishopsgate in 1993. These campaigns were repeated in other cities. On 8 August 1996, the *Guardian* estimated that the repair and building bill following the bombing of Manchester city centre approached £1 billion.

Some of the episodes carried out by Northern Irish republican groups have primarily sought to fulfil public relations objectives. They have attempted to gain publicity and demonstrate their capacity to strike when and where they wished, thus indicating that despite innovations in security policy the public remained vulnerable to random acts of violence. These included the mortar bombing of the garden of 10 Downing Street in 1991 and a series of attacks on Heathrow Airport in March 1994.

The campaign of the Real IRA

The Real IRA's activities were mainly conducted in Northern Ireland and included the Omagh car bomb in 1998 which was the worst atrocity of the 'Troubles' causing the death of 29 persons and two unborn babies. This prompted a ceasefire, but violence was recommenced a year later and included actions in Northern Ireland such as the grenade attack on Derry Police Station in April 2001. Actions undertaken on mainland Britain have mainly been of a secondary nature, and have included the detonation of a car bomb outside the BBC television centre in West London in March 2000, the placing of a bomb outside a Post Office sorting depot in Hendon, North London in March (and again in September) 2000, the planting of a device on the railway track at Twyford Avenue, Acton in July 2000 (which severely disrupted rush-hour traffic), the placing of a bomb on Hammersmith Bridge in June 2000, and a rocket launcher attack directed at the headquarters of M16 in Vauxhall, London in September 2000. These targets were designed to cause the maximum disruption at minimum cost to the perpetrators, although a bomb planted at Ealing in August 2001 perhaps indicated a change of tactics towards an intention to cause the loss of life and injury (in addition to publicity) rather than disruption which had characterised the previous attacks by this organisation.

The main intention of the campaign initiated by the Real IRA on mainland Britain in 2000–2001 was to destroy the Northern Irish peace process. Bombs were planted when the peace process was showing signs of strain. The Ealing bombing in August 2001, for example, occurred when the Northern Irish political parties had been set a deadline to respond to a joint UK–Irish government package of proposals which were designed to reinvigorate the 1998 Good Friday Agreement.

Case study (2): the animal rights movement

The issue of animal rights (as distinct from animal welfare) has been largely ignored by conventional politics and the cause has been chiefly promoted through the use of various forms of extra-parliamentary political action. This brief discussion examines the very wide range of tactics used by those advocating animal rights and also the diverse range of issues which have emerged out of this agenda. The inclusion of organisations concerned with animal welfare and animal rights in a discussion of terrorism is highly debatable. It is not an argument of this book that those engaged in these activities are terrorists but they are included in this chapter as the reaction of the state to the activities of some of those engaged in causes of this nature has been to officially label them as 'terrorist', indicating the difficulty of providing a precise differentiation between direct action (which is discussed in Chapter 2) and terrorism.

The belief of the absolute right of animals not to be harmed by humans resulted in the use of violent tactics against those who transgressed this standard of behaviour. During the 1980s and 1990s vivisectionists and others who used violence against animals (for example in medical research) were targeted in campaigns which included letter bomb offensives conducted by the Animal Rights Militia in the 1980s and the Animal Rights Coalition in the 1990s. Animals were also liberated from research laboratories and factory farms by animal rights activists.

During the 1990s a major campaign was mounted against Huntingdon Life Sciences which tested the safety of new drugs on animals. This involved maintaining a permanent presence outside the firm to lobby staff who worked there, although more violent tactics including physical attacks on staff, their homes and cars were also carried out by some opposed to the organisation's activities. An innovation was to put pressure on corporate shareholders to sell their shares in Huntingdon by tactics which included sending letters and flooding the switchboards of city backers with telephone calls. This action resulted in the collapse of the firm's share prices in 2000, and in 2001 the Royal Bank of Scotland withdrew its support. Additionally, in 1999 a new tactic was used in the campaign against vivisection. Activists from the organisation, British Union for the Abolition of Vivisection Reform Group, turned up on the doorsteps of individual investors in companies which were involved in animal experiments. Those who were 'doorstepped' were asked to either sell their shares or risk having their houses picketed.

In December 2000 a small scale bombing campaign commenced which was attributed to animal rights activists and which involved the use of indiscriminate violence. In February 2001, for example, the targets were diverse and included a chip shop and an estate agents, although a schizophrenic man who had been motivated by animal rights beliefs was subsequently convicted for this campaign. At around the same time a targeted campaign which involved placing incendiary devices under the cars of medical researchers involving animals was carried out. Other targeted activities included sending threatening letters to those engaged in medical research involving animals and protesting outside their homes.

Terrorists and terrorist organisations

Terrorists possess total commitment to a cause for which they are willing to give their own lives; display audaciousness, ruthlessness and (particularly when indiscriminate violence is used) have 'no regard for the sanctity and value of human life' (Blair, 2001). Those who carry out acts of political violence are motivated by a sense of injustice sufferered by those within their own community (Toolis, 1995: 39) and seek to redress this position. The limited number of studies conducted into the reasons why people become terrorists suggest that some recruits who join these organisations had a prior involvement with radical politics and participated in illegal, sometimes violent, events. They sometimes felt they were personally at risk of being arrested and prosecuted because of their participation in radical political activities and thus went underground to avoid arrest (della Porta, 1995: 98, 166–7, 169–70). Although the decision to join an underground organisation could be an individual one, recruitment in political sects is often facilitated by friendship ties, and solidarity with one 'important' friend who had been arrested or forced to go underground was the factor which pushed an individual to enter a terrorist group (della Porta, 1995: 167–8). The death of militants (who thus become martyrs) may also inspire others to join an armed struggle waged by terrorist methods although the widespread level of support in favour of the cause for which a prominent person has died may have the effect (as was the case following the death of the Provisional IRA hunger striker, Bobby Sands, in May 1981) of inducing militant organisations to pursue a political agenda (Kennedy-Pipe, 1997: 107).

Self-fulfilment may also be an inducement for individuals to become terrorists. Some have been deprived of educational and career opportunities (Burton, 1997: 27) and terrorist organisations thus provide them with status, a feeling of importance and a sense of belonging (McDonald, 1999) and the more risks they take the greater is the respect they acquire (Burton, 1997: 27). Many recuits to organisations such as the Real IRA have been very young teenagers. This situation may be a consequence of the discrimination experienced by social groups within a society which prompts some of its members to take up arms. In Northern Ireland the existence of a Catholic underclass has been alluded to: 'marginalised, on the periphery of society, jobless and poorly educated, powerless and voiceless' (Collins, 1998: 10). This explanation has been put forward in connection with some attracted to Muslim fundamentalism which offers an alternative to young men whose efforts to succeed in the field of business have been thwarted and who fail to secure any tangible rewards such as a job. Violence may arise out of what those in this situation perceive as a sense of social injustice (Seabrook, 2002).

However, middle-class, educated young people may also be attracted to these movements. This was the case with West Germany's Baader-Meinhof Gang which grew out of Berlin student demonstrations in the late 1960s and whose activists included young women, many from middle-class homes (Dobson and Payne, 1997: 155). Those who engaged in terrorism in that country were described as persons with middle-class occupations who occupied positions in society which commanded respect (Cobler, 1978: 42). For people from backgrounds such as these, personal experiences of repression by the state, the ruination of professional careers because of attachment to radical politics or a commitment to moral concerns which 'ended up in a radical, cultural critique of the dominant value system' may induce them to endorse violence as a means of political expression (della Porta, 1995: 140 and 148). Most members of the United Kingdom's Angry Brigade were middle class (the exception being Jake Prescott), and the group drew its intellectual inspiration from European radical movements, especially the Situationists and the anarchist 22 March Movement and from student protest in the late 1960s (especially at Essex and Cambridge universities). Some commentators have also drawn attention to the lifestyle adopted by terrorists and suggested that some who join these organisations are attracted by this. A study of West Germany's Baader-Meinhof Gang suggested that some who entered the movement were 'attracted by the combination of excitement and the possibility of sexual pleasure' (Dobson and Payne, 1979: 44).

The remainder of this section will discuss the organisations concerned with violence in connection with the two campaigns which were discussed in the previous section, namely the politics of Northern Ireland and the cause of animal rights.

The Provisional IRA

This organisation was formed in December 1969 following a split in the IRA. The failure of the IRA's border campaign between 1956 and 1962 temporarily discredited the physical force tradition within the republican movement which was replaced by a new strategy, placing emphasis on political mobilisation on social and economic issues rather than violence. It was hoped that this emphasis would forge an alliance in Northern Ireland which would cut across the historic sectarian divide. The onset of sectarian violence in the 1960s undermined this objective and resulted in a resurrection of support for attaining the republican goal of a united Ireland by violent means. This approach was endorsed by those who split from the IRA and formed the Provisional IRA in 1969 (Mitchell and Wilford, 1999: 37–8). This organisation was subsequently involved in a campaign of bombing and shooting in both Northern Ireland and mainland Britain, in which the cell structure was utilised. Its political wing is Sinn Fein.

The Irish National Liberation Army

The official IRA underwent a further split in December 1974 when the Irish Republican Socialist Party broke away. This had a military wing, the Irish National Liberation Army which was described as 'probably the most ruthless of all paramilitary organisations in the province' (Wichert, 1991: 171). This organisation was involved in a number of acts of violence in Northern Ireland, the Irish Republic and on mainland Britain. These included the bombing of a public house/disco in Ballykelly in 1982, and the assassinations of Lord Mountbatten and Airey Neave (both in 1979).

The Real IRA

The Real IRA emerged in 1997. It was opposed to Sinn Fein's decision to sign up to the Mitchell principles that constituted the cornerstone of the Good Friday Peace Agreement. Its recruits included some former members of the Provisional IRA from whom this organisation split, although former members of the Continuity IRA and the Irish National Liberation Army were closely identified with its aims of seeking to derail the peace process, believing that the peace process would not accomplish their desired objective of a united Ireland. The Real IRA's leaders recruited a number of persons with no previous track record in terrorism (who are termed 'lilywhites') to carry out acts of violence which made the task of the police in countering their activities more difficult. The political wing of the Real IRA is the Thirty-Two Counties Sovereignty Movement.

Animal rights and animal welfare movements

The historic view taken of animals was that they were different from human beings: human beings were viewed as a unique species, in particular (as was held by the Church) because they had souls. In post-war Britain, the role of organisations such as the Royal Society for the Prevention of Cruelty to Animals (RSPCA) was confined to securing the decent treatment of animals rather than seeking to establish that they had rights which needed to be recognised.

The view taken of animals historically was that they were creatures whose purpose was to provide humans with food and entertainment in places such as zoos or circuses, to act as fashion accessories or status symbols or to serve humans in the pursuit of scientific knowledge (for example in space flights or medical research). However, in the 1960s organisations such as the League against Cruel Sports emerged which opposed the hunting of mammals with dogs. This issue had not been highlighted by the RSPCA, and although younger militants entered this organisation to change its stance in the 1960s, it endorsed a ban on fox-hunting belatedly in 1976. Opposition to hunting escalated in the 1970s (involving tactics such as trespass) and the animal welfare movement also broadened its agenda in this decade to take on board issues such as opposition to the trade in fur coats (which was viewed as abusing animals for vanity) and factory farming (which was seen as exploiting animals for greed). The issue of animal welfare was also aided by the investigative journalism carried out by the *Sunday People* in 1975 whose exposé of the use of dogs in experiments connected with smoking in an ICI laboratory placed the issue of animals and medical research in the public eye.

The elaborated agenda of animal welfare was influenced by studies conducted into the lifestyle and habits of animals such as chimpanzees (for example Goodall, 1971) which suggested that animals other than humans possessed intelligence, the ability to construct elaborate social relationships and the capacity to develop complex behavioural patterns. The blurring of the line between humans and animals had significant ethical implications which resulted in issues related to society's treatment of animals being reassessed. During the 1970s those concerned with man's treatment of animals acquired a philosophy which was inspired by campaigns against discrimination on grounds of gender or race and sought to end what was regarded as 'speciesism' (Ryder, 1975: 11–19) in which animals were depicted as an oppressed minority in need of protection. Activists also adopted an alternative lifestyle which was based on vegetarianism.

A key role in the development of what became known as the animal rights movement was played by the book, *Animal Liberation* (Singer, 1976). This assumed immense importance by placing the issue of the *rights* of animals (rather than man's benevolence towards them) at the centre of the agenda of what became referred to as the animal rights movement. He depicted animals as the slaves of mankind and asserted that humans had no right to treat animals as inferior creatures. The abuse of animals was placed on a par with the abuse of human beings by regimes such as the Nazis and those who mistreated animals were perceived as torturers or murderers. Humankind's obligations to animals was viewed as the same as their obligations to human beings. The concern for animal rights eclipsed the support historically obtained for animal welfare.

Violent action was enacted by activists associated with the Animal Liberation Front (ALF), a body which lacked any concrete organisation or leadership but which was pledged to protect and release animals in danger and to support economic sabotage of the business and property of animal abusers. Groups willing to endorse more militant tactics (such as the Animal Rights Militia, the Hunt Retribution Squad, Animal Aid, the Animal Rights Coalition and the Justice Department) were associated with the ALF, some of which adopted the cell structure used by some terrorist organisations. Campaigns which used some form of violence involved a relatively small number of people. However, the protests against the export of calves for the continental veal trade in 1995 (which is an issue discussed in Chapter 2) involved large numbers of demonstrators who were new to the animal rights campaign.

Explanations for the emergence of terrorism

Organisations might resort to violence to advance a cause which is unlikely to make headway within a state's existing political framework. This activity may be pursued both from a position of strength (based on a degree of popular support for the cause) or weakness (whereby violence is utilised out of a sense of desperation in the knowledge that other political tactics are unlikely to succeed and that only extreme actions will force governments and public opinion to take notice of a cause or issue which has been consigned to political oblivion and is permanently ignored on political agendas). A country's political culture governs the public's tolerance of violence and may affect the willingness of groups to engage in such methods. In Britain violence has traditionally been viewed as an unacceptable form of political action and those who utilise it frequently find that they lose rather than gain public support. Consequently tactics such as indiscriminate terrorism may engender a 'stiff upper lip' mentality derived from the perception that violence is an illegitimate form of political action. Demands to introduce the death penalty for 'terrorists' rather than to pull British troops out of Northern Ireland have frequently been made in the wake of Northern Irish republican violence on mainland Britain since 1970.

The willingness of individuals and groups to utilise violence to further a political cause may also be governed by the nature of the political system. In totalitarian political systems governments lack popular legitimacy and frequently maintain their hold on power by coercive means. This may justify the use of violence as the only way to change the direction of public policy. However, in liberal democratic political systems a variety of political freedoms exist which groups may utilise to further their beliefs. However, this does not necessarily mean that violence is not utilised by groups seeking reform within these political systems.

It has been argued that 'in both Italy and Germany, two factors legitimised political violence which commenced in the late 1960s – the diffusion throughout the counterculture of an image of a "violent" and "unfair" state, and the radicals' frequent conflicts with the state apparatus'. Activists found a justification for violence 'in the widespread belief that the state had broken the rules of the democratic game and that revolutionary violence was therefore the only way to oppose an increasing authoritarianism' (della Porta, 1995: 158) (the main features of which were discussed by Cobler, 1978: 52–142). Thus violence may occur in liberal democratic political systems because those seeking reform perceive that the state is adopting a policy of repression towards dissent. This may delegitimise the state by creating the belief that it has violated the rules of the political game and is acting unjustly (della Porta, 1995: 163, 214), a situation which may justify the use of violence by those opposed to it, perhaps initially in a defensive posture (della Porta, 1995: 158–9). This issue is further considered in Chapter 6 in connection with banning parties on the extreme right of the political spectrum which have been directly or indirectly associated with racially motivated violence.

The reaction of the state to politically motivated violence

A state's response to various forms of politically motivated violence, including terrorism, cannot be manufactured in a vacuum. It has to take into account both the dynamics of the policy-making process (which requires constantly adjusting responses to terrorist activities) and external pressures which may influence the nature of anti-terrorist policies. The response to violence of this kind has been depicted in a cyclical fashion: the *threat* posed by terrorism emerges from which a *perception* develops which impacts on the state's *decision-making machinery*. This results in the initiation of *policy* which becomes translated into measures which are *implemented*. Implementation creates a reaction by those who use violence which causes the cycle to begin again. This cycle progresses in both directions, emphasising the fluid nature of the tactics used both by those who carry out violence and by the state, and the manner in which either participant to the struggle has the ability to influence the policies pursued by the other. In addition to the cycle of activities is the 'envelope of influences' which is comprised of variables such as a country's environment, history or culture. These external factors influence the component parts of the decision-making cycle (Davidson Smith, 1990: 29–31).

A number of methods have been commonly utilised by liberal democratic governments to respond to campaigns of politically motivated violence. These include the development of new police powers, the imposition of limitations on political activity, the introduction of reforms to the judicial process (especially in connection with trial procedures), the introduction of stiffer penalties for those involved in acts of political violence, the establishment of police units whose specific terms of reference are to respond to terrorism, and the formulation of international cooperation to defeat this form of violence (Gregory, 1976: 2–3, 11–12). Below, the response of successive governments to terrorism on mainland Britain is discussed.

The Prevention of Terrorism (Temporary Provisions) Act (PTA)

The degree of violence associated with terrorism involving injury to persons and damage to property was the obvious rationale for the introduction of legislation in 1974. The response of the British government to terrorism has been to treat these actions as criminal and not to take any political motive into account.

Key provisions of the PTA

The main response to the campaign of politically motivated violence on mainland Britain was the Prevention of Terrorism Act. It was enacted in the wake of the Birmingham public house bombings in 1974 and was replaced by legislation of the same name in 1976. Following recommendations made in 1983, the maximum life of the Act was five years and it was subject to annual approval by Parliament (Jellicoe, 1983). Revisions to this legislation occurred in 1984 and 1989, and a fundamental review of the legislation was initiated in 1995. Additionally, amendments relating to police powers to stop and search vehicles and persons and the creation of a new offence of possessing articles for suspected terrorist purposes were introduced in part VI of the 1994 Criminal Justice and Public Order Act. The Prevention of Terrorism Act also applied to Northern Ireland but was supplemented there by the Emergency Provisions Act, which was initially passed in 1973. Although it was regarded at that time as 'draconian' it remained on the statute book until replaced by the 2000 Terrorism Act.

The Prevention of Terrorism Act contained a number of powers which could be used to combat the activities of paramilitary groups conducting terrorist operations on mainland Britain in connection with the politics of Northern Ireland. The Secretary of State was empowered to proscribe organisations concerned with these activities. This action criminalised membership of these organisations and additionally made it illegal for them to raise funds. It further prohibited the public from contributing money or participating in their meetings. Initially powers to prevent financial contributions to proscribed organisations were directed against localised activity such as collections made in public houses. However, the belief that bodies such as the Provisional IRA obtained money from foreign sources led to new powers. Sections 9–13 of the 1989 Legislation made it an offence to be concerned in any arrangements which facilitated the retention or control of funds for terrorist organisations.

The 1974 Act introduced exclusion orders. This gave the Secretary of State the power to deport any person who was alleged to have been involved in the commission, preparation or instigation of terrorism related to the politics of Northern Ireland. Initially the power to deport was only from mainland Britain. However, the accusation that 'a bomb in Belfast was more acceptable than a bomb in London' resulted in the 1976 revision of the Act making it possible to deport from Northern Ireland to mainland Britain.

The Prevention of Terrorism Act introduced a wide range of powers governing arrest, detention and control of entry. Many of the offences contained in the legislation provided the police with the power to arrest without warrant on reasonable suspicion that a person was involved in the commision, preparation or instigation of acts of terrorism. Low-level intelligence gathering was facilitated by the process of 'examination'. This required travellers entering or leaving Britain or Northern Ireland to fill in forms detailing their movements to enable the authorities to ascertain whether they were concerned with terrorism or were subject to an exclusion order. All underwent this process which was not governed by the criterion of 'reasonable suspicion'. Those unable to fill in such forms or who refused to do so could be detained for a total period of seven days (48 hours at the discretion of the police and a further five days with the agreement of the Secretary of State), at the end of which a person had to be charged or released. The police were also provided with powers to question suspects and search persons and property in connection with the investigation of terrorist offences.

The PTA was the main legislative weapon applied against terrorist organisations which operated on mainland Britain after 1970. However, by the end of the 1990s powers contained in the Prevention of Terrorism Act were not widely used. During 1998, 20 persons were detained in connection with Northern Irish terrorism (down from 31 in 1997), and 25 persons were detained in connection with international terrorism (up from twelve in 1997). Eight of these 45 persons were subsequently charged with an offence. Extensions of detention were granted for 21 persons in 1998, and 600 persons were examined for more than one hour but were not detained. Thirty-eight of these were charged with an offence. Eighty-one of these examinations were in connection with international terrorism. The last twelve exclusion orders were revoked in October 1997 and the power to make them was not included when the Prevention of Terrorism Act was renewed for twelve months in March 1998 (Home Office, 1999).

The 1998 Criminal Justice (Terrorism and Conspiracy) Act

This measure was enacted following the Omagh bomb in Northern Ireland which killed 28 persons. Powers were provided to proscribe organisations operating in Northern Ireland which sought to destroy the peace process. A key provision was directed against terrorist groups operating in the

United Kingdom which were associated with acts of violence against foreign governments. It introduced the new offence of conspiracy to commit acts of violence abroad.

The 2000 Terrorism Act

The 2000 Act replaced the Prevention of Terrorism legislation, the Northern Ireland Emergency Provisions Act and sections 1–4 of the 1998 Criminal Justice (Terrorism and Conspiracy) Act. Unlike the Prevention of Terrorism Act, the 2000 measure was permanent. Under this legislation, the definition of terrorism was extended to embrace 'the use or threat of action ... to influence the government or to intimidate the public or a section of the public' for the purposes of 'advancing a political, religious or ideological cause' by actions which involved 'serious violence against a person ... serious damage to property' or which 'endangers a person's life' or 'creates a serious risk to the health or safety of the public or a section of the public' or which was 'designed to interfere with or seriously disrupt an electronic system'. The latter embraced activities such as hacking or subjecting a corporation to a fax blockade which had been used by some political campaigners (termed 'hacktivists') in pursuit of their objectives.

The Terrorism Act provided a wide array of police powers to combat terrorism. These included provisions related to stop and search (whereby stop and search zones could be established in areas where terrorist activity was suspected for a period of 28 days), and to detention and arrest. Additionally the Act created a number of new offences which included that of incitement of others to commit criminal acts abroad. This was directed at foreign-based groups or individuals operating in Great Britain whose activities were directed against foreign governments. For the first time the legislation enabled domestic as well as Northern Irish-oriented organisations to be proscribed. The ability to utilise exclusion orders (which had lapsed in 1998) was incorporated into the legislation. The legislation embodied emergency powers which existed in Northern Ireland, including the Diplock Courts, although it was envisaged that these would be phased out when the security situation allowed. The Act also made it an offence to provide money or other property which could be used for the purposes of terrorism, for a person not to tell the police if he or she suspected others of doing this and of the possession of any 'article' or 'information' in circumstances which gave rise to reasonable suspicion that they could be used for terrorist purposes.

The 2001 Criminal Justice and Police Act

Activities pursued by animal rights activists prompted further government legislative action. The 2001 Criminal Justice and Police Act strengthened police powers in connection with activities associated with the ALF such as 'doorstepping' and sending intimidatory mail and e-mail to staff engaged in research involving animals or to shareholders in companies involved in these activities. The Act gave the police powers to direct persons to leave the vicinity of a residence if it was reasonably believed that their presence or behaviour there was likely to cause harassment, alarm or distress. Existing provisions related to sending malicious communications were extended to e-mails, and the Companies Act was amended so that the Secretary of State could allow a company director or secretary to have his or her residential address withheld if disclosure was likely to create a serious risk of violence or intimidation.

The 2001 Anti-Terrorism, Crime and Security Act

This measure was enacted following the terrorist attacks in New York and Washington on 11 September 2001. It amended the 2000 legislation, by providing a number of new powers in connection with terrorism and security. These included powers to provide for the forfeiture of cash which was intended to be used for the purposes of terrorism, and to enable the Treasury to make a freezing order to prohibit persons from making funds available to or for the benefit of a persons or persons named in the order. The Act authorised the Secretary of State to issue a certificate in connection with a person whose presence in Britain was deemed to be a risk to security and who was suspected of being either directly concerned or associated with international terrorism. This person could then be detained without a trial pending deportation. Powers were provided in connection with acts of terrorism involving the use of biological, chemical or nuclear weapons which included making it an offence to aid, abet, counsel, procure or incite a person who was not a citizen of the United Kingdom to commit an act of this nature outside of the United Kingdom. Measures were introduced to improve the safety of the aviation industry in connection with matters which included unauthorised presence in a restricted zone or on an aircraft or trespass on an aerodrome, and police powers were extended in connection with the identification of terrorist suspects through means which included fingerprinting, searching, photographing and the removal of disguises.

Other measures to combat politically motivated violence

In addition to the anti-terrorist legislation, a range of other measures have been introduced in an attempt to combat politically motivated violence.

The machinery of central government

The machinery associated with contingency and emergency planning (discussed in Chapter 3) may also be involved in responding to major episodes of politically motivated violence. The remit of the four intelligence committees operating at Cabinet level (the Ministerial Committee on the Intelligence Services, the Permanent Secretaries' Committee on the Intelligence Services, the Joint Intelligence Committee and the Sub-Committee on Security Service Priorities and Performance) includes activities of this nature and the response to specific incidents may require ministerial consent to the use of the military. This is likely to involve the use of specialist units such as the SAS (which rescued 19 captives held at the Iranian Embassy in 1980) or the Royal Marine Commandos (who are responsible for the protection of North Sea oil platforms and with terrorist incidents involving ships in harbour and at sea). Additionally, the Cabinet Office Briefing Room (Cobra), also referred to in Chapter 3, may be activated to aid the progress of operations in connection with politically motivated violence, through securing the coordination of police, military and political responses. It also keeps the Cabinet informed on the progress of measures which are taken.

The police and security service

A major initiative undertaken by the police was to establish a specialist squad to investigate instances of politically motivated violence. This was originally formed as the 'bomb squad' in January 1971 in response to the activities of the Angry Brigade, but was renamed the 'anti-terrorist squad' in 1976. It is part of the Metropolitan Police and is based in London, but the nature of its work involves it in pursuing a national brief. It works closely with intelligence organisations in Britain, Northern Ireland and the Irish republic. It can draw upon specialised firearms support provided by the 'Blue Berets' and sophisticated technical aids supplied by C7, a support branch specialising in surveillance and monitoring. These are of relevance in the response to major incidents such as hostage negotiation.

The work performed by the anti-terrorist squad in countering politically motivated violence is supplemented by both special branch and MI5. The work performed by this latter agency is considered in more detail in the concluding chapter. A dispute between special branch and MI5 concerning prime responsibility for gathering intelligence in this area of activity was resolved in May 1992 when the then Home Secretary, Kenneth Clarke, announced that MI5 would assume the lead role in gathering intelligence on the IRA on mainland Britain. The decision to provide MI5 with this new role was criticised within policing circles on the grounds that MI5 had no operational function and its operatives had no power of arrest. Additionally the agency lacked experience in preparing evidence for the courts. Nonetheless, there have been successful examples of cooperation between the police and security service which resulted in the conviction of perpetrators of acts of violence. This included the arrest and subsequent jailing of two Irish National Liberation Army activists (Martin McMonagle and Liam Heffernan) in 1993. MI5 is also responsible for coordinating intelligence related to political violence which is gathered in Northern Ireland by the army and Royal Ulster Constabulary. The Government Communication Headquarters also established a special unit to target Irish-based political violence in 1993. The provisions of the 2000 Terrorism Act (especially those which apply to the proscribing of terrorist organisations) are likely to further increase the role of MI5 in compiling evidence on which these decisions will be based.

In 1985 an anti-terrorist coordinating committee was set up by the Home Secretary, headed by the Metropolitan Commissioner of Police. This action was prompted by an anticipated bombing campaign in seaside resorts and involved officers from the anti-terrorist squad moving into areas which were suspected of having been targeted. In October 1990 a national anti-terrorist unit was established to coordinate the gathering of intelligence. Additionally, in 2001 a special police unit was established to counter animal rights extremists.

The broadcasting ban

An important role served by all forms of politically motivated violence is to secure publicity for the cause advocated by those who carry it out. The preference of the media for events which are deemed to be 'newsworthy' serves as one inducement for groups to engage in acts of violence to further their political cause. Dramatic violence such as the bombing of a city centre is guaranteed prominent media attention. The terrorist attacks which took place in New York and Washington on 11 September 2001 were prominent news events across the world for many subsequent weeks. The desire for media attention may pose a dilemma for liberal democracies concerning the extent to which open government should be sacrificed to deny publicity to groups utilising political violence and also to ensure that counter measures implemented by the state are conducted in the degree of secrecy required for the attainment of a successful outcome.

One example of an attempt to deny publicity to terrorists occurred in 1988 when the then government introduced a ban on the live broadcasting of interviews given by persons associated with organisations suspected of involvement in acts of politically motivated violence or of being associated with organisations which conducted such activities. Sinn Fein and 10 other organisations were affected by this action. The power to do this was contained in broadcasting legislation and the aim was to deprive those who used violence of the oxygen of publicity.

The 'ring of steel'

A further tactic which was pioneered in Belfast but which was subsequently adopted on mainland Britain was to establish security road checks. These were placed on main roads leading into major cities at which officers (sometimes armed) implemented stop and searches of vehicles. This tactic was deployed in Manchester in December 1992 and on a more permanent basis around the City of London in July 1993, involving the operation of eight checkpoints. Section 81 of the 1994 Criminal Justice and Public Order Act subsequently provided the police with powers to stop and search persons or vehicles in a specified locality in connection with terrorism.

There were problems associated with this tactic. Members of the public whose journeys were impeded might react adversely. It is also possible that the use of this tactic in one area could persuade those engaged in political violence to transfer their activities elsewhere where safeguards of this nature were not in force.

International cooperation

Groups which carry out acts of politically motivated violence increasingly operate in an international arena. Examples of this included the claim that the Hamas suicide bombers who were responsible for a wave of violence in Israel in 2001 had been supplied with explosives by the Basque separatist group, ETA and that a three-way link existed between the IRA, ETA and the Colombian guerrilla movement FARC (the Revolutionary Armed Forces of Colombia) in the early twenty-first century. On 14 September 2001, the *Guardian* reported that the terrorist network of Osama Bin Laden (al-Qaeda) which was held responsible for the 11 September terrorist attacks in America had been identified or suspected to exist in 34 countries. The American government subsequently made it clear that states who failed to suppress terrorist organisations forfeited 'some of the normal advantages of sovereignty, including the right to be left alone inside your own territory' (Haass, 2002).

International cooperation to counter politically motivated violence is pursued at three levels. These are international treaties, actions undertaken by supranational bodies and bilateral arrangements concluded between individual states. International conventions have imposed obligations on the British government which have been translated into legislation including the 1974 Biological Weapons Act, the 1982 Aviation Security Act, and the 1982 Taking of Hostages Act. In 1977 the Council of Europe adopted a European Convention for the Suppression of Terrorism. This sought to ensure that extradition for certain actions (including kidnapping, hijacking and hostage-taking) would not be refused on the grounds that these crimes were considered to be political. However, article 13 retained the possibility to refuse such a request on these grounds and the effectiveness of this initiative was further impeded by the reluctance of a number of states to ratify and implement it (Wilkinson, 1986: 286).

The United Nations is a key agency for broadening the scope of international cooperation against political violence whose actions have included International Humanitarian Law (contained in the Hague Convention no. IV, 1907, the Geneva Conventions, 1949, and the Protocols additional to the Geneva Conventions, 1977). In 1972 an ad hoc committee on terrorism was set up to consider a coordinated policy to counter this form of violence but progress was thwarted by the fundamental political differences which existed between blocks of nations represented on that committee (Wardlaw, 1989: 107). Multilateral action has also been pursued by the Group of Seven (G7) summit meetings, consisting of Canada, France, Germany, Italy, Japan, the United Kingdom and America). In 1984 the London summit issued a declaration which listed a series of objectives designed to counter terrorism. This proposed closer coordination between the police, security organisations and other authorities (especially in the exchange of information, intelligence and technical knowledge) and expressed support for the expulsion of known terrorists from member countries, including those with diplomatic status.

Further policies directed against politically motivated violence have been pursued under the auspices of supranational organisations such as the European Union. In 1976 the TREVI group (Terrorism, Radicalism and International Violence) was established. This consisted of an annual meeting of ministers and more regular liaison between police and intelligence officers from member countries which aimed to improve and coordinate the European fight against politically motivated violence. This cooperation was subsequently enhanced by the development of measures which were collectively referred to as the 'third pillar of the European Union'. These included the 1995 and 1996 Conventions drawn up on the basis of Article K.3 of the Treaty on European Union on Simplified Extradition Procedure between the Member States of the European Union, framework decisions adopted under Article 34 of the Treaty on European Union on the execution in the European Union of orders freezing property or evidence, on joint investigation teams, or on combatting terrorism, and the Convention on Mutual Assistance in Criminal Matters between the Member States of the European Union, and the Protocol to that Convention, established in accordance with Article 34 of the Treaty on European Union. Following the 11 September attack in America, EU ministers attending an emergency summit meeting in Brussels agreed to enhance intelligence links with America by giving new powers to the police agency Europol and to harmonise police and judicial procedures in connection with search and arrest warrants.

Bilateral agreements exist between a number of countries including Britain and the Irish Republic. A particular difficulty with this arrangement has been the reluctance of Irish courts to extradite persons wanted in Britain for terrorist offences in the belief that the crime was political or that the accused would be denied a fair trial in Britain. Additionally, foreign governments may undertake actions helpful to the government of Great Britain in countering a terrorist threat. For example, in May 2001 the American government outlawed the Real IRA and froze its assets in the USA. It became illegal for American citizens to raise money for this organisation and visas for those belonging to the Real IRA or the Thirty-Two Counties Sovereignty Committee would henceforth be refused.

Chapter 7 discusses the role of MI5 in connection with terrorism. Intelligence is an important aspect of a state's response to terrorism whose effectiveness may be greatly enhanced by international cooperation against what is seen as a common enemy. In the western world this was historically viewed as the USSR. However, following the collapse of the Soviet Union, organisations using terror have become subject to international surveillance and fundamentalist Muslim groups have especially been targeted following the 11 September attacks in America. An important development in international intelligence cooperation is the Echelon electronic eavesdropping system which is based in Maryland, USA, but also operates from bases in Australia, New Zealand and Canada, and from GCHQ and the USA's National Security Agency facility in Menwith Hill, Yorkshire, in England. This system has the capacity to intercept all satellite communications (which include phone calls, faxes and e-mails) which are then scanned by computers for key words thus undermining the privacy of those sending such communications. The information gathered is passed to America's National Security Agency, which allegedly has the capacity to store enormous amounts of information on its computer storage system. Its ability to monitor organisations deemed to be subversive was evidenced in 2001 when President Bush allegedly offered to share the information gathered by this system to countries such as Spain who were combating terrorism. Some of the information may have been gathered by monitoring ETA communications originating from its command structure in the South of France.

Evaluation of the state's response

Terrorism requires governments to respond in order to defend the property and lives of their citizens. However, the nature of the response by liberal democratic states is a complex one as it is necessary for a balance to be struck between effective action to prevent violence and the need to avoid activities which threaten the fundamental freedoms associated with liberal democracy. This section considers the principles underpinning the response of a liberal democratic state to terrorism and the specific actions undertaken in Great Britain to deal with activities of this nature.

Reaction and overreaction

A particular concern of a government's response to a campaign of politically motivated violence is to avoid the twin dangers of underreaction and overreaction. A government must respond to a campaign of politically motivated violence especially when this is deployed indiscriminately. This response may include the use of public relations to convince the public that something is being done. In Britain the government's reaction to public outrage occasioned by the Birmingham bombings in 1974 was to pass a piece of legislation calculatedly entitled the *Prevention* of Terrorism Act. A government which adopts an approach to politically motivated violence which is widely seen as too soft may lose credibility. There is the further danger that a government which accedes to the demands of those who utilise this tactic may encourage its further use.

Alternatively, governments must avoid taking actions which are viewed as being too extreme. What is termed the 'hard line' response to terrorism involves governments making no concessions whatsoever to those who carry out violence, but this approach also embraces problems. The Brazilian urban guerrilla, Carlos Marighella, identified how politically motivated violence would succeed if it was able to provoke the government into overreaction. He stated that the aim of violence was to force those in power to transform the political situation of the country into a military one. This would alienate the population since 'the police networks, house searches, arrests of innocent people and of suspects, closing off streets, make life in the city unbearable' (Marighella, 1969: 40). Society would thus become polarised and an ever-increasing spiral of violence would occur in which the government and its opponents utilised force in response to each other's activities. Liberal democracy would be abandoned and the political conflict would become militarised. This tactic was utilised effectively by the Uruguayan urban guerrilla group, the *Tupamaros*. Their activities, conducted against the background of a declining economy, resulted in the abandonment of liberal democracy and the institution of a military regime in 1973. Thus governments need to avoid responses to politically motivated violence which might serve to legitimise the actions of its opponents, in particular in relation to oppressed minorities who might adopt a revolutionary posture in reaction to actions undertaken by the state which they deem to be oppressive (Walzer, 1970: 64).

Governments faced with a campaign of politically motivated violence also need to treat terrorist prisoners humanely and to ensure that they are sentenced appropriately. In order to pose as a defender of 'civilised values' a state must avoid the perception that it is intent on meting out vengeance rather than dispensing justice. In particular it must avoid the creation of martyrs (either as a consequence of state repression or as a deliberate act undertaken by political activists who seek to publicise a cause by causing harm to themselves) since these create support for a cause – 'they provide the basis of legend and so inspiration for others who will continue your resistance' (Elliott-Bateman, 1974: 324). The execution of republican leaders by the British following the 1916 Easter Rising inspired those who participated in the contemporary armed struggle waged by the IRA (Collins, 1998: 36–7) and the later death of Bobby Sands in 1981 boosted support both for the membership and political objectives of Northern Irish republican groups. Governments must also contemplate the effects of their actions on both internal and external opinion. Violence sponsored by the state against its political opponents may result in a propaganda war being lost at home or overseas. British actions undertaken in Northern Ireland to counter politically motivated violence since 1970 (such as interrogation and the alleged 'shoot to kill' policy) have come under the close scrutiny of the governments of the Irish Republic and America and have on occasions had an adverse effect on Britain's standing in the international community.

The response which a government adopts to restore social harmony when this is threatened by politically motivated violence should consist of both military and political dimensions. In particular it is necessary to pursue actions designed to isolate those who carry out acts of violence by seeking to shore up the 'middle ground', thereby preventing the polarisation of society around extreme political positions. Militarily this involves protecting the state and its citizens against physical attack while avoiding any tendency to overreaction by ensuring that the population consents to the measures which the government puts forward to combat violence. Politically it embraces reforms designed to secure or to reinforce the allegiance of significant sections of the population to the economic, political and social status quo.

The diminution of civil liberties

An important aspect of the response of a liberal democratic state to politically motivated violence concerns the extent to which liberal democratic freedoms are departed from. Any significant departure from liberal democratic standards of behaviour may alter the fundamental nature of the state and legitimise further acts of violence designed to overthrow it. Here the discussion is confined to anti-terrorist measures enacted since 1970. The implications of policies concerned with all forms of extra-parliamentary political activity are considered in the concluding chapter.

Criticisms of the prevention of terrorism legislation

The prevention of terrorism legislation was subject to a range of criticisms. One significant problem was that the Act (and subsequent anti-terrorist measures) applied to 'terrorism'. This was a nebulous term which might be utilised when there is insufficient evidence to bring a more specific charge (such as murder or manslaughter) against those suspected of involvement in acts of politically motivated violence. Although there was an understandable desire by the government to protect members of the public against these activities, the vagueness of the term makes it subject to abuse. It has been argued that the extended powers of arrest and detention given to the police in connection with the vaguely defined offence of terrorism resulted in 'fishing expeditions' to gather intelligence (Rose-Smith, 1979: 138). Persons were arrested, detained and questioned to enable the police to extend their information concerning republican activists and sympathisers. For this reason a relatively small percentage of those detained were charged with any offence under the legislation. According to the *Guardian* on 3 September 1993, between 1974 and March 1993, 7193 persons were detained under this measure. Of these only 3 per cent were subsequently charged with offences under the legislation, 5 per cent were charged with other offences and 4 per cent were excluded or deported.

A further erosion of civil liberties concerned the absence of adequate safeguards to protect the civil liberties of those who became subject to the provisions of the PTA. The main defence of civil liberties was provided through the process of annual review of the operations of the legislation. This was initially performed by Viscount Colville who was replaced by Mr J. Rowe, QC in 1994. Persons who were detained under the legislation were denied safeguards contained in the 1984 Police and Criminal Evidence Act, including lack of access to legal advice or contact with someone outside the police station. Adverse criticism was especially levelled against exclusion orders which were initially introduced in the PTA. These were labelled 'internal exile': a person whose freedom of movement was restricted in this manner was never shown the evidence upon which the decision to exclude was based, which handicapped any subsequent appeal. Additionally the PTA was criticised for the absence of judicial review for elongated periods of detention. The Home Secretary determined applications by the police to detain persons who had been in their custody for two days for a further period of up to five days. The ability of a minister to ban a political organisation was criticised as an attack on political rights. It was argued that the criteria used to ban an organisation were too subjective and could be utilised against those whose views were deemed 'offensive' by public opinion or against organisations whose aims conflicted with government policy (Scorer and Hewitt, 1981: 20–2, 64).

A further criticism was that the Prevention of Terrorism Act introduced a range of innovations that were subsequently extended to cover issues which were not originally the subject of the legislation and which were aimed at groups referred to in Chapter 2 which utilised direct action. The 1984 revision of the legislation, for example, introduced the 'international provisions' whereby powers related to arrest and detention became applicable to terrorism in general and were not specifically related to political violence associated with the politics of Northern Ireland. The 1989 Act made it an offence for international terrorists to canvass for funds or arms in Britain. Some of the provisions of this exceptional legislation became applied to 'normal' police work: the 1984 Police and Criminal Evidence Act, for example, made the seven-day period of detention applicable to any arrested person, and the 1994 Criminal Justice and Public Order Act allowed the police to mount roadblocks and stop and search without the safeguard of reasonable suspicion.

Finally, the ability of the media to scrutinise actions undertaken by the state was impeded by provisions which required journalists to disclose the sources of their information. Orders under the Prevention of Terrorism Act were first made in connection with a Channel 4 programme, *The Committee*, in 1992. The company was subsequently charged with contempt of court when it refused to obey the court and destroyed or sent abroad material connected with the programme. However, the courts do not consistently support government interventions in these matters, placing the onus on the police to prove that the material they request is of 'substantial' value to an investigation of terrorism.

Criticisms of the 1998 and 2000 Terrorism Acts

A number of criticisms were levelled against the 1998 Criminal Justice (Terrorism and Conspiracy) Act and the 2000 Terrorism Act. The chief ones included the placing of domestic groups within the scope of legislation in which the definition of terrorism was extended to violence against property as well as to persons. This meant that organisations such as the Animal Liberation Front and environmental activists who carried out direct action involving, for example, the destruction of genetically modified crops, henceforth became labelled as 'terrorist' and thus subject to a wide array of exceptional powers. This represented a significant reduction in the tactics which protesters were henceforth authorised to utilise in their opposition to the policies pursued by governments or commercial organisations and potentially eroded significantly the ability to protest which has been discussed in Chapter 2.

Criticism was also levelled at the new offences of conspiracy and incitement in relation to activities directed against foreign-based governments by individuals or organisations operating in Great Britain. The 1998 Act has been criticised for its uncritical support of foreign governments (particularly those in Algeria and Egypt). The absence of effective civil and political liberties in some foreign countries might compel its critics to use violence as a tactic to bring about political change but under the new legislation the British government was disposed to support established regimes in these circumstances. This legislation would, for example, have made it illegal for support in the United Kingdom to have been given to Nelson Mandela and the African National Congress (ANC) in its campaign of opposition to the apartheid regime in South Africa. It was also argued that making it an offence to possess any 'article' or 'information' in circumstances giving rise to reasonable suspicion that they would be used for the purposes of terrorism could have implications for journalists and that reversing the burden of proof in these (and other circumstances provided for in the legislation) constituted an erosion of civil liberties.

Those who promoted the 2000 Act, however, rejected arguments that it would be used to stifle legitimate protest and dissent in Great Britain and alleged that it improved the defence of civil and political liberties in comparison to the earlier temporary anti-terrorist measures. Thus the establishment of stop and search zones required ministerial approval, and the decision to permit the police to detain a suspected terrorist for more than 48 hours was wrested from ministers and instead given to a stipendiary magistrate or his or her equivalent. This latter change enabled Great Britain to comply with an earlier ruling of the European Court of Human Rights that the previous practice of extended detention contravened the European Convention of Human Rights which the government had ignored through the exercise of derogation. An appeal process was provided in connection with the proscribing of organisations, initially to the Secretary of State, thence to a Proscribed Organisation Appeal Commission and ultimately to the Court of Appeal. Additionally, organisations could only be proscribed following Parliamentary approval for this course of action. Initially 21 groups were proscribed under the 2000 Act in addition to 13 Northern Irish organisations which remained banned. Most of these new groups were Islamic.

Criticisms of the 2001 Anti-Terrorism, Crime and Security Act

A key criticism of the 2001 legislation was that responses to issues of national security were prejudicial to civil liberties. For example, powers related to the seizure, detention and forfeiture of cash on the grounds that it was to be used for the purposes of terrorism placed the onus on the accused to prove that their financial affairs were not of this nature, thus eroding the presumption of innocence until guilt could be proved. The Act also involved the sacrifice of human rights in connection with the introduction of powers to detain suspected foreign terrorists without trial. Aspects of the 1998 Human Rights Act (which is discussed in the concluding chapter) had to be reversed through the process of derogation in order to enable this provision to be introduced. The procedure adopted under this legislation meant that rather than charging persons with the crimes with which they were alleged to have been involved, they could be locked up without any clear evidence being produced against them and denied access to a proper trial. Those subject to this procedure were entitled to a bail hearing and, if this was unsuccessful, could present their case to a Special Immigration Appeal Commission. This, however, was a limited and partly secret process in which the detainee and his or her lawyer were not entitled to see all the evidence and from which they were excluded when the panel considered material deemed to be secret. The case against a detainee did not have to be proved beyond all reasonable doubt, the presumption of innocence did not apply and quality checks on the evidence were missing (Wadham, 2001).

Considerations of this kind prompted the Lord Chief Justice to suggest that the Act, which he regarded as a hastily-conceived short-term measure, should be repealed as soon as possible (Woolf, 2001).

Effectiveness

One historic difficulty with the state's response to terrorism has been the multiplicity of agencies involved in these operations. In the early 1990s, for example, the work of the anti-terrorist branch and special branch (which were under a unified command at Scotland Yard) in this area of activity was supplemented by special branches operating in each of England and Wales's 43 police forces, MI5, the Royal Ulster Constabulary and Army intelligence. This posed the danger of inter-agency rivalries and the possibility of one holding back information from another. This led to the proposal that a national counter-terrorism agency should be set up to coordinate the work of all bodies engaged in activities of this nature

(Annesley, 1992), and in 1992 (as is discussed in Chapter 7) the then Home Secretary, Kenneth Clarke, sought to improve coordination by giving MI5 the lead role in countering terrorism.

The effectiveness of anti-terrorist legislation has also been questioned. The initial Prevention of Terrorism Act was initially passed as a 'knee jerk' reaction to the Birmingham bombings in 1974 when it was important for the government to respond to public anger at these events. The title of the Act was, however, a misnomer: it did not prevent politically motivated violence between 1974 and the enactment of the 2000 Terrorism Act. Similarly the 1998 Act was described as 'an unnecessary panic measure or at best it was symbolic' (Walker, 1999). The effectiveness of other actions undertaken by governments have also been criticised. The broadcasting ban was undermined when television companies used actors' voices to mouth the words of spokespersons of organisations associated with politically motivated violence. The ban was lifted in 1994 following the first IRA ceasefire.

Conclusion

This chapter has discussed a number of general issues which relate to terrorism as the context for considering events of this nature which have occurred in Great Britain since 1970. The terrorist attacks which occurred in America on 11 September 2001 emphasised the contemporary importance of many of the considerations which were the focus of this chapter. These events illustrated the dramatic nature of terrorism which in this instance adopted the ideology of Islamic fundamentalism in an attempt to force onto the political agenda of western nations action to alleviate the plight of poor countries, epitomised by the long suffering endured by the Palestinian Arabs. These developing countries were denied access to any formal mechanism to voice their concerns which resulted in a 'feeling of impotence deriving from degradation and the failure to be heard or understood' (Pamuk, 2001). This action demonstrated the manner in which terrorism is designed to secure empowerment which may occur at two distinct levels.

First, it might be assumed that the deaths of thousands of innocent people occasioned by flying a number of aircraft at key targets in America would ensure that this country subsequently pursued positive measures to remedy the problems the world's poor. Second, empowerment took the form of allowing those who perceived themselves to be victims of American neglect to strike back at their perceived oppressor and thus feel morally uplifted. However, this second form of empowerment was temporary since in the wake of the 11 September attacks in America, an international coalition against terrorism was established which included former historic enemies such as America, Russia and Great Britain together with a number of Muslim states. An American-driven military campaign was subsequently launched and secured the overthrow of Afghanistan's Taliban government which was held responsible for harbouring the alleged architect of the events on 11 September, Osama Bin Laden and his al-Qaeda terrorist network. This military campaign took place without any significant attempts by western nations to seek a greater understanding of the roots of Islamic fundamentalism or to address the concerns which prompted the 11 September attack and thus evidenced that the first form of empowerment entailing a changed relationship between western nations and poorer countries (especially those in the Arab world) failed to occur. This suggests that although terrorism is often practised by groups who perceive that this is the only form of political expression left open to them, it does not necessarily secure their objectives, but may (at least in the short term) serve to marginalise them further.

The use of violence to secure political ends is not confined to the international stage and this chapter has provided examples of terrorism which have occurred in Great Britain since 1970. The following chapter continues with this theme of violence by considering the specific subject of racially motivated attacks which may, in the context of the discussion provided in this chapter, be considered as terrorist activities associated with those who identify with the extreme right of the political spectrum.

Glossary

Cell structure

Cell structures have been employed by many groups pursuing campaigns of political violence operating in urban areas. The Provisional IRA adopted this structure (in what were termed 'active service units') in Northern Ireland and on the streets of mainland Britain since the early 1980s, coinciding with Bobby Sands' hunger strike in 1981 and the use of the 'supergrass' policy by the security forces. A cell consisted of around four or five members one of whom was the quartermaster, one the intelligence officer and at least two were operators who carried out the bombings and shootings (Collins, 1998: 82–3). On the mainland this structure has involved the use of 'sleepers'. These were activists sent to Britain with no previous police record and who blended in with the local population awaiting the call to arms. The cell structure ensured that those called together to carry out a mission had little personal knowledge of each other. This was a defence against information leaks especially from informants (Toolis, 1995: 206) and prevented those who were captured and subsequently interrogated being in a position to reveal details concerning the full membership of a group. The Real IRA subsequently adopted this form of organisation. Cells concentrate on the military struggle rather than on promotional strategies to recruit new activists and often practise a high degree of autonomy. This may, however, be at the expense of the centralised coordination of guerrilla activities, although the ability of groups such as the Provisional

IRA to order truces which are then adhered to by their members suggested that cell structures were subject to central control.

Guerrilla warfare

Individuals and groups engaging in acts of violence to further a political cause often dispute the use of the term 'terrorist' in relationship to their activities. They may more readily identify themselves as guerrilla movements. The distinction between 'terrorism' and 'guerrilla warfare' is hard to delineate precisely. Terrorists do not seek a military victory (Clinton, 2001) and additionally guerrilla movements often fight in accordance with the conventions of war (Wilkinson, 1974: 80) perhaps taking or exchanging prisoners. Terrorists do not do this and their violence is characterised by 'indiscriminateness, inhumanity, arbitrariness and barbarity' (Wilkinson, 1986: 56). A further distinction which may be drawn between guerrilla movements and terrorism is the extent to which violence is utilised in conjunction with other tactics to achieve a political objective. Individuals and organisations may be considered as 'terrorist' when intimidatory violence is pursued to the almost total neglect of other activities and may appear almost as an end in itself. Attempts have been made to justify violence of this nature. Frantz Fanon argued that violence elevated the self-esteem of a downtrodden person and was important both collectively and individually. At the collective level it mobilised the masses and unified the people. At the individual level it was viewed as 'a cleansing force' which 'frees the native from his inferiority complex and from his despair and inaction; it makes him fearless and restores his self respect' (Fanon, 1961: 73–4). This heightened sense of self-esteem would form the basis of bolder revolutionary acts.

Rural guerrilla movements

Rural guerrilla movements are modelled on the success of Mao Tse-Tung in China who utilised this form of warfare as one aspect of the revolutionary struggle. Mao sought to build a revolution through the mass participation and support of the peasantry in which the cities would eventually be encircled by the countryside. Thus what was termed 'phase 1' of the revolutionary war was particularly concerned with persuading as many people as possible to commit themselves to the cause (Griffith, 1978: 18). Rural guerrilla organisations utilise the advantages of a rural terrain to openly exercise freedom of movement in isolated areas which effectively become 'liberated zones' controlled by the guerrillas. Their tactics are particularly directed at those whose operations are deemed essential to the effective functioning of the state. The 1919–21 Irish war of independence witnessed the IRA targeting members of the Royal Irish Constabulary in an attempt to drive the British from Ireland. Between January 1919 and October 1920, 109 police officers were assassinated and a further 174 were injured by the IRA, 484 unoccupied police barracks were destroyed and 2861 armed raids were made, mainly on police stations (Bowden, 1974: 226). The methods of violence are usually those of 'hit and run' enabling the guerrillas to utilise their mobility to their advantage.

Terrorism

Terrorism is a difficult term to define or to differentiate precisely from other forms of political activity ranging from direct action to conventional warfare. It has been described as 'the use of physical force in order to damage a political adversary' (della Porta, 1995: 2). The British Prevention of Terrorism Act (which was originally introduced in 1974) defined the term as 'the use of violence for political ends and includes any use of violence for the purpose of putting the public or any section of it in fear'. However, the emphasis placed on intimidation in this definition could equally be applied to states engaged in conventional warfare which may utilise tactics such as the saturation bombing of civilian populations to advance their cause. This suggests that terrorism is a subjective term whose usage is primarily determined by one's political perspective: one person's terrorist is another person's freedom fighter. The label 'terrorist' is frequently applied pejoratively – it is 'the label used by the threatened' (Morris and Hoe, 1982: 22). However, a distinguishing feature of terrorism from other forms of warfare is that it does not challenge the state directly by seeking a head-on battle with the police or army (Walzer, 1970: 64). Recognising their weakness (in areas such as technology, military or economic power), terrorists alternatively seek to attain their ends by intimidating the public and utilising violence which is not constrained by the conventions of war.

Urban guerrilla movements

Unlike rural guerrilla warfare, urban guerrilla warfare views revolution as an activity advanced by military tactics performed by a relatively small group of activists. The urban terrain makes it difficult for these groups to operate openly and they thus adopt alternative organisational models. Some form of cell structure has frequently been utilised by urban guerrilla movements. A greater variety of tactics are utilised by urban guerrilla movements, which include violence directed against the population in general rather than specifically targeting those deemed essential to the operation of the state. For these reasons it has been argued that urban guerrilla warfare has a far higher 'terrorism potential' than other forms of unconventional warfare (Wilkinson, 1986: 59).

References

Sir H. Annesley (1992) speech to the Police Foundation, Guildhall, London, 22 July
A. Arblaster (1977) 'Terrorism, Myths, Meaning and Morals', *Political Studies*, 25(3), 413–24

T. Blair (2001) statement in the wake of the terrorist incidents in America, 11 September, BBC television

T. Bowden (1974) *Revolt to Revolution* (Manchester: Manchester University Press)

T. Bowden (1977) *Breakdown of Public Security: the Case of Ireland 1916–1921 and Palestine 1936–1939* (London: Sage)

M. Bright (2002) 'Look Back in Anger', *Observer Magazine*, 3 February, 17–22

M. Burton (1997) *Violence Explained* (Manchester: Manchester University Press)

G. Carr (1975) *The Angry Brigade: a History of Britain's First Urban Guerrilla Group* (London: Victor Gollancz)

S. Cobler (1978) *Law, Order and Politics in West Germany* (Harmondsworth: Penguin)

E. Collins (1998) *Killing Rage* (London: Granta Books, 2nd edition)

T. Coogan (1980) *The I.R.A.* (London: Fontana)

B. Clinton (2001) 'The Struggle for the Soul of the Twenty-First Century', the Dimbleby Lecture, BBC1, 16 December

G. Davidson Smith (1990) *Combating Terrorism* (London: Routledge)

C. Dobson and R. Payne (1979) *The Weapons of Terror: International Terrorism at Work* (London: Macmillan)

M. Elliott-Bateman (1974) *Revolt to Revolution* (Manchester: Manchester University Press)

F. Fanon (1982) *The Wretched of the Earth* (Harmondsworth: Penguin, first published 1961)

J. Goodall (1971) *In the Shadow of Man* (London: Collins)

F. Gregory (1976) *Protest and Violence, the Police Response: a Comparative Analysis of Democratic Methods* (London: Institute for the Study of Conflict, *Conflict Studies* No. 75)

S. Griffith II (1978) *Mao Tse-Tung on Guerrilla Warfare* (New York: Anchor Books)

A. Guelke (1999) 'Political Violence and the Paramilitaries', in P. Mitchell and R. Wilford (eds) *Politics in Northern Ireland* (Oxford: Westview Press)

R. Haass (2002) quoted in *Guardian*, 2 April

B. Hoffmann (1995) 'Holy Terror: the Implications of Terrorism Motivated by a Religious Imperative', *Studies in Conflict and Terror*, 18

Home Office (1999) *Statistics on the Operation of Prevention of Terrorism Legislation: Great Britain 1998* (London: Home Office Research, Development and Statistics Directorate, Home Office Statistical Bulletin, Issue 3/99)

Rt. Hon. Earl Jellicoe (1983) *Review of the Prevention of Terrorism (Temporary Provisions) Act, 1976* (London: HMSO, Cmnd 8803)

M. Keith (1993) *Race, Riots and Policing: Lore, and Disorder in a Multi-Racial Society* (London: UCL Press)

C. Kennedy-Pipe (1997) *The Origins of the Present Troubles in Northern Ireland* (Harlow: Longman)

C. Marighella (1969) 'The Minimanual of the Urban Guerrilla', published as an appendix in R. Moss, *Urban Guerrilla Warfare* (London: International Institute for Strategic Studies, 1976)

H. McDonald (1999) 'Boy Soldiers Recruited by Real IRA', *Observer*, 24 October

E. Morris and A. Hoe (1987) *Terrorism, Threat and Response* (Basingstoke: Macmillan Press – now Palgrave Macmillan)

O. Pamuk (2001) 'Listen to the Damned', *Guardian*, 29 September

D. della Porta (1995) *Social Movements, Political Violence and the State* (Cambridge: Cambridge University Press)

B. Rose-Smith (1979) 'Police Powers and Terrorism Legislation', in P Hain (ed.) *Policing the Police*, Volume 1 (London: John Calder)

R. Ryder (1975) *Victims of Science: the Use of Animals in Research* (London: Davis-Poynter)

C. Scorer and P. Hewitt (1981) *The Prevention of Terrorism Act – the Case for Repeal* (London: National Council for Civil Liberties)

J. Seabrook (2002) *Freedom Unfinished, Fundamentalism and Popular Resistance in Bangladesh Today* (London: Zed Books)

P. Singer (1976) *Animal Liberation: Towards an End of Man's Inhumanity to Animals* (London: Jonathan Cape)

K. Toolis (1995) *Rebel Hearts: Journeys within the IRA's Soul* (London: Picador)

J. Wadham (2001) 'Detention under Anti-Terror Act "Utterly Unjust"', www.liberty-human-right.org.uk, 19 December

C. Walker (1986) *The Prevention of Terrorism in British Law* (Manchester: Manchester University Press)

C. Walker (1999) *Current Law Statutes* (London: Sweet and Maxwell, Volume 2, 1998, c. 40)

M. Walzer (1970) *Obligation – Essays on Disobedience, War and Citizenship* (Cambridge, Massachusetts: Harvard University Press)

G. Wardlaw (1989) *Political Terrorism: Theory, Tactics and Counter Measures* (Cambridge: Cambridge University Press, 2nd edition)

P. Wilkinson (1974) *Political Terrorism* (London: Macmillan)

P. Wilkinson (1986) *Terrorism and the Liberal State* (Basingstoke: Macmillan, 2nd edition)

S. Witchert (1991) *Northern Ireland Since 1945* (Harlow: Longman)

Lord Woolf (2001) statement on 31 December 2000, quoted in *The Times*, 1 January 2002

6
Racial Violence

The previous chapter examined the subject of terrorism, defined by the 1974 Prevention of Terrorism Act as 'the use of violence for political ends'. This chapter continues with the theme of politically motivated violence and considers racially motivated attacks as an extra-parliamentary tactic used by those on the extreme right of the political spectrum. The objective in carrying out (or giving legitimacy to) actions of this kind is to further the political objective of destroying a multiracial society. Racially motivated violence furthers this objective either by driving minority ethnic groups out of Great Britain entirely or by serving to create a society which is segregated on racial lines. The nature and rationale of racist violence is discussed and the response of the state to this problem is analysed. Particular attention is devoted to the police service. Perceptions that racial violence was not treated with the seriousness which it merited formed the basis for reforms additional to those proposed by Lord Scarman in 1981 (and discussed in Chapter 4) to improve the relationships between the police service and minority ethnic communities.

Introduction

Racially motivated violence is underpinned by *racism*. This constitutes a denial of humanity to those who are its victims and involves regarding such persons as belonging to an entirely different, subordinate species (Parekh, 1974: 238). The rhetoric of racism frequently downgrades humans to animals or vermin. The denial by one group of another's humanity provides a climate in which violence ranging from genocide to racial attacks will occur and in which *racial prejudice* and *racial discrimination* will be encountered. Racially motivated violence constitutes a most serious threat to social harmony since 'an assault motivated by racism is more socially divisive than any other assault, and if allowed to pass unchecked will begin to corrode the fabric of our tolerant society' (Home Affairs Committee, 1994: 27–8). Historically the victims of such attacks were Jewish people who have continued to be subject to violence directed at communal property such as cemeteries and synagogues, unprovoked assaults and the receipt of anti-Semitic literature.

Members of minority ethnic communities have frequently been subject to various forms of racially motivated violence since 1970, ranging from verbal abuse and incivility to physical attacks on themselves and their property. Racial harassment may be targeted at individuals who become subject to a sustained campaign of intimidation carried out by hostile neighbours or locals (thereby transforming what might appear as routine low-level abuse into something which places a devastating burden of stress on victims) (Beider, 1999), although violence is also randomly directed at individuals. These attacks are inflicted upon individuals or groups purely because of their colour, race, nationality or ethnic and national origins (CRE, 1987: 8) and must be understood in the context of unequal power relationships between white and black people. They challenge the right of ethnic minorities to live in Great Britain, have an adverse effect on the dignity of the person who is subject to them (Holdaway, 1996: 46–7) and constitute a source of 'continual unremitting humiliation' to those who are victim to such actions (Dholakia and Price-Jones, 1993: 6). This situation frequently results in black people being unable, or too scared, to leave their homes, in which they exist as virtual prisoners.

Serious racial violence directed at minority ethnic groups first occurred in the post-war period in 1958 when whites went on the rampage in Nottingham and the Notting Hill district of London and attacked any black person they came into contact with. These events culminated in the racist murder of Kelso Cochrane in Notting Hill in 1959. A severe outbreak of racial violence directed at Asian people took place in Southall in the 1970s (Vogler, 1991: 126), and in East London a report referred to the 'unrelating battery of Asian people and their property' and a 'barrage of harassment, insult and intimidation' to which people were subjected (Bethnal Green and Stepney Trades Council, 1978: 3). Racial attacks have involved gangs of white people indiscriminately attacking blacks, resulting in serious injuries to the victims. The phenomenon described as 'paki bashing' was especially directed at the Bangladeshi community in the East End of London. A number of murders have been committed. These include two Bengali workers who were stabbed to death in 1965 in Newham, the murder of Gurdip Singh Chaggar at Southall in 1976, and the murders of Akhtar Ali Baig in 1980 and Fiaz Mirza and Stephen Lawrence in 1993. The implications of this latter killing and the response of the Metropolitan Police Service to it are discussed in greater detail below.

In 1981 a study estimated that there were 7000 racially motivated incidents reported to police forces in England and Wales in one year and that Asians were 50 times and West Indians 36 times more likely to be victims of such attacks than were white people (Home Office, 1981: 10–11). It was reported that the number of incidents of racial violence reported to the police in England and Wales had risen from 5900 in 1985 to 7734 in 1992 and that for the year 1992–93 such incidents totalled 9762 (Maclean, 1994) rising to 11,878 in the year ending March 1995. Official figures, however, were believed to provide an inaccurate picture of the problem as racial attacks were frequently not reported and many of these were not recorded by the police: one study combining data from the 1988 and 1992 British Crime Survey suggested that Indians were most likely to report racially motivated incidents to the police and African-Caribbeans and Pakistanis were less inclined to report them (Fitzgerald and Hale, 1996: 1). Under-reporting and non-recording has meant that official estimates of the extent of racially motivated violence may greatly underestimate the scale of the problem: one estimate based on a victimisation survey suggested that there were 130,000 racially motivated crimes committed against South Asians and African-Caribbeans in 1991 (Aye Maung and Mirrlees-Black, 1994: 18–19), rising to 143,000 in 1995 (Percy, 1998). It has been suggested that the main reason why minority ethnic groups are likely to be the victims of serious crimes and threats is 'their age structure, their socio-economic characteristics and the type of area they live in' (Fitzgerald and Hale, 1996: 1).

Racist political organisations: their views and support

Those who commit acts of racial violence 'are of all ages ... both male and female, and they often act together, as groups of friends or as families. Some perpetrators may also be involved in other anti-social (non-racial) acts, violence towards other groups or individuals, or crime more generally.' The views of the perpetrators were stated to be shared by the wider communities to which they belonged, which perpetrators saw as legitimising their behaviour. This suggested that the views of the community needed to be addressed in efforts to reduce racial harassment. Expressions of racism were stated often to serve to distract the attention of perpetrators, potential perpetrators and other individuals within the community away from real, underlying concerns which they felt impotent to deal with. These factors included a lack of identity, insecurity about the future and physical and/or mental health problems. Stress, delinquency and criminality were identified as factors which were likely to facilitate racial prejudice (Sibbitt, 1997: vii–viii). The electoral appeal of parties on the extreme right is discussed in greater detail below.

Unlike other forms of extra-parliamentary political activity, racism is frequently articulated by established political parties whose sentiments provide a breeding ground (and perverted legitimacy) for acts of racial violence which may be viewed as a form of direct action to advance the cause of racism. Chapter 4 has discussed allegations of racist conduct by Britain's three major political parties. This section briefly examines those minor parties which place race at the very heart of their political agenda and in so doing serve to stimulate racial violence, giving a perverted form of legitimacy to those who carry it out.

The National Front

The National Front was formed in 1967 following the fusion of a number of groups on the extreme right wing of the political spectrum. These included the League of Empire Loyalists and the British National Party who were supported by some members of the Racial Preservation Society. Later in 1967 these were joined by the Greater Britain Movement which brought into the National Front members who were to become leading activists (including Martin Webster and John Tyndall). The party contested its first by-election in 1968 at Acton and in 1973 gained 16 per cent of the poll at West Bromwich. It secured several good results in local government elections after the second 1974 general election but declined towards the end of that decade. For several years in the 1970s, however, the National Front posed a significant threat to the urban support of the main political parties although it never succeeded in getting any of its candidates elected to local or national political office. Its chief political impact was to force the issue of race onto the political agenda.

The main plank of the National Front's programme was to end immigration and initiate a programme of repatriation. The party blamed the problems faced by contemporary urban society (such as poor housing, low employment prospects and the strains placed on the welfare state) on those who came to Britain from the new Commonwealth countries. Additionally the party placed itself at the forefront of a defence of Britain's national identity by decrying attempts by governments of both parties to foster assimilation, one of whose consequences was depicted as mixed marriages. The 1966 general election, however, evidenced an apparent decline in popular support for racism. Labour recaptured Smethwick (an episode which is discussed in Chapter 4) while Enoch Powell's majority was reduced in SW Wolverhampton.

These considerations, coupled with a toughening Conservative stance on immigration, led the National Front to adopt a populist stance. The party depicted itself as the standard bearer for the views of 'ordinary' members of the general public which were allegedly being ignored by the major political parties said to be dominated by 'unrepresentative liberals'. The National Front argued that this resulted in policies such as immigration, the abolition of capital punishment and abortion (Walker, 1977: 133–77). This populist stance permitted the National Front to expand the scope of its policies by emphasising the alleged manner in which 'ordinary' people suffered as the result of immigration about which they had not been consulted: urban crime, blamed on black youths, was emphasised in this respect. Additionally, the National Front moved into new policy areas by opposing the Common

Market and the power of multinational corporations which were allegedly driven by considerations which were prejudicial to the interests of the working class or those engaged in small business enterprises.

The populist stance of the National Front enabled it to serve as the vehicle for a 'moral backlash'. Citizens who were concerned that society was moving in directions over which they had no control and in ways they disliked thus hankered for a return to the past. They were susceptible to the appeal of a party which pledged to listen to ordinary people and to display effective leadership in restoring 'traditional' ways of life and standards of moral behaviour which were depicted as values upon which Britain's prior greatness had been based. The scapegoating of immigrants was of crucial importance to the National Front as it provided a specific social category upon which to hang the more general concerns affecting the direction in which society was perceived to be moving. The prior existence of racial prejudice made it possible to depict immigrants and their descendants as the source of all unpopular manifestations of social change including the changing character of neighbourhoods and the lack of opportunity affecting some sections of society. Racism also elevated the self-esteem of disadvantaged white people by providing a group which they could 'look down on'.

The National Front further sought to benefit from the economic and political climate of the early 1970s. The extent of industrial unrest (which is discussed in Chapter 3) and the indecisive results of the two 1974 general elections led to calls for a 'government of national unity'. The National Front depicted itself as a movement which could mobilise the support of all classes and political parties and provide firm and effective leadership which would 'save the nation'. In this sense it was able to portray itself not as a political party but as a movement which would serve as a rallying point to save the nation from decline and secure regeneration.

By the end of the 1970s, however, the appeal of the National Front was waning. Several factors contributed to this situation, the first of which was the mobilisation of opposition to what was depicted as a fascist movement by organisations such as the Anti-Nazi League. This was established in 1977 by the Socialist Workers' Party. Its tactics included protest marches, public meetings and rock concerts. It waned with the virtual demise of the National Front but was re-formed in 1992 to respond to the emergence of the British National Party. In 1991 a new organisation, the Anti-Racist Alliance, was formed mainly by black political activists who had been working in the Labour Party. Opposition of a more violent kind has also been mounted by the Anti-Fascist Alliance which was formed in 1985 to confront the BNP both ideologically and physically. One of its 'successes' was to prevent hundreds of skinheads attending a gig by a neo-Nazi group, Skrewdriver, in 1992. Confrontational opposition to the extreme right has also been waged by anarchist groups such as Class War in connection with violence associated with the extreme right at football matches.

Other factors which influenced the decline of the National Front included the nature of its support. Some of its appeal, particularly in the 1974 general elections, had been as a protest vote, which cannot provide a political party with a durable basis of electoral strength (Steed, 1974: 336). Although the National Front succeeded in attracting some trade unionists (including some postal workers at London's Mount Pleasant sorting office) it failed to make any substantial impact on class loyalty which although in decline (Franklin, 1985) remained an important underpinning of the support obtained by both main political parties. The election of Margaret Thatcher as Conservative leader in 1975 resulted in a more pronounced emphasis on issues such as law and order and a less liberal attitude towards immigration which tended to lessen the appeal of the National Front. Internal divisions, often based on personality rather than policy, occurred: successive leaders Chesterton and O'Brien resigned from the party in 1971 and 1972 respectively and in 1975 a further chairman, Kingsley-Read, left and formed the National Party which secured some limited local successes especially in Blackburn. In 1995 this latter party was renamed the National Democrats. In 2001 it was estimated that the National Front had a membership of around 300. Urban disorder in several towns in Northern England in 2001, however, caused this organisation to heighten its activities, seeking to plan racist marches in order to provoke British Asians into violence (Harris, 2001).

The British National Party (BNP)

The British National Party was formed in 1982 following a split within the National Front. Its policies are racist and anti-Semitic. Initially it called for the repatriation of minority ethnic groups and distributed anti-Semitic literature which included the *Holocaust News*. At the 1994 local elections it called for the repeal of all race relations laws and made a facetious demand for the legalisation of golliwogs (Skellington, 1996: 239). The party won a local authority by-election in Tower Hamlets in 1993 and the following year saved a deposit in a Parliamentary by-election at Dagenham. BNP policies subsequently articulated an anti-Muslim message, one reason for this being that targeting minorities on grounds of religion is less likely to pose the party difficulties in connection with race relations legislation (Oldham Independent Review, 2001: 45). This stance was also designed to enable them to profit from perceived anti-Muslim sentiments following the 1990 Gulf War and the September 11 attacks in America which are discussed in Chapter 5. The pragmatic nature of this aspect of BNP policy was demonstrated in 2002 when leading members of Bradford's Sikh and Hindu communities were sent recruiting videos urging them to join with the BNP in a campaign directed at what was depicted as a common enemy, Islam. The BNP expresses support for intensified racial segregation (which is blamed on Muslim communities having high birth rates with the consequent need for communal living space) rather than the policy of compulsory repatriation of all non-whites (although they endorse a policy of voluntary repatriation) and brands Islam as an aggressive religion.

The *Guardian* on 12 February 1994 estimated that the membership of the BNP was 2000. Its sources of funding include aid from American racist extremists. The party's main objective is targeted at winning representation on local authorities rather than in Parliament. At the 2001 general election the BNP polled 47,225 votes, and won three seats in Burnley in the 2002 local elections. It depicts itself as the champion of the white working class which perceives itself to have been neglected by new Labour and whose disenchantment makes them susceptible to the articulation of racism (alleging, for example, preferential treatment given to racial minorities).

Other groups on the far right

Other organisations on the far right of the political spectrum include Combat 18 which was formed in 1992 (although a similar organisation, Column 88, existed in the 1960s) and has been associated with acts of violence against racial minorities which seek to spark 'tit for tat' violence resulting in intensified residential segregation. Combat 18 was initially formed to guard BNP meetings but the relationship between the organisations became less close in the 1990s. The BNP proscribed Combat 18 in 1994 in order to sustain its image as a political party rather than a street gang and because the party officially condemns violence. A more recent organisation, the Order of White Knights, was established in response to riots in 2001. Membership is limited to those with a track record in carrying out acts of racial violence, thereby making police infiltration difficult.

The tactics of the far right

The contemporary tactics of the far right include that of inciting racial minorities into committing acts of violence which result in minority communities and the police becoming involved in street violence. A deliberate attempt to provoke violence resulted in the riot at Southall in 1981 and the tactic was further developed in 2001 by the National Front and Combat 18. It involved gathering in city centres or staging (or threatening to hold) rallies which tied up the police while smaller groups of extremists launched raids on Asian people and their property. The aim of this action (which was most successful in places where there was a pre-history of tensions between whites and minority ethnic communities) (Lowles, 2001: 319) was to provoke Asian people into retaliation (Harris, 2001). Groups on the extreme right then withdraw, leaving the police to battle with Asians and bringing public disapproval on the latter community. The ability of the incitement of violence to achieve the extreme right's political ends was apparent in the results obtained by the British National Party in Oldham's two Parliamentary constituencies in the 2001 general election. In total the BNP polled in excess of 11,000 votes and in one constituency the party leader obtained 16 per cent of the poll.

The extreme right has also been linked to additional forms of disorderly activities. These include football hooliganism, most notably the riot which caused the abandonment of the international match between England and Ireland at Lansdowne Road, Dublin in February 1995. This was allegedly provoked by Combat 18 and other extremist right-wing groups, and after this event Scotland Yard established a special unit to tackle neo-Nazi groups. The connection between the extreme right and football hooliganism seemed justified following police seizures of racist and hooligan literature undertaken in Operation Harvest in 1996. This was designed to tackle potential disruption to the Euro '96 football competition.

The environment underpinning racist violence

Racial violence occurs within a climate which is directly or indirectly supportive of this activity. This section briefly examines explanations put forward to account for the existence of racism in contemporary society which provides an environment which both nurtures and legitimises racial violence.

Racism and the colonial heritage

One explanation of racism is that it must be understood in historical terms: it emerged as the result of the 'dramatic historical encounter between the white and black man in a colonial context' (Parekh, 1974: 239) when it was perceived by white colonisers that it was the divine duty of the Anglo-Saxon race to rule and civilise the world (Bowling and Phillips, 2002: 3). These sentiments provided the underpinnings for the subsequent development of a racist society. Countries of 'the new Commonwealth' had been subjected to occupation and colonial rule during the nineteenth century. This entailed the economies of these countries becoming subservient to the requirements of the imperial power. Economic control was reinforced by cultural domination which alleged that the conquered peoples were backward and would benefit greatly from their association with the British Empire whose advantages included the Christian religion and education. Those who were colonised were constrained to abandon their culture and adopt that of the colonised country – 'the colonised is elevated above his jungle status in proportion to his adoption of the mother country's cultural standards. He becomes whiter as he renounces his blackness' (Fanon, 1952: 18). The right to exert control over conquered people was further justified by social Darwinism and by biological and genetic theories which asserted the superiority of the white race. The perception thus arose that black people were inferior to whites. The subsequent teaching of history in schools glorifying the Empire further reinforced negative images of black people. Those who came to the United Kingdom after 1948 (when the ship, *Empire Windrush*, brought the first African-Caribbean migrants to Britain) were thus subject to sentiments which had been nurtured in literature and history for many decades and passed on almost unquestioningly from one generation to the next, giving rise to a racist culture.

The colonial heritage had an additional consequence for those who entered Great Britain as immigrants. Colonial societies contained numerous tensions. Settlers and natives competed for jobs and land while conquered or enslaved people occasionally rose in revolt. These conflicts affected the attitudes and conduct of both British people and immigrants. British history portrayed these tensions in terms which were derogatory to black people. They were often depicted as heathen savages who wantonly massacred white people who came to live in their lands. Such events suggested to white people that black people were uncivilised, whereas to black people they signified the lack of social justice and a heritage of exploitation suffered at the hands of greedy, usurping whites. Immigration resulted in pre-existing tensions of this kind being translated to the United Kingdom.

Psychological explanations of racism

The extent to which the prejudice of an individual can be solely attributed to the existence of a racist culture has not, however, been universally accepted. All societies contain people who are racially prejudiced and others who are not. This may suggest that the source of prejudice resides in the personality of the individual rather than with the operations of society and the processes of socialisation. One theory suggested that an individual's failure to achieve satisfaction may result in frustration which leads to aggression. Although this anger should be directed at those responsible for such frustration it could be targeted at a scapegoat rather than the genuine source of the individual's problems if the former course of action was impractical (Dollard, 1939). This theory was used as an explanation of white racism in the American Deep South (Dollard, 1957). However, it does not sufficiently explain why aggression assumes a racial form nor does it take into account the extent to which the development of the human personality may be influenced by the social system.

It has been further argued that the theory of frustration and aggression provides a better explanation for oppressed groups rising in revolt rather than accounting for the display of violent conduct towards them (Rex, 1986: 107). Research associated with the Frankfurt School of Critical Theory asserted that racism was a consequence of an authoritarian personality. A measurement was devised to indicate willingness to submit to a form of rigid authority coupled with aggression against those who rejected this. Persons who scored highly on this 'F-scale' were assessed as being likely to display anti-Semitism and racial prejudice (Adorno, 1950). Those with such personalities were, however, in a minority and this theory did not explain the relatively widespread extent of racism which was asserted to exist at that time within American society.

Marxist explanations of racism

Sociological interest in race and ethnicity was closely associated with the analysis of urban development associated with Robert Park and the Chicago School (Rowe, 1998: 21). Marx applied the term 'class' solely to the relationships arising in the labour market. Class membership was determined by an individual's relationship to the means of production. Later sociologists inspired by Weber applied the term more widely, discerning a variety of markets and a wide range of resultant class situations. A class was defined as a number of individuals who shared a particular market situation. Conflict arose between classes when one sought to promote its own interests at the expense of others. According to this argument, people who came to Britain from new Commonwealth countries entered into an existing situation of conflict which was played out in the arena of the city. The competition for space which led groups to compete for housing resources was one important source of conflict between indigenous whites and black immigrants. Particular attention was drawn to the existence of five 'housing classes' which involved differential access to housing provision, creating a hierarchy of class situations which provided the basis for conflict between groups located in different market situations (Rex and Moore, 1967: 36–8). Conflict over housing resources was viewed as one of a number of factors which helped to explain the character of racial encounters in the city. Latterly this form of competition involved other areas, including local government resources, welfare benefits and jobs. Immigration did not cause these social tensions but served to aggravate existing conflicts.

What has been termed the 'sociology of race relations' studies was subsequently challenged by Marxist approaches. Whereas it had formerly focused on highlighting conditions where the various races came into conflict and suggested means to alleviate this, Marxist approaches 'problematise the concept of "race" and seek to explain it critically in a socio-economic context', viewing 'race' as dependent on more fundamental class relations (Rowe, 1998: 21–2, 46). There are, however, considerable differences within Marxism concerning the explanations of race and racism. What has been termed the 'classical Marxist approach' (Rowe, 1998: 23) asserted that racial identities and prejudices were deliberately constructed 'proletarian–bourgeois relations' (Cox, 1948: 336) which could be understood only by reference to the economic relations that existed within capitalist societies. Capitalism relies on the exploitation of labour which depends upon the guaranteed existence of an abundant supply of this commodity coupled with mechanisms to ensure that class conflict can be resolved before it assumes revolutionary proportions.

Immigration was initially designed to secure the abundance of unskilled and semi-skilled labour. Racial prejudice directed at immigrants and their descendants impeded their social mobility and thus ensured that they would continue to perform menial jobs. These were the original members of Britain's underclass (a term which is considered in greater detail in Chapter 4) who were deprived of a range of social rights including adequate employment, housing and education opportunities (Rex and Tomlinson, 1979: 328). Racial prejudice further impaired the development of class consciousness. Problems such as low wages or scarcity of employment resulted in the working class fighting itself on racial lines rather than pooling resources against those who benefited from an economic system which perpetuated social injustice. This aspect of Marxist analysis thus asserted that the bourgeoisie deliberately nurtured racial prejudice in order to justify exploitation and divide the proletariat (Cox, 1948).

Alternatively, the migrant labour model emphasised the processes by which social life became racialised. Its focus was the entry and reception of black people into Britain after 1945 (Phizacklea and Miles, 1980) and sought to explain why migrants from Britain's former colonies were confronted by racism and how this was subsequently maintained. The prior existence of racial prejudice derived from colonialism which depicted black people in a negative light and ensured that newly-arrived immigrants became scapegoats for an urban social setting based upon injustices derived from the unequal distribution of material resources throughout society. Public expenditure cuts affecting employment and the social and welfare services after 1979 tended to intensify the level of prejudice and discrimination directed against those who were blamed for the problems affecting large numbers of the urban working class. This approach accepted that race is expressed through spheres other than the economic, although it accorded a dominant influence to the economic dimension, viewing class relations as the determinant of others. Racism and exclusionary practices were seen as 'a component part of a wider structure of class disadvantage and exclusion' (Miles, 1989: 9). Finally, the relative autonomy model argued that race had a certain autonomy and that there was no simple and consistent pattern between racism and the broader social relationships of capitalism. Attention has been particularly drawn to the local and spatial context within which it arises (Solomos and Back, 1995).

The state's response to racial violence

It is necessary for the state to intervene and counter racial violence in order to fulfil its role of preserving the most fundamental human right of its citizens, the right to life. This section considers the responses which have been initiated to deal with this problem since 1970.

Legislation concerning racial attacks

One potential response to racially motivated violence is to create a specific offence to outlaw activities of this kind. This section briefly assesses the rationale for acting in this manner and the problems it embraces. It also refers to the main legislative developments which took place in the 1990s.

The main argument in favour of the introduction of specific legislation to deal with racial violence was the inadequate protection afforded to those who were subject to it. Although incidents of racial attacks on whites have occurred (including the murder of Richard Everitt by Bengali youths in North London in 1994), black and Asian people are the main target of such violence. One remedy, the use of civil law in connection with issues such as harassment and violence, is often not an appropriate response to a serious problem of this nature. Further, existing criminal law was often subject to interpretation which, coupled with the lenient sentences sometimes given to those found guilty of offences of racial violence, failed to deter racial misconduct. A specific offence of racial violence would serve a useful declaratory purpose, informing the police, courts and the general public of the commitment by the government and Parliament to eradicate this social problem and would also make it possible to monitor the precise extent of this activity.

There was, however, opposition to the introduction of a 'hate crime' to cater for racial violence. It was argued to be unnecessary since it was alleged that there existed sufficient criminal and civil law to deal both with violence in general and racial harassment in particular. This issue is dealt with in more detail in the entry *'racial violence and the law'* contained in the glossary at the end of this chapter. A further problem in creating a specific offence of racial violence was that it might be utilised in a manner not anticipated by its proposers. A main dilemma would be to decide whether this offence was designed to deal only with incidents in which the victim was a member of a minority group (in which case it might result in accusations of preferential treatment being accorded to minorities) or whether the offence could be applied to any crime of an inter-racial nature, which was the proposal of the Select Committee in 1994 (Home Affairs Committee, 1994). This reform was opposed by the then Conservative Home Secretary, Michael Howard, on the grounds that it would provide members of racist parties such as the BNP with a chance to present their members as martyrs to the cause of free speech, thereby increasing the risk of social unrest. This situation had occurred in 1976 when Robert Relf was jailed for contempt of court when he refused to remove a sign outside his house in Leamington Spa which stated 'for sale to an English family'. Eventually, however, Parliament provided legal remedies to deal with racial violence which are discussed below.

The 1997 Protection from Harassment Act

This legislation made it an offence to pursue a course of conduct which amounted to harassment of a person which caused that individual to fear that violence would be used against him or her. The Act created a civil tort against which an order to restrain from harassment could be sought. The criminal courts also had the power to make an order to prevent further harassment, the breach of which would be a criminal offence. This Act was particularly drawn up to offer protection against 'stalking' although it could be applied to any form of harassment including that of a racial nature.

The 1998 Crime and Disorder Act

The 1997 Labour government enacted legislation specifically to deal with racial harassment and violence. The 1998 Crime and Disorder Act introduced a range of provisions to deal with racially aggravated offences of assault, criminal damage, harassment, and public order offences. It was perceived that the stiffer sentences provided for racially motivated crime under the 1998 Crime and Disorder Act would have a significant effect on how offenders were prosecuted and sentenced. Even if a person is not charged with an offence under this legislation, the court was required to impose an increased penalty if it was satisfied that race was an aggravating factor in the crime.

The criminal justice system and racial violence: before 1999

A key issue affecting the state's response to racially motivated violence concerns the way in which agencies operating in the criminal justice system respond to problems of this nature. This section discusses the approach adopted by these bodies in the period which preceded the report by Sir William Macpherson into the botched murder investigation of Stephen Lawrence (Macpherson, 1999). The approach adopted by the criminal justice system in this period must, however, be seen in the context that it was not until 1981 (Home Office, 1981) that racial violence was recognised as a specific social problem (Bowling and Phillips, 2002: 120).

The Crown Prosecution Service (CPS) and racial violence

Perceptions that the CPS had a poor record in dealing with racist violence led the Home Affairs Committee in 1989 to recommend the introduction of a comprehensive scheme of monitoring racial incident cases. This advice was not immediately acted upon although in 1992 the Code for Crown Prosecutors was amended so that a clear racial motive would be regarded as an aggravating feature when assessing whether a prosecution was required in the public interest. The following year the CPS began monitoring racial incident cases.

The courts and racial violence

Accusations of inappropriate treatment by the courts have also been made in connection with racially motivated violence when it sometimes appears that a black life is worth less than that of a white. In 1976 the killer of an Asian in Southall was sentenced to four years imprisonment. Kingsley-Read (then chair of the National Front) subsequently delivered a speech in Newham in which he stated 'one down, a million to go' and referred to immigrants as 'niggers, wogs and coons'. In 1978 he was acquitted of an offence under the race relations legislation. The judge advised him to moderate his language in future and concluded the trial by wishing him well. In 1994 Richard Edmonds, a leading member of the British National Party, received a derisory three-month prison sentence for his part in an attack on a black man which left him scarred for life.

Black people often seem to be dealt with less fairly by the courts whether they are defendants or victims of crime. In 1978 three brothers, the Virks, fought back against National Front attackers, were charged with assault and jailed for a total of 12 years. In 1993 two youths who subjected an Asian teenager to an attack which left him partly blinded in one eye were jailed for only 3.5 years. According to the *Independent* on 22 September 1993, the trial judge admitted that 'we are going to kill you, you smelly Paki' constituted racial undertones but did not amount to an 'aggravating feature'. However, the most publicised examples of racial injustice occurred in 1993 with the murder of Stephen Lawrence (which is discussed in more detail later in this chapter) and the death of Joy Gardner who collapsed following a struggle with police whilst being served with a deportation order. In the latter case an Old Bailey jury cleared two police officers of manslaughter in 1995. A third officer was cleared on the directions of the judge earlier in the trial. The Police Complaints Authority subsequently declined to insist that these three officers should face any form of disciplinary charge.

The attitude of the courts in dealing with cases related to racial violence is not, however, totally biased. Some of those involved in attacks on black people in Notting Hill in 1958 received gaol sentences and an unambiguous rebuke from the trial judge regarding the unacceptable nature of their conduct. There are also examples of those found guilty of racial attacks being given severe sentences. In 1993, for example, two men (one 22 and the other 19 years of age) were jailed for life for the racist killing of an Asian minicab driver, Fiaz Mirza. The judge recommended that one of these men should serve a minimum sentence of 22 years in prison. A significant judicial decision to facilitate a more vigorous state response against racial violence was made in 1994 when the Lord Chief Justice Taylor (in *R v. Ribbans, Duggan and Ridley*) ruled that although the law did not have any specific offence of racial violence, a proven racial motive in any crime of violence could lead the judge to exercise discretion and give an increased sentence. Juries may also provide some defence for those who are prosecuted when seeking to defend themselves against racial violence. In 1982 charges including that of conspiracy brought against 12 Bradford youths involved in a defence organisation were rejected and all defendants were acquitted.

The police and racial attacks

As Chapter 4 argues, the relationship between the police service and minority ethnic communities was viewed as a key explanation for the inner city disorders which took place after 1980 and prompted a number of reforms which were inspired by the 1981 Scarman report. The attitude of the police service to the specific problem of racial violence has a crucial bearing on this relationship since perceived indifference to racial violence by the police is viewed as indicative that those on the receiving end are officially regarded as second class citizens: 'inactivity by the police may be the most serious failure of the state to protect all its citizens equally' (Wilson, 1983: 8). This may erode the legitimacy of the criminal justice system and create the potential for conflicts between minorities who perceive themselves to be treated unjustly and state agencies such as the police.

Numerous allegations have been made of alleged police indifference to black victims of racial violence (Bowling, 1998). An early report criticised the failure of the police to protect black people and accused the police themselves of attacking and harassing them (Hunte, 1965). It has been subsequently alleged that police responses to these actions involved a denial that there was any racial motive to such incidents, a desire to avoid official intervention in favour of treating the incident as a civil dispute between neighbours, the provision of misleading advice or hostility towards victims, and delays in responding to requests for help from victims of these attacks (Bethnal Green and Stepney Trades Council, 1978: 7–8; Gordon, 1983: 48; and the Independent Committee of Inquiry into Policing in Hackney, 1989: 235). A particular problem with the police handling of these incidents was that the alleged perpetrators were interviewed before those who were the victims of such violence. Those subject to racial violence were instructed by the police to look after themselves by undertaking actions such as 'using reinforced plastic to replace glass windows which were constantly being smashed, keeping a dog and never walking home alone at night' (Metropolitan Police Community Relations Branch, 1987: 6–9). Police Monitoring Groups which emerged during the early part of the 1980s scrutinised racial attacks and the police response to them. It has been further alleged that attempts by communities to protect themselves against racial attacks have been met with an unsympathetic police response which resulted in the prosecutions of the 'Bradford 12' in 1982 and the 'Newham 8' in 1983, seeking to criminalise the right of self-defence (Wilson, 1983: 8). A similar problem arose in 1994 when an Asian, Lakhbir Deol, was charged with murder when he sought to defend himself and his property against a racial attack. Accusations of police indifference to black victims of racial violence have also included the allegation of the reluctance of the police to identify crimes in which race was a factor. A report by the Crown Prosecution Service stated that in 1997–98 only 37 per cent of incidents with a racial element were flagged up as such by the police (Kirkwood, 1998).

The police and racial attacks: case studies. Accusations of an inappropriate response by the police service to the victims of racial violence are illustrated in the following examples which occurred in the 1970s.

- '29 December 1976. A 15-year-old Bengalee boy is attacked by a gang of four to five youths as he is walking down Aldgate High Street at around 4 pm. The Bengalee boy was initially sworn at by the white youths, and he swore back. The youths then attacked the boy and knocked out one of his front teeth. They then ran off. The boy attended the London Hospital, Whitechapel, the following day for treatment. Six days later the incident was reported to police at Bethnal Green station by the boy's teacher. The station officer refused to enter the incident into his record book, according to the teacher who was our informant. The teacher also complains in her report of the incident that the duty officer took a sceptical and sneering attitude over the incident and suggested that it was often Bengalees who started fights'. (Bethnal Green and Stepney Trades Council, 1978: 65–6)
- 'Late August 1977. A forty-year-old male was shot in the eye with an air-gun by a group of whites travelling in a car down Woodseer Street, E1. The man was taken to the London Hospital, Whitechapel, within half an hour of the attack which occurred at around 5 pm. The doctor informed the wounded man that he was lucky not to be blinded. At 9.30 pm a CID officer arrived at the wounded man's home. The officer is believed to have asked the man only if he remembered the car registration number and wrote nothing down. The victim of the attack has heard nothing from the police'. (Bethnal Green and Stepney Trades Council, 1978: 67)
- '15 October 1977. A Bengalee family of six living in Wakeling Street, E14, has a lighted firework, wrapped in a piece of cloth, pushed through their letterbox. A car directly outside is heard driving off. The family has been subject to constant harassment in the past: windows of their home have been broken and every night stones are put through their letter box and fireworks are set off directly outside the front door. On the evening of the firework attack (15 Oct.) two police officers from Arbour Square Police Station visited the home at 11 pm – three hours after the incident took place. The officers refused to take a statement and said they would not report the incident – dismissing it as the work of children'. (Bethnal Green and Stepney Trades Council, 1978: 68)

Explanations of police attitudes towards racial violence.   One explanation which might be offered for the stance adopted by the police towards racial attacks is the negative attitude which officers allegedly have of black people because of their association with crime such as mugging, drugs, prostitution (Gutzmore, 1983: 27; Tompson, 1988: 21) and disorder. This resulted in the use of stop and search powers in a random fashion against black persons which were rarely justified by the legal requirement of reasonable suspicion (Fitzgerald, 1999). Senior officers have sometimes been associated with public comments which are perceived as racist. In 1982 crime statistics published by the Metropolitan Police for the previous year drew attention to the increase of 'mugging' which allegedly involved a disproportionate number of black persons. The linkage of race and crime was further made in 1995 when the Metropolitan Commissioner, Sir Paul Condon, stated that 80 per cent of 'muggings' in high crime areas including Harlesden, Stoke Newington and Lambeth were carried out by young black men. This statement implied that the colour of a person's skin and not socio-economic factors such as poverty and high unemployment were responsible for certain types of crime, and it was these actions allegedly undertaken by black persons which were prioritised by senior officers who failed to attach similar importance to combating racial violence. These negative connotations of black people serve to weaken the trust which minority communities have of the police service and undo the good which might derive from community policing initiatives which were pursued after 1981 throughout the police service.

The acceptance of the relationship between crime and the colour of a person's skin by the police service made it difficult for officers to view black youths as the victims of crime and also accounts for other practices which discriminate against ethnic minorities. The Commission for Racial Equality (CRE) investigated accusations that black juveniles were more likely to be referred by the police for prosecution rather than being cautioned or diverted from the courts in some other way. It was concluded that there was a higher prosecution rate for minority ethnic young offenders which did not arise from the seriousness of offences committed or past record (CRE, 1992: 7, 25). Specific allegations of mistreatment included deaths in custody and abuse of power when it appeared that police conduct towards persons from minority ethnic communities departed from the principle of minimum force (Bowling and Phillips, 2002: 132) and which sometimes included the use of oppressive control techniques (Institute of Race Relations, 1991). The acquittal of police officers in 1995 involved in the death of Joy Gardner who choked on her own vomit whilst restrained in a body-belt led the late Bernie Grant MP to articulate the sense of outrage of many black people when he stated in the *Guardian* on 17 June 1995 that the tendency for the deaths of black people in custody to go unpunished suggested that 'a black life is worth nothing'.

There are, however, alternative opinions which question police bias in dealing with racial violence. It might be argued that the random nature of many racial attacks makes it hard for the police to mount effective operations designed to combat them, even if the violence is clustered in certain areas. Additionally, the frequent absence of corroborating evidence is an impediment to the successful detection of those involved in racial attacks and securing their subsequent prosecution.

Reforms to the police handling of racial violence. In order to respond to criticisms which have been referred to in the previous section, the Association of Chief Police Officers (ACPO) published *Racial Attacks – ACPO Guiding Principles* in 1985. The following year a common reporting and monitoring system for these incidents was established, supervised by the Inspectorate. Although problems arose with the practices which were adopted (especially the degree of subjectivity involved in assessing whether an incident had been racially motivated) this initiative indicated a desire on the part of the police hierarchy to take positive action on this issue. However, in 1986 the Home Affairs Committee argued that the police had failed to make racial attacks a priority and urged that this should be done, and it was recommended that the police should receive special training in handling racial violence (Home Affairs Committee, 1986). In 1988 the Home Office required all police forces to record details of 'racial incidents'. This approach has been criticised for relating to any incident of an inter-racial nature rather than only to violence perpetrated by white persons on members of ethnic minorities (Gordon, 1996: 21).

Individual police forces pursued additional initiatives which included the establishment of specialist race attack squads in some north London police stations, the setting up of victim 'hot lines' and attempts to improve the relationship between police and public by transforming community contact work into mainstream policing. This approach involves the abandonment of discrete community contact departments and the enhanced use of area constables in multi-ethnic urban areas. Additionally the emphasis of the Home Office on a multi-agency response to racial violence and harassment (which was formalised with the establishment of the Inter-Departmental Government Working Party in 1987) resulted in police involvement in a range of local level initiatives designed to tackle these problems. One difficulty with such approaches, however, is that they may result in individual agencies absolving themselves of their own responsibilities (Gordon, 1993: 174–5).

In 1993 the newly-installed Metropolitan Commissioner of Police indicated that his force had to be 'totally intolerant' of racially motivated attacks and of those who used racial hatred for political ends (Condon, 1993). Problems including the low clear-up rate for incidents of this nature prompted a Parliamentary committee to assert that while progress had been made by the police service in dealing with this type of crime, it was necessary for the Home Office to re-emphasise to all chief constables that tackling racial incidents should be regarded as a priority task (Home Affairs Committee, 1994: 11). Subsequent initiatives included the involvement of CRE officers with the Police Staff College at Bramshill in 1995 to develop and deliver a two-and-a-half day training course for police officers on the policing of racial incidents, and cooperation between the CRE and ACPO in 1996 to develop management standards for police forces around the country concerning responses to racial harassment.

The Stephen Lawrence murder: a catalyst for change

The murder of the black teenager Stephen Lawrence in 1993 eventually provided the impetus to change the way in which the criminal justice system responded to ethnic minorities in general and to racially motivated violence in particular. This agenda for change was provided in a report written by Sir William Macpherson (Macpherson, 1999). The background to this report, its main recommendations and their implementation are discussed in this section.

Background to the Macpherson Report

Developments which have been described above failed to provide a totally effective police response to racial violence and harassment. In 1997 the HMIC expressed a number of concerns in connection with this issue, stating that many officers remained unaware of the definition of a racial incident initially laid down by ACPO in 1985, and that there were widely different interpretations of what it meant among those who believed that they did know (HMIC, 1997: 30). It was argued that there was continuing evidence of 'inappropriate language and behaviour by police officers', which was unchecked by sergeants and inspectors (HMIC, 1997: 9), and that the links constructed between the police and minority ethnic communities were limited in scope and relied heavily on 'formal links with a narrow (and possibly unrepresentative) section of the minority community' (HMIC, 1997: 26). It was thus recommended that all forces should undertake community and race relations audit, that sensitivity to community and race relations should be positively recognised in the recruitment, promotion, staff appraisal and the posting and deployment of staff, and that a community and race relations dimension should be explicitly included in all relevant training (HMIC, 1997: 59). These criticisms prompted ACPO to establish a task force to examine issues surrounding police/race relations in 1998, and the Metropolitan Police to set up a Racial and Violent Crimes Task Force in the same year whose work was aided by the formation of Community Safety Units at borough level.

Racist murders in the 1990s

Further reforms to the police service in addition to those discussed in Chapter 4 were eventually initiated in response to a number of violent attacks on persons from minority ethnic groups in the 1990s. On 24 February 1999, the *Guardian* published a list of 25 black and Asian people (in addition to Stephen Lawrence who is discussed in more detail below) who had been murdered in racially motivated attacks since 1991. The police response to this extreme form of racial violence, however, seemed inappropriate. It was argued that murderers of black people were less likely to be caught than those of white or other ethnic groups: in 1996–97 and 1997–98 'there was a much higher proportion (40%) of homicides with black victims where there was no suspect than for white (10%) or Asian (13%) victims' (Home Office, 1998: 27).

A particular criticism levelled against the police service in connection with serious cases of this kind was that officers were often disinclined to view any racial motive in murders involving members of minority ethnic communities. In one case (involving the death of Michael Menson in 1997), the Metropolitan Police failed for 18 months to perceive the incident as murder at all, instead viewing the attack as a self-inflicted injury. Similarly, in the case of 'Ricky' Reel, in 1997 the Metropolitan Police insisted that his death had been a tragic accident and vetoed the PCA's decision that the Surrey police (who were investigating a complaint regarding the Metropolitan Police Service's handling of the incident) should also investigate the death itself. In November 1999 an inquest jury formally rejected the Metropolitan Police's argument that his death had been an accident by recording an open verdict.

However, the murder of Stephen Lawrence, on 22 April 1993 proved to be a major catalyst which emphasised the need for change in the way in which the criminal justice system, and especially the Metropolitan Police, responded to racially motivated violence. Criticisms of the manner in which the subsequent investigation was handled included officers at the scene failing to assess any racial factor in the murder, and the delay in arresting suspects. The first arrests occurred on 7 May, although important information regarding the identity of the murderers was received by the investigating team soon after the murder had taken place. Two persons were subsequently charged with murder but the CPS dropped the charges on 29 July on the grounds of insufficient evidence. In 1994 the CPS again declined to prosecute on the grounds of insufficient evidence. The Lawrence family subsequently initiated a private prosecution against three youths allegedly involved in the attack which broke down in 1996 when the trial judge ruled that the identification of two of the defendants by a person who had been attacked with Lawrence was contradictory and contaminated. In 1997 an inquest jury returned a unanimous verdict that 'Stephen Lawrence was unlawfully killed in a completely unprovoked racist attack by five white youths.'

The Macpherson Report

In 1998, the Labour government initiated an inquiry into the Metropolitan Police Service's handling of the Stephen Lawrence murder investigation. It was chaired by a retired judge, Sir William Macpherson. In the hearings which were held in connection with this investigation, Ian Johnston, the assistant commissioner of the Metropolitan Police apologised to the Lawrence family for their shortcomings regarding the investigation into the murder of their son. In 1999, Macpherson's report was fiercely critical of the police handling of this matter (Macpherson, 1999). He examined three specific allegations in connection with it – that the Metropolitan Police were

- incompetent
- racist
- corrupt

Macpherson judged that the Metropolitan Police Service was guilty of the first two accusations, enabling it to draw cold comfort from the fact that he did not endorse the charge of corruption. Sir William stated that the investigation had been fundamentally flawed and 'marred by a combination of professional incompetence, institutional racism, and a failure of leadership by senior officers' (Macpherson, 1999: 317). Sir William believed that the police were guilty of gross negligence in their investigation of Stephen's murder, an accusation which hinged on the failure of the police to make early arrests which was stated to be 'the most fundamental fault in the investigation of this murder' (Macpherson, 1999: 95).

Institutional racism

The concept of institutional racism was developed in the struggles of black Americans for civil rights. Despite courtroom victories and the enactment of legislation such as the 1965 Civil Rights Act and 1965 Voting Act, the condition of most black Americans failed to change for the better. This gave rise to the term 'institutional racism' which suggested that racism should be analysed not only from the perspective of an individual act of prejudice but at the level of a racist power structure within society. It was argued that institutional racism was akin to a system of internal colonialism in which black people stood as colonial subjects in relation to white society (Carmichael and Hamilton, 1967). This term was subsequently defined to embrace established laws, customs, and practices which systematically reflected and produced racial inequalities and the interactions of various spheres of social life to maintain an overall pattern of oppression (Blauner, 1972).

As is argued in Chapter 4, Lord Scarman's report in 1981 adopted the 'bad apple' approach to racism in the police service (Crowther, 2000: 98) which attributed this problem to personal attitudes which were held by a minority of officers. Macpherson, however, went further than this, effectively arguing that racism existed throughout the Metropolitan Police and that the problem was organisational rather than one which affected a small number of individuals. He put forward the concept of 'institutional racism' which his report defined as:

> the collective failure of an organisation to provide an appropriate and professional service to people because of their colour, culture or ethnic origin. It can be seen or detected in processes, attitudes and behaviour which amount to discrimination through unwitting prejudice, ignorance, thoughtlessness and racist stereotyping which disadvantage minority ethnic people. (Macpherson, 1999: 28)

Although this term has been criticised for sidestepping questions of causality and for asserting racism to be the sole or primary cause of black disadvantage (thus ignoring other processes relating to class and gender), it is useful as it directs attention to how 'racist discourses can be embodied within the structures and organisations of society' (Singh, 2000: 29, 38) and provides explanations for practices which derive from either unwitting or uncritical racism (S. Smith, 1989: 101).

Reforms proposed by the Macpherson Report

Macpherson's report suggested a number of reforms (70 in total) which were designed to ensure that the criminal justice system (and especially the police service, to which 60 of the recommendations applied) operated in a manner which was perceived to be fairer to minority ethnic communities by addressing racism and enhancing the effectiveness of measures to combat racial violence. These recommendations included:

- *A drive to rebuild the confidence of the ethnic minority communities in policing.* The proposal that a ministerial priority 'to increase trust and confidence in policing amongst minority ethnic communities' (Macpherson, 1999: 327) should be established for all police forces was Macpherson's first recommendation. This emphasised the government's role in bringing about improved relationships between the police service and minority ethnic communities. It was proposed that the performance indicators which could be used to monitor its implementation included the existence and application of strategies for the recording, investigation and prosecution of racist incidents, measures to encourage incidents of this kind to be reported and the extent of multi-agency cooperation and information exchange.

- *Definition of racist incidents.* These should be defined as 'any incident which is perceived to be racist by the victim or any other person', and the term should be understood to include both crimes and non-crimes in policing terms. Both should be recorded and investigated with equal commitment. This recommendation was designed to make the police service victim-orientated.

- *The recruitment of more black and Asian police officers.* In 1998 the minority ethnic population comprised 5.6 per cent of the total population. However, there were only 2483 black or Asian police officers in all English and Welsh police forces (which constituted below 2 per cent of the total personnel of 124,798) (Home Office, 1998: 37). This was a particular problem in London where minority ethnic communities comprised 25.5 per cent of the population but only 3.4 per cent of the Metropolitan Police's 26,411 officers were drawn from these communities, although minority ethnic groups were more adequately represented in the Special Constabulary and the civilian support staff (HMIC, 2000: 8). Research also revealed that rates for resignation and dismissal from the police service were higher for minority ethnic officers than for white officers (Bland et al., 1999) and that in March 1999 only 14 per cent of minority ethnic officers had been promoted compared to 23 per cent of white officers (Bowling and Phillips, 2002: 218). Macpherson thus proposed that the Home Secretary and Police Authorities' policing plans should include targets for recruitment, progression and retention of minority ethnic staff (Home Office, 1999: 334).

- *To consider whether the use of racist language and behaviour and the possession of offensive weapons in a private place should become a criminal offence.* This recommendation was prompted by evidence obtained from a police surveillance video which showed some of those accused of Stephen Lawrence's murder acting in a violent manner and using racist language. It would extend the scope of the criminal law into the home and to other venues such as clubs and meeting places. This course of action, however, seemed unlikely to be acted upon as it would inevitably lead to accusations of Britain having a 'thought police'.

- *Freedom of information legislation should extend to most areas of policing.* Disclosure would be withheld subject only to the test of 'substantial harm'. This proposal was designed to make allegations of incompetence and prejudice easier to prove in the future, and went further than the recommendation in the 1998 white paper on this subject which included documents relating to the administrative functions of the police whilst excluding material related to their investigation and prosecution responsibilities.

- *Reform of the 1976 Race Relations Act.*   This reform was designed to combat institutional racism. It would bring the entire public sector within the scope of the legislation, thus enabling the CRE to launch investigations into individual police forces. This reform would leave individual officers facing claims for damages for discrimination from Asian or black suspects whom they had arrested.

- *To consider the abolition of double jeopardy.*   Double jeopardy ensures that defendants are not subject to repeated trials and encourages the police and prosecutors to be diligent at the outset of a case. This reform would enable the Court of Appeal to permit a person to be re-tried, having initially been acquitted, if fresh and viable evidence subsequently became available.

- *The introduction of a tougher police disciplinary regime.*   It was proposed that racist words or actions should lead to disciplinary proceedings which would normally result in an officer's dismissal from the service. Scarman had put forward a similar proposal in 1981 but although section 101 of the 1984 Police and Criminal Evidence Act required Police Discipline Regulations to be amended to make racially discriminatory behaviour a specific disciplinary offence, resistance from the police service prevented it from being acted upon. It was also proposed that disciplinary action should be available for at least five years after an officer had retired. This latter suggestion was especially influenced by the fact that four senior officers whose conduct with regard to the Lawrence investigation had been criticised by the PCA had retired from the police service and were thus unable to face neglect of duty charges. Only one officer subsequently faced a disciplinary hearing over the investigation and in July 1999, following a tribunal ruling that he had been guilty of two counts of neglect of duty, received the lightest sentence possible (a caution for each of the two counts).

Responses to the Macpherson Report

The damning nature of the criticisms made of the criminal justice system in general and of the police service in particular regarding its response to the needs of minority ethnic communities, especially regarding racial violence, ensured that the recommendations made by Sir William Macpherson would be acted upon. This section examines the responses made to this report by the police service and the Labour government.

The police service

The need to improve the relationship between the police and minority ethnic communities which was articulated in Macpherson's report was further endorsed by the Inspectorate. A report published in March 1999 investigated the progress which had been made in implementing the recommendations made in an earlier HMIC report, *Winning the Race*, published in 1997. It asserted that 'there has been a general improvement but the overall picture is patchy. There is a lack of consistency and the pockets of good work identified tend to be the product of a committed few rather than representing corporate endeavour' (HMIC, 1999: 3). Only 11 forces had conducted any form of community and race relations audit (HMIC, 1999: 40) and only 16 forces reported that they had a community and race relations strategy (or equivalent) in place, with a further 10 forces in the developmental stage (HMIC, 1999: 37). The officer who led the inspection commented that 'we were disappointed to find that progress has been less than satisfactory, with many of the original recommendations largely ignored and few forces placing the issue high on their agenda' (Crompton, 1999).

Following the publication of the Macpherson report, a package of measures entitled *Protect and Respect* was announced by the Metropolitan Police Service. These included:

- *Random testing of officers to assess racist attitudes.* This reform involved the use of black undercover officers to ensure that officers behaved in a courteous and correct fashion regardless of the colour of a complainant or witness.
- *The fast-tracking of racially motivated crimes through the forensic system.* This recommendation was designed to improve the investigation of these crimes and heighten the possibility of securing the convictions of those responsible for them.

- *Improved reporting rates of racially motivated crime.* An important aspect of the attempt to improve the level of reporting of these incidents was for officers to be more aware of what constituted such an incident.

In March 1999, the Metropolitan Police Service published a report, *A Police Service for all the People* which put forward a 15-point plan designed to tackle institutional racism. One objective was to have a fifth of senior posts held by minority ethnic officers which would be achieved by introducing a special career development scheme for officers of the rank of inspector and above. In 1999, only four of the 873 minority ethnic officers in this force were of superintendent rank. The issue of recruitment was addressed through suggestions that fellowships could be made available to minority ethnic students in their final year of study to encourage them to join the police service following graduation, and the retention of these officers was to be tackled by establishing network groups of 30–35 ethnic minority officers across London, each with career development officers attached to them. Mentoring schemes would also be introduced to aid ethnic minority officers.

Police reservations concerning the Macpherson Report. The nature of the criticisms made against the police service in the Macpherson Report made it unlikely that it would be universally accepted within the service. The deputy chief constable of Kent, Robert Ayling (who had headed a PCA-supervised enquiry into the Metropolitan Police's handling of the Lawrence murder investigation in 1993) asserted in the *Guardian* on 9 March 1999 that the evidence to support the charge of institutional racism was limited. Other observations included the perception that the complexity of murder inquiries was underestimated in the report, and that some of its conclusions (such as ending double jeopardy and legislating in connection with racist conduct in the home), while understandable in the specific context of the Lawrence murder investigation, posed significant problems for civil liberties as well as for their implementation. The chair of the Metropolitan Police Federation argued that the real issue was not institutional racism but deficiencies in management whereby a review of the murder inquiry ordered by the then senior officers of the area was 'signed off, accepted as correct, passed up the chain of command and then relied upon as a shield to deflect criticism. That single act has let down every single Metropolitan officer' (Smyth, 1999).

A subsequent report which alluded to problems affecting murder investigations in the Metropolitan Police Service also implied that institutional racism might not be the full explanation for failures by the Metropolitan Police to apprehend perpetrators of serious crimes. It was revealed that murder investigations did not have a specific priority in that force. The report asserted that the lower than average rate for the detection of murders in the ten-year period 1989–98 (84 per cent compared to the national average of 92 per cent) was 'largely attributable to the level of resources assigned to investigation rather than to the expertise or competence of detective officers' (HMIC, 2000: 11–12). It thus recommended that the Metropolitan Police should carefully consider the maximum case load appropriate for Senior Investigating Officers to manage, having regard to the varying complexity of cases (HMIC, 2000: 161). Poor liaison with the CPS in the early stages of a murder investigation was also highlighted. It was asserted that close cooperation between the police and the CPS was required to ensure that the investigation was steered along the correct path so that the best evidence was available in court. It was recommended that a structure for formal liaison between the Metropolitan Police and the CPS should be established as a matter of urgency (HMIC, 2000: 12, 162).

The government's response

In March 1999 the then Home Secretary, Jack Straw, announced the government's response to the proposals of the Macpherson Report which were contained in an 'action plan'. This was presented to the House of Commons on 23 March 1999, and included the issues which are discussed below.

Recruitment, retention and promotion.   Jack Straw had formerly endorsed proposals for a national target of 7 per cent for minority ethnic police officers, which could be exceeded in inner city areas. In the wake of the Macpherson inquiry, he formally committed himself to imposing targets governing recruitment, promotion and retention of black and Asian officers at a speech delivered to the Black Police Association in October 1998. These would act as performance indicators in connection with the ministerial priority proposed by Macpherson and adopted by the Home Secretary. In April 1999 the Home Office issued targets which required police forces to recruit black and Asian officers in proportion to the ethnic mix of the local population. This would amount in total to in excess of 8000 officers from these communities over the next ten years in order to kickstart 'the police service attaining a proper ethnic balance' (Straw, 1999a).

Definition of racist incidents.   Macpherson's definition of a racist incident as 'any incident which is perceived to be racist by the victim or any other person' (Macpherson, 1999: 328) was accepted, although this would only be used in the initial reporting of an incident and would not determine the issue of racial motivation when someone was charged and tried.

Race relations legislation.   The government introduced legislation in 1999 to bring the police service within the scope of the Race Relations Act. Initially it was proposed to make direct racism alone challengeable in the courts which is notoriously hard to substantiate. However, in February 2000 the Home Secretary amended his Bill to include indirect discrimination. The 2000 Race Relations (Amendment) Act placed a duty on the entire public sector (including the police, prisons and immigration service) to promote equality.

Freedom of information legislation. The Home Secretary's 2000 Freedom of Information Act did not include many of Macpherson's recommendations. Information obtained during police investigations was exempt from release, subject to the force's discretion. Other policing agencies consisting of MI5, MI6 and GCHQ (whose work is discussed in the concluding chapter) were exempt from the provisions of this Act. The measure also contained no powers whereby the Information Commissioner could order the disclosure of information in the exempt categories (including criminal investigations) on public interest grounds.

Racism awareness training. In 1994 the Police Training Council had put forward proposals for the delivery of community and race relations training. These had not been fully or effectively implemented by all forces. It was thus proposed by the government that all forces should respond positively to the 1994 proposals. In October 1999 new training courses of this nature were introduced by the Metropolitan Police.

Police discipline. New regulations which came into effect in April 1999 meant that racist behaviour by any officers would result in their dismissal. The proposal that disciplinary action should be available for five years after an officer retired was to be considered by the Home Secretary, and he would also consider legislation to enable forfeiture of police pensions for serious disciplinary offences.

Stop and search. The Home Secretary would consider whether a written record with reasons for all stops should be given to those searched.

An independent complaints system. The government was sympathetic to an independent system for investigating complaints against the police, and a feasibility study was conducted into the costs of such a system. Proposals were subsequently put forward by the Home Secretary to introduce a stronger independent element into the system of investigating complaints against the police (Home Office, 2000b), and a subsequent white paper promised legislation to replace the Police Complaints Authority with an Independent Police Complaints Commission which would investigate serious complaints (Home Office, 2001: 24).

Double jeopardy. The issue of reforming double jeopardy was referred for review to the Law Commission, and reservations were expressed concerning the practicability of banning racist language and possessing offensive weapons in private places. In 1999 the Law Commission published an interim consultation paper which suggested that exceptions might be made to this rule in exceptional circumstances as when new evidence emerged which was substantially stronger and could not have been obtained before the first trial. This change would apply only to serious offences punishable by at least three years imprisonment and where there was a strong likelihood of obtaining a conviction. All retrials would require the permission of the High Court with the right of appeal to the Court of Appeal. In 2000 the Home Affairs Committee lent its support for the relaxation of this rule for offences which carried a life sentence and where new evidence emerged which made the previous acquittal unsafe. It also proposed that the relaxation of this rule should be retrospective. Following the 2001 general election, the new Home Secretary, David Blunkett, announced the government's decision to press ahead with the recommendation of the Law Commission to allow senior judges to overturn acquittals and order a retrial in murder cases when compelling new evidence emerged.

Evaluation of the state's response to racial violence

Statistics suggested that racial violence was on the increase following the publication of the Macpherson Report. The total of racist incidents in 1997–98 was 13,878 (HMIC, 1999: 27). Throughout England and Wales there were 47,814 racist incidents reported to and recorded by the police in 1999–2000, compared with 23,049 recorded in the previous year. This included 21,750 offences created by the 1998 Crime and Disorder Act (Home Office, 2000a: 49). Serious acts of racial violence included the murder of the ten-year-old school boy, Damilola Taylor in November 2000, for which four youths were arrested in June 2001 but acquitted in 2002. These figures suggest a significant rise in racial crimes which has been affected by the adoption of Macpherson's suggestion to record offences as racial crimes when the victim used this designation. However, recording methods (whereby one incident may generate several offences or several incidents one offence) have also influenced these statistics. This section examines the effectiveness of reforms which were introduced following the Macpherson Report in connection with racially motivated violence.

Legal reform

One solution to the continued extent of racial violence in the late twentieth and early years of the twenty-first centuries would be to introduce new legislation to deal with this problem in addition to the provisions of the 1998 Crime and Disorder Act which have been referred to above. There are several approaches that could be adopted to secure this objective.

Proscribing racist political parties

A number of arguments can be presented in favour of banning racist political parties. This action would demonstrate a commitment by both the executive and legislature to a multiracial society in which the articulation of racism is deemed an unacceptable form of social and political behaviour. The activities of racist parties directly or indirectly create a climate in which racial violence is likely to occur. The number of these incidents rose sharply in SE London after the BNP moved its headquarters into the area in 1989 (Makenji, 1995). Disorder at Oldham in 2001 took place when the National Front sought to inflame racial tensions by marching through areas which contained large Asian populations and the leader of the British National Party stood as a Parliamentary candidate in one of the city's constituencies. Here the extreme right sought to gain political benefit from existing racial tensions. If it could be proved that parties on the extreme right utilised or encouraged violence to further their political ends they could be adjudged 'terrorist' organisations under the definition given to this term in the 1974 Prevention of Terrorism Act and be banned on the grounds that they were anti-constitutional organisations. Banning might also save police resources which have often been expended on demonstrations and processions involving racist parties and their opponents.

However, there are problems associated with this course of action. Banning a party is likely to have the effect of driving it underground which poses problems for the police who need to monitor its activities. It may also result in the organisation pursuing more violent tactics to further its political objectives since it is no longer constrained by the need to court political support in a conventional manner. There is also a danger that a party which is banned may secure popular sympathy by being viewed as an 'underdog', denied the liberal democratic right of freedom of speech. The extent to which this is likely to occur may depend on whether the public discern any dignity in the cause espoused by that party. It can also be argued that as major political parties have, on occasions, shown themselves willing to pander to racism it is unfair to pick upon selected organisations for such extreme treatment. Banning racist parties may also be unnecessary since it is possible to utilise existing legislation to deal effectively with the activities of their members. Finally, while banning racist parties may have immense symbolic importance, it would not prevent groups articulating racist sentiments taking to the streets, since technological developments such as the internet facilitate the organising of such events with no need for the kind of organisation that a political party was formerly required to provide.

Racism and the internet

Racist views are circulated on the internet as well as by political parties. On 24 November 2000, the *Guardian* quoted a report from the EU's Racism Monitoring Unit which asserted that there were 2100 racist and anti-Semitic web sites and that these were responsible for reinvigorating racist movements and for increasing the number of acts of racially motivated violence. In order to combat this problem, the industry-financed Internet World Foundation announced plans to target internet sites which published criminally racist material. As a first step the internet service provider would be contacted in the belief that this action would usually secure the removal of the offensive material. If this failed to happen, there would be liaison with the industry and the law enforcement agencies. In the United Kingdom the 1986 Public Order Act could possibly be used as an ultimate sanction, since this makes it an offence to publish material designed or likely to stir up racial hatred.

EU law reform

In 2000 the European Parliament passed European Union-wide laws based on Article 13 of the 1997 Treaty of Amsterdam which sought to ban racial harassment and victimisation and to introduce protection against racial discrimination in education, employment, access to education grants, social protection and social security. A main feature of these laws was the reversal of the burden of proof from complainant to respondent in civil race discrimination cases thereby requiring those who were accused to prove their innocence. These incorporated a definition of indirect discrimination which included a situation 'where an apparently neutral provision is liable to adversely affect a person or group of particular racial or ethnic origin'. Indirect discrimination previously existed in British law but not in the domestic law of most other EU countries.

The criminal justice system

Effective action to discourage and punish racial violence relies on these issues being treated seriously by the key agencies in the criminal justice system. This section considers the effectiveness of reforms which have been introduced since the Macpherson Report.

The Crown Prosecution Service

The Macpherson Report recommended that the police service and the CPS should ensure that care was taken at all stages of a prosecution to recognise and include reference to any evidence of racial motivation. In particular it should be the duty of the CPS to ensure that this evidence was referred to at both the trial and in the sentencing process. Additionally, the CPS and counsel should ensure that this evidence should not be excluded as the consequence of 'plea bargaining'. It was also proposed that the CPS should ensure that all decisions to discontinue a prosecution should be carefully and fully recorded in writing (Macpherson, 1999: 331). In 1999–2000, 2417 defendant cases involving racist incidents were identified by the CPS. Of these, 1834 (76 per cent) were prosecuted: most defendants pleaded guilty (66 per cent) and the overall conviction rate, including not guilty pleas, was 79 per cent (Home Office, 2000: 49). Additionally, it has been observed that defendants of African, Caribbean and Asian origin were more likely to have their cases terminated by the CPS either because the evidence presented by the police was weak or because it was against the public interest to prosecute (Bowling and Phillips, 2002: 239).

However, accusations of racism within the CPS had an adverse impact on the image of this organisation and its desire to pursue a rigorous approach towards racial violence. Between 1993 and 2000, 22 claims by minority ethnic lawyers alleging racial discrimination by the CPS were launched, and in February 2000 an employment tribunal awarded £30,000 to a minority ethnic crown prosecutor, stating that the organisation's conduct had fallen below the standards which would have been expected from a corner-shop. In October 1999 a tribunal made the third finding of racial discrimination against the CPS in less than a year and in December 1999 the Commission for Racial Equality proposed a formal investigation into allegations of racism within the CPS in connection with decisions to prosecute and its employment (including promotion) policies. The CPS was able to have this investigation suspended by initiating an independent investigation in January 2000 conducted by Sylvia Denman.

The conclusions of Denman's report stated that the CPS had responded slowly to modern equal opportunities legislation and practices and that although ethnic minority staff were well represented overall, they were 'seriously under-represented in both the higher administrative grades and the higher lawyer grades' because barriers to ethnic minority recruitment and progression persisted. It was reported that 'a significant number' of ethnic minority staff had experienced racial discrimination at one time or another within the CPS although most failed to report it, and that the concept of institutional racism was not generally understood or acknowledged. It was, however, accepted that 'modest progress' had been made during the period of the inquiry in seeking to ensure that the CPS developed a national culture which embraced all sections of the community and that there was 'a very clear commitment to change at the most senior levels' (Denman, 2001: 13–14). It was thus recommended that positive action should be taken to redress the current under-representation of minority ethnic staff at the lower and middle management grades and that monitoring should be used to achieve change in the CPS, especially in relation to setting targets. It was proposed that external investigation of equal opportunity complaints should be implemented immediately and that an external mediation service should be available to all staff (Denman, 2001: 15).

Additionally, the CRE launched its own separate, formal, investigation into allegations that staff at Croydon, Surrey, were working in racially segregated teams. The subsequent report argued that separation on racial lines had occurred at this office (race being 'a not insignificant factor' in accounting for this situation), and additionally that the few internal complaints of discrimination that were made were inadequately investigated or not dealt with within a reasonable period of time. It was concluded, however, that these facts did not support a finding on unlawful segregation within the meaning of the 1976 Race Relations Act as there was no evidence that the CPS had acted to keep staff apart on racial lines or that this situation was maintained or supported by specific acts of direct discrimination. It was accepted, however, that had the 2000 Race Relations (Amendment) Act been in force during the period under investigation the outcome could have been different since the CPS might have been in breach of its statutory obligation to pursue actions to bring about race equality, end unlawful discrimination and promote better race relations (CRE, 2001: 6).

The courts

According to the *Guardian* on 29 September 1999, between May 1997 and September 1999 five judges were disciplined by the Lord Chancellor for making offensive racial remarks. One development concerned with attempts to alter the culture of the judiciary took place in 1999 when an Equal Treatment Bench Book was launched by the Lord Chancellor and the Lord Chief Justice. This aimed to increase the sensitivity of judges to issues of race and their awareness of Britain's multi-cultural society. Every judge in England and Wales was to be issued with this guide which advised them to avoid gaffes such as referring to black people as 'coloured', stereotyping particular communities as 'crime-prone' and asking followers of minority religions for their 'Christian' names. They were told never to use terms which included 'Paki', 'negro', 'ethnics' or 'half-caste'. The guide provided judges with a brief history of the main ethnic minorities in Britain including their religions, customs, festivals, special apparel and dietary rules.

However, the perception that the courts were insufficiently sympathetic to minority ethnic victims of racial violence was evidenced in April 2001 in trials involving two Leeds United Footballers who had been accused of attacking an Asian student, Sarfraz Najeib. The first trial collapsed following the publication of an article in the *Sunday Mirror* based on an interview with the victim's father which the trial judge held to make it impossible for the jury to reach an unbiased decision. Although the Crown Prosecution Service had previously decided not to pursue racism as a motive for the attack, the trial judge, Mr Justice Poole, went out of his way when delivering his judgement to abort the trial, to criticise the recommendation contained in the Macpherson Report regarding the definition of a racial incident. In the second trial, one of the two footballers was found guilty of affray (the other being acquitted of all charges by the all-white jury) and sentenced to 100 hours community service. Although another participant was jailed for six years, the lenient sentence given by the judge to the footballer was ill-judged to discourage others from carrying out violence of this nature. Perceptions that the action taken to protect members of minority ethnic communities from violence remained insufficient should be seen in the context that on conviction black people were more likely to receive custodial sentences and that these were longer for black and Asian persons than for whites (Bowling and Phillips, 2002: 240).

The police service and the Macpherson Report

The recommendations of the Macpherson Report were especially directed at the police service. This section evaluates the initial effectivenes of these reforms.

The confidence of ethnic minorities in the police.   The government responded to Macpherson's recommendation that a ministerial priority should be put forward to rebuild the confidence of minority ethnic groups in the police service by making this a police national objective in 2000/2001. A major problem with achieving this aim was the image of the police. In 1999 a *Guardian*/ICM poll showed that one in four members of the general public believed that the police were racist, 31 per cent of the 18–24 year old age group believed that most police officers were racist or very racist, 33 per cent of respondents believed that the police failed to treat black or Asian people fairly, and only 45 per cent disagreed with this proposition. It might be concluded that unless the image of the police is dramatically improved targets to increase recruitment of ethnic minority officers will inevitably fail.

The recruitment of police officers from minority ethnic communities.   Progress in recruiting more police officers drawn from African-Caribbean and Asian communities was initially slow. Detailed information on recruitment was compiled by the *Guardian* from answers to Parliamentary questions put by the Liberal Democrat MP, Simon Hughes and published on 3 August 2000. This indicated that in the two years from March 1998 to March 2000, the number of ethnic minority officers had increased from 2483 to 2754. However, police forces were required to recruit 826 officers from minority ethnic communities each year for 10 years to meet the Home Secretary's target. Progress in key forces was limited. In West Yorkshire the overall number of minority ethnic officers had declined in this two-year period and the Metropolitan Police (which needed to recruit 566 ethnic minority officers each year over 10 years) had only succeeded in attracting 125 between March 1999 and March 2000. By early 2002, this force had 1205 officers drawn from minority ethnic communities, 4.42 per cent of the total (Hopkins, 2002).

One difficulty with attaining this objective was the financial constraints imposed on police forces which compelled some (including West Yorkshire which policed multi-ethnic Bradford) to scale down recruitment. An additional problem was the wastage rate of minority ethnic officers who were twice as likely to resign and three times more likely to be dismissed than their white peers. The then Home Secretary argued that ways had to be found to stop this 'exodus' (Straw, 1999b). Additionally, a survey conducted by the *Guardian* which was published on 24 February 2000 also revealed that 20 forces had no tests in place to measure whether officers had racist attitudes and that only 17 forces had complied with Macpherson's suggestion that all officers should be trained in racial awareness and cultural diversity.

The reform of police culture.   Numerous accusations of the existence of a racist police culture have been articulated. In 1999 a long-serving black police officer, Leslie Bowie, brought a claim for racial discrimination against the Metropolitan Police. His evidence (reported in the *Guardian* on 19 February 1999) included allegations that when he first joined the police service in 1973 he had been driven around in a police vehicle with a golliwog tied to its blue light on the roof. He alleged that 'words like nigger, coon, wogs, spick...were constantly bandied about in general conversation, no matter where officers were or who was present'. He was subsequently awarded £7000 by an industrial tribunal in November 1999 for racial discrimination.

Macpherson's emphasis on institutional racism pointed to the urgent need to address the culture of the police service. Police culture has a crucial impact on the ability of the police service to move positively in the direction outlined in the Macpherson Report. Before the publication of the report, some senior officers expressed support for root and branch reform of the police service to restore public confidence in it: Ian Blair (then the chief constable of Surrey) called for the modernisation of the 'homogenous and traditional' police culture, which he believed was old-fashioned and had to be changed in order for the police to serve a multicultural and modern nation. He particularly drew attention to minority ethnic officers feeling that they had to adopt the 'mores of a white culture' (Blair, 1999).

Attempts to eradicate racism within police forces were traditionally directed at the external issue of police–public relationships. Key pronouncements regarding quality of service expressed concern with ensuring that members of the public did not receive less favourable treatment from the police 'on the grounds of race, colour, nationality, or national or ethnic origins or were disadvantaged by conditions or requirements which could not be shown to be justifiable' (ACPO/CRE, 1993: 9). However, 'absolutely no critical attention is given to the features of the occupational culture that redefine what...are "good" and desirable features of a work environment...but exclude minority ethnic officers from full and active membership' (Holdaway, 1996: 171).

An alternative approach would be to concentrate on the internal characteristics of the police service, involving an examination of police culture, one core characteristic of which is alleged to be racial prejudice (Reiner, 1985: 100–3) which mobilises the lower ranks of the police service to resist progressive change. This approach would go beyond attempts designed to stop the use of racialist language (Holdaway, 1991: 168) and address the manner in which the key features of police occupational culture 'construct and sustain racialised relations within the police' (Holdaway, 1996: 169). Tackling those processes which cause and reproduce racism (particularly the marginalisation of black officers) within police forces is seen as an indispensable requirement for eliminating the public display of such behaviour towards members of minority ethnic communities. This approach will ensure that reforms to police recruitment and training policies were advanced within an organisational climate which was supportive of initiatives to eradicate racism.

One key initiative to affect the working environment of police forces has been developed by minority ethnic police officers. In 1994 a Black and Asian Police Association was formed within the Metropolitan Police. This 'may strengthen the racialised identity of its members and, realising their collective strength, unite them through both a shared experience of social exclusion ... and ... a positive commitment to policing' (Holdaway, 1996: 196). Critics, however, believe that this may have divisive consequences, diverting energy into internal police affairs to the detriment of the provision of a service to the public (Broughton and Bennett, 1994).

Additional methods to alter the culture of the police service have included pursuing with greater vigour equal opportunities policies within police forces promoted by the Home Office. In 1995 the Inspectorate conducted an equal opportunity inspection of 13 police forces and subsequently accepted aid from the CRE in this area of work. A key problem with this approach is the absence of positive discrimination legislation making it impossible to change the composition of police forces by methods which include the use of employment quotas. Police forces could pursue a more active role to eliminate racism by making greater usage of the sanction in section 101 of the 1984 Police and Criminal Evidence Act whereby Police Disciplinary Regulations were amended to provide for a specific disciplinary offence of racially discriminatory behaviour, one penalty for which was dismissal from the police service. This sanction could be directed at police behaviour both to their colleagues as well as to members of the public. Currently police officers are rarely punished for this behaviour.

Following the Macpherson Report a number of significant changes were made in police forces to respond to the criticisms which were put forward, in particular that of institutional racism. In the Metropolitan Police area the slogan of 'protect and respect' was adopted in order to indicate changes in police attitudes towards ethnic minority communities, and specialist community safety units were set up in each division to investigate complaints of racial crimes. In line with Macpherson's recommendation that the police service should adhere to the victim's view that a crime was of a racist nature, the ethos of these community safety units was victim-orientated. Aided by changes spearheaded by community safety units, the reporting and arrests for racial crime increased as did intelligence on these crimes. Additionally, the Metropolitan Police established an Understanding and Responding to Race Hate Crime project whose role was to analyse and review data to give the force a clearer understanding of the issue.

However, problems continued after 1999 which implied that progress in changing the culture of the police service (especially in London) had not been entirely successful. There remained concerns about the disproportionate rates of attention paid by police officers to persons from minority ethnic backgrounds (especially concerning the use of stop and search powers) and a lack of confidence in policing particularly in connection with the service received by persons from minority communities (Clancy et al., 2001). A number of well-publicised episodes occurred regarding the treatment of Asian and African-Caribbean persons by the police which seemed to go beyond the abberant actions of a few officers and suggested that institutional racism remained a problem for the service, especially the Metropolitan Police. In October 1999, a lay advisory group which had been set up following the Macpherson Report suspended its work after claims that two of its members were racially abused by police officers when they attended the scene of the Paddington rail disaster to counsel the families of black and Asian victims. Complaints were also voiced that senior officers had failed to attend the group's meetings. In January 2000 Stephen Lawrence's father, Neville, lodged a complaint against this force after he was stopped, searched and questioned about a street robbery and in connection with the car he was driving. Later that month the Bishop of Stepney, John Sentamu, was stopped and searched by the Metropolitan Police. This was the eighth time this internationally respected figure (who is also a trained lawyer) had been inconvenienced in this manner. Duwayne Brooks, who had been with Stephen Lawrence when he was murdered, was subsequently arrested on six occasions without being convicted. In March 2000 a judge threw out the latest charge laid against him (that of indecent assault) before it was allowed to proceed to open court. In 2000 the Metropolitan Police announced an inquiry into the alleged harassment of Delroy Lindo (a friend of Winston Silcott who had been wrongly convicted of murdering a police officer in the Broadwater Farm riots in 1985). He had been charged on 19 occasions since 1996 and cleared each time.

The effectiveness of changes to police procedures to deal with racial violence in London was queried in a report by the Inspectorate. This praised the role performed by officers in specialist units but argued that more needed to be done to win over the hearts and minds of non-specialist police officers. Reference was made to 'a pervasive feeling ... among some staff that what is seen as special treatment to the victims of racial attacks can only be delivered by prejudicing service to the broader community'. The report thus urged that this issue should be addressed in community and race relations training courses (HMIC, 2000: 6). This opinion was underpinned by resentment felt by many rank-and-file officers that they had been effectively 'sold down the river' by senior management accepting Macpherson's view that the service was institutionally racist which they did not believe was the case. The resistance of some officers to this view took numerous forms, including advising white victims of crime involving members of ethnic minority groups that theirs was a racial crime.

Accordingly, since the publication of the Macpherson Report, there has been a rise in the number of white persons who have been victims of such attacks: according to figures published in the *Guardian* on 11 May 2001, between 1997 and 1998 the Metropolitan Police recorded 27 per cent of victims of racial attacks as white, 27 per cent as black and 37 per cent as Asian, but between 1999 and 2000 the number of black victims rose to 29 per cent and the number of white victims to 31 per cent. Similarly there has been an increase in the number of black suspects of racial incidents. Between 1997 and 1998, 71 per cent of suspects of racial incidents were white. This figure fell to 67 per cent between 1999 and 2000, and during the same period the percentage of black suspects rose from 16 per cent to 20 per cent. This has led to suggestions that this is perverse reporting by officers actively conniving in a white backlash against the recommendations of the Macpherson Report (Fitzgerald, 2001). It has also had the consequence of overloading community safety units with casework.

Problems with the elimination of institutional racism in the police service have also occurred outside London. Disorder at Oldham in 2001 occurred against the background of accusations of police indifference to racist attacks in which Asians were the victims coupled to assertions made by the local police commander in June 2001 that Asians committed the majority of incidents of racial violence. This resulted in the formation of self-defence groups. Further, accusations of inadequate police responses to racially motivated violence continued to be made. The inquest into the death of Errol McGowan (who had been found hanged in Telford in July 1999) in 2001 heard evidence that he believed a campaign of harassment and threats had been directed against him but that the West Mercia police had failed to provide him with an effective remedy. In 1999 Jay Abatan was the victim of a racial attack in Sussex. No person was convicted of this crime. Two suspects had charges of manslaughter dismissed before the case could go to court and a year later lesser charges were also dismissed. Subsequently a report into the way in which the Sussex police handled the investigation was conducted by the Essex police. This drew attention to 57 inconsistencies, failures and inexplicable decisions taken by the Sussex force, following which it made a public apology to the family of the murder victim.

Institutional racism – what more needs to be done? A further reform affecting police culture might be secured by subjecting the police service to enhanced accountability. On 24 February 1999, Jonathan Freedland, writing in the *Guardian*, suggested it would have been inconceivable that the Stephen Lawrence investigation would have been handled so incompetently had the Commissioner of Police been accountable to the voters of London with its 25 per cent minority ethnic electorate. He stated that 'if he had to face the voters, as police chiefs do in some of America's biggest cities, would he not have realised his job was on the line?' He further suggested that if, alternatively, the Commissioner was accountable to a mayor (as is the case in New York) this episode would not have arisen either since the mayor would have sacked the police chief in order to keep his own job. Although London elected its first mayor (Ken Livingstone) in 2000, he does not appoint the Commissioner of Police, and neither is this official elected by the London voters. However, the enhanced role of local government in police affairs provided for in the 1998 Crime and Disorder Act, and the appointment of a police authority for London under the provisions of the 1999 London Government Act present the possibility of increased accountability of the police to their local public. Other reforms introduced by the Labour government, including the reform of the Race Relations Act and the endorsement of an independent system for investigating complaints against the police, will also erode the autonomy of the organisation and make it more susceptible to the views and opinions of the general public.

The probation service

The probation service may have to deal with those found guilty of racially motivated crimes. Towards the end of the 1990s the West Midlands probation service pioneered anti-racism offending behaviour programmes, which were directed at convicted racists. This scheme, entitled *Murder to Murmur: Working with Racially Motivated and Racist Offenders*, sought to expose racist offenders and tackle their attitudes and behaviour in order to prevent further acts of violence. Probation officers were enjoined to be observant of, and to challenge, racism wherever they observed it. However, a subsequent report into the operations of the probation services stated that few had produced detailed guidelines for working with racially motivated offenders and that no commonly accepted definition of what constituted a racially motivated offender existed across the services (HMIP, 2000).

The prison service

The number of racist incidents in prison in 1998–99 was 293 for prisoner on prisoner, 379 for prisoner on staff, and 218 for staff on prisoner. In February 2000, the prison service adopted the definition of a racist incident provided in the Macpherson Report and from August 2000 four new racially aggravated offences were introduced into Prison Rules (Home Office, 2000: 50). However, major problems persisted with the ability of the prison service to deal with the problem of racial violence in their institutions and it has been argued that the 'stereotyping of black people as "violent" and "dangerous" legitimises violence against them, and allows their mental and physical health needs to be overlooked when in the care of the police and prison services' (Bowling and Phillips, 2002: 241). In March 2001, Zahid Mubarek (whose crime was that of a minor theft and interfering with a motor vehicle) was made to share a cell with a racist psychopath with a history of violence at Feltham Young Offenders' Institution. Mubarek was subsequently murdered by this inmate.

Conclusion

This chapter has examined the issue of racially motivated violence as an extra-parliamentary tactic used, endorsed or encouraged by extreme right-wing parties and organisations in Britain. Violence of this nature is based on a denial of the shared humanity between white and minority ethnic persons and is designed either to drive minority ethnic groups into segregated areas akin to the situation which persisted during South Africa's apartheid system or to force them to leave the country.

Violence directed against persons from minority ethnic groups requires the intervention of the state, and this section has discussed the deficient way in which key agencies operating in the criminal justice system traditionally responded to actions of this nature and how the tragic murder of Stephen Lawrence in 1993 provided an agenda for change. The response of the state to racial violence is underpinned by the consideration of political toleration which has been discussed in the introductory chapter. However, any restriction on political actions raise questions regarding civil and political liberties and this topic forms the basis of the concluding chapter which seeks to assess how responses by the state to the various forms of extra-parliamentary political activity discussed in Chapters 2–6 have affected the nature of liberal democracy in Britain.

Glossary

Racial discrimination

Racial discrimination involves the acting out of negative feelings felt towards a minority group (which may be defined in a number of ways including race, ethnicity, culture, language, sex or gender) so that they become disadvantaged in a wide range of areas by virtue of the 'unequal, unfavourable and unjustifiable treatment' which they receive (Bowling and Phillips, 2002: 38). Discrimination can be of two types. Direct discrimination entails explicit actions (often enshrined in law) which disadvantage persons from minority groups, whereas indirect discrimination is concerned with actions which have a disadvantageous outcome for a minority group even though these seem to provide formal equality for all groups.

Racial prejudice

Racial prejudice may be defined as blind and irrational hatred based upon the victim being assigned stereotypical characteristics. The term has been more fully defined as 'a readiness to act, steming from a negative feeling, often predicated upon a fixed over-generalisation or totally false belief and directed towards a group or individual members of that group' (Kleg, 1993: 114).

Racial violence and the law

Prior to the passage of the 1998 Criminal Justice and Public Order Act, there were a number of Acts which related to violence which might be applied to racial attacks. These included the 1861 Offences against the Person Act, the 1953 Prevention of Crime Act, the 1968 Firearms Act, the 1971 Criminal Damage Act, sections 137 and 222(a) of the 1972 Local Government Act, the 1977 Protection from Eviction Act, the 1985 Housing Act and the 1988 Malicious Communications Act. The 1991 Football (Offences) Act made indecent or racialist chanting illegal actions. Additionally common law charges of common assault and occasioning bodily harm could be pursued. The offence of incitement to racial hatred contained in the 1986 Public Order Act was of particular importance. This made it an offence to use threatening, insulting or abusive words or behaviour with the intention of stirring up racial hatred, or if it could be proved that actions of this kind were likely to stir up racial hatred whether intended or not. The law also covered the publication and broadcast of racially inflammatory material through media such as films, video and sound recordings. The consent of the Attorney General remained a requirement for a prosecution to be initiated. The offence relating to disorderly conduct in section 5 of the 1986 Act might also be utilised in relation to threatening, abusive or insulting behaviour of a racial nature. In 1986 the Racial Harassment Bill sought to declare racial harassment an offence, and would have required landlords to take action against perpetrators in specific circumstances. It also placed duties upon local authorities to investigate all complaints of racial harassment. One criticism of this measure was that it placed too much emphasis on action by landlords rather than by the police (CRE, 1987: 29). It failed to pass the House of Commons and was substantially redrafted in 1992. In 1994 the Racial Hatred and Violence Bill proposed extra penalties in cases where a racial motivation could be established and the creation of a new offence of racial harassment. This also failed to become law. In 1994 the Home Affairs Select Committee called for legislative reforms to make it easier to prove a racial motivation for an act of violence in court and which would increase the penalties for racial crimes. Under the Select Committee's proposals, a charge of violent assault in which there was evidence that the attack had been motivated by colour, race, nationality or ethnic or national origins could result in an additional and consecutive sentence of up to five years' imprisonment for the racial element of that offence (Home Affairs Committee, 1994: 29). No legislation was enacted to specifically criminalise racial violence although the 1994 Criminal Justice and Public Order Act introduced the new offence of intentional harassment to deal with persistent problems of this nature.

Racism

Racism is a social construction which seeks to justify the control which one set of individuals wish to exert over another. It emerges from an unequal power relationship between black and white people which it serves to perpetuate.

References

ACPO/CRE (1993) *Policing and Racial Equality* (London: Association of Chief Police Officers and the Commission for Racial Equality)

T. Adorno, E. Frenkel-Brunswick, D. Levinson and R. Sanford (1950) *The Authoritarian Personality* (New York: Harper and Row)

H. Beider (ed.) (1999) *We Can't All Be White – Racist Victimisation in the UK* (London: Joseph Rowntree Foundation)

Bethnal Green and Stepney Trades Council (1978) *Blood on the Streets: a Report by Bethnal Green and Stepney Trades Council on Racial Attacks in East London* (London: Bethnal Green and Stepney Trades Council)

I. Blair (1999) speech to the Social Market Foundation, London, 18 February, quoted in *Guardian*, 19 February

N. Bland, G. Mundy, J. Russell and R. Tuffin (1999) *Career Progression of Ethnic Minority Police Officers* (London: Home Office Research, Development and Statistics Directorate, Home Office Police Research Series Paper 107)

B. Bowling (1998) *Violent Racism: Victimisation, Policing and Social Context* (Oxford: Oxford University Press)

B. Bowling and C. Phillips (2002) *Racism, Crime and Justice* (Harlow: Longman)

R. Blauner (1972) *Racial Oppression in America* (New York: Harper and Row)

F. Broughton and M. Bennett (1994) quoted in the *Guardian*, 27 September

S. Carmichael and C. Hamilton (1967) *Black Power* (New York: Vintage)

A. Clancy, M. Hough, R. Aust and C. Kershaw (2001) *Crime, Policing and Justice: the Experience of Ethnic Minorities* (London: Home Office, Home Office Research Study Number 223, Findings from the 2000 British Crime Survey)

Commission for Racial Equality (1987) *Living in Terror: a Report on Racial Violence and Harassment in Housing* (London: Commission for Racial Equality)

Commission for Racial Equality (2001) *The Crown Prosecution Service, Croydon Branch: Report of a Formal Investigation* (London: Commission for Racial Equality)

P. Condon (1993) quoted in *Guardian*, 1 March

O. Cox (1948) *Caste, Class and Race* (New York: Doubleday)

D. Crompton (1999) quoted in *Guardian*, 2 March

C. Crowther (2000) *Policing Urban Poverty* (Basingstoke: Macmillan Press – now Palgrave Macmillan)

S. Denman (2001) *Race Discrimination in the Crown Prosecution Service: Final Report* (London: Crown Prosecution Service)

N. Dholakia and A. Price-Jones (1993) 'Introduction and Opening Address', in P. Francis and R. Matthews (eds) *Tackling Racial Attacks* (Leicester: Centre for the Study of Public Order, University of Leicester)

J. Dollard (1939) *Frustration and Aggression* (Yale: Yale University Press)

J. Dollard (1957) *Caste and Class in a Southern Town* (New York, Doubleday)

M. Fitzgerald (1999) *Searches in London under Section 1 of the Police and Criminal Evidence Act* (London: Metropolitan Police Service)

M. Fitzgerald (2001) *Crime, Disorder and Community*, quoted in *Guardian*, 11 May

M. Fitzgerald and C. Hale (1996) *Ethnic Minorities, Victimisation and Racial Harassment* (London: Home Office Research and Statistics Directorate, Research Findings Number 39)

M. Franklin (1985) *The Decline of Class Voting in Britain: Changes in the Basis of Electoral Choice* (Oxford: Clarendon)

P. Gordon (1983) *White Law: Racism in the Police, the Courts and Prisons* (London: Pluto Press)

P. Gordon (1993) 'The Police and Racist Violence in Britain', in T. Bjorgo and R. Witte (eds) *Racist Violence in Europe* (Basingstoke: Macmillan Press – now Palgrave Macmillan)

P. Gordon (1996) 'The Racialisation of Statistics', in R. Skellington (ed.) *'Race' in Britain Today* (London: Sage, 2nd edition)

C. Gutzmore (1983) 'Capital, Black Youth and Crime', *Race and Class*, XXV(2), Autumn, 13–30

P. Harris (2001a) 'Far Right Plot to Provoke Race Riots', *Observer*, 3 June

P. Harris (2001b) 'Revealed: Secret Plot to Stir Riots', *Observer*, 22 July

Her Majesty's Inspectorate of Constabulary (1997) *Winning the Race: Policing Plural Communities, HMIC Thematic Inspection Report on Police Community and Race Relations 1996/97* (London: Home Office)

Her Majesty's Inspectorate of Constabulary (1999) *Winning the Race: Policing Plural Communities Revisited: a Follow up to the Thematic Inspection Report on Police Community and Race Relations 1998/99* (London: Home Office)

Her Majesty's Inspectorate of Constabulary (2000) *Policing London: 'Winning Consent', a Review of Murder Investigation, Community and Race Relations Issues in the Metropolitan Police Service* (London: Home Office)

Her Majesty's Inspectorate of Probation (2000) *Thematic Inspection Report, Towards Racial Equality* (London: Home Office)

S. Holdaway (1996) *The Racialisation of British Policing* (Basingstoke: Macmillan Press – now Palgrave Macmillan)

Home Affairs Select Committee (1981) *Racial Attacks* (London: HMSO, House of Commons Paper 106)

Home Affairs Committee (1986) *Racial Attacks and Harassment* (London: HMSO, House of Commons Paper 409)

Home Affairs Select Committee (1994) *Racial Attacks and Harassment* (London: HMSO, Volume 1, House of Commons Paper 71–1)

Home Office (1998) *Statistics on Race and the Criminal Justice System* (London: Home Office Research, Development and Statistics Directorate)

Home Office (2000a) *Statistics on Race and the Criminal Justice System* (London: Home Office Research, Development and Statistics Directorate)

Home Office (2000b) *Complaints against the Police, a Consultative Paper* (London: Home Office Operational Police Unit)

Home Office (2001) *Policing a New Century: a Blueprint for Reform* (London: Home Office, Cm 5236)

N. Hopkins (2002) 'Met Winning the Battle against Prejudice', *Guardian*, 22 February

J. Hunte (1965) *Nigger Hunting in London?* (London: West Indian Standing Conference)

Independent Committee of Inquiry Commissioned by the Roach Family Support Committee (1989) *Policing in Hackney 1945–1984* (London: Karia Press)

Institute of Race Relations (1991) *Deadly Silence: Black Deaths in Custody* (London: Institute of Race Relations)

A. Kirkwood (1998) *Crown Prosecution Service: Racial Incident Monitoring, Annual Report 1997–1998* (York: Crown Prosecution Service, Amended Version)

M. Kleg (1993) *Hate, Prejudice and Racism* (Albany: State University of New York Press)

N. Lowles (2001) *White Riot: the Violent Story of Combat 18* (Bury: Milo Books)

D. Maclean (1994) written answer to Ms Corston, 14 July, *House of Commons Debates*, 6th Series, Volume 246, column 692

Sir William Macpherson (1999) *The Stephen Lawrence Inquiry: Report of an Inquiry by Sir William Macpherson of Cluny* (London: TSO Cm 4262)

N. Makenji (1995) quoted in *Guardian*, 18 April

N. Aye Maung and C. Mirrlees-Black (1994) *Racially Motivated Crime: a British Crime Survey Analysis* (London: Home Office Research and Planning Unit)

Metropolitan Police Community Relations Branch (1987) *Racial Harassment Action Guide* (London: Metropolitan Police)

R. Miles (1989) *Racism* (London: Routledge)

Oldham Independent Review (2001) *One Oldham, One Future* (Manchester: Government Office for the North West)

B. Parekh (1974) 'Postscript', in B. Parekh (ed.) *Colour, Culture and Consciousness: Immigrant Intellectuals in Britain* (London, George Allen and Unwin)

A. Percy (1998) 'Ethnicity and Victimisation: Findings from the 1996 British Crime Survey', *Home Office Statistical Bulletin*, 6/98, 3 April (London: Home Office)

A. Phizacklea and R. Miles (1980) *Labour and Racism* (London: Routledge and Kegan Paul)

R. Reiner (1985) *The Politics of the Police* (Brighton: Harvester Press)

J. Rex (1986) *Race and Ethnicity* (Milton Keynes: Open University Press)

J. Rex and R. Moore (1967) *Race, Community and Conflict: a Study of Sparkbrook* (Oxford: Oxford University Press)

J. Rex and S. Tomlinson (1979) *Colonial Immigrants in a British City* (London: Routledge and Kegan Paul)

M. Rowe (1998) *The Racialisation of Disorder in Twentieth-Century Britain* (Aldershot: Ashgate)

R. Sibbitt (1997) *The Perpetrators of Racial Harassment and Racial Violence* (London: Home Office Information and Publications Group, Home Office Research Study Number 176)

G. Singh (2000) 'The Concept and Content of Institutional Racism', in A. Marlow and B. Loveday (eds) *After Macpherson* (Dorset: Russell House Publishing)

R. Skellington (ed.) (1996) *'Race' in Britain Today* (London: Sage, 2nd edition)

J. Solomos and L. Back (1995) *Race, Politics and Social Change* (London: Routledge)

D. Smith and J. Gray (1983) *Police and People in London: Vol IV, The Police in Action* (London: Policy Studies Institute)

S. Smith (1989) *The Politics of 'Race' and Residence: Citizenship, Segregation and White Supremacy in Britain* (Cambridge: Polity)

G. Smyth (1999) letter to the *Guardian*, 10 February

M. Steed (1974) 'The Results Analysed', in D. Butler and A. King (eds) *The British General Election of February 1974* (London: Macmillan)

J. Straw (1999a) speech at Gloucester, 1 March, quoted in *Guardian*, 2 March

J. Straw (1999b) speech to a conference of chief constables, Southampton, 14 April

K. Tompson (1988) *Under Seige: Racial Violence in Britain Today* (Harmondsworth: Penguin Books)

R. Vogler (1991) *Reading the Riot Act: the Magistracy, the Police and the Army in Civil Disorder* (Milton Keynes: Open University Press)

M. Walker (1977) *The National Front* (London: Fontana)

A. Wilson (1983) 'Conspiracies to Assault', *New Statesman*, 105(2710), 22 February

7
Conclusion: Extra-Parliamentary Politics and Civil and Political Liberties

The previous chapters have considered a range of extra-parliamentary political activities which have been utilised by political parties and organisations since 1970 in Britain. Each chapter has specifically examined the reaction of the state to the activity or activities which formed its focus. This concluding chapter examines the implications of these interventions on the exercise of political and civil liberties in particular, but also on political expression and individual privacy. It focuses on two key considerations both of which have major implications for the nature of liberal democracy in Britain. These are whether changes to policing as the result of extra-parliamentary political action have undermined the traditional British concept of policing by consent and, in particular, have restricted the freedom of political expression expressed through extra-parliamentary means, and whether the gathering of intelligence by state agencies on organisations which utilise various forms of extra-parliamentary political action (on the grounds of defending the state against subversion) have threatened basic liberal democratic freedoms, in particular, privacy.

Changes affecting policing

A number of criticisms have been made of the initiatives introduced by the police service to respond to the various forms of extra-parliamentary political activities which have been referred to in Chapters 2–6. Some have dubbed these changes 'paramilitary policing', which has been defined as 'the application of (quasi) military training, equipment and organisation to questions of policing (whether under central control or not)' (Jefferson, 1990: 16). The main features of what has been described as paramilitary policing (centralisation, standardisation and aggressive police behaviour) are considered in greater detail below.

Centralisation and standardisation of policing

Policing has become more standardised and uniform throughout the country as the result of the emphasis placed on the policing of public order events since 1970. Chapter 3 has discussed allegations of central control being exerted by a body then named the National Reporting Centre over major public order situations, especially in connection with the 1984–85 miners' dispute. The publication of the *Public Order Manual* in 1983 was accompanied by the formation of an ACPO body, the Public Order Forward Planning Group, to review all new developments and emerging tactics. Other developments (including the formation of a Central Intelligence Unit during the 1984–85 miners' dispute to analyse intelligence gathered by officers on the ground) followed this initial ACPO initiative. The deployment of officers from across the country in specific crowd situations generated further pressures for enhanced levels of standardisation in both equipment and training. All forces were subsequently required to train a number of Police Support Units according to common standards, one advantage being that an officer from one force could effectively command PSUs drawn from different forces. Central government supported these ACPO initiatives which were especially detrimental to the role exerted by police authorities over policing. Home Office circular 40/1986, for example, made it possible for the Home Office to override the refusal of a police authority to supply riot equipment to a local force, provided that the chief constable's request for such material was supported by the HMIC.

The emphasis placed on public order in police training programmes since the 1980s (which are now provided in a basic form to all officers), and the actual involvement of officers in confrontational situations, may have a detrimental effect on the performance of regular police duties performed by officers in their local communities. It may result in forces having to devote resources to issues which are of limited relevance to its local population or in having to abandon their local responsibilities in order to respond to central pressures to police major public order events (an issue which is discussed in more detail in Chapter 3). Contemporary debates concerning the introduction of armed response vehicles, the use of batons rather than the traditional truncheon, and the introduction of pepper sprays may be seen to have derived from the development of new methods to police crowds in a more coercive manner.

Allegations of aggressive police conduct

A number of criticisms have been made of the police methods utilised in public order situations after 1970. These have been discussed in more detail earlier in this work (especially in Chapters 2 and 3). A response by the police which is perceived as overly aggressive by those on the receiving end may result in alienating sections of the population from the police. It was in this sense that one chief constable argued in 1981 that the appropriate response by the police to inner city disorders was to 'talk hearts and minds, not CS gas and plastic bullets' (Alderson, 1981). An additional danger is that the presence of police officers at a specific incident, dressed and equipped as if they were 'looking for trouble', has the potential to exacerbate violence (Jefferson, 1987: 51–3) and may actually provoke it or legitimise the use of violence by a crowd (Saunders, 1996: 118).

Various explanations might be offered for allegations of aggressive police behaviour in public order situations. It might be suggested that in violent situations the control exercised by senior police officers breaks down, or that aggression can be explained by fear, triggered by the violence to which police officers are often subjected. However, an equally important consideration concerns the political environment in which the police response to public disorder is shaped. In the 1980s the police were aware that their actions in events such as industrial disputes had the full support of the Conservative government. This may have resulted in a tendency to act in an aggressive manner in the knowledge that the government would defend this course of action. The so-called 'battle of Orgreave' evidenced an aggressive response of this nature which involved the use of 'tortoise' formations of man-sized riot shields operating with snatch squads to seize demonstrators, and the deployment of mounted police – one of whom was infamously pictured about to smash his baton into the head of a terrified woman who was luckily rescued by a demonstrator.

The new policing methods and liberal democracy

Those who are critical of changes made to the policing of crowd situations since 1970 assert that they imply a departure from the concept of minimum force that threatens to erode the principle of policing by consent which historically underpinned policing in Britain. In its place, it is argued, a more coercive style of policing has been substituted. The image of managing public order events by the traditional method of 'conventionally uniformed officers tolerantly pushing and shoving in defensive formation against lines of pickets or demonstrators' (D. Waddington, 1996: 1) was argued to have been replaced in the 1980s by a police service which was 'armed with new powers, possessing new equipment and coordinated on a national basis … they appear unfamiliar and discomfiting: less a part of society: more apart from it' (Brewer et al., 1996: 6).

The changes which have been made to police organisation, tactics and weaponry could serve to limit the ability to engage in extra-parliamentary political activity. Demonstrators may be deterred from taking to the streets if they believe that the police would use the pretext of the imminent breakdown of public order as a justification for deploying all the coercive resources at their disposal against those wishing to protest. Accusations of this nature were levelled at the 'zero tolerance' approach adopted by the police at the May Day anti-capitalist protest in London in 2001 in which demonstrators were heavily outnumbered by police officers. It has thus been argued that developments associated with paramilitary policing indicate a departure from the concept of minimum force (Brewer et al., 1996: 22), are incompatible with fundamental freedoms traditionally associated with liberal democratic political systems and are more appropriate to the treatment of subjugated populations under colonial regimes (Northam, 1989; Jefferson, 1990). These new methods were allegedly developed as a deliberate attempt to prevent the articulation of protest and dissent. It has been argued that the extent of political dissent in the 1970s and early 1980s led the state to concentrate attention on 'the enemy within'. These were the working class who had borne the brunt of the fall in living standards through inflation and who were the first to experience unemployment (Bunyan, 1977: 277). Orgreave, 1984, witnessed 'the unveiling of colonial policing tactics in mainland Britain' (Northam, 1989: 59), influenced by the methods adopted by the Hong Kong police (Northam, 1989: 39–40).

The following sections elaborate on arguments which suggest that new policing methods were designed to curtail the ability of citizens to engage in various forms of extra-parliamentary political activity (as have been put forward in connection with the 'strong state' thesis) and then examine counter arguments which assert that these developments pose no threat to the political liberties traditionally associated with liberal democracy.

The 'strong state'

Allegations related to the erosion of civil and political liberties in the 1980s were associated with the crisis affecting capitalism in that period. The economic climate is a key consideration affecting social harmony. In post-war Britain the development of the welfare state was a key mechanism utilised to 'sell' an essentially unfair economic system to the public at large. It represented an 'institutionalised class compromise' which provided 'workers with economic security whilst also allowing capitalists profitability' (Jenkins, 1995: 28). However, during the 1970s the post-war boom came to an end. Economic growth slowed down and inflation became a major problem by the mid-1970s. Unemployment and the cost of living rose and successive governments introduced policies designed to reduce public expenditure and control prices and wages. External factors including the rise in the price of oil and a worldwide trade recession aggravated the United Kingdom's economic difficulties. Attempts to solve the crisis facing capitalism were especially associated with Margaret Thatcher's Conservative administrations which pursued economic policies which resulted in deteriorated circumstances for those at the bottom end of the social ladder who experienced unemployment and the dismantling of the welfare state. A major political problem became that of responding to the inevitable dissent which would emerge from groups who felt they were being denied their rights especially the 'right' to work and access to an ever-expanding level of services provided by the welfare state.

It has been alleged that there were three possible responses which the bourgeoisie could implement to counter threats to social harmony (Ackroyd et al., 1980). They might lend their weight to fascist political ideology, institute military intervention in politics, or encourage a range of piecemeal political reforms designed to curb civil and political rights, especially the ability to express dissent. The latter approach could take place behind the façade of liberal democracy and would constitute no overt attack on the liberal democratic political system even though the piecemeal reforms which were introduced altered its fundamental nature. These changes could be introduced with a degree of popular support derived from carefully orchestrated moral panics which involved scapegoating those at the lower end of the social ladder who were alleged to display moral failings or exhibit unacceptable social habits. The term 'strong state' was coined to describe what was depicted as the inevitable consequence of the free market in which the state and its agencies developed the capacity to be able to counter effectively the opposition of those who were adversely affected by economic policies or who sought to orchestrate challenges to them (Hall, 1979; Gamble, 1988). The police were thus given new powers and developed more robust tactics to deal with crowd situations to enable them to intervene aggressively on behalf of the state whose legitimacy was threatened by 'a whole panoply of public order challenges' (Brewer et al., 1996: xiv) including protest, industrial disputes and riots (which are discussed in Chapters 2, 3 and 4). However, the perception that policing had become less consensual and more politicised (Reiner, 1985: 4) in the sense of acting as 'partisan enforcers of minority needs' and 'agents of political control' (Brewer et al., 1996: 214) had an adverse effect on the image of the police and its relationship with the general public (Brewer et al., 1996: xiv–xv).

The compatibility of new policing methods and liberal democracy

The assertions made above in connection with the 'stong state' thesis suggest that economic factors forced changes to the nature of the liberal democratic state which restricted the citizens' ability to engage in various forms of extra-parliamentary political activity by imposing restrictions on the freedoms of expression and assembly. Arguments which alleged that the diminution of civil and political liberties is an inevitable consequence of capitalism in crisis are associated with Marxist analysis and have been challenged from other political perspectives. In particular the new right argued that 'rolling back' the frontiers of the state enhanced personal freedom. The condemnation of the increased coercive capacity of the state was especially associated with those who sought to reassert its role in social and economic affairs, viewing these interventions as key social rights.

However, the negative views expressed concerning the nature and consequence of changes to the policing of crowd situations which were introduced after 1970 are not universally accepted. It has been asserted that reforms to policing have not always been of a paramilitary nature and have included developments such as intelligence gathering, tension indicators and improved command and control structures (Brearley and King, 1996: 87–93). It has further been argued that changes to police methods in these circumstances were prompted in response to the violence to which police officers were often subjected. Extreme disorder at the 1976 Notting Hill Carnival (when police officers were compelled to defend themselves with dustbin lids) resulted in the introduction of riot shields (which were first used at Lewisham in 1977 at an event attended by the National Front and its opponents) and the use of petrol bombs by rioters in 1981 resulted in the provision of flameproof overalls to police officers (Reiner, 1991: 171). This argument thus rejects the view that changes in police methods were introduced in order to prevent protest and, alternatively, views them as a reactive response by the service to violence initiated by those engaged in various forms of extra-parliamentary political activity. Nor is there total agreement as to the significance of changes that were introduced after 1970. It has been argued that the stance adopted by the police when dealing with public order is substantially unaltered. In particular, the concept of minimum force remains (although the base line has altered so that the level of force which constitutes 'minimum' has been pushed upwards) and police actions continue to be based upon the under-enforcement of the law and the use of discretion (Reiner, 1998: 46).

The argument that changes introduced to policing are contrary to the exercise of freedoms traditionally associated with a liberal democratic political system is also rejected by some observers. What has been termed paramilitary policing is viewed as a selective summary of changes to policing methods since 1970 which have included intelligence gathering and planning (in particular the use of new command and control structures at public order events, as discussed in Chapter 3) in addition to the use of specialist equipment and training (P. Waddington, 1987). It has been contended that the improved central planning and supervision of public order events by police forces which entails the use of intelligence and trained personnel acting 'under hierarchical command in accordance with a formulated strategy and tactics' (P. Waddington, 1993: 366) has resulted in an improved level of protection to demonstrators who are not subject to ad hoc and contradictory police managerial decisions (which was a major problem at Red Lion Square) and are less likely to experience indisciplined actions by junior police officers (P. Waddington, 1996: 124–5). Improved management, new tactics and the availability of weaponry may further give the police confidence to let events go ahead which previously they would have prevented because of uncertainties as to whether public order could be maintained (P. Waddington, 1994: 201).

The development of 'political policing' in Great Britain

In addition to changes affecting the nature of police work in Great Britain, an enhanced level of attention has been devoted by the state to the regulation of political ideas and opinions as opposed to dealing with 'ordinary' crime and lawlessness. This is termed 'political policing' and threatens fundamental political freedoms and civil liberties associated with liberal democracy, most notably the freedom of expression, the ability to protest and the right to privacy. The rationale for the state's interest in these activities is that ideas may be translated into actions which threaten the stability of the state. Accordingly the justification of *subversion* has been put forward to justify the state's right to intervene in the political and private lives of its citizens. Chapter 5 discusses restraints in political and civil liberties introduced in connection with terrorism and this section furthers this discussion by considering the nature of subversion and examining the operations and accountability of those agencies which are involved in this area of work.

Subversion

The main difficulty with the concept of subversion is that it may encompass a wide range of extra-parliamentary political activities including direct action (which is discussed in Chapter 2) and industrial disputes (which are the focus of Chapter 3) in addition to activities such as terrorism (which are the concern of Chapter 5). The allegation of communist party involvement in industrial unrest and protest has often been used to justify the involvement of MI5 in activities of this nature (Geary, 1985: 60). In 1985 a former *Security Service (MI5)* intelligence officer, Cathy Massiter, revealed that CND had been closely monitored by the agency. This was initially justified by the belief that it was a 'communist dominated organisation' and, latterly, a 'communist penetrated organisation'. This might suggest that the advocacy of the abandonment by Great Britain of its independent nuclear deterrent was viewed by agencies such as MI5 as a subversive proposition (since the consequence of this policy would have been to weaken its defences) or it could suggest that extra-parliamentary political activities associated with CND and the peace movement in general (which are discussed in Chapter 2) were the source of the state's concern.

It has been argued that subversion was used as a pretext to justify state intervention on a scale which involved redrawing the boundaries of the liberal democratic tradition 'by declaring to be illegitimate political and industrial activities which had previously been thought to have distinguished a liberal democracy from an authoritarian or fascist society' (State Research, 1979: 4). Agencies such as Special Branch, MI5 and the Government Communications Headquarters (GCHQ) may find themselves accused of operating in the manner allegedly adopted by the American intelligence agencies. These, it has been argued, 'invaded the privacy of countless citizens, have seriously inhibited the freedom of expression, have arrogated to themselves the making of policy decisions in the most sensitive areas and have been employed by the administration in power for political purposes'. At one point they became virtually a fourth branch of government, functioning beyond civilian control (Emerson, 1983: 270). John Alderson, then Chief Constable of Devon and Cornwall, pointed to the dangers posed to progressive politics through the association of subversion with 'anything which is designed to change society' (quoted in Davies et al., 1984: 34).

The agencies responsible for defending the state against subversion

Although it can be argued that 'ordinary' crime is subversive as it poses a threat to the work ethic, the role of the police in countering subversive thoughts and actions is limited and primarily carried out by *Special Branch*. The main agencies concerned with defending the state against subversion are the Security Service (MI5) and the *Government Communications Headquarters (GCHQ)*, although additional bodies including the Defence Intelligence Staff (housed within the Ministry of Defence) and the Secret Intelligence Service, MI6 (which is part of the Foreign Office) may also be involved in activities of this nature. Commercial bodies may also be involved in this work, their main advantage being that they can be disowned by state agencies if their operations become public knowledge. On 27 January 1985, for example, the *Observer* alleged that a firm called Zeus Security had mounted a surveillance operation on individuals and groups at the Sizewell enquiry who opposed the nuclear industry. The newspaper claimed that such information was being obtained at the behest of British intelligence, although the company denied this allegation.

Case study: MI5, GCHQ and the miners' dispute 1984–85

The extent to which extra-parliamentary political activities are threatened by the actions of state agencies countering actions which are perceived as subversive may be illustrated by events which took place in the 1984–85 miners' dispute (see also Chapter 3).

MI5 was responsible for monitoring key members of the National Union of Miners (Arthur Scargill, Peter Heathfield and Mick McGahey) during this dispute as they believed that they were using the strike for subversive purposes. One rationale for this assumption was that the Soviet Union supported the strike (Rimington, 2001), although this argument could justify MI5 involvement in almost every industrial action undertaken after 1970 since, with the sole exception of the 1974 Ulster Workers' Council strike, 'every major strike in Britain was supported by the CPGB' (Norton-Taylor, 2001). An accusation of joint operations conducted by GCHQ and the American organisation, the National Security Agency (NSA), was made in the context of attempts by foreign governments, particularly the Soviet

Union (USSR), to donate money to the NUM during the 1984–85 miners' dispute (Milne, 1995: 4). The threat of sequestration made it imperative to obtain funds to keep the union afloat. However, the British government was able, through international surveillance of the NUM bank accounts and union officials, to keep abreast of attempts by the USSR to donate money even when this aid was sent indirectly (from Moscow initially via Switzerland and latterly via Warsaw) to avoid damaging relations with the British government. The belief that the NUM strike threatened to destabilise the government prompted it to utilise GCHQ to monitor a British target.

The control and accountability of agencies defending the state against subversion

A balance has to be struck between the operational freedom which bodies responsible for defending the state against subversion require in order to carry out their duties, and the preservation of liberal democratic political values and civil liberties. This emphasises the need for state security to be compatible with the political and civil rights normally associated with liberal democratic political systems rather than such rights being subordinated to security considerations (Lustgarten and Leigh, 1995). This objective is secured by ensuring that bodies such as Special Branch, MI5 and GCHQ have to answer for their activities as opposed to pursuing their own objectives without being subject to the mechanisms of accountability which are a fundamental feature of public agencies operating in a liberal democracy. This issue is discussed in more detail below.

The requirement of operational independence

Traditionally governments shied away from seeking control over agencies concerned with countering subversion. The 1952 Maxwell Fyfe directive emphasised that MI5 should be kept free from any political bias or influence and that nothing should be done 'that might lend colour to any suggestion that it is concerned with the interests of any particular section of the community, or with any other matter than the defence of the realm as a whole' (quoted in West, 1983: 243). Contravention of the spirit of this directive might result in agencies being accused of advancing the interests not of the state but of the government, an accusation which was made in connection with the activities of MI5 and CND in the 1980s. MI5 was accused of liaising with a unit within the Ministry of Defence (DS 19) which sent information to Conservative candidates in the 1983 general election on the political affiliations of members of the CND leadership.

The problem of ineffective accountability

The main difficulty with public agencies being insufficiently accountable for their actions is that they may determine their own roles (which is referred to as 'self-tasking') and the manner in which they perform them.

Their function as 'guardians of the state' may induce agencies concerned with combating subversion to elevate themselves above elected politicians or governments in the belief that these are pursuing subversive activities. Accusations that a group of MI5 officers plotted to get rid of the 1974–76 Wilson government because they suspected the Prime Minister of being excessively sympathetic to the Soviet Union were made by a former MI5 officer (Wright, 1987: 368–72) and although he subsequently withdrew these allegations on a BBC television programme, *Panorama*, televised on 13 October 1988, a subsequent television programme, *Secret History*, shown on 15 August 1996 asserted that the Wilson administration of 1974–76 suffered from operations carried out by MI5 operatives to discredit ministers. Other sources have alleged that its targets were Judith Hart (Leigh, 1988: 228–9) and Tony Benn, who was alleged to have been subjected to a 'stop Benn' campaign in 1979 (Walsh, 1982: 38). Activities of this nature undermine the right of citizens to choose who governs them which is an indispensable aspect of liberal democracy.

The problem of self-tasking was compounded by the manner in which the security services historically recruited personnel. Both MI5 and MI6 made extensive use of the 'old boy' network rather than using established civil service rules and procedures. This tended to mean that staff operating in these agencies were not socially representative and possessed views and attitudes that were likely to be conservative (unless, of course, they happened to be Soviet spies!). However, the conviction in 1985 of an MI5 agent, Michael Bettaney, for trying to pass information to the Soviet KGB led to reforms in recruitment and personnel management culminating with the open recruitment of graduates in 1995.

A further difficulty arising from ineffective accountability concerned the manner in which MI5 discharged its responsibilities. Some aspects of MI5's work were allegedly carried out by the use of 'dirty tricks' which might include tactics designed to undermine, smear or hound those individuals or groups which MI5 believed to be its political opponents. There have been several recent allegations of the use of tactics of this nature. In 1973 MI5 replaced MI6 as the lead agency for intelligence coordination in Northern Ireland, a role performed through the office of the Director and Coordinator of Intelligence. It was linked to a secret operation termed 'Clockwork Orange', which was initially designed to undermine the morale of the IRA and extreme loyalist groups but later extended to leading politicians in Northern Ireland and Britain. Colin Wallace (who was associated with covert work of this nature but subsequently distanced himself from it) was allegedly framed by MI5 for the manslaughter of his friend in 1980. In 1996 the Appeal Court quashed this conviction. The chief executive of the National Union of Miners during the dispute of 1984–85, Roger Windsor, was alleged to have been an MI5 undercover agent whose activities included making false allegations of corruption against the union president, Arthur Scargill, which were designed to destablise and sabotage the union (Milne, 1995: 5). Although it was subsequently denied that Roger Windsor was an MI5 agent, it was asserted that other agencies such as Special Branch or the police could have been involved in activities of this nature (Rimington, 2001).

There are also practical complications which arise from the lack of effective mechanisms of accountability. The funding arrangements for agencies involved in countering subversion were not historically disclosed and difficulties arose because of secrecy in this matter. MI5 faced perpetual problems due to its lack of adequate financing which resulted in the agency having to seek funding from the Americans for the development of technological innovations (Wright, 1987). It is also likely that when agencies operate under 'a cloak of secrecy', accusations can be made concerning their actions which are not necessarily accurate but which result in the erosion of 'the basic trust, confidence and tolerance upon which a democratic society must rest' (Emerson, 1982: 278). The accusation, strongly denied by West Mercia police, that the death of the anti-nuclear campaigner, Hilda Murrell, in 1984 could be attributed to the work of the security services provided an example of official secrecy providing an environment in which sinister and damaging accusations concerning the operations of agencies of the British state could be made (Murray, 1993).

Mechanisms of accountability (1): the historic position

The mechanisms to provide for the accountability of agencies involved with defending the state against subversion were traditionally viewed as being inadequate and thus incompatible with the operations of public bodies in a liberal democratic state. They were not, however, non-existent. This section discusses the situation before reforms were introduced in the 1980s.

Executive control

In their day-to-day operations, the intelligence and security agencies operated under the immediate control of their respective heads who were responsible to ministers. Traditionally (until the passage of the 1989 Security Services Act) the Director General of MI5 was responsible to the Home Secretary, but in practice the agency enjoyed almost total operational freedom with ministers being informed by the director general on a 'need to know' basis.

The methods used to gather intelligence, principally telephone tapping and mail opening were governed by warrants issued by senior ministers, usually the Home Secretary. The precise circumstances surrounding the issuance of a warrant were revealed in a white paper issued in 1980. This stated that the police and customs and excise could only obtain a warrant in connection with a serious offence when normal methods of policing had either been tried and had failed to produce any evidence or would be unlikely to succeed in producing information, and when there was reason to believe that an activity of this nature would lead to an arrest and conviction. Warrants set out the name and address or telephone number of the person or organisation subject to interception and were subject to a time limit of up to two months which could be renewed. Different criteria applied when MI5 or the police were conducting a 'counter terrorist' operation involving the investigation of a major subversive, terrorist or espionage activity which was capable of constituting a threat to the realm. The material gathered had to be of direct use in compiling information laid down by MI5 to carry out its tasks as laid down in directives given to its Director General (Home Office, 1980). Ministers also issued guidelines governing other activities performed by the security services. Bugging was not referred to in the 1980 white paper although the Home Secretary, William Whitelaw, insisted that it occurred only with his knowledge. Guidelines were drawn up in 1977 affecting CID and Special Branch whereby a chief constable could authorise bugging in connection with investigations seeking to dispel a suspicion of serious crime.

Legislative accountability

The ability of Parliament to hold accountable those bodies concerned with monitoring subversive thoughts and actions was traditionally limited. There was no annual debate on the security services and their budget was not subject to Parliamentary scrutiny. The Speaker was able to prevent matters affecting the security services from being discussed, including covert operations allegedly carried out by the SAS (Lindsay, 1980: 77). The new system of select committees introduced in 1979 aided Parliament's investigatory function and has spasmodically been used to examine the role of the security services. One example of this was the investigation of Special Branch by the Home Affairs Committee in 1984.

Legal accountability

Members of the general public who perceived they had suffered from improper actions by the security services could theoretically seek redress in the courts. However, their ability to intervene was restricted by factors which included MI5 not possessing a legal basis until 1989 and safeguards such as warrants and guidelines issued by ministers lacking statutory authority. Additionally the procedures adopted in cases involving official secrecy (such as the use of Crown privilege or the convention whereby judges refused to allow the cross-examination of witnesses which might be contrary to the national interest) hampered the ability of individuals to prosecute cases or defend themselves if they were the subject of proceedings initiated by the state (Lindsay, 1980: 83). The European Commission and Court of Human Rights sometimes intervened to protect individuals against the operations of the security services until (as is discussed later in this chapter) the 1998 Human Rights Act provided domestic courts with powers to act in these matters.

Organisational accountability

Special Branch is a part of the police service and outside London is theoretically accountable to both the police authority and the chief constable. Police authorities, however, have not greatly involved themselves in this aspect of work and their ability to elicit information has been impaired by chief constables being able to deny requests for information not deemed essential to the discharge of their functions. Chief constables have rarely intervened in the operations of the Special Branch. One exception to this was John Alderson when Chief Constable of Devon and Cornwall betweeen 1973 and 1982. He recorded the tendency of Special Branch to 'record almost anything, however remotely connected it may be with activity which might in the loosest sense be regarded as subversive'. Such included '"X" had a meal with Wedgwood Benn' (quoted in Davies et al., 1984: 34).

Media scrutiny and published accounts of the operations of the state security services

The role of the media as the 'fourth estate' provided a theoretical check on the ability of the state and its agencies to conduct themselves in an overbearing manner which was prejudicial to the operations of a liberal democratic state. Investigative journalism could be used to expose the activities and methods utilised by state security agencies. However, the ability of the press and television media to expose the workings of such bodies was restricted. The 'D' notice system could be used by a government to prevent sensitive stories being made public. This was augmented by the Official Secrets Act which discouraged media stories or first-hand accounts of the operations of the security services from being published. Section 1 of the 1911 Official Secrets Act permitted court proceedings to be held in camera, and section 2 of this Act made it an offence both to disclose any form of information which was attributable to a person's employment in government service and also to communicate this information to a wider audience. The sanction of a fine or imprisonment could be applied both to journalists and to former government employees who sought to provide the public with accounts of the activities of the security services. The battles which took place in the Australian courts between 1986 and 1988 in connection with Peter Wright's account of the work of MI5 in his book, *Spycatcher*, demonstrated the extent to which the government was willing to go to prevent public knowledge of the work of these bodies.

Mechanisms of accountability (2): reforms introduced since 1980

Accusations that political and civil liberties in Britain were being undermined by the actions of the intelligence and security agencies prompted a number of reforms which were introduced in the 1980s. These were designed to reassure the public that civil and political liberties were not being unnecessarily restricted by making the agencies undertaking work of this nature more accountable for their activities. This section discusses the reforms which were implemented after 1980.

Telephone tapping

The 1980s witnessed a considerable volume of interest displayed in telephone tapping. This practice constituted an invasion of privacy which was justified by the need of the state to monitor individuals and organisations whose actions could be deemed as subversive. Two related problems can be identified in the debate concerning telephone tapping – the impact of technology on telephone tapping and a belief that the extent of the practice was more widespread than the government was willing to admit.

Traditionally, telephone tapping assumed two forms. The first was an attempt to build up information on a suspect's contacts which was done by logging calls made by that person. The second involved either listening to a suspect's telephone conversations when they were made or recording them and subsequently listening to a whole series of them. The latter practice (which initially involved 'taps' being placed in local telephone exchanges but was performed by computer from a central BT facility in Shropshire when the country's telephone network became totally digital) was extremely costly in terms of the personnel required to monitor and transcribe intercepted telephone calls. Technology considerably increased the capacity of the state to conduct telephone tapping. The introduction of System X exchanges during the 1980s meant that information such as who telephoned whom and for how long could be generated automatically. The use of terrestrial microwave systems by major carriers including British Telecom has facilitated widescale tapping (Fitzgerald and Leopold, 1987: 89–90) while the development of key-word computerised transcription and voice recognition computers made it easier to sift through vast quantities of recorded telephone conversations to elicit material of relevance to the agency undertaking an enquiry (Campbell, 1981: 21). A further development affected telephone calls made on mobile phones which can be intercepted by scanning equipment normally used in connection with radio transmissions. Although these scanners usually lose the call after a few seconds additional equipment makes it possible for entire conversations to be intercepted.

Governments were traditionally loath to admit the extent to which telephone tapping was practised. There was a gap in official information between the publication of the Birkett Report in 1957 and a white paper issued in 1980. The latter revealed that the number of warrants authorising telephone taps had risen from 129 in 1958 to 467 in 1979 (Home Office, 1980: 8). However, the relatively small size of this figure was the subject of debate. It was unclear whether the figure quoted in the 1980 white paper was the annual total of all warrants in operation or whether it comprised the annual total of new warrants issued in each year. It was further admitted in Parliamentary debate that the document made no reference to

Northern Ireland, where different criteria applied, it omitted the work of the Defence Intelligence Staff and MI6 (Campbell, 1981: 44–8) and did not refer to GCHQ whose operations were governed by informal guidelines issued by ministers. These concerns resulted in the government appointing Lord Diplock to examine the interception of communications by the police, post office and MI5. His first report in 1981 expressed general satisfaction that the procedures outlined in the 1980 white paper were being adhered to (Diplock, 1981).

The Interception of Communications Act, 1985.   Perceptions that the general public were not adequately protected against the misuse of powers related to telephone tapping by the police or security services arose in relation to the case of James Malone in 1984 in which evidence obtained from telephone taps was used against him in a court case involving the handling of stolen goods. In court Malone challenged the legitimacy of the operation by arguing that as a telephone subscriber he had rights of privacy and property over his conversations, and although this argument was lost in the English courts, the European Court of Human Rights subsequently found in his favour on two of the three issues brought before them, arguing that telephone tapping was illegal as there was no statute specifically authorising it. The European Commission subsequently found the United Kingdom government in breach of Articles 8 and 13 of the European Convention of Human Rights.

The controversy related to the Malone case resulted in the 1984 Telecommunications Act, providing redress through the courts for illegal tapping. This procedure was almost immediately amended by the 1985 Interception of Communications Act. This measure was based upon proposals contained in a white paper published in 1985. This referred to 538 warrants having been issued by government ministers during 1984 and proposed amended regulations to regulate this process (Home Office, 1985). These were incorporated into the 1985 Act and thus placed telephone tapping on a legal basis. Interception of communications would usually require a secretary of state to issue a warrant. This would normally last for two months but could be cancelled at any time and was also renewable. Section 2(2) stipulated that warrants could be issued in the interests of national security, to prevent or detect a serious crime or to safeguard the economic well-being of Great Britain. Under this legislation, warrants could include an address or series of addresses used by the person named in the warrant. Additionally the secretary of state should consider whether the information required could be obtained by other means, thus diluting the previous requirement that normal methods of investigation had been tried and failed (Home Office, 1980). Usually the telecommunications which were authorised to be intercepted were internal to the United Kingdom, the main exception being investigations designed to prevent or detect terrorism. Warrants dealing with international issues (which would be carried out by GCHQ) did not have to identify a person or address but instead could describe the kind of material information was required on (such as arms).

The Act also introduced safeguards into this system. The secretary of state was required to ensure that procedures related to the use of intercepted material were followed. These included disclosure to a limited group of persons involved directly in the surveillance operation. The Act further established a tribunal which would investigate claims of interception by aggrieved members of the general public. Its role was to establish whether a warrant had been issued and if so to ensure that the correct procedures had been followed. The tribunal possessed the power to quash warrants and acccompanying certificates, to direct the destruction of intercepted material and to direct the secretary of state to pay compensation. Finally, the legislation established the office of commissioner to monitor the legislative arrangements, thus placing the role initially performed by Lord Diplock and latterly by Lord Bridges on a statutory basis. The commissioner could investigate alleged violations which were not the subject of an individual complaint and had the power to issue reports to the Prime Minister and also to publish an annual report to Parliament.

The 1984 and 1998 Data Protection Acts

The ability of a citizen to access information stored on him or her by the state is an important aspect of liberal democracy. It is underpinned by the right to individual privacy and has significant implications for the freedom of expression. The 1984 Data Protection Act provided access for citizens to personal data held on them by data users. It established a Data Protection Registrar to maintain a register of data users who was responsible for ensuring that the data protection principles embodied in the Act were upheld by users and empowered to serve an enforcement notice to require compliance with them. Ultimately the sanction of deregistration could be deployed for non-observance of these principles. The 1984 Act also established a Data Protection Tribunal. There were, however, exceptions to a citizen's access to personal information, which included material where secrecy was necessary to safeguard national security. The 1998 legislation developed the previous Act of 1984. The Data Protection Registrar was renamed the Data Protection Commissioner. The tribunal established under the 1984 Act remained essentially the same save that an appeal was provided against a ministerial certificate allowing access to personal data to be withheld on grounds of national security. Appeals of this nature were held before a special national security appeals panel.

The 1989 Security Service Act

The background to this legislation was considerably influenced by allegations made in 1985 by Cathy Massiter, a former MI5 operative, concerning that organisation's activities in tapping the telephone of Dr John Cox, then a vice president of CND and a Communist Party councillor. This activity broke MI5's guidelines which stated that the target should be involved in a criminal activity which would carry a prison term of at least three years or that the target was involved in a major subversive terrorist or espionage activity. These guidelines did not justify telephone tapping merely because the target was a communist or an alleged subversive.

The 1989 legislation placed MI5 on a statutory basis. Section 1 of this Act defined its role as that of protecting national security and in particular its protection 'against threats from espionage, terrorism and sabotage, from the activities of agents of foreign powers and from actions intended to overthrow or undermine parliamentary democracy by political, industrial or violent means'. Additionally MI5 was charged with safeguarding the economic well-being of Great Britain against threats posed by the actions or interests of persons outside the British Isles. This Act confirmed MI5 to be under the control of the Home Secretary who determined the responsibility of the Director General of MI5. The 1989 Act authorised the issuance of warrants permitting the 'entry or interference with property' by MI5 personnel. Warrants to 'bug and burgle' were issued for a period of six months and could be renewable. However, the legislation failed to offer any definition as to what the terms 'national security', 'terrorism' or 'serious crime' actually consisted of. Mechanisms of accountability included the annual report prepared by MI5's Director General, and provisions whereby complaints against the service could be investigated by procedures similar to those provided in the 1985 Act in connection with the interception of communications. A Security Services Tribunal consisting of three legally trained persons investigates complaints and a Security Services Commissioner, appointed by the Prime Minister from a person who had held high judicial office, reviews the issuance of property warrants by the secretary of state. The commissioner makes an annual report which is normally laid (in whole or in part) before Parliament. The 1994 Intelligence Services Act placed MI6 and GCHQ on a similar legal footing to MI5 and enabled the secretary of state to issue warrants authorising interference with property or wireless telegraphy.

The 1998 Human Rights Act

A major development in the defence of political and civil liberties was provided in the 1998 Human Rights Act which placed the European Convention of Human Rights onto the statute book. Political freedoms were enshrined in Article 10 (which guaranteed the freedom of expression), and Article 11 (which established that everyone had the right to freedom of peaceful assembly and to associate with others). A particularly important provision relevant to the concerns of this chapter was Article 8. This guaranteed to all persons 'the right to respect for his private and family life, his home and his correspondence' and stipulated that there should be no interference by a public authority with the exercise of this right 'except such as is in accordance with the law and is necessary in a democratic society in the interests of national security, public safety or the economic well-being of the country, for the prevention of disorder or crime, for the protection of health or morals, or for the protection of the rights and freedoms of others'. This meant that all policing methods which interfered with the privacy of the individual required a legal basis which was provided for in the 2000 Regulation of Investigatory Powers Act.

The 2000 Regulation of Investigatory Powers Act

As has been stated above, this measure was designed to ensure that all police practices which interfered with the rights of the individual had a legal basis so that they would not contravene the 1998 Human Rights Act. This legislation superceded earlier measures concerned with the interception of communications (most notably the 1985 Act). The new legislation authorised the interception of a wide range of communications which would be affected by the issuance of warrants: warrants to intercept communications required a warrant signed by a minister but other methods of surveillance could be authorised by senior police officers. The main innovations introduced by this Act permitted forms of communication either not available or not widely used when the 1985 Act was enacted (such as e-mails and the internet) to be monitored by the state, enabled bodies not officially in existence (such as MI5 and GCHQ) or not established (such as the National Criminal Intelligence Service, NCIS) to apply for warrants to intercept communications, and also coordinated the arrangements set up under the 1985 Act and subsequent legislation (such as the 1989 Act) providing for the accountability of agencies which carried out various forms of interception.

In order to monitor e-mails, the Act required internet service providers to instal 'black boxes' so that every scrap of data traversing their networks could be scrutinised by the newly-created Government Technical Advice Centre. This was housed in the MI5 building and was operated by the NCIS. This form of interception did not require any specific warrant and the police were further given the power to demand the keys to encrypted data. The Act further authorised covert surveillance, embracing methods which were catered for in the earlier 1997 Police Act but including other forms (such as the use by the police of informants or 'covert human intelligence sources') which were not. Covert surveillance by agencies such as the police service, MI5 and MI6 was exempted from challenge in the courts for breaching the right to privacy which was guaranteed in the 1998 Human Rights Act. Ministers were also empowered to issue orders to allow other agencies (such as the DSS and the DTI to conduct covert surveillance).

The 2000 Act established safeguards in connection with interceptions. A tribunal was established to investigate complaints from members of the general public. A Technical Advisory Board was formed to represent the interests of those on whom obligations might be imposed by the Act.

Additionally, provisions of the Act sanctioned the appointment of an Interception of Communications Commissioner (a post set up by the 1985 Act), an Intelligence Services Commissioner (an appointment established in the 1989 Act) and provided for the new post of an Investigatory Powers Commissioner for Northern Ireland. The activities of these officials were coordinated by the new post of Chief Surveillance Commissioner.

Executive accountability

The Prime Minister exercises overall responsibility for intelligence and security matters and is supported in this role by the secretary of the Cabinet. Accountability within the executive branch is also secured through the Joint Intelligence Committee. This is housed within the Cabinet Office and is responsible for setting Great Britain's national intelligence requirements and for producing regular intelligence assessments for ministers and officials. The Cabinet Office also has an intelligence coordinator whose role is to advise the secretary of the Cabinet on the coordination of intelligence machinery and its resources and programmes (Cabinet Office, 1996).

Legislative accountability

In 1993 the Home Affairs committee argued that MI5 should be more closely monitored because of its new role in connection with Irish terrorism. It was pointed out that its annual budget was secret and that the official figure of £185 million a year was almost certainly an underestimate (Home Affairs Committee, 1993). Such arguments ultimately resulted in the 1994 Intelligence Services Act, establishing the Intelligence and Security Committee to examine the expenditure, administration and policy of MI5, MI6 and GCHQ. It consists of nine cross-party MPs and peers appointed by the Prime Minister. However, it lacks the power to summon 'persons and papers' and its ability to increase public awareness of the role of these agencies has been hampered by its members being subject to the duty of silence imposed by the Official Secrets Act. This committee issues an annual report to the Prime Minister who decides what aspects of it may be disclosed to Parliament.

Bugging

Bugging has become a widely used mechanism of intrusive surveillance. There are numerous forms of bugging devices. Direct Intelligence Access Listening (DIAL) systems are powered from a telephone and can operate for many years without the need for maintenance. Others may be powered by batteries. Video–audio bugs which are used by the intelligence and security services are relatively new devices. These are placed in television sets or clock radios. However, bugging is subject to no meaningful regulation: the 1949 Wireless Telegraphy Act made it an offence to transmit without a licence but as the signals transmitted by bugging devices are too weak to interfere with emergency services and public networks the provisions of this legislation have not been applied.

The regulation of bugging was traditionally provided by guidelines (in the form of circulars) issued by the Home Secretary. In 1984 new guidelines were issued by the Home Secretary, Leon Brittan, following the use of this method of surveillance by the North Wales police in a public telephone box in Talysarn in 1981 (Davies et al., 1984: 41–3). These instructed police forces to cease bugging public facilities. The *Guardian* on 20 December 1984 stated that these revised guidelines imposed further conditions on a chief constable's decision to authorise the use of bugging. These were that the investigation concerned a serious crime, other methods of investigation had either failed or were deemed unlikely to succeed, and there was a good chance of an arrest and conviction under the Prevention of Terrorism legislation.

The practice of bugging was formally recognised in the 1989 Security Services Act when provisions were made regarding the circumstances under which this method of surveillance could be used.

The impact of reforms initiated since 1980 on civil and political liberties

Reforms initiated since 1980 were designed to respond to criticisms made of the role, and particularly the methods, utilised by the security services which were alleged to be undermining the operations of liberal democracy in Great Britain by imposing restraints on political expression and activity and invading individual privacy. These have resulted in a greater degree of openness affecting the operations of MI5 which have been evidenced in the decision to name the Director General in 1991 and in the publication in 1993 of a booklet (*MI5, The Security Service*) which gave information on its activities. The existence of agencies such as MI5, MI6 and GCHQ is now publicly acknowledged and information concerning their work has been made available. There is also a greater degree of openness concerning expenditure (the budget for MI5, MI6 and GCHQ for 1996/1997 being £751 million) (Cabinet Office, 1996: 11) which is planned to rise to £941 by 2003 (Norton-Taylor and Hopkins, 2001). However, the effectiveness of innovations introduced in the 1980s to defend civil and political liberties has been disputed. This issue is discussed in more detail below.

Telephone tapping

Telephone tapping is a major intrusion into an individual's privacy, but the extent to which it takes place remains the subject of debate. On 14 June 1991 the *Guardian* alleged that 35,000 telephone lines were tapped each year. The disparity between this figure and the number of warrants issued (which was less than 600) suggested that a warrant named either a person or an organisation so that each warrant authorised the tapping of a large number of telephone lines relevant to the named individual or members of a target organisation. It also suggested that the figures which were issued referred only to new warrants which were issued and ignored existing warrants (some of which were alleged to be of a permanent nature).

The adequacy of safeguards to protect the privacy of members of the public from the abuse of power by the security services has also been disputed. Warrants to intercept communications and to permit MI5 to break into a person's home or vehicle and plant bugs are issued by the Home Secretary, acting on the advice of the Civil Service rather than the judiciary, which is a separate branch of government. The tribunals established by the 1985 and 1989 legislation were merely required to satisfy themselves that correct procedures had been followed. It is not necessary for them to produce evidence to convince a complainant that its findings are justified or to give reasons for its decisions. Lord Allen informed the House of Lords on 25 June 1996 that since 1989 the tribunal had considered 187 complaints against MI5 and had dismissed each one. The weaknesses of this system became public knowledge in connection with Alison Halford's complaint alleging that her telephone calls from her home and office had been tapped while she was in dispute over alleged sex discrimination by the Merseyside police in 1990. The tribunal refused to clarify whether tapping had taken place or whether it had been authorised by a warrant issued by the Home Secretary. The European Human Rights Commission ruled in 1996 that such a reply of this nature gave her no effective redress as was required by Article 13 of the European Convention on Human Rights.

The 2000 Regulation of Investigatory Powers Act provided agencies such as MI5 with powers to scrutinise e-mails and internet web sites. The ability of state agencies to undertake actions of this kind infringed the privacy of the individual which was enshrined in the 1998 Human Rights Act but could be justified on the grounds that criminals (such as paedophiles) and political campaigners used these methods of communication to organise and recruit. The decisions of the tribunal established by this Act were not subject to challenge in the courts, although this might be in contravention of the right to a fair trial provided for in the 1998 Human Rights Act.

Data protection legislation

Data protection legislation also offers defences to members of the public whose civil and political liberties are jeopardised when state agencies gather and store information on them regarding their political views, affiliations and activities. However, MI5 has been effectively outside the scope of the 1984 Data Protection Act (which gave individuals the right of access to information held by the security and intelligence agencies). Although MI5 registered its intelligence computer system in 1995, disclosure has been resisted on the assertion that this would threaten national security. Additionally, the effectiveness of safeguards designed to protect civil and political liberties which were introduced by this legislation have been questioned. In 2001 the data protection tribunal's special national security appeals panel considered a case involving a Liberal Democrat MP, Norman Baker, who had sought access to any material which MI5 had kept on him. The agency refused to confirm or deny that it held a file on him and the agency's desire to impose a blanket ban on disclosure of any information related to its personal files on the grounds of safeguarding national security was supported by the Home Secretary, Jack Straw, who had signed a public interest immunity certificate to this effect. It was argued before the tribunal that this action contravened Article 8 of the European Convention of Human Rights which guaranteed the right to privacy. Additionally, a blanket ban of this nature presumably covered all the operations conducted by MI5 including its newer role in connection with serious crime. In 2001 the special national security appeals panel ruled that the government's blanket ban preventing anyone from knowing whether MI5 held information on them was illegal.

The 1989 Official Secrets Act

The ability to scrutinise and debate the actions undertaken by public agencies is a key feature of liberal democratic political systems. This would ensure, for example, that incursions into civil and political liberties were justified through mechanisms of accountability. However, the reforms which have been introduced since 1980 have not significantly altered the climate of secrecy within which agencies whose work may infringe civil and political liberties operate. The state retains the capacity to cloak the work of the security services in secrecy. The 1989 Official Secrets Act amended section 2 of the 1911 measure and made it an offence for a person who was (or had been) a member of the security or intelligence services without lawful authority to disclose any information, document or other article related to security or intelligence which was (or had been) in that person's possession by virtue of their being a member of such services. This meant that those who were members of the security and intelligence services were subject to a lifelong duty of confidentiality and the Act contained no provision whereby a person in this position could seek to justify disclosure on the grounds of public interest. A minister was empowered to apply this provision of the Act to any other person. Additionally, the Act made it an offence for Crown servants and government contractors to make 'damaging disclosures' concerning the security or intelligence services, defence and international relations. It also became an offence for Crown servants and government contractors to make disclosures concerning crime and special investigation powers. The 2000 Freedom of Information Act also contained a blanket ban on the disclosure of information relevant to the purpose of national security regardless of any public interest consideration.

The Official Secrets Act, disclosure and freedom of the press

One danger with the Official Secrets Act is that it could be used against journalists and writers to require them to name their sources thus preventing the media from discharging its role of raising issues of genuine public concern and enabling agencies of the state to be held publicly accountable for their actions. It is also arguable that this Act is incompatible with the freedom of expression guaranteed in Article 10 of the European Convention of Human Rights.

In 1997 a former MI5 agent, David Shayler, disclosed information and MI5 documents to the *Mail on Sunday*. He justified his actions by arguing that allegations of wrongdoing and incompetence by MI5 were in the public interest. He was subsequently charged under the Official Secrets Act. In July 2000 the Appeal Court ruled that the *Guardian* and *Observer* newspapers did not have to hand over to the police any information they possessed in relation to David Shayler on the grounds that it infringed the freedom of speech. At the trial Lord Justice Judge asserted that this right was enshrined in common law. This was regardless of the impact which the 1998 Human Rights Act would have on this situation when it became law in October 2000. The ruling that journalists did not have to hand over material would make it difficult for the police henceforth to find evidence that the Official Secrets Act had been breached.

The new role of MI5

In the last decade of the twentieth century, the role of MI5 extended beyond its historical concern with subversion. The changes which extended the role of MI5 pose additional threats to civil and political liberties, especially in relation to individual privacy and political expression. This issue is discussed below.

Background to extending MI5's role

The extended role of MI5 needs to be seen in the context of other developments concerned with the introduction of units with a national remit operating across police force boundaries. In 1992 the National Criminal Intelligence Service (NCIS) was established to perform 'a supply and support role in relation to agencies which do have enforcement and investigative functions' (Walker, 2000: 202). It brought together under one roof a number of existing units concerned with gathering intelligence on specific problems (such as football hooliganism) which operated on a national basis.

The end of the Cold War resulted in MI5 straying from its initial brief. In 1992 it was assigned the lead role in countering terrorism on mainland Britain. The bulk of MI5's resources were devoted to this function which provided the main reason for the agency's continued existence. Approximately half of its resources were devoted to Northern Irish terrorism (Rimington, 1994). This brought the agency into contact with provincial police forces' special branches rather than confining its relationship to the Metropolitan Police's Special Branch as had been the case previously, but tended to remove this area of work from the scrutiny of Parliament. The IRA ceasefire necessitated the development of new areas of responsibility. Accordingly, the 1996 Security Services Act allocated MI5 the responsiblity for dealing with 'serious crime' in addition to its existing functions. This development could be partly attributed to the microelectronics revolution. Electronic data processing and communications became vulnerable to disruption from a range of sources which included fraudsters, hackers, eavesdroppers, disrupters and extortionists (Clutterbuck, 1990: 17–21), blurring the boundary between 'ordinary' crime and terrorism. It has also been argued that the prior formation of a national criminal intelligence-gathering unit was an important prerequisite to the extension of the role of MI5 into 'ordinary' crime and further served as a building block for the establishment of a national policing organisation, the National Crime Squad (NCS) (Walker, 2000: 224). This unit was based on the existing regional crime squads (established in 1965) which were absorbed into the NCS in 1998. Its role was to prevent and detect serious crime which was of relevance to more than one police area in England and Wales. These developments provided Britain with national policing organisations subject to a considerable degree of central government control, which, in connection with the NCS, embraced a wide array of strategic, oversight, instructional, personnel, budgetary, regulatory and coordinative powers (Walker, 2000: 218).

The 1996 Security Services Act

The 1996 Security Services Act theoretically gave MI5 a broad remit since serious crime was defined as an offence which carried a sentence of three years or more on first conviction or any offence involving conduct by a large number of persons in pursuit of a common purpose. Theoretically, therefore, 'mugging', obstruction of the highway and various forms of extra-parliamentary political activity discussed in Chapters 2–6 could become concerns of MI5. This posed the problem of demarcation disputes arising between the police and MI5 although the relatively small size of MI5 (which has approximately 2000 staff) made it unlikely that the agency would usurp mainstream policing roles. The role to combat serious crime contained in the 1996 measure was contentious. Civil libertarians expressed concerns that this term was broad and that the Act provided no definition of the categories of persons liable to surveillance, failed to place limits on the activities which were subject to scrutiny, and gave no definition of the conditions under which any information gathered would be retained. The most severe criticism was levelled by a former chief constable, John Alderson. He argued that it was fatal to involve MI5 with ordinary crime because of its lack of accountability. He argued that this organisation worked by infiltrating organisations, people's jobs and lives, operating 'almost like a cancer...destroying trust and security between people'. He accused the Home Secretary of seeking to turn Britain into a police state with MI5 becoming an East German-style Stasi force with half the population spying on the other half (Alderson, 1996). Although it might be argued that allocating MI5 a role regarding serious crime would be beneficial to its accountability since its traditional use of public immunity certificates to mask the sources of its evidence and how it was obtained would be difficult to employ in 'ordinary' criminal cases, other time-honoured methods associated with the agency (including 'dirty tricks', and the provision of disinformation) might become tactics employed against serious crime especially when the perpetrators could not be taken to court.

The 1997 Police Act

The police service was concerned about developments which extended the remit of MI5. In contrast with the NCIS, MI5 had statutory recognition. Unlike ACPO or individual chief constables, the Director General of MI5 had direct access to ministers who might give operational directions to this agency. ACPO responded to suggestions that MI5 should become involved in areas such as drugs and organised crime by supporting the formation of a national police squad to deal with serious crime, acting as the operational arm of the NCIS. The police service was concerned that MI5 would assume the lead role in these matters and become a de facto national police organisation, the British equivalent of the American FBI. Fears concerning MI5 dominance in dealing with serious crime arose as only this agency had specific legal power (granted by the 1996 Security Services Act) to enter a person's premises and plant a bugging device to effect surveillance. Although the House of Lords was informed on 20 January 1997 that the police regularly undertake such actions, the absence of specific legal sanction was in probable breach of the right to privacy enshrined in Article 8 of the European Convention on Human Rights. This made it problematic to produce the transcripts of bugged conversations as evidence in a trial. Accordingly, ACPO and the NCIS urged police powers in connection with bugging to be placed on the same legal footing as MI5's, thereby extending the state's ability to interfere with individual privacy. This innovation was introduced in the 1997 Police Act which provided the police with powers to 'bug and burgle' in order to prevent or detect serious crime. The legislation defined this latter term as offences involving the use of violence, which resulted in substantial financial gain likely to result in a prison sentence of at least three years, or which involved conduct by large numbers of persons in pursuit of a common purpose.

The 1997 Police Act established a new system for the authorisation of intrusive surveillance such as bugging which had previously been governed by Home Office circulars. Under the new system, a chief constable could authorise the police to trespass on land to carry out or plant a surveillance device, but if there was a need to trespass in a dwelling house, hotel or office the authorisation of surveillance commissioners (who are High Court judges) was required. However, the Act did not embrace all listening devices such as long-range sensitive microphones or 'wired' undercover police officers, and the Act did not apply if the police had consent to enter premises and plant a bug (perhaps from a hotel manager, for example). Other forms of surveillance were outside the scope of this legislation such as the use of informants or undercover officers which were instead regulated by Home Office and ACPO guidelines but which lack any basis in law. This legislation also asserted the primacy of the police service in work concerned with serious crime. The security service would be tasked by the NCIS which would also coordinate this type of work.

Conclusion

This chapter has examined two issues related to the ability of citizens to engage in extra-parliamentary political activities. The first of these concerned the changing nature of policing in connection with activities discussed in Chapters 2–6 and to assess whether what was termed 'paramilitary policing' restricted extra-parliamentary political activities. The discussion which took place here and in preceding chapters (especially Chapters 2 and 3) suggested that citizens remain able to engage in a wide range of extra-parliamentary actions but that the state has the capacity to intervene more effectively and prevent crowd situations developing into disorder. As Chapter 2 argued, this new capability may be used on occasions to stifle protest or to neutralise its impact.

The second issue discussed in this chapter concerned the operations of those agencies whose role is to monitor the political views and opinions held by individuals and organisations. Although this activity might be justified by the belief that views and opinions can be translated into actions which threaten the security and well-being of the state, the methods that are used to gather intelligence in connection with these concerns undermines individual privacy and threatens the freedom of political expression both of which are crucial underpinnings of a liberal democratic state. Additionally, the safeguards which have been introduced to defend individuals from unwarranted intrusions into their civil and political liberties are often ineffective and fail to provide those who have been targeted by agencies such as MI5 with adequate means to defend themselves against charges made or to secure redress when mistakes are made. The accountability of these agencies is further impeded by the state's use of official secrecy to limit public discussion of their work.

The introductory chapter asserted the importance of extra-parliamentary political activity, the various forms of which were then discussed in Chapters 2–6. It may be that the state has a sceptical view of actions of this kind, and that through the use of technology it now possesses the capability to monitor the views and opinions of those who endorse the use of these activities to a greater extent than was previously possible. Additionally, changes to police methods mean that it has the enhanced ability to respond to events of this nature. Thus the state has an enhanced potential to undermine key liberal democratic values (especially the right to privacy and the freedom of political expression) in connection with extra-parliamentary political activities through the use of both pre-emptive and reactive methods. The challenge to these values requires the introduction of improved safeguards affecting the work performed by the police service and the other agencies, especially MI5, which have been discussed in this chapter, which will enable those who deem voting to be an inadequate or irrelevant mechanism to continue to utilise various forms of extra-parliamentary political activity in order to secure political change.

Glossary

Government Communications Headquarters (GCHQ)

The origins of this organisation stem from the First World War when Signals Intelligence (SIGINT) was set up to break enemy ciphers: the designation GCHQ was adopted during the Second World War. During these hostilities its work extended beyond code breaking to the interception of enemy signals and sending and receiving British secret wartime communications. Following the end of the war GCHQ became part of a multinational pact to enable the 'free world' to intercept and monitor radio, radar, telex, teletype and microwave transmissions, telephone calls and satellite communications made within and between communist countries. Interception of this kind was carried out using spy satellites and listening posts throughout the world. Although the role of GCHQ was historically confined to the interception of international communications between foreign governments, international companies or private individuals, the increased use by companies such as British Telecom of microwave radio transmissions to relay telephone conversations across the country led to accusations that the equipment operated by GCHQ could be applied to internal matters.

The Security Service (MI5)

The Security Service (usually referred to as MI5) was established in the early years of the twentieth century. Its initial concern was to foil the spying activities conducted by foreign powers within Great Britain. It is controlled by a Director General appointed by the Prime Minister and is accountable to the Home Secretary. Initially MI5 had no legal status and neither its role nor duties were defined by statute. The fullest guide to these matters was provided in the Maxwell Fyfe directive of 1952 which stated that MI5 was part of the defence forces of the United Kingdom whose task was the defence of the realm 'from external and internal dangers arising from attempts of espionage and sabotage, or from actions of persons and organisations whether directed from within or without the country, which may be judged to be subversive to the state' (quoted in West, 1983: 243). As has been discussed above, MI5 was placed on a statutory footing by the 1989 Security Service Act. Special Branch and MI5 have traditionally enjoyed a close working relationship. This was especially apparent in the procedures adopted to implement the positive vetting of state employees and contractors. This procedure was introduced in 1952 and sought to ensure that members of the communist party or those with communist sympathies were not employed in connection with secret state work. Cooperation between the two agencies is also required as MI5 officers lack the power of arrest. Administrative links between Special Branch and MI5 exist centrally through the Home Office and regionally through an MI5–police liaison officer (Davies et al., 1984: 31–2). Although some areas of activity overlap, Special Branch tends to concentrate on short-term activities whereas MI5 handles longer-term surveillance (Aubrey, 1981: 40).

Special Branch

Special Branch is a branch of the police service. It was established in 1883 from members of Scotland Yard's CID to combat the Fenian bombing campaign in London. Historically it was based in London but its remit was subsequently extended across England and Wales through the development of special branches in provincial police forces which although nominally answerable to their chief constables had a direct reporting link to Scotland Yard (Bunyan, 1977: 128). It is responsible for a wide range of surveillance work affecting foreign communities living in Britain and played a major role in the process of positive vetting and the enforcement of the prevention of terrorism legislation. It has a tradition of working closely with MI5, and in 1975 a proposal (which was not acted upon) was made to create a new centralised intelligence agency which would coordinate the work of a number of intelligence gathering agencies including MI5 and Special Branch (Geary: 1985: 95–6).

Subversion

Subversion lacks any objective definition. It is, instead, a nebulous term whose meaning has become extended in response to the growth of extra-parliamentary forms of political activity since 1970. Until the 1970s Lord Denning's definition of subversion was generally accepted as the 'official' one: he defined the term as 'an act which contemplated the overthrow of government by unlawful means' (quoted in Aubrey, 1981: 16). During the 1970s the fear of internal upheaval by extreme left-wing groups prompted a redefinition of subversion by Lord Harris in 1975 entailing 'activities which threaten the safety or well being of the state' and which were 'intended to undermine or overthrow parliamentary democracy by political, industrial or violent means' (quoted in Davies et al., 1984: 33–4). This definition (which did not necessarily involving breaking the law) was subsequently confirmed by Merlyn Rees in 1978 when he stated that Special Branch (whose role is referred to above) was concerned with collecting information on those 'whom I think cause problems for the state' (quoted in Davies et al., 1984: 34). Later, in 1982, the then Home Secretary, William Whitelaw, indicated that state surveillance of individuals who were active in a political movement was justified 'not because of the views they hold but because the activities of the group could be such as to encourage public disorder' (quoted in Reeve and Smith, 1986: 15).

References

C. Ackroyd, K. Margolis, J. Rosenhead and T. Shallice (1980) *The Technology of Political Control* (London: Pluto Press, 2nd edition)

J. Alderson (1981) evidence submitted to Lord Scarman's Enquiry into the Brixton Disorders, 2 September, quoted in G. Northam (1989) *Shooting in the Dark: Riot Police in Britain* (London; Faber and Faber, 2nd edition)

J. Alderson (1996) 'A Fair Cop', *Red Pepper*, 24

C. Aubrey (1981) *Who's Watching You? Britain's Security Services and the Official Secrets Act* (Harmondsworth: Penguin)

J. Brewer, A. Guelke, I. Hume, E. Moxon-Browne and R. Wilford (1996) *The Police, Public Order and the State* (Basingstoke: Macmillan Press – now Palgrave Macmillan, 2nd edition)

T. Bunyan (1977) *The History and Practice of the Political Police in Britain* (London: Quartet Books)

Cabinet Office (1996) *Central Intelligence Machinery* (London: HMSO)

D. Campbell (1981) *Phonetappers and the Security State* (London: New Statesman)

R. Clutterbuck (1990) *Terrorism and Guerrilla Warfare: Forecasts and Remedies* (London: Routledge)

J. Davies, Lord Gifford and T. Richards (1984) *Political Policing in Wales* (Cardiff: Welsh Campaign for Civil and Political Liberties)

Lord Diplock (1981) *The Interception of Communications in Great Britain* (London: HMSO, Cmnd. 8191)

R. Emerson (1982) 'Control of Government Intelligence Agencies: the American Experience', *Political Quarterly*, 53, 273–91

P. Fitzgerald and M. Leopold (1987) *Stranger on the Line: the Secret History of Phone Tapping* (London: Bodley Head)

A. Gamble (1988) *The Free Market and the Strong State* (Basingstoke: Macmillan Press – now Palgrave Macmillan)

R. Geary (1985) *Policing Industrial Disputes, 1893–1985* (London: Methuen)

S. Hall (1980) *Drifting into a Law and Order Society* (London: Cobden Trust)

Home Office (1980) *The Interception of Communications in Great Britain* (London: HMSO, Cmnd. 7873)

T. Jefferson (1987) 'Beyond Paramilitarism', *British Journal of Criminology*, 27, 47–53

T. Jefferson (1990) *The Case against Paramilitary Policing* (Milton Keynes: Open University Press)

J. Craig Jenkins (1995) 'Social Movements, Political Representation, and the State: an Agenda and Comparative Framework', in J. Craig Jenkins and B. Klandermans (eds) *The Politics of Protest: Comparative Perspectives in States and Social Movements* (London: UCL Press)

M. King and N. Brearley (1996) *Public Order Policing: Contemporary Perspectives on Strategy and Tactics* (Leicester: Perpetuity Press, Crime and Security Shorter Study Series: No. 2)

D. Leigh (1988) *The Intelligence Service and the Discrediting of the Prime Minister 1945–1976* (London: Heinemann)

K. Lindsay (1980) *The British Intelligence Services in Action* (Dundalk: Dunrod Press)

L. Lustgarten and I. Leigh (1995) *In from the Cold: National Security and Parliamentary Democracy* (Oxford: Oxford University Press)

S. Milne (1995) *The Enemy Within: the Secret War against the Miners* (London: Pan Books)

G. Northam (1989) *Shooting in the Dark: Riot Police in Britain* (London: Faber and Faber)

R. Norton-Taylor (2001) 'Truth but not the Whole Truth', *Guardian*, 11 September

R. Norton-Taylor and N. Hopkins (2001) 'Secret Services Struggle to Get Up Speed', *Guardian*, 16 October

G. Reeve and J. Smith (1986) *Offence of the Realm: how Peace Campaigners Get Bugged* (London: CND Publications)

R. Reiner (1985) *The Politics of the Police* (Brighton: Wheatsheaf)

R. Reiner (1991) *Chief Constables, Bobbies, Bosses or Bureaucrats?* (Oxford: Oxford University Press)

R. Reiner (1998) 'Policing Protest and Disorder in Britain', in D. della Porta and H. Reiter (eds) *The Control of Mass Demonstrations in Western Democracies* (Minnesota: University of Minnesota Press)

S. Rimington (1994) The Richard Dimbleby Lecture, *Security and Democracy – Is There a Conflict?*, BBC television, 12 June

S. Rimington (2001) *The Open Secret* (London: Hutchinson)

M. Saunders (1996) 'A Preventive Approach to Public Order', in C. Critcher and D. Waddington (eds) *Policing Public Order: Theoretical and Practical Issues* (Aldershot: Avebury)

State Research (1979) 'Introduction', in E.P. Thompson, *The Secret State* (London: Independent Research Publications, State Research Pamphlet No. 1)

N. Walker (2000) *Policing in a Changing Constitutional Order* (London: Sweet and Maxwell)

D. Waddington (1996) 'Key Issues and Controversies', in C. Critcher and D. Waddington (eds) *Policing Public Order: Theoretical and Practical Issues* (Aldershot: Avebury)

P. Waddington (1993) 'The Case against Paramilitary Policing Considered', *British Journal of Criminology*, 33, 353–73

P. Waddington (1994) *Liberty and Order: Public Order Policing in a Capital City* (London: UCL Press)

P. Waddington (1987) 'Towards Paramilitarism? Dilemma in the Policing of Public Order', *British Journal of Criminology*, 27, 37–46

P. Waddington (1996) 'Public Order Policing: Citizenship and Moral Ambiguity', in F. Leishman, B. Loveday and S. Savage (eds) *Core Issues in Policing* (Harlow: Longman)

L. Walsh (1982) *CIA Infiltration of the Labour Movement* (London: Militant)

N. West (1983) *MI5 1945–1972: a Matter of Trust* (London: Coronet Books)

P. Wright (1987) *Spycatcher: the Candid Autobiography of a Senior Intelligence Officer* (New York: Heinemann)

Index